Palgrave Macmillan's
Postcolonial Studies in Education

Studies utilizing the perspectives of postcolonial theory have become established and increasingly widespread in the last few decades. This series embraces and broadly employs the postcolonial approach. As a site of struggle, education has constituted a key vehicle for the "colonization of the mind." The "post" in postcolonialism is both temporal, in the sense of emphasizing the processes of decolonization, and analytical in the sense of probing and contesting the aftermath of colonialism and the imperialism which succeeded it, utilizing materialist and discourse analysis. Postcolonial theory is particularly apt for exploring the implications of educational colonialism, decolonization, experimentation, revisioning, contradiction, and ambiguity not only for the former colonies, but also for the former colonial powers. This series views education as an important vehicle for both the inculcation and unlearning of colonial ideologies. It complements the diversity that exists in postcolonial studies of political economy, literature, sociology, and the interdisciplinary domain of cultural studies. Education is here being viewed in its broadest contexts, and is not confined to institutionalized learning. The aim of this series is to identify and help establish new areas of educational inquiry in postcolonial studies.

Series Editors:

Antonia Darder holds the Leavey Presidential Endowed Chair in Ethics and Moral Leadership at Loyola Marymount University, Los Angeles and is Professor Emerita at The University of Illinois, Urbana-Champaign.

Anne Hickling-Hudson is adjunct Professor of Education at Australia's Queensland University of Technology (QUT) where she specializes in cross-cultural and international education.

Peter Mayo is Professor, in the Department of Education Studies at the University of Malta where he teaches in the areas of Sociology of Education and Adult Continuing Education, as well as in Comparative and International Education and Sociology more generally.

Editorial Advisory Board

Carmel Borg (University of Malta)
John Baldacchino (Teachers College, Columbia University)
Jennifer Chan (University of British Columbia)
Christine Fox (University of Wollongong, Australia)
Zelia Gregoriou (University of Cyprus)
Leon Tikly (University of Bristol, UK)
Birgit Brock-Utne (Emeritus, University of Oslo, Norway)

Titles:

*A New Social Contract in a Latin American Education Context*
Danilo R. Streck; Foreword by Vítor Westhelle

*Education and Gendered Citizenship in Pakistan*
M. Ayaz Naseem

*Critical Race, Feminism, and Education: A Social Justice Model*
Menah A. E. Pratt-Clarke

*Actionable Postcolonial Theory in Education*
Vanessa Andreotti

*The Capacity to Share: A Study of Cuba's International Cooperation in Educational Development*
Anne Hickling-Hudson, Jorge Corona González, and Rosemary Preston

*A Critical Pedagogy of Embodied Education*
Tracey Ollis

*Culture, Education, and Community: Expressions of the Postcolonial Imagination*
Jennifer Lavia and Sechaba Mahlomaholo

*Neoliberal Transformation of Education in Turkey: Political and Ideological Analysis of Educationsal Reforms in the Age of AKP*
Edited by Kemal İnal and Güliz Akkaymak

*Radical Voices for Democratic Schooling: Exposing Neoliberal Inequalities*
Edited by Pierre W. Orelus and Curry S. Malott

*Lorenzo Milani's Culture of Peace: Essays on Religion, Education, and Democratic Life*
Edited by Carmel Borg and Michael Grech

# Lorenzo Milani's Culture of Peace

## Essays on Religion, Education, and Democratic Life

Edited by
*Carmel Borg and Michael Grech*

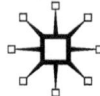

LORENZO MILANI'S CULTURE OF PEACE
Copyright © Carmel Borg and Michael Grech, 2014.

All rights reserved.

First published in 2014 by
PALGRAVE MACMILLAN®
in the United States—a division of St. Martin's Press LLC,
175 Fifth Avenue, New York, NY 10010.

Where this book is distributed in the UK, Europe and the rest of the world, this is by Palgrave Macmillan, a division of Macmillan Publishers Limited, registered in England, company number 785998, of Houndmills, Basingstoke, Hampshire RG21 6XS.

Palgrave Macmillan is the global academic imprint of the above companies and has companies and representatives throughout the world.

Palgrave® and Macmillan® are registered trademarks in the United States, the United Kingdom, Europe and other countries.

ISBN: 978–1–137–38210–8

Library of Congress Cataloging-in-Publication Data

    Lorenzo Milani's culture of peace : essays on religion, education, and democratic life : / edited by Carmel Borg and Michael Grech.
      pages cm
    Includes bibliographical references and index.
    ISBN 978–1–137–38210–8 (hardcover : alk. paper)
     1. Milani, Lorenzo. 2. Peace—Religious aspects—Catholic Church.
    3. Religion. 4. Education. 5. Democracy. I. Borg, Carmel, editor of compilation.

BX4705.M5526L68 2014
261.8′73—dc23                                                        2013045797

A catalogue record of the book is available from the British Library.

Design by Newgen Knowledge Works (P) Ltd., Chennai, India.

First edition: May 2014

10 9 8 7 6 5 4 3 2 1

To Bruce Kent, Giovanni Franzoni, and Dionysius Mintoff.
Three wise men engaged in the struggle for peace in the former centre, current outskirts, and perennial periphery of the empire.

# Contents

*Series Editors' Preface* ix

*Acknowledgments* xiii

*Notes on Contributors* xv

Introduction 1
Carmel Borg and Michael Grech

## Part I  Peace and Religion: Then and Now

1 The Catholic, Italian, and Tuscan Ecclesiastical Contexts
  of Don Milani's "Letter to the Military Chaplains" 13
  Carmel Borg and Michael Grech

2 Peace and the Religions in a Changing World: From Consensus to
  Difference 29
  Darren J. Dias

3 Vatican II's Teaching on Peace and War: A Contribution to
  Conciliar Hermeneutics 41
  Michael Attridge

4 The Church as a Sacrament of the Future 53
  Brian Wicker

## Part II  Peace, Memory, and Education

5 The History of World Peace in 100 Objects: Visualizing Peace
  in a Peace Museum 65
  Peter Van Den Dungen

6 Responding to the Call of Peace: In Memory of a Future That
  Might Have Been 77
  Clive Zammit

7 Peace Education in a Culture of War 91
  Antonia Darder

8 On Education, Negotiation, and Peace 97
  Marianna Papastephanou

9  From Conflict to Conflict Resolution: Teaching the History of
   Cyprus in the Buffer Zone                                          111
   *Isabelle Calleja Ragonesi*

10 Beyond Reality Dissonance: Improving Sustainability of
   Peace Education Effects                                            131
   *Yigal Rosen*

11 Because "I Care": From an Encounter to a Political Option          147
   *Francois Mifsud*

### Part III   Peace, Democracy, Sexuality, Gender, and Aesthetics

12 Peace Education and Critical Democracy: Some Challenges in
   Neoliberal Times                                                   161
   *John P. Portelli*

13 Does Democracy Promote Peace? A Rancière Reading of Politics
   and Democracy                                                      175
   *Duncan P. Mercieca*

14 Peace and Sexuality—Two Reflections                                187
   *Mario Gerada, Clayton Mercieca, and Diane Xuereb*

15 On Art and Politics: Exploring the Philosophical Implications
   of the Creative Order of Art on the Organization of
   Social Relations                                                   195
   *Mark Debono*

16 Can We Learn from Comparing Violent Conflicts and
   Reconciliation Processes? For a Sociology of Conflict and
   Reconciliation Going beyond Sociology                              203
   *Nicos Trimikliniotis*

17 The "Modern" Muslim Woman in the Arab Peoples'
   Revolution of Freedom and Dignity                                  219
   *Nathalie Grima*

Critical Epilogue: Making Sense of Lorenzo Milani's Antiwar
Project in Our Times                                                  233
*Carmel Borg and Michael Grech*

*Index*                                                               245

# Series Editors' Preface

Last year (2013) marked the ninetieth anniversary of the birth of Don Lorenzo Milani, a Roman Catholic priest and conscientious objector who dedicated his life to the education of poor children in Italy. He is best known for his direction of the School of Barbiana and his *Lettera a una Professoressa* (Letter to a Teacher). Yet despite his vital educational project, few educators outside of Italy or the European South are aware of his tireless efforts to critique war and the impact of militarization on the education of students in his country. With this in mind, *Lorenzo Milani's Culture of Peace* focuses on the inspiration of this leading European critical pedagogue to a postcolonial pedagogy of peace. Toward this end, this book includes a broad range of his writings, hitherto not translated (into English) such as *Esperienze Pastorali* and the letters to the Military Chaplains and Judges, *L'ubbidienza non è più una virtù* produced in English translation by James T. Burtchaell with the title of *A Just War No Longer Exists: The Trials and Tribulations of Don Lorenzo Milani*.

True to Milani's *Lettera ai cappellani militari* (Letter to the Military Chaplains), which offers an ethical defense of the right to be a conscientious objection, the urgency of Milani's message is resurrected in the spirit of the text. It is urgent for various reasons, not least of which is the hegemonic politics of militarisation, witnessed constantly over the last century. Furthermore, despite the fall of the Berlin Wall and the process of formal decolonization of nations, which occurred after the Second World War until the late 1970s (with the independence of Portuguese colonies in Africa and elsewhere), growing disparities in standard of living betwen West and East and North and South persist, with little signs of abating. Yet, colonialism has not gone away, having morphed into more subtle and covert political forms.

Milani, together with his students at Barbiana, called into question the issue of a "Just War," which they argued no longer exists. In so doing, he provided a critical process of reading and teaching history against the grain, challenging officially santized versions of public wartime discourses. He also examined the nineteenth-century movement for Italian unification, the Risorgimento—referred to by certain commentators of Gramscian inspiration as a case of a failed revolution—the wars which characterized it, and the duplicitous politics that ensued.

Milani accomplished the same feat with his interrogation of imperialist wars in Africa during the second wave of European imperialism in the nineteenth and early twentieth centuries, and the concurrent pedagogy of duplicity and dishonesty at the core of the pro-war school curriculum at the time, which coincided with Milani's own period of schooling. He recalls the way students were socialized and conditioned to blindly rejoice for the Empire in its wars of colonial expansion in Africa, without being told that it was Ethiopia who held the moral high ground. This was so, given that Ethiopians had done nothing to provoke the Italians, who employed outlawed poisonous gas on their crusade of conquest.

The Letter produced by Milani and his students is also instructive in considering the ways history can be taught from an anti-imperial stance,— a pedagogical approach that is most relevant today, an age where the "War on Terror" persists and blood is often traded for oil. In this regard, the letter connects with some of the writings that emerge from Critical Pedagogy around these themes. Henry Giroux's antimilitaristic arguments, for instance, in *Hearts of Darkness* and *Against the New Authoritarianism: Politics after Abu Ghraib*, easily comes to mind.

What emerges in this book then is the important contribution that a critical pedagogy, based on a powerful reading of history, can make to the lives of students. In this instance, it equips them with the knowledge and confidence to say "No" to a politics of militarization and the spread of imperial interests and the loss of innocent human lives, as witnessed in Iraq, among other places, in the last decade. Moreover, it is worth noting that at the time when Milani wrote the Letter, many within the Catholic tradition considered absolute obedience to the authority of the Church a fundamental virtue.

This discourse also extended itself to issues concerning citizenship and the State; citizens were to regard obedience as a political and social virtue in the interests of the Homeland. Obedience also became a virtue in both Fascist and post-Fascist Italy, especially, in the latter case, in the armed forces. Milani, in direct contrast, argued that "obedience is no longer a virtue," the very message that appears as the book title of the volume in Italian, which first included the letter to the military chaplains and judges. As might be expected, Milani was vilified for his stance, but vindicated posthumously. This change of heart is apparent in more recent years, when youth have been accorded the right to engage in community work anywhere in the world, many in the South, in lieu of military conscription. And although mandatory conscription was recently removed, young Italian men and women still have the right to obtain state funding to carry out work in Italy and various other parts of the world.

In 2010, for example, a meeting was held with popular educators in a shanty town on the outskirts of Rio de Janeiro, which involved a number of Italian youth who benefited from this provision and their involvement with emancipatory Freirean work in the South. This seems to point to a significant change in policy with respect to the former military expectation, that Milani and his students inveighed against, when writing in defense of conscientious objection. One might argue that, in contexts such as these, there is the potential for shifts from a onetime imperial military policy to a postcolonial one—one that tackles the negative aftermath of colonialism particularly in the global South. However, this seldom happens without much labor and struggle, given the common glorification of military culture in capitalist societies.

Carmel Borg and Michael Grech have carefully pulled together an edited volume that provides a worthy and varied examination of many of the same issues linked to war and peace once raised by Milani. The contributions to this collection are truly written in the spirit of Milani's work as an organic intellectual, although authors do not all necessarily speak directly to his contribution. As such, these essays encompass a variety of perspectives from Christian to non-Christian, which critically engage a variety of areas and touch upon a number of academic disciplines, including history, political theory, philosophy, theology, and sociology. At the heart of this compilation is found a deep attention to the conditions of subaltern classes and an understanding that education must function as a decolonizing project, where students and their communities learn to critically question, challenge, and transform their everyday lives, as they together work to reshape the contours of civil society.

# Acknowledgments

This work would not exist had it not been for the invaluable help of: Father Lawrence Attard who translated into English works that were originally in Portuguese; Joe Bezzina who provided critical feedback on some of the papers; Antoinette Pace who proofread a late version of the manuscript; and Father Zelio Belloni, Father Vincenzo Caprara, Valerie Flessati, Bruce Kent, Gianfranco Riccioni, Luigi Sandri, Nevio Santini, Father Aldo Tarquini, and Frei João Xerri who provided logistic and moral support.

## Contributors

**Michael Attridge** is Associate Professor of theology at the University of St. Michael's College in Toronto. He researches the Second Vatican Council and most recently the intersection of Vatican II and the Canadian Church and society. Some recent publications include: *Vatican II: Expériences canadiennes/ Canadian Experiences* (University of Ottawa Press, 2011); and *Jews and Catholics Together: Celebrating the Legacy of Nostra Aetate* (Novalis, 2007).

**Carmel Borg** is Associate Professor of Sociology of Education and Curriculum Studies at the Faculty of Education, University of Malta. He is the author, co-uthor, and editor of a number of books, papers in academic journals, and chapters in books that foreground the relationship between education, democracy, and social justice.

**Isabelle Calleja Ragonesi** obtained her doctorate in politics from the London School of Economics. She is presently head of the Department of International Relations, University of Malta, where she lectures in international politics.

**Antonia Darder** is the Leavey Endowed Chair of Ethics and Moral Leadership at Loyola Marymount University, Los Angeles. An internationally renowned Freirian scholar, her books include *Culture and Power in the Classroom* and *Reinventing Paulo Freire: A Pedagogy of Love*.

**Mark Debono** holds an MA in Philosophy and is a lecturer at the University of Malta, Junior College. His interests include continental philosophy, and the interaction of philosophy with politics, art, science, and the environment.

**Darren Dias** is assistant professor at St. Michael's College, University of Toronto. A scholar of the thought of Bernard Lonergan, his research interests include: the relationship between Trinitarian theology and religious diversity; and the intersection of doctrinal development and its reception in the life of the Church.

**Mario Gerada** is a qualified social worker. He is a published poet and contributing author to a number of web-based magazines. He is one of the founders of the Maltese LGBTI Christian group Drachma, and is invited regularly to lecture and discuss gay and Christian themes in academic and other settings.

**Michael Grech** teaches Philosophy at the Junior College, University of Malta. Grech published and coedited works concerning religion and a number of social issues like racism, immigration, liberation theology, and radical multiculturalism.

**Nathalie Grima** holds an MA in Sociology. Her fieldwork for a research-based dissertation focused on political transnationalism among first generation, foreign residents in Malta from the MENA region.

**Duncan Mercieca** is lecturer in Philosophy of Education and head of the Depratment of Education Studies, Faculty of Education, University of Malta. His research interests include: continental philosophy and education; diversity and otherness; inclusion and disability; the concept of becoming in educational contexts; children's literature and philosophy; and the process of writing and reading.

**Clayton Mercieca** holds a bachelors degree in Social Work and a masters in Creativity and Innovation. Besides his full-time profession working with the Government of Malta on EU Funded Projects, he is actively involved in Drachma (the Christian LGBTI organization) and JCI (Junior Chamber International) Malta.

**Francois Mifsud** holds a degree in Philosophy from Bologna University and a masters degree in Catholic Education from the University of London. While working on a PhD in Education he is Chaplain at St. Michael's College, University of Toronto.

**Marianna Papastephanou** has studied and researched in Cardiff (Wales) and Berlin (Germany). She teaches Philosophy of Education at the University of Cyprus, and is the author of books and articles on various education-related topics.

**John P. Portelli** has been teaching since 1975, and joined OISE at the University of Toronto in 1999, after having taught at many other universities and educational institutions. Portelli's main research and teaching interests are in philosophy of education and educational leadership and policy.

**Yigal Rosen** is a Senior Research Scientist at Pearson Education. He has previously taught educational leadership, technology, and peace education at the University of Haifa, the Open University of Israel and Ben-Gurion University.

**Nicos Trimikliniotis** is associate professor of Law and Sociology and director of the Center for the Study of Migration, Inter-ethnic and Labor Relations at the University of Nicosia. He has researched and published on ethnic conflict, reconciliation and resolution, constitutional and state theory, human rights, multiculturalism, migration, and Labor law, among other areas.

**Peter Van Den Dungen** has been lecturing in Peace Studies at the University of Bradford since 1976. He is the founder (1992) and general coordinator of the International Network of Museums for Peace (INMP). He has published extensively on peace history and peace museums.

**Brian Wicker** has lectured in the Department of Adult Education at the University of Birmingham. He has been involved in various initiatives that concern peace and was chairman and vice president of Pax Christi International, as well as chairman of the Council of Christian Approaches to Defence and Disarmament.

**Diane Xuereb** is of Maltese nationality, presently living in the Netherlands, former co-president of the European Forum LGBT Christian groups (2009–2013) and a qualified photographer.

**Clive Zammit** is senior lecturer in the Department of Cognitive Science at the University of Malta. He is currently interested in issues related to memory, myths, archives and their bearing on creative performance. Zammit has contributed to publications on performing arts, contemporary Maltese society and Maltese philosophers.

# Introduction

*Carmel Borg and Michael Grech*

As we approach the fiftieth year since Don Lorenzo Milani (1923–1967) wrote a rejoinder in response to a letter sent to the newspaper—*La Nazione*—by a group of retired military chaplains, in which they referred to conscientious objection as "an insult to the fatherland and to the Fallen" (Burtchaell, 1988, p.17), this book offers a stark reminder that Milani is not simply a man of his times but a prophet that speaks of the absence of today's peace in a global context marked by savage inequalities and asymmetries of power. As illustrated by a number of contributions to this book, the war on the poor has intensified. Simultaneously, the various manufacturers of consent continue in their quest to persuade us that the real war is on terror. Milani's legendary letters, alongside his radical reading of the gospels, translated into his conscious and deliberate, preferential option for the poor, and his educational vision, reflected in educational projects that welded critical literacy with transformative action, focus on the link between peace and social justice. They denounce blind obedience to hegemonic discourses that alienate the poor from the real threats to lasting peace, luring them into a war culture that ultimately leads them to shed their blood in wars against their fellow poor. His call for resistance and subversion by the oppressed is echoed in this book which, through most of its chapters, clearly distinguishes between authentic peace and pacification, that is, between just peace and a pseudo-peace arrangement that violently reproduces the social and economic status quo on a global scale.

## Lorenzo Milani—Profile of a Peace Maker

Born into a prestigious, Florentine family, on May 27, 1923, Lorenzo Milani Comparetti's boyhood unfolded within a distinctively upper-bourgeois context, marked by privilege, economic comfort, social networking, and intellectual stimulation.

Milani was born when Italy was still a Kingdom. The fascist regime had marched on Rome on October 29, 1922, and effectively ruled the country from then on. While Mussolini consolidated his grip over Italy, another concentric political ring was forming around the Kingdom and the rest of Europe. On January 30, 1933, Hitler was appointed chancellor of Germany. This event was of direct relevance to the Milani family—Lorenzo's mother, Alice Weiss, was of Jewish descent. Essentially agnostic, his parents turned to the Catholic church for protection. A marriage of convenience, choreographed by Don Vincenzo Viviani, a family friend from the parish of San Pietro in Mercato, followed, on the same day (June 29, 1933) by Lorenzo's baptism, was meant to shield the family from the anti-Semitic rhetoric, vandalism, and violence that characterized the years leading to the Second World War (Borg et al., 2013).

Writing about school, several years later, Lorenzo denounced his schooling as a process that socialized students into assimilating and absorbing the fascist ideology. He also accused his former teachers of acting as organic intellectuals to the fascist bloc by legitimizing "common sense" (read fascist) knowledge within schools.

Lorenzo continued to live a bohemian life until the end of his schooling years in 1941. Breaking with family tradition, Milani spent a year in art school instead of going to university. To his family's shock, Lorenzo underwent a silent and largely mysterious religious conversion that led him to the seminary in 1943.

Lorenzo's antipathy toward the school's socialization process, the fact that his social-class position brought him in direct contact with social, cultural, and economic privilege and dominance, his awareness that his own social class had delegated political powers to Mussolini, his close contact with poverty on the streets of Florence and Milan, coupled with an early understanding of the social injustice that characterized society in which he lived, constituted the prelude to a journey that led him to: a radical reading of the gospels; his eventual preferential option for the poor; a pastoral life that was characterized by an obsession with coherence (close to his ordination, Lorenzo renounced his family's inheritance, a deeply symbolic gesture of how he wanted to live his pastoral years) and social justice; a commitment to a liberatory vision and project; and his antiwar stance (Borg et al., 2013).

Milani's twenty years of pastoral leadership in Tuscany (1947–1967) unfolded against a sociopolitical backdrop marked by Pius XII's crusade against communism; a crusade that was partially responsible for the polarization of Italian society. Milani refused to foreground anticommunism in his pastoral work. He considered communists as children of a common Father God. As a priest, Milani felt morally obliged to reach out to all, irrespective of one's ideological or denominational background.

Lorenzo's radical teaching and action were energized by Tuscany's wealth in projects that addressed peace and social justice. Some of these projects were led by radical Catholics such as Don Primo Mazzolari, Giorgio La Pira, Don Bruno Borghi, Ernesto Balducci, and others from the circle of *Testimonianze*, a well-established Catholic periodical. Aldo

Capitini, whose reflections and action were inspired by the philosophy of passive resistance of Mahatma Gandhi, was also highly influential within Catholic circles in Tuscany (Schettini, 2008).

Milani's pastoral journey started at the parish of San Donato di Calenzano, a small community near Prato, 15 kilometers away from Florence. Characterized by high levels of illiteracy, unemployment, and exploitation of child labor, and by a crisis in accommodation, San Donato was populated by farmers and textile workers.

His pastoral leadership at San Donato mirrored the principles that informed his entire pastoral journey: coherence between action, reflection, and spirituality (Schettini, 2008); dominance of moral law over predominance of power; and a life dedicated to others, particularly those who were living in poverty (Fiorani, 1999).

San Donato's cultural landscape was mainly defined by what Milani considered as low levels of analysis, weak organization of ideas, and poor communication skills. Shyness was also understood by Milani as a major roadblock to the community's emancipation. Against such a backdrop, Milani's educational project at San Donato, which consisted mainly of a *scuola serale* (evening school), was meant to reclaim the community members' humanity by engaging in a process of "locating and dislocating oppression" (Freire, 1973; Ledwith, 2005).

True to Milani's inclusiveness, the educational context of San Donato was nondenominational in nature. Milani rejected the confessional school. For Milani, school constituted a space for genuine dialogue and for active engagement with issues that were profound, relevant, immediate, and potentially transformative in nature. Milani argued that the search for truth and genuine dialogue were not possible within a school climate that was partisan and exclusive (Borg et al., 2013).

Language was central to Milani's pedagogy of freedom. He understood that one cannot read the "world" without mastering the "word" (Freire, 1995). Milani referred to language as the "ghostly key" that opens every door, including the door of sovereignty. For Milani, proficiency in the language of power is intimately tied to the struggle for democracy, equity, peace, and social justice.

Milani's students at San Donato and, later, at Barbiana, engaged in emancipatory action research. The students were the subjects and protagonists in the process of research and writing. Blending archival research with direct, experiential knowledge, the writing phase served to collectively bond them with the contents of their analysis. In the true spirit of social theology, the ultimate goal of writing was to help the community transform the conditions that facilitate material as well as cultural domination. As a result, the writing had to be kept simple and sieved of any flowery language that tends to colonize rather than emancipate the reader.

Milani's radical pastoral approach at San Donato disturbed the comfort zone of a number of parishioners, ecclesiastics in the vicinity and the ecclesiastical authorities in Florence. Milani's radical option for the poor, his readiness to problematize, question and challenge established practices, his willingness to venture into hazardous territories, his openness to all, irrespective of political allegiances, his controversial sermons, some of which included references to upcoming elections and twice, in 1951 and 1953, provided clear indications of his voting preferences, his critique of parish priests in the area and of communists for their alienating practices, rendered his transfer to another community a foregone conclusion (Borg et al., 2013).

On December 6, 1954, seven years into his priesthood, Don Milani arrived at his new parish—*Sant'Andrea a Barbiana*. Situated in the hills of the Mugello region, Barbiana was a hamlet that lacked most of the basic services, including an access road, water, and electricity that was introduced in 1965, two years before Milani's death.

While "exile" was meant to silence and isolate Milani, the Barbiana phase proved to be the most productive, radical, public, and controversial of the two pastoral experiences. It was characterized by his total dedication to an educational project—the school of Barbiana—that served students, ranging in age from 11 to 18, 12 hours a day, 7 days a week, public holidays included.

The educational life of children born at Barbiana followed a definite script—they would come out of the *quinta elementare* semiliterate, timid, and with poor self-esteem. In fact, most of the children who would later attend his school would "have either failed their exams and left school or were bitterly discouraged with the way they were taught" (Rossi and Cole, 1970, p.10).

Given the fact that the formal education system had shortchanged most of his students, Milani acted with a sense of urgency. The school at Barbiana had to quickly equip students with relevant skills while preparing them for the formal exams imposed by the official system. It was a parallel curriculum that addressed official expectations as well as what Milani perceived as real needs. From the eyes of one of his former students, real needs were skills in critical and active citizenship; a curriculum aimed at equipping citizens with the necessary analytical competence and courage to challenge and subvert the root causes of symbolic and real violence.

Barbiana's school ethos is best captured in its motto. Written in English—"I Care"—it provided an antidote to dominant educational practices where individualism, achievement, and selection were symptomatic of a system that reproduced dominant cultures and asymmetrical relations of power on the basis of specific class, gender, and linguistic lines. Not only did pupils care but their caring also took the form of a pedagogical experience in which they were both teachers and learners, a political and pedagogical principle that Freire would develop, almost simultaneously, in Brazil (Mayo, 2007).

The Barbiana experience revolved around a very important principle—schools should not fail students. Milani and his students considered failure as the weapon used by schools to perpetuate a "caste system," as the root cause of most of the intra-class hatred, and as politically unsustainable and unconstitutional. Exclusionary practices were discriminatory since they acted as sorting machines that ultimately pushed students from disadvantaged backgrounds out of the education system, possibly readying them for exploitation, including overrepresentation at the war front.

Visually and symbolically, the logic of inclusion was expressed in a different way at Barbiana. While at San Donato the crucifix was removed to create an open, nondenominational space for all, at Barbiana the holy cross reappeared on the wall, next to other symbols—Gandhi, Confucius, and a Cuban poem. While not using the term "intercultural dialogue," Milani's curriculum centered around the affirmation and valorization of difference. Difference was perceived by Milani as an essential ingredient in the formation of human beings as well as in the development of democratic and authentically peaceful societies.

Milani's obsession with language became more apparent at Barbiana. Milani conducted 1–3 hour-a-day reading sessions. These sessions were consciously meant to sharpen the students' use of the Italian language and to provide them with a backdrop to read, understand, and write the world from the point of view of the oppressed. During these sessions, students were exposed to narratives of revolutions, wars, resistance, liberation movements, trade unionism, and social movements, among others. These narratives were analyzed against a historical backdrop that ranged from the war experience of their grandparents and parents to the Russian revolution or the wars of liberation in Africa and Asia. These reading sessions centered around Milani's idea that those who could not read and understand the first page of the newspaper were easily pushed to sports pages and doomed to a life of subordination. Such an approach to reading, which also included books like Gandhi's autobiography, "Apartheid" by Angelo Del Boca, and the letters of Claude Eatherly (Martinelli, 2007), contrasted heavily with the fascist practice of using newspapers and periodicals for propaganda. Such was the case in 1936 and 1941, during the occupation of Ethiopia and the first defeats in Africa respectively. Fascist propaganda was also disseminated in schools by Balilla and GILE.

Barbiana's curriculum was also characterized by the struggle against ethnocentricity and monoculturalism (Toriello, 2008). Starting from 1959, Don Milani hosted a number of young foreigners with whom his students could interact in English, French, or German. Those who demonstrated sufficient knowledge of any of the foreign languages were normally encouraged to spend some time abroad. The experience of travelling abroad added credibility to the intercultural dimension of Barbiana's curriculum as it was through such an experience that language genuinely served as an instrument of social relations, real exchange, culture, and negotiation (Toriello, 2008).

Critical literacy and Milani's obsession with mastery of language/s converged in a series of letters that were meant to sharpen his students' analytical skills as well as provide possibilities for action. One of the letters,

*Lettera a una professoressa* (Letter to a Teacher), constitutes a critique of the education system, written by eight of his students, all boys and in their teens. In their *Lettera*, the authors distinguished between a teacher whose attitude and action contributed to their exile to a life of labor in the fields and a teacher, like Milani, who loves unconditionally to the point of going on a hunger strike to reclaim a child who was taken away from school by his parents (Abbate, 2008).

The anger that characterizes *Lettera a una professoressa* is partially attributed to the boys' recognition of the fact that the school system served to reproduce vertical inequalities rather than liberate students. What appeared to be an innocent and apolitical system, intended to offer equal opportunities for all, was, in effect, a school system that sorted, classified, and labeled students, before sending them to different life trajectories, including serving the colonial ambitions of the fascist regime.

Don Milani and his schoolboys were well aware that parents could play a decisive role in the struggle for quality education. The *Lettera* directly addressed parents, encouraging them to stand up to a system that was engineered to perpetuate the hierarchical structure of society; a system that was ironically funded by the work of the poor.

The *Lettera* foregrounds the different fortunes of two boys—Pierino and Gianni. Pierino, a generic name, represents the privileged students who are rewarded and promoted by the education system, and eventually by an "occupational hierarchy" (Bowles and Gintis, 1976) that is essentially credentialist in nature. Scholastic life is easy for Pierino as he comes to school already equipped with the psychophysical discipline, the cultural capital and the mental attitude expected from school. Gianni, another generic name, mirrors the authors' background and fortunes. He represents the low-socioeconomic status students who have been pushed out by the education system and forced into internalizing a complex of inferiority and low self-worth; an education system that did not respect their culture and was at war with the poor.

In response to the analysis of their own exclusion, the Barbiana boys favored a broad-based, curricular experience where the rights of citizenship, the right to be listened to, included and respected, are affirmed (Borg et al., 2013).

*Lettera a una professoressa* appeared on the book shelves in May 1967, a month before the death of Milani on June 26, 1967.

## Milani—Story of a Peace Activist

*Lettera a una professoressa* was written in the shadow of a major controversy that started in 1965. A group of retired military chaplains published a letter in *La Nazione* denouncing those who refused service in the Italian army on the grounds that they were conscientious objectors. The chaplains considered conscientious objection as an insult to the nation and to those who had died defending it. They also referred to conscientious objection as something alien to the Christian commandment of love and an expression of cowardice.

Considering the chaplains' letter as diametrically opposed to his educational philosophy, one based on critical reading of the world rather than passive acceptance of cultural invasion, Milani, in conversation with his students at Barbiana, wrote a letter that linked obedience with support for a string of unjust and repressive wars waged by Italian State that served only the privileged. His historical analysis led him to conclude that the liberal-bourgeois monarchy, from 1862 to its downfall, waged wars but did very little for the poor. He also questioned the chaplains' faith by asking: "Is it God or men that we ought to obey?" (Burtchaell, 1988, p.27). Milani's letter ended:

> Let us respect suffering and death, but let us not dangerously confuse the young people who look to us, about good and evil, about truth and error, about the death of an aggressor and the death of his victim.
>
> Let us say, if you will: we pray for those unfortunate people who have, through no fault of their own, been poisoned by a propaganda of hatred, and have sacrificed themselves for a misunderstood ideal of Fatherland, while unwittingly trampling underfoot every other noble human ideal. (Burthchaell, 1988, p.28)

Milani's letter was immediately condemned by the veterans of war. The public confrontation that developed as a result of the two letters, including the *autodifesa* (self-defence) that followed, attracted a lot of attention on Milani and his school, both locally and internationally, including that of Eric Fromm who sent his secretary, Clara Urquhart, to the parish (Martinelli, 2007).

In this particular period, Barbiana became an educational experience where research, critical and historical analysis, an ongoing process of writing and rewriting dialogue, and external critical input informed the daily life of the foregoing community of learning. Such an experience socialized the Barbiana students into militating against social injustices and to confront immoral practices head-on. In one particular case, when one of his students of conscription age was eventually conscripted, Milani urged him to object to any orders that he regarded as evil. The boy did exactly so and was sent back home after a short stay at the barracks.

Milani and his school were publicly isolated in their objection to forced conscription and in their challenge to the Church to come clean in its glorification of obedience even if it meant that "hapless farmers or workers...were turned into aggressors by military obedience" (Burtchaell, 1988, p.27). The only periodical that published Milani's letter in its entirety was *La Rinascita*, the communist publication edited by a childhood friend—Luca Pavolini. It was published several days after Milani had distributed it to a number of potential publishers. According to Milani, he was left with no option but to publish in the aforementioned periodical. All Catholic press refused to publish the letter (Burtchaell, 1988). Milani himself describes the days following the publication of his letter:

> Dozens of anonymous letters arrived, full of insults, threats, signed with only a swastika or the Fascist symbol. We were misused by some journalists who conducted "interviews" that were dishonest. Then followed incredible conclusions drawn on the strength of those "interviews" by people who never bothered to check their accuracy. We were poorly understood by our own archbishop (Letter to the Clergy, 14 April 1965). And our letter has now become the object of criminal proceedings. (Burthchaell, 1988, p.57)

Don Milani and his publisher were tried on charges of incitement to and advocacy of the crime of desertion and the crime of military disobedience. When the trial began, in autumn 1965, Milani was no longer able to travel to Rome to defend himself. Instead, he submitted letters of defence to the Tribunal of Rome, to be read at the trial.

In his long letter to the judges, Milani affirmed the importance of learning peace by doing peace. He confirmed that the events leading to the trial provided him with a pedagogical opportunity to teach students:

> how a citizen reacts to injustice. What it means for a citizen to enjoy freedom of speech and of the press. How a Christian reacts when it is a priest or even a bishop that has gone amiss. How each one ought to hold oneself responsible for everyone else.(Burthchaell, 1988, p.56)

He also contrasted the school with the courtroom, maintaining that in schools:

> we must form in them, on the one hand, a sense of lawfulness (in this our work resembles yours), and arouse in them, on the other hand, a desire for better laws: a political sense, if you will (and in this our work differs from yours). (Burthchaell, 1988, p.58)

The court of first instance acquitted Don Milani on the grounds that he and his publisher co-defendant simply were exercising their rights of free speech. However, the acquittal was overturned by an appeals court in 1967. The court decreed that:

> The publication of the letter had "inflicted damage upon the public order, and...it is in the interest of the state to repress any activity which has been found to subvert the people's readiness to observe the law." (Burtchaell, 1988, p.107)

By the time the decree was issued Milani was dead.

## Milani and the Struggle for Peace Today

This book honors Milani's religious, educational, and political memory; his struggle for institutions that enable rather than obstruct social justice and genuine peace.

As the world becomes increasingly dominated by an economic system that concentrates wealth and power in the hands of a global ruling class that is served by selectively porous states, this book reminds us that Milani's project of subverting the world that is, with the hope of inventing a world that is not, is a dream worth perpetuating and struggling for.

While all inspired by Milani's biography, the 18 chapters that constitute this book take different trajectories in promoting and/or problematizing peace, confirming the complex and multifaceted nature of the struggle for authentically peaceful social relations. Ranging from the struggle over the creation of memories to repositioning peace artifacts within museums, from rewriting history textbooks to exposing the limits of peace programs, from interrogating symbolic violence to exposing real violence in different contexts wherein social class intersects with gender, religion, ethnicity, and sexuality, from promoting subversion as a viable democratic act to reimagining a Church for the post-internet and post-climate–change world, and from an understanding of peace as a community-in-difference to deconstructing peace/peace education and the cosmopolitan self, among several other issues, the book aims to engage readers in reclaiming the right to dream of a world that disowns fatalism; a world that refuses to accept uncritically the core reasons for violence, that is, colonization of human beings and their resources on a local and global scale.

As editors, we hope that, through this book, the memory of Lorenzo Milani continues to inspire prophets of peace to act now and in dialogue with both oppressors and oppressed.

## References

Abbate, G. (2008). "La scuola di Barbiana: orientamenti e prospettive didattiche." In G. Abbate (Ed.), *Don Milani. Tra scuola e impegno civile*. Naples: Luciano Editore.

Borg, C., Cardona, M. & Caruana, S. (2013). *Social Class, Language and Power: "Letter to a Teacher"—Lorenzo Milani and the School of Barbiana*. Rotterdam and Taipei: Sense Publishers.

Bowles, S. and Gintis, H. (1976). *Schooling in Capitalist America*. New York: Basic Books.

Burthchaell, J. T. (Ed. and Trans.) (1988). *The Teaching and Trial of Don Lorenzo Milani*. Notre Dame, IN: University of Notre Dame Press.

Fiorani, L. (1999). *Don Milani. Tra storia e attualità*. Vicchio, Florence: Centro Formazione e Ricerca Don Lorenzo Milani e Scuola di Barbiana.

Freire, P. (1973). *Education for Critical Consciousness*. New York: Continuum.

Freire, P. (1995). "Learning to Read the World. Paulo Freire in Conversation with Carlos Torres." In C. A. Torres (Ed.), *Education and Social Change in Latin America*. Melbourne: James Nicholas Publishers.

Ledwith, M. (2005). *Community Development. a Critical Approach*. Bristol: Policy Press.

Mayo, P. (2007). "Critical Approaches to Education in the Work of Lorenzo Milani and Paulo Freire." *Studies in Philosophy of Education*, 26, pp. 525–544.

Martinelli, E. (2007). *Don Lorenzo Milani. Dal motivo occasionale al motivo profondo*. Florence: Società Editrice Fiorentina.

Rossi, N. and Cole, T. (1970). *Letter to a Teacher. By the School of Barbiana*. Victoria, Australia: Penguin Books.

Schettini, B. (2008). "Don Lorenzo Milani: l'inquietudine della fede, la passione per l'uomo." In G. Abbate (Ed.), *Don Milani. Tra scuola e impegno civile*. Naples: Luciano Editore.

Toriello, F. (2008). "Lettera a una professoressa quarant'anni dopo: una lettura interculturale." In G. Abbate (Ed.) *Don Milani. Tra scuola e impegno civile*. Naples: Luciano Editore.

# Part I

# Peace and Religion: Then and Now

# 1

# The Catholic, Italian, and Tuscan Ecclesiastical Contexts of Don Milani's "Letter to the Military Chaplains"

*Carmel Borg and Michael Grech*

## Introduction

This writing will suffer from an obvious defect. It will attempt to sketch one single and concise picture out of the different approaches to peace and war among the varied, heterogeneous, contradictory, and multifarious phenomena that were to be found among the Catholic clergy and laity in Italy and Europe in the late nineteenth and early and mid-twentieth centuries. Hence, it will inevitably be characterized by oversimplification and overgeneralization. In addition, in certain parts, it might appear to suffer from another defect; a voluntaristic and idealistic emphasis on the thoughts of eminent thinkers and figures, as though the history of the thoughts, sentiments and ideas of millions of Catholics could be synthesized in the beliefs and notions of a few individuals. Moreover, it might appear to detach these from the variegated social, economic, and political formations from which they stem or, at least, not to give sufficient importance to these. We wish to do none of this, though given the lack of space and the vastness of the subject, this might be inevitable.

Our intent is only to paint a few brushstrokes that will hopefully give the reader an idea of the contexts (at least the intellectual and ecclesiastic ones) in which Milani grew and formed his beliefs, opinions, and character. The emphasis will be on the Catholic Church, its institutions and milieu, with a particular emphasis on the Italian and indeed the Tuscan churches.

## The Post/Counter Revolution Church

One cannot understand Milani's context without referring to the dominant Catholic "worldview/s" in the late nineteenth and early-mid twentieth centuries. Following the French Revolution and the Napoleonic wars, the Church[1] gradually became the champion of those who attempted to restore the *Ancien Regime* or at least to resist the bourgeois-democratic ideals stemming from the Revolution of 1789 that were spreading throughout Europe. This role was cemented by the pontificate of the once-"liberal" Pius IX. In this period the Church generally denounced bourgeois-democracy, stressed the people's duties to their kings and "intervened" in political affairs through alliances and exchanges with various thrones. The bourgeois tide in the major European centers, however, could not be stemmed. Moreover, the arrival on the political scene of a new protagonist, the working class movement, entailed not merely an alliance between the church and some sectors of the bourgeoisie with which it was previously at loggerheads, but, generally, a tactical, programmatic and at times ideological *aggiornamento*. For instance, rather than opposing parliamentary-democracy *tout court* as it had done in some cases, in major European Catholic nations the Church started to back political groups and parties; generally monarchist, conservative, and increasingly nationalist; that opposed the demands of those bourgeois still intent on curtailing the Catholic Church's privileges and on furthering the rights stemming from the ideals of 1789, as well as of those workers' movements hoping for even deeper change.

Christian-Democratic parties; appealing to Church-abiding Catholics, who were sensible to social issues and who sought to deal with social problems in the light of the Church's social teachings, also became popular, although they generally became the Church's "political vehicle" in some European nations but not in others. In countries like France, Spain, Portugal, and in the Austro-Hungarian empire, Christian-Democratic parties remained marginal, at least prior to the Second World War, and the Church's hierarchy and the Catholic faithful electorate generally preferred monarchist, conservative, and nationalist alternatives.[2] Even where Christian-Democratic discourse got hold, these parties could easily be sacrificed to nationalist, monarchist, and conservative groups, if an alliance with the latter were deemed to be more convenient to the Church. This occurred in Italy to the *Partito Popolare Italiano* in the early 1920s, when the Church saw Fascism as a better alternative to the Partito Popolare Italiano (PPI) in combating Socialism, and to the Centre Party in Germany following the signing of the Concordat with the Nazi regime.

The "discourses" of all these parties favorable to the Church generally shared two different features. First they were discourses that appealed to the masses. Secondly they downplayed the class struggles and contradictions that characterized industrial societies, attempting to reconcile these "idealistically" or to present "external" solutions to internal contradictions and shortcomings.[3] Some mass parties, particularly in France in the nineteenth and Spain in the nineteenth and twentieth centuries, went further than this, preaching a radical/reactionary reversal to institutions, structures, and concepts that promote ideas that predate the revolution of 1789.[4]

## Peace and a Marriage of Convenience

While the Catholic Church upheld peace as an ideal, it did not endorse Pacifism. A common assumption among many Catholics was that peace could be achieved in a true and lasting manner only if a Christian World Order were established.

The notion of a Christian World Order had two main aspects. The first is a practical aspect, related to a person's morals and conduct. In this regard, it is pertinent to go back at least to St. Augustine who divides humanity into two communities, two "cities," the City of God—meaning the community of those humans living a spiritual, God-fearing, life, and the City of Man—people who give priority to the material world and its pleasures. Only the former may achieve and promote true and lasting peace, and exhibit what Augustine considers to be the fundamental virtue, "Charity," meaning unlimited, altruistic, love. The City of Man includes pagans and possibly even Christians (including Churchmen). Only God-fearing individuals may be members of the City of God.

The notion of a Christian World Order had another aspect, an institutional one, an aspect related to the Church, to states and to their arrangement and relationship. A state may be just only if it follows Christian principles and precepts, principles and precepts that are imparted by the Church. This attitude generally stemmed from the belief that "anything positive, benevolent, true, just and pure, both on an individual and on a collective level,... is directly or indirectly traceable to Christianity."[5] On international level, this seemed to entail that lasting and genuine peace may only be achieved if states followed Christian principles.

In the light of this, many theologians and religious affirmed the superiority of the Church over the state, and promoted the belief that the Church is set above such nations, and, if need be, should act as an arbiter between them. Obviously, this raises problems when not all nations are Christian or for that matter "good Christian Nations" (those Christian nations, for instance, who strayed away from Catholicism in theory and/or in practice, or from papal favor and approbation[6]). Not only was there the belief that no true and lasting peace may be achieved in such a situation, the logical conclusion to be drawn from the belief that genuine peace arises only if people abide by Christian principles, but the problem cropped up as to what legal, political, moral, and practical approaches to adopt in dealing with non-Christian nations or with Christian nations that had strayed away from the right path. Should one take an "active" stance and attempt to bring these within the right fold? Or should one take a more resigned attitude, in the hope that the inevitable failure of their attempts to build peaceful and prosperous societies according to non-Church inspired mores, might induce them to turn to Rome for guidance?[7]

Moving to the nineteenth and early twentieth centuries, the Church finally ceased to exist as a sovereign political power. Yet, this did not immediately entail a change in outlook or ambitions. Even with regards to peace and war, not only did it continue to uphold the Medieval Just War theory, the theory which holds that, provided certain conditions, sovereigns could and indeed might be duty-bound to declare war, but, in many cases, it allowed Nationalists and Conservatives of different ilks to intertwine Nationalistic rhetoric emphasizing duties to one's fatherland with Catholic doctrines and beliefs. This included instances when this nationalistic rhetoric referred to sacrifices to this fabled fatherland and implied duties of unquestionable or almost unquestionable obedience to it. At times, this enthusiasm for one's country did not limit itself to those instances when the "fatherland" was threatened by others; it extended to the support of expansionist wars as well as to violent rebellion against "red" governments and progressive movements, as in Spain in the 1930s.

Already at this time however, there were Catholics who saw beyond this marriage of convenience between Catholicism and Nationalism. The American Catholic activist Dorothy Day was a case in point. For instance, she refused to take sides in the Spanish Civil War, a war which a lot of Catholics considered as a God-sanctioned Crusade. Through her paper *The Catholic Worker* she promoted pacifism. Day was also highly engaged in her country's labor movement, and explicitly linked the ideal of peace to the promotion of social justice and the causes of labor and the poor. Following the Second World War, she and her followers also denounced most Cold-War rhetoric, and claimed that, given the destructive nature of modern military technology, no war could be just in a modern scenario. In Europe, the German Cardinal Michael Von Faulhaber (a recipient of the Iron Cross during the First World War) and the Jesuit Auguste Valensin among others had been harboring similar thoughts prior to the Second World War.[8]

In Austria, the humble sacristan Franz Jägerstätter, the illegitimate son of a farmer, did not have the intellectual training of Von Faulhaber or Valensin, nor the broad and articulated views as to how the world and society ought to be organized that Day and her movement had. Yet, in his simplicity, he debunked the myths that emphasized the purity and integrity of the German peoples, myths that ideologically buttressed Nazism in Germany and Austria. Jägerstätter claimed that it is the blood Christ spilled on the cross, not Aryan or German blood, that can bring redemption to people. He denounced those Austrian Catholics who had succumbed to this pagan rhetoric and in 1939 refused to serve in the German army, despite the opinion to the contrary of his village priest, the insistence of his family and the assurance by local officials that he would be assigned to a noncombatant post and, later, that he would be immediately dismissed on answering the call. Jägerstätter was guillotined on August 9, 1943. He was raised to the altars by Pope Benedict XVI.

One can therefore see that apart from the Nationalistic and Conservative character of a lot of Catholic thinking prior to the Second World War, there were already Catholics who: (1) questioned the just war theory, or its applicability; (2) supported or practiced some form of conscientious objection; and (3) linked peace to social justice.

## Italy

The situation was different in Milani's Italy at the dawn of the twentieth century. One major difference concerned the nature of Italian Nationalism and its relationship to the Catholic Church. The Italian state, formed in 1860 under the leadership of the Royal House of Savoy, was not recognized by the Holy See for almost 70 years, until the 1929 Concordat and the Lateran Pacts. To come into existence, the Italian state had to annex and bring to extinction the papal states, a process culminating in the Savoyard invasion of Rome in 1870. The Pope of the day, Pius IX, not only refused to recognize the Italian state, claiming that the Savoyard Kingdom had usurped his rights as a sovereign and head of the Catholic Church, but through his *Non-Expedit* issued in 1870, encouraged Catholics not to participate in Italian politics. This notwithstanding, many Italian Catholics, including a number of clerics, took/had to take a more pragmatic approach to the new nation, and gradually started to collaborate with it and to participate in state affairs. The *Non-Expedit* was relaxed by Pope Pius X in 1904 through the encyclical letter *Fermo Proposito*. It was formally lifted by Pope Benedict XV in 1919. One reason for this gradual settlement was the electoral success of the *Partito Socialista Italiano,* which had been founded in 1892, a success that undoubtedly favored some form of rapprochement between the Church and the bourgeois elites that had dominated politics in the nascent state. Even though the Vatican did not yet recognize the Italian state and prior to the formal lifting of the *Non-Expedit*, a priest like the Sicilian Luigi Sturzo could stand for local elections and be elected vice-mayor of his hometown Caltagirone. Clerics also undertook missionary work in the new Italian colonies of Eritrea (1890) and Libya (1912). Some started to serve in the army as chaplains.

Many of the latter could combine Catholic pastoral activity among soldiers with Nationalistic fervor and rhetoric, even before the Italian state and the Holy See were reconciled with each other. Such Nationalistic rhetoric however, was not limited to military chaplains. Sturzo, the founding father of the West's largest Christian-Democratic party (the Partito Popolare Italiano or PPI), claimed in 1904 that *"nazionalismo"* was one of the ideals of his movement,[9] and supported the Italian invasion of Libya in 1912 as well as Italy's intervention in the First World War on grounds that Italy should support the Allies' ideals of liberty, justice, and civilization.[10] Sturzo could thus embrace "colonial policies enhancing the Nation's interest"[11] while at the same time promoting a "Society of Nations...that would arbitrate, abolish secret treatises...(and) promote universal disarmament."[12]

Others went even further and adopted a fiercer Nationalistic rhetoric. Notwithstanding Pope Benedict XV's condemnation of the First World War as *Inutile Strage* (something that earned him the aversion of Italian Nationalists, who started to call him "Maledetto XV" and accusing him of instilling defeatism in Italian troops), clerics like Don Agostino Gemelli (later to found the Catholic University at Milan and, in the words of Antonio

Gramsci, to be entrusted with organizing the Church's cultural hegemony following the 1929 Concordat), talked of an "Anti-Teutonic Crusade." The Vatican newspaper *L'Osservatore Romano* emphasized that it is a Catholic's duty to resist his motherland's enemies.[13] Even a mild priest like Angelo Roncalli, later to become Pope John XXIII and to inaugurate the Second Vatican Council, would claim that: "A sacrifice for one's country is a sacrifice for God and for our brothers"[14]

To a number of clerics, the First World War started to appear as an event that had a redemptive function, many of them comparing it to a "Long Good Friday" and drawing analogies between the wives and mothers of dead soldiers and Mary standing beneath Jesus' cross. Some even claimed that the sacrifice and suffering war entailed served quasi-redemptive purposes.[15]

Despite these advances, not all Italian Nationalists accepted the Catholic-Nationalistic rhetoric of Gemelli and the rest. After all, the Italian state had been formed in opposition to the Vatican and a good number of anticlericals and freemasons played a prominent part in the process of unification. Many of these were suspicious of and resisted Catholic overtures to the "Patria." Pope Benedict XV's stand during the conflict did not endear him to them either. No wonder that a good number of Italian Nationalists, including the Nascent Fascist movement, still saw Italian Nationalism and Catholicism as fundamentally incompatible.[16]

Yet, the "Red threat," manifested particularly in the years 1919–1920, forced the two sides to come nearer to each other. The mass unemployment and the economic and political crises that followed the war, as well as the example of the Russian Soviets, together with other causes, led to a number of strikes and worker takeover of various industries. These were mostly crushed by Fascist militias, leading many anti-Socialists, including a good number of Catholics, to see Fascism as the only bulwark against Communism and/or anarchy. Moreover, Mussolini could and did abandon his movement's anticlericalism in order to widen Fascism's consensus and strengthen his hold on Italian people. The 1929 Lateran Pacts blessed and fostered this rapprochement, and in some quarters led to "'Clerico-Fascism," an ideological hotchpotch of Fascist politics and Conservative-Catholic philosophy. The endorsement by many Catholics of the aggressive ambitions of the Italian Fascist state was perhaps exemplified in one episode; Cardinal Schuster of Milan blessing the banners of Italian troops on their way to brutally colonize Ethiopia in October 1935. The Cardinal described the war as a new Crusade, a Crusade that would bring new converts to the Catholic Church. The invasion supported by most Italian clerics and apparently endorsed by the Vatican itself, with Pope Pius XI commenting that "the hopes, the demands, the needs of a great and good people [Italy] should be recognised and satisfied"[17] when the League of Nations discussed sanctions against Italy following the latter's aggression against Ethiopia.

The enthusiasm for this war, however, was infectious among all strata of Italian society, and not just within Catholic and Nationalist circles. Milani himself, at this stage still an agnostic Jew, admits to having been overjoyed when, following the defeat of Ethiopia by Italian forces, as a 15-year-old student he and his friends listened to the proclamation of the Italian Empire on May 9, 1936.

## Rays of Hope

Already at this time however, there were Catholics, including priests and other religious, who took a different approach to Christianity, war, Nationalism, and the relationship between these. Some denounced the Fascist regime, without necessarily condemning the concept of war as such. Others went even further. In this regard, the work of Primo Mazzolari clearly stands out. Although he supported Italian intervention in the First World War (on grounds that German militarism had to be stamped out and that there was the need to establish a democratic order throughout Europe) and was a military chaplain on the French front, Don Primo gradually started to adopt a different approach to war and to social and international issues. Mazzolari denounced:

> The pagan celebration of war, which falsely presents armed conflict as a celebration or an undertaking that is essential to the glory of the fatherland...when in fact it may only be a terrible necessity brought about by private and national self-love.[18]

He later "refined his view to war as an 'evil which at times may be necessary' and finally become firmly critical of all wars, including defensive ones, identifying war as the anti-thesis of humanity."[19] This seemed to mean that no war may be just, regardless of how right or aggrieved a party is.[20]

Mazzolari publicly opposed Fascism during the regime's heyday, and was censured by both state and church. Rather than seeing Fascism as the movement that might restore Italy to its past glory or to some mythical golden age, as Fascists and certain currents within the Church maintained, Mazzolari argued that what Italian society required was cultural and moral restructuring, based on the ideals of justice, solidarity, and fraternity of human beings; ideals that were foreign to Mussolini and his regime. Mazzolari's "patria":

> began to be identified with the ascent of the popular masses...(with) a civil and participative dynamism.[21]

His opposition to Fascism was not tempered by the signing of the Concordat, lamenting that this event entailed that "we (the clergy) no longer are what we were up to yesterday; the only break to nationalistic enthusiasm."[22] As with Dorothy Day and others, his activity for peace was intertwined with his commitment to social justice (calling peace and social justice two sides of the same coin), a commitment that was not deaf to the arguments of those on the Left who clamored for a social order where the instances of workers and the downtrodden are recognized and acknowledged.

An important collaborator of Don Primo, Guido Miglioli worked along these lines.[23] A Catholic trade-unionist, a firm opponent of huge landowners during the *biennio rosso* and a member of the *Partito Popolare Italiano* as from 1919, Miglioli was expelled from the party in 1924 because of his radical social ideals and, subsequently, had to flee Italy during the Fascist *ventennio*. Following the Second World War, he founded a political movement called *Movimento Cristiano per la Pace* (Christian Movement for Peace), a movement that supported the Socialist-Communist coalition in the 1948 elections.

Mazzolari, Miglioli, and similar minded Catholics were not the only ones to propose a different "world-view" from the one that Fascism and clerico-Fascism promoted. Another important figure who opposed the regime and was a major influence in debates about peace, even in Catholic circles, was Aldo Capitini. Capitini helped popularize Gandhi's thought in Italy and held that violence cannot be justified, even as a way of dealing with injustice. His refusal to use violence was not merely a pragmatic expedient, but stemmed from a nonviolent philosophy, which inspired his world-view. In light of this philosophy Capitini adopted vegetarianism and, though remaining a fervent Christian and a deeply spiritual person, abandoned Catholicism. He renounced Catholicism not merely because of its pragmatic compromises with brutal regimes like Fascism,[24] but also because of certain doctrines and doctrinal points, like the Catholic Church's insistence on the eternity of hell and its portrayal of the devil, which he considered to be incompatible with Christianity's nonviolent convictions.[25] Despite these unorthodox thoughts, Capitini still exerted an influence in some Catholic quarters.

## Second World War and the End of Fascist Rhetoric

The terrible consequences of Fascism's bellicose rhetoric were felt during the Second World War. War came to be seen by many for what it was: a "strage" as Pope Benedict XV had called it in 1917 and something through which "everything is lost" in the words of Pius XII—the Pontiff that sat on Peter's throne during the conflict. The glory of war and the beauty of dying on the battlefield, flaunted by many Fascists and by some members of the clergy, came to be seen as the tragedy they were. Still, patriotic rhetoric persisted even after the war had ended, so much so that some postwar historians attempted to depict resistance to Fascism in patriotic terms, notwithstanding the fact that this resistance prominently featured Socialist, Anarchist, and Communist groups sporting an internationalist character and outlook. Resistance was pictured by Conservative and Moderate historians as a war against "foreign" invaders, the German Nazis, forgetting that it was first and foremost a civil war, with as many Italian youths enrolled on the Nazi-Fascist side as in the antifascist resistance.[26] This patriotic rhetoric was used as a popular and legitimizing coagulate that, following the war, Conservative and bourgeois intellectuals and politicians used to counter the popular and widespread discourse of left-wing parties and organizations. No wonder that even following the Second World War many Italians still thought that pacifist and internationalist discourses were a left-wing exclusive!

There was indeed a strong pacifist tradition on the Left. A good number of Socialists, Anarchists and others had viewed the First World War as a struggle between the various bourgeois elites in different nations, a war in which the working class should not play any part. Most members of the PSI favored neutrality in the First World War, though the party also contained an interventionist wing. This wing included Benito Mussolini who would later roam in different pastures.

Following the Second World War, one cannot fail to mention the movement of the "Partisans of Peace" inaugurated in Paris in 1949. This movement exerted an important influence on the Italian Left. Among other things, the movement sought to combat imperialism, ban atomic weapons, limit the size of armies, support pacifist initiatives, oppose racial hatred, help victims of war and lobby the five major world powers to agree on a "pact for peace" that would avoid a new world war. The founding members included Pablo Picasso, Albert Einstein, Pablo Neruda, Pietro Nenni, Henri Matisse, and the Nobel Prize winner Frédéric Joliot-Curie. The movement was labeled as "communist" by many Western governments and by many Catholic prelates, even though it included members who were famous for their non-Marxist credentials. No wonder that in 1959 the Jesuit *Civiltà Cattolica* thundered against those Catholics who were fooled by "the illusion of Co-existence" between Western and Communist Europe; the latter regimes being characterized by "seduction" and "deception."[27] In many Catholic circles, this suspicion stemmed not merely from the belief that communism and anything that smacks remotely of it cannot be redeemed, but also from the conviction that even with the best of intentions, secular and non-Catholic individuals, organizations and initiatives cannot achieve peace.[28] The idea that peace may only be achieved through an international Christian World Order was still very much alive. In the words of the Bishop of Montalcione, Ireneo Chelucci:

> Having completely failed to achieve the 'peace of man; we have no option but the peace of God....(After all) at the heart of every war there is a moral disorder, it is futile to wish to achieve peace without addressing the latter.[29]

Those Catholics that espoused themes similar to those of these secular peace movements raised the suspicions of the hierarchy and of their religious brethren. This notwithstanding, their voice grew and became more articulate as years went by and the Cold-War unfolded.

Within the Catholic Church, a movement aimed at reconciling French and German peoples was born in 1946. This movement, Pax Christi

International, gradually widened its network, scope and perspectives, and is still influential today. In Milani's Italy a foremost voice for peace was Giorgio la Pira, a Sicilian who had championed human rights during Fascism and published various journals that were suppressed by the regime. La Pira entered parliament in 1948 and, together with Giuseppe Dossetti, Amintore Fanfani, and Giuseppe Lazzati, was a prominent part of the ruling Christian-Democratic party's "left-wing." His "leftist" and redistributive initiatives as mayor of Florence, led many Conservatives to accuse him of being a "white-communist," a fellow-traveler to Marxists and Communists.

La Pira made Florence a center of peace. In this regard he initiated a number of peace initiatives aimed at enhancing East-West, North-South, and Christian-Muslim-Jewish dialogue. These included a roundtable conference promoting disarmament, initiatives aimed at voicing the concerns of Africa and the third world, and an active support of decolonization. La Pira visited Moscow in 1959 and addressed the Soviet Supreme on the theme of disarmament. In 1965 he visited Vietnam when the country was at war with the United States. Here he met Ho Chi Minh and together with the North Vietnamese leader, drafted the blueprint of a possible agreement between the two warring parties. (This agreement, which was much more favorable to the United States than the actual peace agreement the Americans were forced to sign eight years later, was rejected by President Johnson.) Most of La Pira's initiatives attracted the ire of conservative quarters within the Church and society. He was however, supported by "liberal" clerics like the Florence-based David Maria Turoldo.

Primo Mazzolari was still active in the 1950s, publishing his *Tu Non Uccidere* in 1955, his major and most articulate protest against war and violence. The Catholic Action and the Catholic Scout movement also took an interest in affairs beyond Europe, particularly the movement for African independence. The ideas that peace may be achieved through the promotion of justice (including social justice on a national and international level) and democracy (and not simply through political and international treaties), as well as the belief that peace may not be achieved from "the above" but by working at a grassroot level, were gaining ground. One implication this "entailed was going beyond the notion that peace necessarily...(requires) a 'Christian World Order'"[30] Indeed, inside:

> ecclesiastical circles...[the]...growing concern about rearmament...led to the gradual acceptance that Catholics should sustain wider peace initiatives, even those that might be ideologically 'tinted.'[31]

The Vatican seemed to give its "blessing" to this trend with the publication of Pope John XXIII's groundbreaking encyclical *Pacem in Terris*. The encyclical was groundbreaking not merely because it was addressed to all people of goodwill (and not just to Catholics), regardless of their belief, if any, but also because it did not pose adherence to Catholicism and to the guidelines/guidance of the Catholic Church as the presupposition of what it considers as the goal (Peace) that humans have sought and longed for throughout the ages.

Rather than beginning with belief in God or Catholic Faith, the encyclical opens with what it takes (in terms which sound pre-Kantian and pre-Darwinian) to be the: "marvelous order predominates in the world of living beings and in the forces of nature."[32] The interpretative key to such order is not metaphysics or Catholic Doctrine but "modern research and the discoveries of technology" and " it is part of the greatness of man that he can appreciate that order." [33] In contrast to this idyllic picture of nature, there is: "disunity among individuals and among nations which is in striking contrast to this perfect order in the universe." The encyclical considers those who "think that the relationships that bind men together could only be governed by force," an opinion that was upheld by many Catholic theologians, and confutes it by maintaining that "the world's Creator has stamped man's inmost being with an order revealed to man by his conscience; and his conscience insists on his preserving it. Men show the work of the law written in their hearts."[34]

The recipe to rectify this "disunity" is not a "Catholic World Order," wherein the Holy See is an arbiter between states, or a situation where states "return" to a Church that emanates *diktats* or anathemas (very much the spirit of nineteenth and early twentieth-century encyclicals), but rather a "world-wide community of nations"; be these Christian or not.[35]

Referring indirectly to Marxism, the Encyclical affirms that:

> It is perfectly legitimate to make a clear distinction between a false philosophy of the nature, origin and purpose of men and the world, and economic, social, cultural, and political undertakings, even when such undertakings draw their origin and inspiration from that philosophy. True, the philosophic formula does not change once it has been set down in precise terms, but the undertakings clearly cannot avoid being influenced to a certain extent by the changing conditions in which they have to operate. Besides, who can deny the possible existence of good and commendable elements in these undertakings, elements which do indeed conform to the dictates of right reason, and are an expression of man's lawful aspirations?[36]

It is: "Men's common interests [that] make it imperative that at long last a world-wide community of nations be established." When there is "a clash of interests among States, each striving for its own development...When differences of this sort arise, they must be settled in a truly human way, not by armed force nor by deceit or trickery. There must be a mutual assessment of the arguments and feelings on both sides, a mature and objective investigation of the situation, and an equitable reconciliation of opposing views." The encyclical makes a deep plea for disarmament,[37] expresses skepticism at the belief in mutual rearmament,[38] and advocates disarmament, negotiation, and dialogue between people.[39]

## Conscientious Objection

Still, not all new currents within the Catholic Church entailed that those involved in them supported conscientious objection. Conscientious objection is not mentioned in *Pacem in Terris*. Even a movement sympathetic to peace and peace initiatives like the Catholic Action tended, in the 1950s and 1960s, to raise doubts about conscientious objection, holding that "obligatory conscription constitutes a positive contribution by citizens; a consolidation of values... the ideals and spirit of sacrifice with military life promotes."[40] Roberto Massimiliani, Bishop of Civita Castellane, Orte and Galalese, could still reiterate that:

> It is a common doctrine amongst Catholics that conscientious objection violates duties to legal justice as well as our obligations towards our society, from which we receive benefits and to which we have duties. The common good requires that citizens share the benefits as well as the burdens of collective life, including the obligation to military service.[41]

One of the first prominent Catholics to support conscientious objection was the Tuscan Ernesto Balducci, a presbyter-intellectual who was involved in various political and social activities, as well as in many peace and third world initiatives initiated by La Pira and others. Balducci was one of the very first Catholics who defended conscientious objection in 1963. In an article on *Il giornale del mattino,* Balducci argued for the primacy of conscience over any law enacted by the state. Like Milani, he was also put on trial. He kept working for peace until the 1980s, focusing on themes like the promotion of human rights, environment, and disarmament.

The foremost sign of openness by the *magisterum* probably came with the Apostolic Constitution *Gaudium et Spes* of 1965 (the year when the Tuscan military chaplains and Milani wrote their letters). The Apostolic Constitution is lovingly concerned with the "joys, hopes, griefs and anxieties" of human beings in the modern world and, apart from encouraging cultural and economic progress, promoting the rights of the poor, advocating the avoidance of war, linking peace to justice and abetting the idea of an international community, recognizes in a qualified manner the legitimacy of those who choose to renounce to actively serving in armies for reasons of conscience.

In the first years of the twentieth century up to the time of Milani's letter, Italian Catholicism contained a number of different and at times divergent lines of thought regarding the issue of war, the military, and the "patria." Apart from Conservative, patriotic, and nationalist variants, there were currents that criticized war, some going as far as claiming that no war may be just today, if not denouncing altogether the whole concept of just war. This notwithstanding, even within the Catholic "Left," many had strong doubts about the notion of conscientious objection, though a number of individuals begged to differ.

## Notes

1. In what follows, by "Church" we shall understand the Catholic Church, and more precisely the organized structures of the religious ordained to teach, administer, and rule the faithful, under the guidance of and in communion with the Bishop of Rome (i.e., the Pope). Many, ourselves included, would normally contest this definition of "Church"; understanding by Church the community of all faithful, both ordained and secular. However, since the previous institutional understanding of the term is colloquially more popular, at least in our part of Europe, we shall use the word in this way.
2. See Kalyvas. S. N. (1996). *The Rise of Christian Democracy in Europe* (London: Cornell University Press).
3. As an example of the former one can mention those Christian-Democratic discourses that emphasized the "accidental" or indeed "man-made and malicious" nature of class antagonism and preached the "essential" harmony of interests of all parties in a social formation. As an example of the second, one may mention colonialism and settlement in colonies for "poor" locals.
4. Obviously not all Catholics shared this intent. Christian Democrats, for instance, generally tended to see democracy and certain rights that stemmed from the French Revolution as a *fait accompli,* and as a positive legacy.
5. Triofini. P. (2009). "Il mondo cattolico italiano tra guerra e pace dal Patto atlantico al Concilio Vaticano II," in P. Trionfini, *Tu Non Uccidere—Mazzolari e il Pacifisimo del Novecento* (Brescia: Morcelliana), p.86.
6. Many a time, this discourse about a Christian World Order coincided with the Papacy's politics and international role. From simply being the seat of the bishop of Rome, the Papacy gradually widened its claims, vision, and ambitions regarding the Western Roman Empire, Christendom, and the World at large. An early indication of the Pope's claims and ambitions was the forged "Donation of Constantine," an eighth-century forgery claiming that emperor Constantine the great had handed Pope Sylvester his imperial crown which, though refused, signified that the emperor (and by implication any secular ruler) received his power from the Church. In the Middle Ages, saints like Bernard of Clairvaux would claim that the Pope "had received the whole world to govern and it was the task of his vicar 'to direct princes, to command bishops. To set kingdoms and empires in order'" (Duffy. E, *Sinners & Saints: A History of the Popes,* [Yale: Nota Bene, 2003], p.138) This could take different forms; from sanctioning the deposition of a king or ruling house and the installation of another (as in the Carolingian takeover of the French throne, William the Conqueror's invasion of Britain and the recognition of Norman rule in Southern Italy), to playing the role of arbiters or mediators.
7. The attitude adopted generally depended on Rome's ability to mobilize kings, Christians, and armies.
8. Trionfini, "Il mondo cattolico," p.43.
9. Sturzo. L. (2004). "La Croce di Costantino" quoted in G. Fanello Marcucci, *Lugi Sturzo—Vita e battaglie per la libertà del fondtore del Partito Popolare Italiano* (Milan: Le Sice Mondadori), p.30.
10. Marcucci, *Vita e battaglie,* p.44.
11. Ibid.
12. Ibid.
13. Peter Hebblethwaite (2000), *John XXIII Pope of the Century* (London: Continuum). p.41.
14. Sergio Luzzato (2009), Padre Pio—Miracoli e politica nell'Italia del Novecento (Torino: Einaudi), p.75.

15. Luzzato, S., *Padre Pio—Miracoli e politica nell'Italia del Novecento*, p.6. Not all those who served on the front shared this nationalist enthusiasm. A case in point was: "Clemente Rebora (1885—1957)…[who] would eventually enter the Catholic Church…When war came, he was drafted and sent to the Isonzo. He likened military service to a 'mission,' like pastoral care, and praised the soldier's 'patient sweet humanity.' As a soldier and poet, he was determined to spare himself nothing amid the 'seas of mud and freezing bora, and putrefaction'. He was tormented at having to send his men…to almost certain death. 'what a stench from our unburied dead, while our own artillery kills us off by mistake!' he exclaimed, in a letter…On 1 December 1915, shortly before he was invalidated away form the front, Rebora wrote to his mother: 'It is a blessing for your peace of mind and comfort that you know nothing about the moral mire, the pity and horror of what's happening; and only know the news through the yellow press that deceives the fatherland—and you mothers!' The physical suffering was awful, but the inward torment was much worse." Thompson. M. (2008), *The White War—Life and Death on the Italian Front 1915—1919* (London), p.182f.
16. An article by Mussolini on the *Popolo d'Italia* in 1916 called for the "re-crucifixion of Christ" and the Fascist political program of 1919 was riddled with anticlerical rhetoric. It also contained provisions against bishops and against the religious orders.
17. Pius XI quoted in Hebblethwaite. P. (2000). *John XIII Pope of the Century* (London: Continuum), p.73.
18. quoted in Ibid., p.40.
19. Trionfini, "Il mondo cattolico," p.65.
20. A position later adopted by other clerics, even some clerics located in the highest stages of the hierarchy like Evaristo Calli, the bishop of Parma, who in 1949 warned that the conditions that may render a war just, no longer hold in the twentieth century.
21. Trionfini, "Il mondo cattolico," p.31. Mazzolari was later to take part in the Resistance movement against the Fascists and the German forces in Italy during the Second World War.
22. Primo Mazzolari quoted in Trionfini, "Il mondo cattolico," p.40.
23. Even Milani collaborated with Mazzolari, writing articles for a journal (*Adesso*) that the latter published.
24. On the occasion of the Concordat, Capitini commented that Christians did indeed owe Mussolini something, the fact that he showed them that religion is one thing and religious institutions quite another.
25. Franzoni. G. (2008). *Il Diavolo Mio Fratello* (Rome: Rubbettino), pp.82–85.
26. See Bartolini, A., *Per la patria e la liberta'. I soldati italiani all'estero nella resistenza*, Milan 1986. To this day, about 60 percent of students in Lombardy associate the concepts of "resistance" and "patriotism." See www.anpi.it/milano_confst_indagine.htm. An example of how this patriotic rhetoric was in many cases far off the mark, is evident from the testimony of ordinary individuals like Massimo Redina "A Catholic…who had no aspiration to fight and kill. Indeed, to an interlocutor who asked him whether 'Catholics prefer suffering death rather than inflicting it?', he answers 'Yes. To this day I'd rather die than inflict death'. Yet, on the 9th of September, when the Nazis had occupied Turin, he made the decision to take part in the Resistance movement, given the death-spree of the German army…This was exemplified in one episode at Porta Susa, where a soldier killed two or three women in cold-blood after some of them shouted 'Leave.'" A. Del Boca (2006). *Italiani Brava Gente?* (Vicenza: Neri Pozza), p.262.
27. Trionfini"Il mondo cattolico," p.89.

28. Ibid., p.100.
29. Quoted in Ibid., p.106.
30. Ibid., p.96.
31. Ibid., p.92. Notable in Florence at the time, was the base community of l'*Isolotto* (a popular district of the city) founded by Don Enzo Mazzi; a community founded to promote "the fundamental needs of the person; happiness, well-being, solidarity and peace." See www.comunitaisolotto.org/chisiamo.htm. The community was noteworthy for the support it gave to disabled people, former prisoners, as well as Catholics who did not endorse the politics of the Christian-Democratic party. The community was later very active in and supportive of the 1968 movement.
32. The author of the encyclical seems awestruck by the order he perceives in the universe; an order that seems to entail some kind of economy and/or design. He is apparently oblivious to the chaos that exists in the universe, the cruelty and waste that characterize life, the Darwinian narrative as to how the order we now witness came into being and Kant's philosophical insight as to the order and design we perceive in the universe being something that our mind imposes on the data it receives, serving practical and heuristic purposes, rather than providing insight into the way in which the world exists independently of us. Otherwise, he would have at least confuted these opinions.
33. Though it also affirms that "what emerges first and foremost from the progress of scientific knowledge and the inventions of technology is the infinite greatness of God Himself, who created both man and the universe." *Pacem in Terris*, p.3.
34. Other writers like La Pira went further than simply not accepting that human relations may only be governed by the use of force. Using, once more, a "teleological" sounding language, this time in relation to human beings, he writes that "[w]ithin human history, beneath the chaotic surface, there are great and mysterious forces pulling towards a precise and definite goal: 'unity' and peace." La Pira. G, *Il Sentiero di Isaia* quoted in A. Cortesi and A. Tarquini (2009). *Mediterraneo Crocevia di Uomoini e di Religioni* (Firenze: Nerbini), p.23. He envisages "an 'optimistic' finalism of history…history has a sense, this sense being peace and unity amongst all people" (ibid.).
35. Indeed, it is only when the human order: "is formed on a basis of rights and duties, (that) men have an immediate grasp of spiritual and intellectual values, and have no difficulty in understanding what is meant by truth, justice, charity and freedom…Inspired by such principles, they attain to a better knowledge of the true God—a personal God transcending human nature. They recognize that their relationship with God forms the very foundation of their life—the interior life of the spirit, and the life which they live in the society of their fellows." The "better knowledge of God" is not the necessary starting point.
36. No wonder that the encyclical was dubbed *Falcem in Terris* in some conservative quarters; the word *Falcem* being a pun on "falce"; the Italian word for "sickle"; which together with the hammer is the symbol of many Communist movements.
37. "We are deeply distressed to see the enormous stocks of armaments that have been, and continue to be, manufactured in the economically more developed countries. This policy is involving a vast outlay of intellectual and material resources, with the result that the people of these countries are saddled with a great burden, while other countries lack the help they need for their economic and social development." *Pacem in Terris*, p.109.
38. "There is a common belief that under modern conditions peace cannot be assured except on the basis of an equal balance of armaments and that this factor is the probable cause of this stockpiling of armaments. Thus, if one country increases its military strength, others are immediately roused by a competitive spirit to augment

their own supply of armaments. And if one country is equipped with atomic weapons, others consider themselves justified in producing such weapons themselves, equal in destructive force. Consequently people are living in the grip of constant fear. They are afraid that at any moment the impending storm may break upon them with horrific violence. And they have good reasons for their fear, for there is certainly no lack of such weapons. While it is difficult to believe that anyone would dare to assume responsibility for initiating the appalling slaughter and destruction that war would bring in its wake, there is no denying that the conflagration could be started by some chance and unforeseen circumstance. Moreover, even though the monstrous power of modern weapons does indeed act as a deterrent, there is reason to fear that the very testing of nuclear devices for war purposes can, if continued, lead to serious danger for various forms of life on earth." *Pacem in Terris,* pp.110–111.
39. "Hence justice, right reason, and the recognition of man's dignity cry out insistently for a cessation to the arms race...Everyone, however, must realize that, unless this process of disarmament be thoroughgoing and complete, and reach men's very souls, it is impossible to stop the arms race, or to reduce armaments, or—and this is the main thing—ultimately to abolish them entirely." *Pacem in Terris,* pp.112—113. "We are hopeful that, by establishing contact with one another and by a policy of negotiation, nations will come to a better recognition of the natural ties that bind them together as men. We are hopeful, too, that they will come to a fairer realization of one of the cardinal duties deriving from our common nature: namely, that love, not fear, must dominate the relationships between individuals and between nations. It is principally characteristic of love that it draws men together in all sorts of ways, sincerely united in the bonds of mind and matter; and this is a union from which countless blessings can flow." *Pacem in Terris,* p.129.
40. *Pacem in Terris,* p.111.
41. Masimlaini, R. "Non Ammazare," quoted in Trionfini, "Il mondo cattolico," p.111.

# 2

# Peace and the Religions in a Changing World: From Consensus to Difference

*Darren J. Dias*

## Introduction

Lorenzo Milani never faced the issue of interreligious dialogue, perhaps because a recognition of its importance did not gain momentum until shortly before his death or perhaps because his context was more monocultural and monoreligious than the multicultural and multireligious world of today. However, given his interest in building inclusive communities, whether at San Donato or Barbiana, his coherence between reflection, action, and commitment, his advocacy for alternative modes of deploying of power and his privileged option for the poor,[1] an article on peace and the world's religions resonates with his life and ministry.

This chapter explores the evolution of the religious meaning and praxis of peace in the Christian West. Since this evolution is historically and contextually determined, the reality of religious diversity must be taken into account in ascertaining what "peace" could mean today. I develop the discussion in six sections. In the first section I trace the major contours in the historical development of the notion of "peace" in the Christian West. Next, I briefly acknowledge the diverse opinions on the status of "religion" today. In the third section I argue that peace in contemporary Catholic thought is underdeveloped because responsibility for peace has been relegated to the modern nation-state and its various organisms. Religion in the West is merely supportive of the peace agenda set by nations and international coalitions. Peace in the modern era has been rooted in a consensus on common values. The fourth section examines the contemporary Roman Catholic approach to the encounter of the world's religions. In the fifth section I explore the theological approach to interreligious dialogue. In the final section, I propose a heuristic for a transformative dialogical process toward the establishment of a religious community-in-difference that celebrates the difference that constitutes religious diversity.

This article addresses peace in a multireligious context. I write as a Roman Catholic Christian and from the privileged position of a Western academe. Nevertheless, believers from other religious traditions may also consider how peace has been understood in their own tradition, whether or not the heuristic proposed resonates with them.

## Peace in the Roman Catholic Tradition

Like any concept and practice peace has been understood differently in different eras and contexts. In Jewish thought peace is generally understood as the result of God's gift of salvation and of being in the right relationship with God and with one another.[2] Peace means reconciliation, wholeness, life, harmony, unity. Unlike later notions of peace, it is not understood negatively as the opposite of war.

For Christians, it is Jesus Christ who gives the peace that this world cannot give. It is Jesus who says, "Peace I leave you, my peace I give you. I do not give to you as the world gives" (John 14:27a). Through his cross and resurrection, Jesus reconciles the world unto himself to achieve a unity that comes from God alone. This is an alternative to the peace achieved through the violent revolution that Jesus' followers might have expected in relation to Jewish attempts to free themselves from Roman domination. Jesus establishes the Kingdom of God, "a kingdom of holiness and grace, a kingdom of justice, love and peace"[3] that will be fully realized only at his second coming. Thus, peace has a partial and incomplete character in this time between the first and second comings of Christ. Final eschatological peace will be the fruit of the Kingdom fully realized. Meanwhile, the Church is commissioned to carry on Jesus' ministry of reconciliation.

With the Edict of Milan in 313 CE, which made Christianity a tolerated religion of the Roman Empire, and then the 380 CE declaration making Christianity the official religion of the Empire the notion of peace was altered significantly. Peace resulted from the collaboration between secular and ecclesial power. The Empire needed the Church to sanction political power and the Church needed political authority to enforce church unity and mission.[4] The collaboration of Church and state colored the Christian understanding of peace throughout the medieval period. Divine law was interpreted and administered by the Church while human law was ensured by secular powers.[5]

The tenth century CE phenomenon of the Peace of God movement is an interesting example of the collaboration of Church and state for peace at a time when international treaties and mutually agreed upon borders did not exist. The disruptive violence that plagued France became the subject of several church councils.[6] Though these were initially moved by self-interest in protecting the Church from the violence, they also evidenced a concern for pilgrims, peasants, townspeople, and their property.[7] The pronouncements of the councils, which made those responsible for unjust aggression liable to excommunication, resulted in the civil authorities attempting to restore peace in the region.[8] Just war, on the other hand, needed to meet three criteria: war had to be waged for a just reason, decided by a legitimate authority and motivated by peace.

While there are many instances of the Church working for peace in the medieval period, history is rife with examples of its collusion in violence. An incendiary pamphlet of the late thirteenth century CE accuses the Church of being the cause of violence because of its political interests.[9] The Church's involvement in the Crusades, Wars of the Holy Leagues, Reconquest of the Iberian Peninsula, and colonization of the Americas are well-known counterexamples to the claim that the Church was always moved by the desire for peace. In 2011, Pope Benedict XVI acknowledged that all violence perpetrated in the name of the Christian faith throughout history was a source of "great shame."[10]

With the rise of the nation-state the Church's involvement in assuring peace was radically altered as the state alone became the guardian of peace (and war) among nations. Peace was possible due to human reason. It was intertwined with morality, technological and scientific progress, and economics.[11] During the period of the rise of the nation-state, several important pacifist Christian denominations emerged such as the Mennonites and Quakers.

For the *Magesterium* the question of peace was renewed after the Second World War. Pius XII maintained just war ethics but also the principles of justice and the common good that had been central to the medieval notion of true peace. He criticized the excessive accumulation of goods and power that lead to the great wars. Pius cautiously warned of the limitation of just war theory in an age when the consequences of war could be far worse than the situation that led to war in the first place.

Faced with the threat of nuclear war Pius' successor, John XXIII, resolutely condemned nuclear armament. Nuclear disarmament became central to the Church's teaching on peace. In his 1963 encyclical *Pacem in Terris*, the Pope writes that peace is the result of an order whose "foundation is truth, and it must be brought into effect by justice" (p.37). This order is perfected by love and flourishes in freedom. This period marks a clear return to a more biblical and holistic understanding of peace.

At the height of the Cold War, Pope Paul VI addressed the United Nations calling for an end to war, indicting nuclear armament as sinful and unjust, and exhibiting concern for the poor.[12] His 1967 encyclical *Populorum Progressio* maintains that lasting peace is based on the integral development of the human person and the elimination of social and economic inequities.[13] In that same year the Pope committed the universal church to pray for peace by observing an annual World Day for Peace on January 1. John Paul II developed the teaching on the dignity of the human person and concomitant human rights as the basis for peace.[14]

The evolving understanding of peace reflects the fact that it is responsive to historical and social conditions. A significant factor in considering peace today is the encounter of the world's religions. In this regard, returning to a biblical notion of peace—a notion that includes not merely the absence of war, but also justice, the option for the poor order and wholeness—enables the Church to make the most of the opportunities this encounter presents.

## Religion and Violence

Literary theorist René Girard makes the socio-anthropological claim that the foundation of religion is in breaking cycles of violence through an act of healing violence.[15] Thus, if this interpretation is correct, far from being the cause of violence, as many today claim, religion is the solution to violence. Charles Kimball claims religions deviate from their original purpose and tend to violence when they make absolute truth claims, demand blind obedience, name an "ideal time," claim that the end justifies the means and call for holy war.[16] William Cavanaugh argues that the violence religions to which may be prone is the same as any other Western institution that make "religious" claims upon people, albeit replacing God with another object of devotion and loyalty (such as the state or military power or consumerism). The phenomenon of religion complexifies conflict situations because religion can personalize conflict, mobilize believers, justify aggression, spiritualize struggle, absolutize issues, demonize the other, and sacralize violence.[17]

Defining and evaluating religion is problematic when one considers the variety and diversity of religious beliefs and practices. It is outside the scope of this chapter to enter into debates as to whether religions are inherently irrational, false, and violent—clearly this is not my position. Generally, two conclusions may be drawn from contemporary sociological evaluations of the relationship between religion and peace from those sympathetic to religion. First, "authentic religion never causes or contributes to violent conflict; only 'flawed' or 'bad religion' does that."[18] Secondly, economic and political factors cause violent conflict not religion. However, the implication of this claim is that political and economic conditions ought to be addressed in the interest of promoting peace as "religion is at best a supplementary or secondary part of the solution."[19]

## The Encounter of Religions in the International Arena

The Parliament of the World's Religions met for the first time in Chicago in 1893. At this conference the universal dimension of religious beliefs was highlighted. It was not until 1988 that the Parliament was revived and it now meets every five years. The purpose of the Parliament is "to cultivate harmony among the world's religions and spiritual communities and foster their engagement with the world and its guiding institutions in order to achieve a just, peaceful and sustainable world."[20] In 1993 the Parliament issued its Declaration toward a Global Ethic. In the document religious leaders admit that "peace eludes us."[21] However, they affirm "a common set of core values is found in the teachings of the religions, that these form the basis of a global ethic."²² The document points to the Golden Rule as an example of a common value that unites religions.

While the document does not deny the importance of difference among the world's religions, it concentrates on "fundamental consensus on binding values."²³ Without downplaying the nuances of the document, consensus and common values are prized over difference and diversity. For example, it states, "we must sink our narrow difference for the cause of the world community, practicing a culture of solidarity and relatedness."²⁴ Later the document states, "We do not wish to gloss over or ignore serious differences...However, they should not hinder us from proclaiming publicly those things we already hold in common and which we can jointly affirm, each on the basis of our own religious or ethical grounds."²⁵

Global leaders in a 1996 document titled *In Search of Global Ethical Standards* maintain that: "Religious institutions will command the loyalty of hundreds of millions but secularization and consumerism command even more support. The world is also afflicted by religious extremism and violence preached and practiced in the name of religion."²⁶ Political leaders encourage religious leaders to cooperate in persuading states to promote a global ethic since religions can agree on solutions to social problems believers and nonbelievers face.

Examples abound of the positive implications of the involvement of religions in peace-making and peace-building. Cases in point are the Bosnia-Herzegovina Inter-religious Council and the Interreligious Coordinating Council in Israel. The last two decades have seen fruitful cooperation between international organizations, religious and civil, in the promotion of peace whether at the regular meetings of the Council of the Parliament of World's Religions or the UN Millennium World Peace Summit of Religious and Spiritual Leaders. However, in these discussions there is no consideration of what the actual encounter of the world's religions in itself could mean and how their differences can contribute to peace processes. Though there is a call for profound transformations of consciousness, there is no hint about what this might entail.

## Contemporary Catholic Approaches to Dialogue

Today the religions of the world encounter one another unlike in any previous era. With the end of official colonialism in the 1960s,²⁷ non-Western cultures and non-Christian religions have begun to encounter one another as equals and partners. Onetime colonies became independent nations and peoples appropriated and celebrated their own cultures and traditions. This was the context within which bishops from around the world participated in the Second Vatican Council from 1963 to 1965.²⁸

In the document *Gaudium et Spes* the Council Fathers clearly return to a primitive Christian understanding of peace. They teach that peace is not merely the absence of war but, positively, that it is the result of a just order. Peace is achieved when personal wholeness and true community through reconciliation and unity. A hallmark of a peaceful community is to be found in the protection of the weakest members of society. And while the sin of disunity and violence is ever present, the cross and resurrection of Jesus Christ makes accessible the peace that flows from the gift of God's love that "goes beyond what justice can provide" (*Gaudium et Spes*, p.78).

Aware of the changing world order and of the role that Catholic Christians should play in it, the Council encourages Catholics to engage people of other religions in order to build a just and peaceful society. In engaging the other, Christians should "learn by sincere and patient dialogue what treasures a generous God has distributed among the nations of the earth" (*Ad Gentes*, p.11). In the document dealing explicitly with the Church's relationship to non-Christian religions the bishops teach that dialogue requires that we "recognize, preserve and promote the good things, spiritual and moral, as well as the socio-cultural values found among these men [of other religions]" (*Nostra Aetate*, p.2). All religious believers of the time faced challenges such as decolonization, war, and the nuclear arms race. The Council states that "to those in quest of peace, she wishes to answer in fraternal dialogue, bearing them the peace and light of the Gospel" (*Ad Gentes*, p.12). Thus, dialogue is the Church's answer to the quest for peace.

In 1964 Pope Paul VI established the Secretariat for Non-Christians, renamed the Pontifical Council for Interreligious Dialogue (PCID) in 1991. The mission of the Council is to (1) "promote mutual understanding, respect and collaboration between Catholics and the followers of other religions," (2) "encourage the study of other religions," (3) "promote the formation of persons dedicated to dialogue."[29] Interestingly, addressing sociopolitical issues is explicitly omitted from the purview of the PCID. Instead, the Pontifical Council for Justice and Peace established in 1967 responds to issues touching upon economic development, war, and human rights.

Since the long papacy of John Paul II spanned the contemporary phenomenon of globalization that brought peoples of different cultures and religions into contact in unprecedented ways, this Pontiff was particularly attentive to the encounter of the world's religions and to their role in promoting peace. Through the PCID, the Pope brought together 160 religious leaders representing 32 different Christian churches and ecclesial communities and 11 non-Christian religious traditions to pray for peace at Assisi in 1986. This is the most significant sign of the Church's outreach to promote peace through interreligious encounter.

In his Assisi address to the leaders of the world's religions John Paul gave an anthropological and eschatological rationale for implicating religions in the peace process. All religions, he says, "share a common respect of and obedience to conscience, which teaches us...to make peace among the nations."[30] Conscience demands that people "respect, protect and promote human life...especially for the weak, the destitute, the derelict: the imperative to overcome selfishness, greed, and the spirit of vengeance."[31] Peace is a common human imperative because all humans share something at the depth of their being. The Pope sees peace in its eschatological dimension as "an anticipation of what God would like the developing history of humanity to be: a fraternal journey in which we accompany one another towards the transcendent goal which he sets for us."[32] Both the anthropological and eschatological dimensions of peace are intensely historical, rooted in actual and concrete human living.

## Dialogue: A Theological Approach

Just as "religion" is a complex and contested concept, so is "dialogue." For the sake of simplicity, I rely on the thought of respected scholar and experienced practitioner of interreligious dialogue, Leonard Swidler. He defines dialogue as "a two-way communication between persons who hold significantly differing views on a subject, with the purpose of learning more truth about the subject from the other."[33] He goes on to say that no one side has a monopoly on the truth.[34] Dialogue partners must be open to learn from one another, each must possess knowledge of his or her own religious tradition and a willingness to learn about the dialogue partner's tradition.[35] The goal of dialogue is not to convince the other that he or she holds a wrong or inferior position but to "learn and change accordingly."[36]

Swidler devised the "Dialogue Decalogue" that describes the rules for engaging in dialogue. First, partners learn, change, and grow in understanding. Next, dialogue takes place not only between religious communities but within them as well. Third, dialogue partners must be honest and sincere and open to hearing one another. There must also be equality and mutual trust between dialogue partners. In addition, each dialogue participant must define himself or herself and recognize himself or herself in the other's description of him or her. Further, only analogous things should be compared (e.g., ideals to ideals and practices to practices). Next, participants must be self-critical and critical of his or her religious tradition. Last, each participant must attempt to experience the other's religion "from within."[37]

Swidler maintains that dialogue begins with learning what dialogue partners share in common and then "more comprehensively what our differences are."[38] Differences according to Swidler "should be cherished and celebrated for their own sakes." This insight contrasts the emphasis of many approaches to interreligious dialogues, for peace eschews difference once there is consensus on what is commonly shared so that worthwhile ethical actions may then be undertaken.

*Dialogue* and *Proclamation,* a 1991 document of the PCID, echoes Swidler's theology in two ways. First, it states, "While keeping their identity intact, Christians must be prepared to learn and to receive from and through others the positive values of their traditions. Through dialogue they may be moved to give up ingrained prejudices, to revise preconceived ideas, and even sometimes to allow the understanding of their faith to be purified."[39] Thus, Christian self-identity is transformed as much as an understanding of the other is altered and enlarged through dialogical encounter.

Second, the document states that "Sincere dialogue implies, on the one hand, mutual acceptance of differences, or even of contradictions, and on the other, respect for the free decision of persons taken according to the dictates of their conscience."[40] Thus, even contradictory differences must be accepted and respected.

The notion of peace and the role of religions in peace-making and peace-building has been largely determined by the agenda of nation-states and the violent conflicts that have plagued them. Indeed, the supportive role that religions provide sociopolitical peace processes is invaluable. As Hans Kung says, "there will be no peace among the nations without peace among the religions" and moreover, "there will be no peace among the religions without dialogue and cooperation among the religions and civilizations."[41] In the brief space that follows, I will outline a heuristic dialogical process that aims to build community among the world's religions. It is a complement to the current patterns of interreligious dialogues based on consensus and aimed at peace. This process is based on a theological notion of peace that extends toward the establishment of a community-in-difference of religions.

The model of community-in-difference that Swidler and the PCID encourage requires a rethinking of the differences that make religious diversity possible. As M. Shawn Copeland argues, difference can be experienced and interpreted as "deviation, division, discrepancy, discord, incongruity, incompatibility, inconsistency, anomaly, contrariety, aberration and misunderstanding."[42] Within this understanding differences should be neutralized and eradicated (unfortunately this is an undercurrent of the Western approach to intercultural and interreligious dialogue). Alternatively, we can understand difference as the "struggle for life in its uniqueness, variation and fullness; difference [as] a celebrative option for life in all its integrity, in all its distinctiveness."[43]

Difference should not be reified or reduced into a category that functions like Aristotle's hyle, as it is the case for some postmodern theorists of difference.[44] Such a function "stands outside the context of intelligibility," and is a contingency without a cause.[45] Difference is the condition of possibility for dialogical encounter as well as interdependence and mutuality among religions. Difference need not function as a barrier to relationality, "an unbridgeable and absolute chasm"[46] or as a concept that reduces otherness to the same, where "[U]nder the banner of difference, the same secretly rules."[47] Difference is not absolute, outside of the context of intelligibility, but relational and relative, meaningful and intelligible.

## Dialogue for Difference

The dialogical process I will outline can be contextualized in any number of settings and could integrate the various dimensions of interreligious dialogue because it is heuristic and derived from an analysis of human development. Thus, it is not tradition-specific. *Dialogue and Proclamation* describes four types of dialogue. The first is the dialogue of life "where people strive to live in an open and neighborly spirit, sharing their joys and sorrows, their human problems and preoccupations" (42). The second is the dialogue of action that aims at the "integral development and liberation of all people" (42). Next, is dialogue of theological exchange, when specialists seek to understand each other's religious tradition. Finally, there is dialogue of religious experience "where persons, rooted in their own religious traditions, share their spiritual riches" (42). The various dimensions that this heuristic can integrate are the cognitive/intellectual, the ethical, the affective and aesthetic, and the holistic.[48]

Theorist Bernard Lonergan proposes a fourfold pattern of normative, recurrent, and related operations that yield cumulative results in human development.[49] This is a human process of knowing and responsible living. Individuals and groups may embark on such process consciously or unconsciously. In becoming aware of such a process and in appropriating it, individuals and communities are able to transcend one horizon and move into a new one. One's horizon is the limit of one's field of vision, scope of knowledge, and range of interests at any given moment.[50] Yet, one's horizon is also the springboard for a wider vision, for further knowledge and expanded interest. The dialogical process moves one into an expanded horizon without necessarily destroying one's previous horizon.

The first level in the process of human development is the empirical level of experiencing data, of sensual perception, feelings, and imaginings. The second level is the intellectual, the level of inquiry into the data experienced, of understanding and the expression of understanding. The next level is the rational when one weighs evidence in order to make a judgment of fact. One answers here the question: is my understanding correct? Last, there is the level of responsibility when the one decides whether or not to act in accordance with the knowledge gleaned from the previous levels. Each level is accompanied by what Lonergan terms, the transcendental precepts: be attentive to the data of experience, be reasonable in understanding, be rational in making judgments and be responsible in the decision to live according to what is known to be the case.

The dialogical process begins with attentiveness to data, whether the data gleaned through understanding differences or else the data of self-understanding brought to encounter. The new knowledge about self and the religiously-other that is appropriated alters one's horizon. One becomes attentive to data, obtains a wider range of data, and new and different ways of understanding it.

Attentiveness to the data of experience grounds the entire dialogical process. Data is assembled, interpreted, compared, reduced, and classified.[51] The range of data to be considered could be limitless. Yet, one should arrive at a point where one has enough data to make a reasonable interpretation and judgment. In comparing assembled data, affinities and oppositions, similarities and differences are revealed. Reduction attempts to find the underlying root of similarities and differences by examining like similarities and like differences. Classification determines which similarities or differences result from dialectically opposed horizons and which do not. Finally, selection chooses the similarities and differences rooted in dialectically opposed horizons. In the dialogical process it is entirely possible that individuals rooted in distinct religious horizons and worldviews will attend to the same data and yet render different interpretations.

Once differences are known they must be classified, lest they become reified or exaggerated. Lonergan enumerates three types of differences: complementary, genetic, and dialectic. Complementary differences are not self-sufficient but require a complement in order to function within a larger whole. Genetic differences grow over time in successive stages. Dialectical differences can be either contradictory or contrary.[52] Contraries can be "reconciled within a higher synthesis" while contradictories exclude one another.[53] A higher synthesis is a complex notion that is capable of preserving differences and holding them in tension. Frequently, contrary differences have disintegrated into contradictories.

A goal of dialogue is to acknowledge difference as "a celebrative option for life in all its integrity."[54] Far from being impediments to forming community, difference is a critical category required to form real community amongst the religions of the world. Hence, the process in which difference is ascertained and the appropriation of difference into a religious horizon is central to the dialogue that draws different religious traditions and faith groups into a relationship that favors reconciliation and unity; that does not extinguish difference.

## Conclusion: Peace as Community-in-Difference

The primitive Christian concept of peace resonates with the Roman Catholic Church's post-Vatican II understanding. Peace is a rich concept that includes justice, the common good, personal and communal wholeness, reconciliation, unity, and the protection of the weak. A contemporary understanding of peace includes yet moves beyond the absences of war. What remains underdeveloped in the concept of peace is a *deep* appreciation of difference. Such an appreciation is furnished in the encounter of the world's religions and a dialogical process that privileges a transformation of consciousness. This is what the encounter of the world's religions brings to the discussion of peace, one that moves away from static consensus to life-giving difference.

## Notes

1. Borg, C., Cardona, M., and Caruana, S. (2009). "Introduction." In *Letter to a Teacher: Lorenzo Milani's Contributions to Critical Citizenship* (Malta: Agenda), pp.6–7.
2. Dwyer, J. A. (1991). "Peace." In Joseph A Komonchak, Mary Collins, Dermot A. Lane (eds.), *The New Dictionary of Theology* (Collegeville: The Liturigcal Press), p.749.

3. Preface for the Mass of the Feast Christ, King of the Universe, *The Roman Missal*.
4. Matthais Mettner (1996). "Paix," trans. A. Disselkamp, *Nouveau Dictionnaire de Théologie*, dir. Peter Eicher (Paris: Les Editions du Cerf), p.649.
5. Ibid., p.651.
6. Johnson, J. T. (2003). "Aquinas and Luther on War and Peace." *Journal of Religious Ethics* 33, 11.
7. Ibid., p.11.
8. Ibid.
9. Mettner, "Paix," p.652.
10. Benedict XVI (2011). "Address at the Meeting for Peace in Assisi," available at: www.vatican.va/holy_father/benedict_xvi/speeches/2011/october/documents/hf_ben-xvI_spe_20111027_assisI_en.html, accessed February 29, 2012.
11. Mettner, "Paix," p.654.
12. Paul VI (1965). "Address to the United Nations," available at: www.vatican.va/holy_father/paul_vi/speeches/1965/documents/hf_p-vI_spe_19651004_united-nations_fr.html, accessed February 29, 2012.
13. Dwyer, "Peace," p.752. See Paul VI (1967). *Populorum Progressio*, available at: www.vatican.va/holy_father/paul_vi/encyclicals/documents/hf_p-vI_enc_26031967_populorum_en.html, accessed February 29, 2012.
14. John Paul II (1979). "Address to the United Nations," available at: www.vatican.va/holy_father/john_paul_ii/speeches/1979/october/documents/hf_jp-iI_spe_19791002_general-assembly-onu_en.html, accessed February 29, 2012.
15. Girard. R. (2004). "Violence and Religion: Cause or Effect?." In *The Hedgehog Review* 6.1, 8–12.
16. Kimball, C. (2011). *When Religion Becomes Evil* (Hoboken: Jossey-Bass).
17. Juergensmyer, M. (2004). "Is Religion the Problem?." In *The Hedgehog Review* 6.1, 29–30.
18. Little, D. (2005). "Religion, Conflict and Peace." *Case Western Reserve Journal of International Law*, 98.
19. Ibid., p.98.
20. Parliament of the World's Religions, available at: www.parliamentofreligions.org/index.cfm?n=1&sn=1, accessed February 29, 2012.
21. Parliament of the World Religions (1993). "Declaration Toward a Global Ethic" (1993), p.1, available at: www.parliamentofreligions.org/_includes/FCKcontent/File/TowardsAGlobalEthic.pdf, accessed February 29, 2012.
22. Ibid.
23. Ibid.
24. Ibid., p.2.
25. Ibid., p.6.
26. InterAction Council (1996). "In Search of Global Ethical Standards," available at: http://interactioncouncil.org/in-search-of-global-ethical-standards. InterAction Council is a grouping of former heads of government from around the globe.
27. I am referring to the dismantling of Western empires in the post–Second World War period in Asia and Africa beginning most significantly with India's independence in 1947. Decolonization reached a climax in the 1960s. However, the end of "official" colonialism does not mean the end to the global cultural, economic and political forces of neocolonialism and neo-imperialism that remain a serious challenge today.
28. For a detailed account of the development of church teaching on the topic of peace, see the contribution of Michael Attridge in this book.
29. Pontifical Council for Interreligious Dialogue, "Profile," available at: www.vatican.va/roman_curia/pontifical_councils/interelg/documents/rc_pc_interelg_pro_20051996_en.html.

30. John Paul II (1986). "Address to the Representatives of Christian Communities and Ecclesial Communities and the World Religions," p.2, available at: www.vatican.va/holy_father/john_paul_ii/speeches/1986/october/documents/hf_jp-I_spe_19861027_prayer-peace-assisi-final_en.html, accessed February 29, 2012.
31. Ibid., p.4.
32. Ibid., p.5.
33. Swidler, L. (2009). "Doing Effective Dialogue and Loving It." In Rebecca Kratz Mays and Leonard Swindler (eds.), *Interfaith Dialogue at the Grass Roots* (Philadelphia: Ecumenical Press), p.11.
34. Ibid., p.11.
35. Ibid., p.12.
36. Ibid., p.13.
37. Ibid., p.20.
38. Ibid., p.13.
39. Pontifical Council for Inter-religious Dialogue (1991). "Dialogue and Proclamation," p.49, available at: www.vatican.va/roman_curia/pontifical_councils/interelg/documents/rc_pc_interelg_doc_19051991_dialogue-and-proclamatio_en.html, accessed March 3, 2012.
40. Ibid., p.41.
41. Hans Kung (2005). "Global Ethic and Human Responsibilities," available at: www.scu.edu/ethics/practicing/focusareas/global_ethics/laughlin-lectures/global-ethic-human-responsibility.html, accessed February 27, 2012.
42. Copeland, M. S. (1996). "Difference as a Category in Critical Theologies for the Liberation of Women." In Elisabeth Schussler Fiorenza and M. Shawn Copeland (eds.), *Feminist Theology in Different Contexts* (Maryknoll: Orbis Books), p.143.
43. Ibid.
44. Lawrence, F. (1993). "The Fragility of Consciousness: Lonergan and the Postmodern Concern for the Other." In *Theological Studies* 54, p.82.
45. Ibid.
46. Wiggins, J. B. (1996). *In Praise of Religious Diversity* (New York: Routledge), p.13.
47. Tracy, D. (1987). "Christianity in the Wider Context: Demands and Transformations." In *Religion and Intellectual Life* 4, p.12.
48. Swidler, "Doing Effective Dialogue and Loving It," pp.10–11.
49. Lonergan, B. J. F. (1972). *Method in Theology* (New York: Herder and Herder), pp.13–14. This process is termed the transcendental method or the generalized empirical method.
50. Ibid., p.236.
51. Ibid., p.250.
52. This is a distinction in Lonergan's notion of dialectic by Robert Doran. See Robert Doran, M. (1990). *Theology and the Dialectics of History* (Toronto: University of Toronto Press), p.10.
53. Ibid., p.10.
54. Copeland, "Difference as a Category," p.143.

# 3

# Vatican II's Teaching on Peace and War: A Contribution to Conciliar Hermeneutics

*Michael Attridge*

## Introduction

At the same time that Don Lorenzo Milani was most active and outspoken as an advocate for the poor and the marginalized, the Roman Catholic Church was undergoing its most significant transformation in four hundred years—one that would eventually renew the Church in its teaching, life and worship. It is noteworthy (to say the least), and perhaps prophetic, that Fr. Milani would publish his first book, *Pastoral Experiences*, in spring 1958,[1] and that the newly elected Pope John XXIII would announce his intention to hold a worldwide "pastoral" council of the Roman Catholic Church only nine months later.[2] Further, considering the substance of the Council's teaching now, almost 50 years after its closing, it is striking that this advocate for peace who died in 1967 at the young age of only 44 was put on trial in 1965 for advocating "conscientious objection."[3] That same year Pope John XXIII's council would promulgate one of its most important documents, the "Pastoral Constitution on the Church in the Modern World" (*Gaudium et Spes*), wherein the legitimacy of conscientious objection was recognized.

This worldwide, ecumenical council, known as the Second Vatican Council, or Vatican II, formulated as official Church teaching changes that had been occurring within the Roman Catholic Church for centuries. Among these, it gave expression to a renewed understanding of the nature of the Church, which in turn opened new ways of understanding the relationship between the Catholic Church and other Christian churches. It taught that wherever truth and goodness may be found in the other religions of the world, Christians had a duty to acknowledge, preserve and promote the spiritual and moral goods of these religions. It offered a renewed form of the liturgy that emphasized the full, conscious, and active participation of the laity and permitted the use of the local language in worship celebrations. It articulated a theology of Revelation that was historically grounded, presenting God's outreach to the world and humanity's response in terms of interpersonal relationship. Most importantly, Vatican II showed the human community that the Church was not above or indifferent to the sufferings of all people. Nowhere is this more evident than in the constitution *Gaudium et Spes*.

*Gaudium et Spes* was Vatican II's statement to the world in 1965 about the Catholic Church's relationship with the human family. Its opening words capture the sentiment of the Council:

> The joys and hopes, the griefs and the anxieties of the people of this age, especially those who are poor or in any way afflicted, these too are the joys and hopes, the griefs and anxieties of Christians. Indeed, nothing genuinely human fails to raise an echo in their hearts.[4]

It was the Council's announcement to the world that we all stand together in one brotherhood and sisterhood. The document continues by laying out an anthropology in theological terms in its first half, and propounds statements on "problems of special urgency" in the second. The titles of the chapters in the second part illustrate the comprehensive vision of the Council in 1965. It also shows what was on the mind of the bishops at the time: marriage and the family, the development of culture, socioeconomic life, the political community; promoting peace and encouraging the community of nations. It is this last chapter that is most closely related to the work of Don Milani.

In recent years, the state of the question in Vatican II research has been whether or not the Catholic Church changed its teachings at Vatican II. The question is one of conciliar hermeneutics. How are we to interpret Vatican II? Is the teaching of Vatican II in continuity or discontinuity with the Church's teaching prior to the Council? The debate has been characterized by two contrasting sides. One side, associated to the *Instituto per le scienze religiose* of Bologna, drew together some of the world's best-known historians and theologians under the directorship of the late Giuseppe Alberigo and produced the detailed and comprehensive five-volume work titled *History of Vatican II*.[5] Its overall hermeneutic, similar to that of Alberigo's own,[6] was that the Council was primarily a moment of discontinuity in the history of the Church's teaching. On the other side, there are a number of theologians and authors, often associated to the Roman Curia, who have argued—against the Bologna approach—for a hermeneutic of continuity.[7] In 2005, Pope Benedict entered the debate offering what could be seen as middle ground—a "hermeneutic of reform." However, as scholars have noted, this position is not unlike that of "continuity" in its privileging of a systematic-theological reading of history. [8]

Looking at the two sides, it would be an overstatement to say that one side holds its position and entirely excludes the other. Neither side has ever claimed this. Instead, what distinguishes them is the role of history in relationship to theology, the former attributing a central place to history in its methods; the latter upholding "a systematic-theological principle as a basis for historiographical research."[9]

The purpose of this paper is not to resolve this debate. Its purpose is to examine the Council's teaching on peace and war and to do so in the light of the current hermeneutical debate. What did the Council teach? Was it different from what the Church had taught before the Council? If so, why? Are there exigent factors that ought to influence the Church in its teaching? In this way, the paper intends both to honor Don Milani, an advocate of peace who was active during the time that the Church was discussing this topic, and also to make a contribution to the current discussion.

## Vatican II's Teaching on Peace and War

*Gaudium et Spes*'s chapter on peace has three sections: the nature of peace, the avoidance of war, and the need to construct an international community. Though each of these is important, for the purpose of this paper I restrict myself to three issues: "what is peace?"; "is war ever justifiable?" and; "what does the Council teach about non-violence and conscientious objection?"

Though the Council begins almost immediately with a definition of peace, it first frames this definition by making two statements about what peace is not; both statements clearly refer to war and to the arms race. First, it says that peace is not "merely the absence of war" (Art. 78). In other words, we cannot say that real peace has been achieved when fighting has stopped. Second, it says that peace cannot be "reduced to the maintenance of power between enemies" (Art. 78). Real peace is not achieved either by stockpiling arms or other military resources, or simply by negotiating the disarmament of both sides. Instead, the Council ties peace to order and justice. It says that "peace results from that harmony built into human society by its divine Founder, and actualized by human beings as they thirst after ever greater justice" (Art. 78). In making this statement, the Council followed the Church's traditional teaching, expressed by Augustine of Hippo in the fourth century that "peace is the tranquility that comes from order."[10] For Augustine, as for the Council, "order is not a certain mechanical behaviour imposed by a despotic power... but an inner force of justice and love... that takes into account both the individual human person and the community, the whole of humanity" as well as the reality that change will occur in all of them. According to the theologian René Coste, the Council here hoped that this description of peace would gain the approval of all people of goodwill "including those in the uncommitted nations, and in the communist states."[11] Concretely, it was recommending the establishment of an international authority that would help to bring about this kind of order.

In the absence of peace and of an international authority that could help to bring it about, the Council teaches that under certain conditions war is justifiable: "As long as the danger of war remains and there is no competent and sufficiently powerful authority at the international level, governments cannot be denied the right to legitimate defense once every means of peaceful settlement has been exhausted" (Art. 79). However, it continued, when it comes to the use of "scientific" weapons, their use must be restricted since they "can inflict massive and indiscriminate destruction far exceeding the bounds of legitimate defense" (Art. 80).

Moral theologian J. Bryan Hehir observes three things about the Council's teaching.[12] First, the term "just war," which has been found so often in Catholic theology since Augustine, does not explicitly appear in *Gaudium et Spes*. However, the "moral logic" for it does, since the Council allows for the possibility of "legitimate defense." Second, the Council places certain conditions on the meaning of "justifiable"—for example, it says that all peaceful means must already have been exhausted. Third, there must be rules such as rules placing limitations on the means by which the sides engage in war. Hehir says that among other things, "the categories which legitimize some forms of force and prohibit others...rely upon the principle of proportionality." As such, the use of scientific or nuclear weapons must be controlled (Art. 80).

Finally, the Council addresses the role of nonviolence in promoting peace. It says that in the spirit of calling and working for peace "it cannot fail to praise those who renounce the use of violence in the vindication of their rights...provided that this can be done without injury to the rights and duties of others or of the community itself" (Art. 79). And further, with respect to rights in relation to those who object to war, it goes further by saying that "it seems right that laws make humane provisions for the case of those who for reasons of conscience refuse to bear arms, provided however, that they accept some other form of service to the human community" (Art. 79).

For Coste, these approaches together with their qualifications strike the right balance. On the one hand, nonviolence for Christians, expressed either as pacifism or conscientious objection ought to be the norm. Christians are called to commit themselves to nonviolence "to the very limits of possibility." This, he writes, is certainly obvious to the weak, to children, to the poor, to the sick, and to the elderly.[13] On the other hand, nonviolence cannot be made an absolute universal principle. Catholic tradition has held that Christ did not promote nonviolence to the point of denying people legitimate defense, especially when it extends to the innocent. As Coste writes: "in a humanity profoundly marked by sin...it can unfortunately be necessary to meet force with force in order to break force and so prevent to some extent the law of the jungle becoming the only law."[14]

## Church Teaching on Peace and War before Vatican II

Was Vatican II's teaching on just war, nonviolence, and conscientious objection consistent with was taught prior to the Council? In order to answer this, we need to look at the period before Vatican II. There is not sufficient space to present a detailed and exhaustive overview of the history of Church's teaching in a paper such as this, nor is it necessarily required. Therefore, I limit myself to the teachings of Popes Pius XII (1939–1958) and John XXIII (1958–1963).

For almost sixteen hundred years, the Catholic Church had taught that war can be justified. This "just war" theory is not exclusively a Christian teaching, but it has been "most extensively cultivated within the Roman Catholic moral tradition."[15] According to J. Bryan Hehir it is possible to see three stages of development prior to that of Pope Pius XII: Augustine in the third and fourth centuries; Thomas Aquinas in the thirteenth century; and, the Spanish Scholastics—Vitoria and Suarez—in the sixteenth and seventeenth centuries.[16]

Along this lengthy trajectory, Pius XII's position on just war represents both a continuation and a modification. His teaching upheld the Catholic tradition in support of just war and at the same time made some changes. Traditionally, the arguments to justify war had been to vindicate offenses, to recuperate things that were taken or to defend.[17] But Pius XII, having lived through the Second World War, was not unaware of the destructive capabilities of global conflict. Therefore, he reduced the legitimate causes of war to one: the defensive war. However, there is a political dimension to the Pope's position. As William Au adds, Pius XII's concession to allow a defensive war is:

> predicated on the absence of an international authority with the power to adjudicate disputes and protect the rights of nations.[18]

Pius XII used traditional just war standards to assess modern weaponry. For him, atomic, biological, and chemical weapons were not intrinsically evil, but there were limits on their use. Nuclear weapons were quantitatively different from others, but not qualitatively different. As such, he "did not rule out in principle the use of nuclear weapons; rather he assessed their moral significance in terms of proportionality."[19] William Au reminds us that Pius was writing at the start of the nuclear age. There was not yet widespread public awareness of the potential devastation of nuclear weapons, or the stockpiling of such.[20]

One of the most significant things to note about Pius's teaching vis-à-vis our topic here is his clear refusal "to provide moral justification for a Catholic position supporting conscientious objection."[21] This appears most clearly in the Pope's 1956 Christmas Message:

> If therefore, a body representative of the people and the government—both having been chosen by free election in a moment of extreme danger decide, by legitimate instruments of internal and external policy, on defensive precautions, and carry out the plans which they consider necessary, they do not act immorally; so that the Catholic citizen cannot invoke his own conscience in order to refuse to serve and fulfill those duties the law imposes.[22]

According to John Courtney Murray, the occasion was a controversy, particularly in Germany, that was giving rise to pacifist movements. Pius was concerned that the exercise of individual conscience could undermine the democratic process that had emerged in the country post–Second World War.[23] Regardless of his reasons, opposition to conscientious objection and to pacifism was a general principle for the Pope.

Pope John XXIII's 1963 encyclical *Pacem in Terris* is dependent upon the teaching of Pius XII but also moves beyond it.[24] One of the important ways in which it does so is in its evaluation of nuclear weapons. *Pacem in Terris* "conveys the substantive judgment that nuclear weapons present a qualitatively new moral problem to Catholic teaching."[25] Recognition of the destructive capability of nuclear weapons by the Pope and that even their limited use could cause an escalation of violence resulting in devastating consequences, called into question the legitimacy of a limited use of force—traditionally a central premise of just war theory. In light of this, the encyclical says that "in this age of ours, which prides itself on its atomic power, it is irrational to think that war is a proper way to obtain justice for violated rights."[26] The encyclical is in fact silent on whether a nation possesses the right to legitimate defense. As Hehir notes, this omission is puzzling: "since the apparent challenge it poses to the just-war position is not complemented by any alternative position."[27] It may be, however, that writing only months after the Cuban Missile Crisis the Pope did not want to be misunderstood as possibly legitimizing war, especially since he had played such an important role in reconciling the two sides.[28]

It must be noted that John XXIII does not explicitly endorse a pacifist position in *Pacem in Terris*. He does, however, as Hehir argues, offer a sufficient basis to provide the conditions for it as a possibility.[29] Three things in the Pope's encyclical move us in that direction. First, it strongly criticizes the arms race and recognizes that the world lacks an international political and legal system that could oversee military matters. Second, as already mentioned, it offers no explicit support for the right to self-defense. Finally, considering the statement from *Pacem in Terris* above that says that it is unimaginable that atomic weapons could be used to obtain justice, the very rationale for such a thing as a just war, seems to be in question. For clarity, this does not mean that scholars are in agreement that, after *Pacem in Terris*, there are no longer grounds for a just war; there are differing interpretations of what *Pacem in Terris* meant. But as Hehir concludes, even if it is reasonable to assume that the encyclical does not condemn the use of force under some strict conditions, this is now to be considered as a "toleration" of the use of force and not as a "moral endorsement" for it.[30]

## Did Vatican II Change Church Teaching?

From the foregoing we can see a clear development in the Church's teaching around issues related to just war and conscientious objection from Pope Pius XII to Vatican II. Pius XII supported just war but restricted justification for it to defense alone. Turning to the battlefield and questions related to how war may be conducted, the Pope showed some concern about nuclear weaponry. During his pontificate, nuclear technology advanced its potential as a weapon became realized, and—at the end of the Second World War, at Hiroshima and Nagasaki—its effects became known. But the bigger potential of these weapons and the longer-term effects had not yet become understood. Moreover, stockpiling was not considered a problem. In light of this, Pius XII could see that there was a quantitative difference between atomic weapons as well as biological and chemical ones and therefore their use ought to be limited. However, he did not see a qualitative difference and therefore did not rule out their use.

Conscientious objection was not an option for Pius XII. Peace was desirable but it was not permissible to appeal to one's own conscience and refuse to serve. John Courtney Murray connected this decision by the Pope to the political situation in Germany in the decade that followed the end of the war. But regardless of the particular circumstances, his position was framed in general and universal terms.

The 1963 encyclical *Pacem in Terris* is a bridge between Pius XII and Vatican II. In it, John XXIII had clearly on his mind the devastating potential of nuclear weaponry. Written in April 1963, only months after the Cuban Missile Crisis when the world came the closest to nuclear conflict between the two Cold War superpowers, the document is noteworthy for several reasons. First it goes beyond Pius XII in its assessment of atomic weapons. They are not simply quantitatively different but also qualitatively so. Second, in light of the fact that they exist, and that they represent something different than the world had ever seen before in warfare, John XXIII questions whether war can still even be justified: "it is irrational to think that war is a proper way to obtain justice for violated rights." This, together with the absence of any statement in the encyclical supporting the right of nations to defend themselves, has led some to this conclusion, namely that war could no longer be justified. At a minimum, the encyclical does not provide a moral justification for war. Third, the document does not offer an alternative to just war.

Regarding nonviolence, *Pacem in Terris* does not repeat the teaching of Pius XII in condemning conscientious objection, but neither does it explicitly endorse it. Instead, as Hehir shows, it provides the conditions for the possibility to allow for conscientious objection, opening the way to a Catholic pacifism.

Two years later, the Second Vatican Council would issue its teaching on these matters in its pastoral constitution, *Gaudium et Spes*. Once again the justification of war would appear, but without explicit use of the term "just war." At the same time, though, the Council would put in place the condition that war was only justifiable after all means of peaceful settlement have been exhausted. The Council did not call for the banning of nuclear weapons, since it recognized that their presence can act as a deterrent to enemy attack (Art. 81). However, at the same time it did not endorse them.

Most noteworthy is the Council's explicit support for nonviolence and conscientious objection. Indeed the Council had placed conditions on these teachings such as "not injuring the rights and duties of others;" but it was still new. In the words of William Au, while the Council's teaching was not a ringing endorsement, "it was the first official recognition in modern Church teaching of pacifism as a legitimate option for Catholics."[31]

## The Importance of Context

From this overview and summary, we can indeed say that the Church did change its teaching at Vatican II on some issues related to war and peace. Most clearly, it granted official permission for the first time, for Catholics to exercise nonviolence as a means of peace, which opened up new ways of thinking and acting. A new chapter for issues of war and peace would begin at this time. In the decades that followed, two distinct lines of Catholic thought would emerge: one "in the direction of a Catholic style of non-violence and pacifism" and; the other that would maintain an ethic of limited war but with significant restrictions on modern warfare.[32]

But, at the same time that we recognize that the Church changed its teaching, we must also ask an important question: "Why" did it do so? Why did the bishops feel the need to formulate a position that was clearly not the teaching of Pope Pius XII and allow for pacifism/conscientious objection? To answer this question we can turn to some of the work that has been done on interpreting Vatican II.

In the recent debates surrounding continuity, discontinuity, and Vatican II, three articles published in three volumes of the journal *Theological Studies* have helped to advance the hermeneutical discussion significantly.[33] Each of the authors acknowledges that there are elements of both continuity and discontinuity in the Council's teaching. However, their emphasis is on discontinuity.

Of the three, the most relevant article for us here is the one by Stephen Schloesser. Schloesser takes an overall historical approach but does so through the lens of the broader global social and political context in which the Council was held. He reminds us that Vatican II did not happen in a vacuum, apart from a context. There were reasons why the bishops reached some of the decisions they did. He writes: "the Council was a response to the cataclysmic shifts in the mid-20th century."[34] Examples include: the holocaust; a global war that claimed between 50 and 60 million lives; the establishment of communism in China in 1949 and in Cuba in 1959; the Korean War; the Bay of Pigs fiasco; the Cold War in which the world was divided into two superpowers; the Berlin Wall; the Cuban Missile Crisis; the assassination of both presidents, Ngo Dinh Diem of South Vietnam and John F. Kennedy in 1963; and decolonization and the end of the Western hegemony. One of the results of this last point was that the "world was fragmenting into smaller entities."[35]

While all of this was swirling about, the question of nuclear weaponry was in the foreground, intensified by the Cuban Missile Crisis in 1962. As Schloesser put it, this was a time when the world learned "what it meant to be only minutes away from the nuclear annihilation of millions."[36] But the problem also had a larger context. The United States had demonstrated its nuclear capability at Hiroshima and Nagasaki in 1945, and just a few years later the Soviet Union tested its first atomic weapon, showing the United States that it did not have a monopoly in this area. In 1954, under the code name "Operation Castle" the Americans responded by testing a thermonuclear weapon with a destructive capability 750 times that of the Hiroshima bomb. Soon after, Soviet scientists concluded that "the detonation of just a hundred hydrogen bombs could create on the whole globe conditions impossible for life."[37]

The Council was therefore faced with: the horrors of the Second World War; the new, emerging—and possibly unstable—global political landscape; the expansion of nuclear weaponry and its devastating potential; and in the midst of all of this the search for ways to ensure peace. It is not surprising that it changed its teaching to allow for a pacifist, nonviolent solution. As Schloesser wrote: in the post-1945 world, the Church changed its teaching because it had an ethical imperative to do so.[38]

## Conclusion

I conclude with some very brief comments regarding ecclesiology, ethical responsibility, and Church teaching. In doing so, I hope to offer something to the discussion on conciliar hermeneutics and the continuity/discontinuity question. Certainly there is continuity. Vatican II preserved much of the Church's teachings on fundamental issues central to Christian identity. However, there is also discontinuity, especially from the standpoint of the Church and its responsibilities to the world.

The Church is not only a mystery abstracted from the world, as the opening chapter of Vatican II's constitution on the Church describes it. It is also—according to the same constitution—a historical reality; a gathering of God's faithful who are called to work for justice and to transform the world. As such, these People of God must be involved in the world and be aware of the needs of all people. Wherever they recognize situations of injustice, poverty, inequality, and so on—individually or communally—they must find ways to correct these conditions. By virtue of our baptism, we have a moral imperative to do so. This, I believe, Don Milani knew well.

In the midst of this, bishops, as leaders in the Church, have a special responsibility to formulate teachings that guide the community of believers along the right path. This is certainly true on a daily basis and at the level of the local Church and of each individual bishop. But it is all the more true at the level of an ecumenical council, which is called infrequently, and at a time when the Church needs to confront particular issues, concerns or crises. It is at such times above others, that bishops, in representing the needs of their dioceses and facing the exigencies of the global Church and the world, need to be particularly attentive. This is a unique opportunity to show the people of the world that they are not alone, that the Church cares for them. If ever there is a time for the Church to change, it is, above all, then.

## Notes

1. Milani, L. (1958). *Esperienze pastorali* (Firenze: Libreria editrice Fiorentina).
2. Angelo Roncalli was elected on October 28, 1958, taking the name Pope John XXIII. He announced his intention to convoke the Council three months later on January 25, 1959.
3. Milani, L. (1965). *L'obbedienza non è più una virtù* (Firenze: Libreria editrice Fiorentina).
4. All references to *Gaudium et Spes* are taken from Abbott, W. M. (ed.) (1966). *The Documents of Vatican II* (New Jersey: New Century Publishers, Inc).
5. Alberigo, G. and Komonchak, J. A. (eds.) (1995–2007). *History of Vatican II*, 5 vols (Maryknoll, NY: Orbis).
6. For Alberigo's hermeneutic, see: Alberigo, G. (1992). "Crieères herméneutique pour une histoire de Vatican II." In Mathijs Lamberigts and Claude Soetens (eds.), *À la veille du concile Vatican II: Vota et reactions en Europe et dans le Catholicisme oriental*, Instrumenta Theologica 9 (Leuven: Peeters), pp. 12–33.
7. See, for example, Marchetto, A. (2005). *Il concilio Ecumenico Vaticano II: Contrappunto per la sua storia*, (Città del Vaticano: Libreria editrice Vaticana).
8. See Schelkens, K. (2008). "*Lumen Gentium*'s 'Subsistit In' Revisited: The Catholic Church and Christian Unity After Vatican II," *Theological Studies* 69, 4, p.881.
9. Ibid., p.880.
10. *De Civitate Dei* XIX, 13, 1; See: Coste, R. (1969). "Commentary on Chapter V." In Herbert Vorgrimler (ed.), *Commentary on the Documents of Vatican II, Vol. V* (New York: Herder and Herder), p.348.
11. Coste, "Commentary on Chapter V," p.348.
12. Hehir, J. B. (1980). "The Just-War Ethic and Catholic Theology: Dynamics of Change and Continuity." In Thomas A. Shannon (ed.), *War or Peace? The Search for New Answers* (New York: Orbis), p.22.
13. Coste, "Commentary on Chapter V," p.350.
14. Ibid., p.351.
15. Hehir, "The Just-War Ethic," p.15.
16. Ibid., pp. 16–17.
17. Murray, J. C. (1959). "Remarks on the Moral Problem of War." In *Theological Studies*, 20, 1, March, 46, n. 12.
18. Au, W. (1986). "Papal and Episcopal Teaching on War and Peace: The Historical Background to The Challenge of Peace: God's Promise and Our Response." In Charles J. Reid Jr. (ed.), *Peace in a Nuclear Age: The Bishop's Pastoral Letter in Perspective* (Washington: Catholic University of America Press), p.99.
19. Hehir, J. B. (1982). "Foreword." In Robert Heyer (ed.), *Nuclear Disarmament: Key Statements of Popes, Bishops, Councils and Churches* (New York: Paulist Press), pp.3–4.
20. Au, "Papal and Episcopal Teaching," p.100.
21. Hehir, "Foreword," p.4.

22. Pope Pius XII, "Christmas Message," 1956, cited in James R. Jennings (ed.), (1973). *Just War and Pacificism—A Catholic Dialogue* (Washington, DC: United States Catholic Conference), p.8.
23. Murray, C. (1959). "Remarks on the Moral Problem of War," p. 53; For the official text of "Christmas Message" see: *Acta Apostolicae Sedis* 49, p.19.
24. Pope John XXIII, *Pacem in Terris,* Vatican Website, available at: www.vatican.va /holy _father/john_xxiii/encyclicals/documents/hf_j-xxiiI_enc_11041963_pacem _ en.html., accessed January, 26, 2012.
25. Hehir, "Foreword," p.4.
26. *Pacem in Terris*, p.127.
27. Hehir, "Foreword," p.5.
28. For an account of the Pope John XXIII's involvement in the Cuban Missile Crisis, see: Fogarty, G. P. "The Council Gets Underway." In Giuseppe Alberigo and Joseph A. Komonchak (eds.), *History of Vatican II, Vol. II* (New York: Orbis), pp. 94–106.
29. Hehir, "The Just-War Ethic," p.20.
30. Ibid.
31. Au, "Papal and Episcopal Teaching," p.103.
32. Hehir, J. B. (2005). "Conflict and Security in the New World Order." In John A. Coleman and William F. Ryan (eds.), *Globalization and Catholic Social Thought: Present Crisis, Future Hope* (New York: Orbis), p. 75.
33. O'Malley, J. W. (2006). "Vatican II: Did Anything Happen?" *Theological Studies,* 67, 1, March, pp. 3–33; Schloesser, S. (2006). "Against Forgetting: Memory, History, Vatican II," *Theological Studies* 67, 2, June, pp. 275–319; and Ormerod, N. J. (2006). "The Times They Are a 'Changin': A Response to O'Malley and Schloesser," *Theological Studies,* 67, 4, December, pp.834–855.
34. Cf. Schloesser, "Against Forgetting," pp.279—285.
35. Ibid., p.284.
36. Ibid., p.282.
37. Gaddis, J. L. (2005). *The Cold War: A New History* (New York: Penguin), p. 65.
38. Ibid., p.278.

# 4

# The Church as a Sacrament of the Future

*Brian Wicker*

## Terrorism and the Church

This chapter continues the thinking that I began with my chapter on *Just War and State Sovereignty* in the recent book, which I coedited with David Fisher (2010) called *Just War on Terror? A Christian and Muslim Response*. That book is a reflection, from Christian and Muslim standpoints, on the moral implications of the attack on the twin towers in New York in September 2001. My own chapter in it is a theological exploration of the long-term implications of this globally significant event and its ramifications in terms of the way humanity is politically organized (or disorganized) in the twenty-first century. It attempts to put some flesh on the concept of the Church as the sacrament of a globalized future, in the light of a key twenty-first-century fact: namely that the allocation of virtually every human being on this planet to membership of one or other "sovereign state" is now unsustainable. For the institution of the sovereign state is itself dying, despite the contrary claims of governments of such states. To avoid perishing through climate catastrophe or suicidal mass-destructive war, the human race has to find another way of organizing itself. And I maintain that the Church is the sign, or sacrament of what we have to do.

Before elaborating my argument I need to clarify what I mean by "the church." This might upset some people. So let me be clear. For purposes of this chapter by "the church" I mean the empirical human community commonly known as the "Roman Catholic Church." I shall say relatively little about other Christian communities or "denominations" or their relations with the Roman Catholic Church. This is not because these relations are not important, but because it is impossible to understand the church as *the sacrament* of the future as long as we think of it as divided into competing, even mutually incompatible, communities. I have no difficulty with calling many other groups and denominations "ecclesial communities" or even "churches," as the Second Vatican Council's Decree on Ecumenism does. And I have no difficulty in accepting what Hans Kung said, in his book on *The Church* in the aftermath of that decree, about the meaning of "unity" and "catholicity" and the need for all Christians to think critically about the community they themselves belong to before casting stones at the others. However, Kung does not say enough about the ethical and political, as distinct from the ecclesiological, differences between these communities. This is why, for my present purposes I shall concentrate on the Roman Catholic Church and what it teaches at the ethical level. Those who think differently about the teachings of Christianity on these issues must make up their own minds about what I shall say in this chapter.

To say that the church is the sacrament of the future may seem odd to some readers, especially if they are used to the old talk about the seven "sacraments" as if these were separate activities that go on in the church, independent of the rest of the Church's life. It is essential therefore to say that the seven "sacraments" are only the tips of the living iceberg which is the church itself, that is, *the sacrament* of God's kingdom: the sign, created by God, of how people should be. As Herbert McCabe OP wrote, this sign, or sacrament, reveals to us a new reality that "makes present Christ himself and shows him to us by signs which indicate what he is, the unity of his faithful in charity." [1]

It matters to the church's being the sacrament of the future that the teachings of the church, to which every member of it is committed, should be *true*. Indeed, if the teaching of the church were not true it would be wrong to belong to it. And given the history of cruelties, corruptions, and crimes done in its name by Roman Catholicism over the centuries, it might even be criminal to join it. However, distinguishing the *teachings* of the church from the mass of opinions, prejudices, assumptions, and cultural baggage that Roman Catholics from the Popes downwards (along with other Christians) tend to accumulate, is an immensely difficult theological task. Furthermore, the teachings themselves are constantly "developing" (to use Newman's phrase) over time and as the needs of humanity itself develop. Nevertheless, I shall maintain that "the church" does propound *teachings*, and that these are *truths* about how matters stand for human beings the world over. And I hope that my argument will be taken in the light of this basic fact, or alleged fact.

## The World of Sovereign States

Let me start by a resume of what I have said in the chapter of the book referred to above. Today the human race is still divided into distinct "sovereign states" and virtually everybody has to be a citizen of one state or another. And everybody is supposed to owe allegiance and loyalty, not to mention having an emotional attachment, to his or her own state, if necessary at the expense of attachment to the citizens of other, competing states. This obsolescent pattern of states has been inherited from the wars of sixteenth-century Europe, and the consequent expansion by imperialism and conquest into other parts of the planet. The mediaeval world, and indeed the classical world before it, did not consist of sovereign states. Of course its many communities were culturally and geographically distinct from each other. But they did not see themselves as sovereign in the modern sense. And certainly the planet as a whole (which people were hardly aware of as such) was not divided into separate sovereign states.

The emergence of the sovereign state system was no doubt a progress of a kind, since it temporarily solved, by international treaties (Augsburg 1555, Westphalia 1648), the conflicts which had beset Europe since the Reformation and the Renaissance. But today it has outlasted its usefulness, and has indeed engendered far worse wars of its own. The Long War of 1914–1989 marked the slow nadir of the sovereign state system. And since then, and emerging very rapidly in the last 25 years or so, many quite new factors have undermined the sovereign state as an institution. Among these we may include the following: (1) the probability of catastrophic global climate change unless, as seems unlikely, states are prepared to collaboratively reverse their pollution of our common life; (2) the emergence of instantaneous global communication and the impossibility of keeping any information private to the state or its government (the Internet, massive and uncontrollable electronic "leaks" from every sort of interstate dialogue, the indiscriminate instantaneous spread of scientific and other information and gossip, true or false, throughout the world); (3) the invention of mass-destruction weapons capable of obliterating whole cities or even states at the press of a button (thus making war, once the characteristic activity of the sovereign state in pursuit of its own ends, virtually impossible between the major players); (4) the inability of states to protect their increasingly porous boundaries against the invasion of money, ideas, immigrants, and tourists from any part of the planet; (5) the globalization of the world's finances, so that no state can properly control its own economy, and a serious financial mistake in one place can immediately infect the rest, leading to possible worldwide banking and economic collapse. All of these developments, which have happened at breakneck speed in the decades since the end of the Long War, manifest the obsolescence of the sovereign state system, which existed to protect its citizens and their governments against just such dangers but can do so no longer. As Audrey Kurth Cronin has observed in her book *How Terrorism Ends*, the twenty-first-century state is mutating into something different from the nation-state.

Given that human beings will always and necessarily wish to live in communities located in one or another portion of the planet, how should this fact be squared with the foreseeable collapse of the sovereign state system? How might we organize ourselves in a different and better way? This is the crucial question we have to answer in the (possibly short) time we have to tackle it. And my suggestion is that the Catholic church is the sign or sacrament of what is required for the future.

## The Church as the Body of Christ

The church originated in Palestine, and soon developed into a set of Christian communities dotted around the Middle East, largely as the result of St. Paul's missionary work. These communities formed themselves around overseers, or "bishops," who were the focus of what each community held in common. So each was "catholic" in that it was the *whole* Christian community, or church, for that piece of planetary territory. And what made each community "catholic" in this sense was that it was rooted in the person, mission, death and resurrection, of Jesus. So faith in Jesus, his message and his resurrection was what united each community, and also what brought these communities into union with each other despite the physical boundaries that separated them. The defining activity of this faith in Jesus, that is, what made these various churches into empirically identifiable communities that could be encountered by would-be members, was the public celebration of the Eucharist, or breaking of bread in a common sacramental meal, as Jesus had commanded on the day before he was executed.

Eventually, as the sacramental language of these communities developed, it came to be recognized that each of these groups of people was the *body* of the living, resurrected Christ in that place. In addition, it came to be understood that the whole collection of these communities was potentially global: the universal body of Christ for all human beings. Hence a further development of the concept of the church as *catholic*.

Furthermore it came to be understood that this unity and catholicity of the church was *sacramental*, in that the new "body" of Christ was *the sign* given to us of how all human beings should live together. For obviously the church was not literally the physical body of the resurrected Jesus (following the "ascension" that was now with God), but was a community of human bodies living on this earth. Yet neither was this term "body" just a metaphor. On the contrary, it was rooted in a new kind of language, in which words, as signs, somehow "embodied" the very reality that they were signs of. Hence the development of *sacramental* language, which is the distinctive contribution of Christianity to our understanding of ourselves. Thus the one community of communities or church understood itself as the sacrament that "embodies" in itself the corporeal reality of Jesus, and does so for our good while we live in this time before the consummation of things in the "Kingdom of God." Hence the church as the sacrament of the future. And hence its necessary unity.

## The Church and Its Territorial Organization

Now the original communities were of course based on certain territories, or as they gradually became recognized, *dioceses*. The global church consisted of these territories, collected together into the one body of Christ. Because the church was thus embodied in dioceses, and because human beings thought of themselves as already organized into territorially self-defined "nations" or "tribes," it was practically inevitable that the church's various communities should slowly become associated with these nations or tribes. After the accession of Constantine this process became the norm. And hence, in the very long run, the assimilation of these various catholic churches to the territories in which "nations" or "tribes" lived. And hence, even later but practically inevitably, the bishops of the various dioceses in these territories or "states" banded themselves together to form an identifiable church leadership in each state. Sovereign states thus eventually acquired national "bishops" conferences' designed to speak collectively for their members in each state. And this is the situation we have today. It is the obvious way in which the church manifests itself in a world of sovereign states.

However, this is not the whole truth. For many centuries there have been other ways in which the church has organized itself, without direct reference to territories, dioceses, or even sovereign state boundaries. For example, the church still does not consistently recognize sovereign state territories in Britain. Scotland has its own distinct bishops' conference, although legally it is part of the sovereign state of the "United Kingdom." Ireland has a bishops' conference for the whole island of Ireland, practically ignoring the fact that "Northern Ireland" is part of the United Kingdom whereas the rest of Ireland is a separate sovereign state. But the most obvious examples of organizations that run counter to sovereign state territories are the regular religious orders, of which the Benedictine, Franciscan, Dominican, Jesuit, Carmelite, and so on are only the most obvious. These global orders are ecclesiastical organizations responding to human needs and hopes that cannot be met by the state or "nation," for these needs are potentially, and in some cases actually, global in scope. Hence the nonterritorial organization of the religious orders. In addition, there are many other nonterritorial organizations of the church. One example is the existence in many states, such as Britain, of "military" bishops and chaplains who minister to the state's military forces wherever they happen to be, not only at home but anywhere on the planet. Prison chaplains similarly exist to minister to prisoners wherever they are, irrespective of diocesan boundaries. These organizations do not coincide with the boundaries of the sovereign state.

Such nonterritorial forms of church organization could be enormously multiplied. If the military forces can have their own bishops and their own church organization, why not Walmart or Greenpeace? There is no good reason why all global activities should not have their own church-presence, answering to the needs of their members. There is no limit to the possible profusion of such nonterritorial forms of church. The territorial diocese may become a minority form. The multiplicity of global activities proliferates while sovereign states disintegrate. For a global crisis needs global remedies. So the church, as sign or sacrament of the future, may need to rethink itself as global in a new way: not primarily in a "vertical" way as territorial churches or dioceses dotted all over the planet with its head in Rome, but rather "horizontally" as a network of Christian responses to people's multifarious needs spread out over the planet.

Of course this "horizontal" church would still require some system of ecclesial regulation designed to focus on what is most important, and to distinguish genuine from fake responses to global human hopes. And of course each network would still have to be a sacramental or eucharistic body: that is the body of Christ, rooted in faith in the death and resurrection of Jesus and practicing the liturgy. But the "organs" of this horizontal Catholic body would be social organizations designed to promote certain kinds of human activity, rather than territorially defined "limbs" located in particular places. And this would mean that the collections of bishops currently organized according to the territorial principle, that is, within the patchwork of sovereign states, would have to be rethought as bodies of bishops gathered together as heads of organizations formed according to the mutual interests and hopes of their respective members. The bishops of various peace or environmental or educational or other organizations could be brought together in groups to promote their own work within the global church, alongside or instead of conferences of bishops of sovereign states.

## The Church and the Good of All

An important reason for this rethinking of the church is that it is generally accepted today that the church has to be global in its teaching and outreach. That is to say, as Pope Benedict VI has constantly insisted, the social and political role of the church is to minister to the common good of *all*. And this inevitably means for *everybody*, wherever they live, and regardless of the interests of sovereign states or governments. As the Second Vatican Council said in *Gaudium et Spes* 36 members of the church "by their competence in secular disciplines...(should) vigorously contribute their effort so that created goods may be perfected by human labour, technical skill and civil culture for the benefit of all." There is a conflict here with the present international patchwork of sovereign states, especially of democratic states. For the government of a state elected by its citizens is practically bound to look after the interests of those electors first, rather than for the common good of all humanity. For example, the prime minister of the United Kingdom, David Cameron, in announcing the contribution that Britain was to make to the "bailout" of the Irish banks, stated publicly that Britain was doing this "in the British national interest." In other words it was helping the Irish to remedy their broken economy for the sake of British citizens, and *not* (except perhaps as a side-effect) for the benefit of the Irish themselves. The British government *had* to say this because, if it did not put the interest of British citizens first, it was thought unlikely to be reelected the next time round. Exactly the same point has been made by successive British governments about the presence of British troops in Afghanistan. They are there, we are told, for the security of the British. If that were not the primary reason they might be withdrawn. The security of the Afghans is a matter for the Afghans themselves, not for "us," although we may remain temporarily in Afghanistan to help them to help themselves.

Of course the same goes for any other democratically elected government of a sovereign state. This is because we live in a condition of permanent competition between sovereign states. And it is no surprise that when this competition cannot be peacefully resolved states have hitherto resorted to violence. This is why war is a characteristic of the sovereign state. And it is also why, at the present time, when war between the major players is becoming ever more unthinkable, even impossible, the whole of the sovereign state system is under threat, and needs to be replaced. Nuclear deterrence between these major players, the current substitute for war between them, is no answer because it does not exist for the common good of *all*, but only for the (alleged) protection of the deterrer—and even then only as long as the deterrer is willing to mass-murder innocents of the enemy state "if necessary" in order to protect itself.

In the early 1980s, when nuclear war fighting was widely recognized as the possible consequence of the deployment of new weapons systems, there was a major crisis for the church in its teaching about nuclear deterrence. For in these new circumstances, there was an outcry by millions of people in the nuclear-armed states about the dangers of the deterrent policy. The church had to respond. But of course, this response came from the bishops' conferences, who could not agree with each other about what was to be said or done. Such disagreement was inevitable, given the competition between states that had given rise to the problem in the first place. Various documents were produced by the conferences of bishops in the nuclear states and their allies, on both sides of the iron curtain. They were all unsatisfactory in various ways; again not surprisingly since they attempted to square the teaching of the church with promotion of national interests. The resultant confusion—which has never been resolved—led to Pope John Paul II's making a statement to the United Nations, which attempted to reconcile some of the differences. A key point in his response to the problem was that deploying nuclear weapons could be tolerated *only* as long as it was a step toward a progressive disarmament—which of course it has never been. A British decision to renew its Trident missile system for the next 30 years or more would therefore be a flagrant breach of papal teaching, and a manifest injustice for that reason. And even then this minimum is not enough because, as the Pope pointed out, there is the constant danger of "explosion."[2]

As I wrote in a Catholic Truth Society pamphlet at the time (*Nuclear Deterrence: What Does the Church Teach?* 1985) even this papal response was itself unsatisfactory for various reasons, and was soon misused by various governments to justify their own policies. The implication of all this confusion on a key question of ethics soon became clear. For the church to formulate its ethical and political teaching through the institution of bishops' conferences designed to promote the interest of their own states leads to intolerable uncertainties. The clear teaching of the Popes, that the church has to promote the common good of *all*, entails a critique of the organization of the modern world into competing and often incompatible state polities, and of the church as dependent on this form of world organization.

There has to be a different way. Despite the obvious problems of the Vatican itself as a sovereign state, the Pope himself is able to articulate teachings that are very far from being confined to the interests of any state, and has consistently done so in the field of nuclear weapons policies since the end of the Long War of 1914–1989. Indeed, promoting global nuclear disarmament and the abolition of nuclear weapons is today the evolving teaching of the church on this question. It is worth noting that the only conference of bishops which, in recent decades, has consistently followed the teaching of the Holy See is that of the Scottish bishops, who thereby show that they do not accept the line taken by the nuclear-armed British government or the fence-sitting line hitherto taken by the bishops' conference of England and Wales. They prefer to follow the teaching of the Holy See.

## The Church and Ethical Dilemmas

At the present time, the church is also faced by a somewhat different set of ethical problems. These focus on sex and sexuality. One of these concerns sexual orientation. Today the issue of homosexuality is prominent in public discourse. A key question is whether homosexuality is "natural" or acquired. If the homosexual orientation, whether for a lesbian or "gay" person, is "natural" in the sense that he or she is homosexual for genetic rather than cultural reasons, then it would seem quite inappropriate to condemn it as ethically unacceptable. To do so would make nonsense of any appeal to "natural law." It is not clear to me at any rate whether homosexuality is genetically determined or acquired after birth. This question needs urgent study. Yet in many parts of the world Christians are prominent is condemning homosexuality as such, whether or not it is genetically determined. The Anglican church is especially vulnerable to difficulties in this area at the present time. The ordination in the United States of an openly homosexual bishop has caused widespread scandal, as was the proposal of an equivalent step in Britain in the case of Dr. Geoffrey John. And several Anglican bishops in Africa have vowed to break away from the parent church if it openly tolerates homosexuality in any way. The Roman Catholic Church has not yet had to face this sort of scandal on the global plane. Gay priests are expected to keep quiet on their sexuality. But it might quite easily have to be opened up in the not too distant future, for it has certainly been the catholic tradition to regard homosexuality as a sin. Perhaps this will have to change as we discover more about it.

To take another cause of concern, the Roman condemnation of contraception has long been a bone of contention. The case against it was closely scrutinized and found logically wanting by many theologically and scientifically well-informed Catholics in the 1960s. Nothing has happened since to refute the argument that the condemnation of contraception was fallacious as well as inappropriate, despite the continuing assertion that it is always a sin. However, Benedict XVI issued a statement that in certain circumstances, in order to avoid infecting a partner with AIDS, the use of condoms can be justified. It remains to be seen how far this relaxation of the long-standing ban will go. Is it merely a concession to cope with the effects of a form of prostitution which is itself unacceptable? Is it the thin edge of a potentially large ethical wedge? We do not yet know, and will have to wait and see.

The key point in all this is that the involvement of territorial dioceses (certainly in the Anglican examples) is central to these disputes. For in the relevant American diocese the ordination of a homosexual bishop has been widely welcomed as a "progressive" step. Much the same could have happened in the British case. But the opponents, on whose opposition the issue may lead to schism in the Anglican church, are diocesan African bishops, who claim support from their state authorities. In other words, the problem is partly caused by the organization of the church into different sovereign state territories or dioceses. And something parallel to the confusion which arose over nuclear weapons in the 1980s among Catholic bishops, is happening over sexuality among Anglican bishops, and could easily spill over into the Roman church.

A further issue concerns the ethics of stem cell research and in vitro fertilization (IVF), and its potential benefits in curing diseases and promoting the creation of healthy children the world over. For this is itself a global question, since it concerns people simply as members of the human race, not as citizens of any state. For example, women are now able to buy embryos for implantation into themselves from anywhere on the planet. The ethics of this practice and other new developments is not confined to any single country or its population. The same is true of IVF and associated technologies, which are not limited to any particular parts of the human community. The Internet disseminates technical information about it all over the globe at the touch of a button. So scientific developments of this kind can no longer be kept within territorial boundaries. Whatever may be taught about the ethics of all this has to be thought through globally, and cannot be dealt with except on the basis of what is for the common good of *all*. For such activity is itself global, and has global consequences for the whole of humanity.

## The Church as Sacrament of the Future

Consideration of all these issues leads to one quite obvious conclusion: the way the church has been organized for the last three hundred years or more is no longer viable, in this post–Long War, postclimate change, postinternet age. It seems increasingly inappropriate for the church to think of itself as a multinational company centrally organized from Rome, with the Pope as its managing director and the various states in which this company operates as his subordinate managers. That bishops are still widely regarded in the first place as teachers of the citizens of their *own states* cannot continue without drastic modification, because of the disintegration of the sovereign state system on which such teaching rests. There is nothing new about this. The church has developed a variety of models of organization over the millennia, and can do so again in the changed world of the twenty-first century. Indeed it is one of the strengths of Christianity that it has persisted for so long, in so many different cultural contexts. And its treasure, namely its sacramental language, is well able to take the strain.

The point of saying that the church is the *sacrament* of the future is that we as the church can *do* what it says on the tin. A sacrament is not just a sign or a model of how things might be. It is a *promise* of something which could be put into practice if only the will and the virtues for it were mustered. To those who are stuck in the old sovereign state order, the notion of a global world order of government, in which justice and peace prevailed, seems hopelessly utopian, perhaps even undesirable. But the fact that the catholic church is the sacrament of just such a global order of justice and peace is a challenge to this utopianism. It says that the utopia is doable if we want to do it. For global justice and peace is simply human friendship writ large and divinised. Now friendship is always sharing, a matter of being loved, not just among ourselves but with God. And we must abide in this love, we must put it before anything else.[3] If we were to do this, global peace and justice could happen. We would be doing what it says on the tin. Of course, that the church itself has lamentably failed to live up to its own sacramental reality in the past is manifest. For after all the church is made up of ordinary people with all their failings. But despite all this the church is still the body of Christ and shares in His divinity. This is what it means to say that the church is the sacrament of what is possible. What prevents this sacrament from being realized in practice is lack of the necessary virtues and willpower, or (to put it another way) lack of faith; not any irresistible political, economic, or cultural counterforce. Hence my claim that if humanity is to survive its own worst crisis the church can and must be the sign of what is to come. Far more work needs to be done to put flesh on the bones of my case: something which I doubt that I myself can do. Let's hope that others will be able to take up the baton and run with it into the future.

## Notes

1. McCabe, H. (2002). *God Still Matters* (London: Continuum), p.116.
2. For a summary of the church's teaching about nuclear weapons and nuclear deterrence since Vatican Council II see the speech by Mgr. Francis Chullikat (the current Vatican Representative to the United Nations), available at: http://ncronline.org/news/peace/text-archbishop-francis-chullikat%E2%80%99s-speech-nuclear-disarmament.
3. McCabe, H. (2003). *Jesus and Sanctity in God, Christ and Us* (London: Continuum), pp. 47–52.

## Reference

Fisher, D. and Wicker, B. (2010). *Just War on Terror? A Christian and Muslim Response*. Aldershot: Ashgate.

# Part II

# Peace, Memory, and Education

# 5

# The History of World Peace in 100 Objects: Visualizing Peace in a Peace Museum

*Peter Van Den Dungen*

In 2010, Neil MacGregor, the director of the British Museum in London, presented "a history of the world in 100 objects," the latter having been carefully chosen from the Museum's vast collection. His talks on BBC Radio, as well as the accompanying publication[1] were widely praised as being among the cultural highlights of the year. It is interesting to note that whereas "war," "weapons," and "armor" all appear in the index of his substantial book, "peace" does not—although there is an entry "Pax Mongolica." Considering the artifacts themselves, only a few have a direct bearing on peace such as the inscription concerning Emperor Ashoka, and the "throne of weapons," a chair made of decommissioned weapons from the war in Mozambique. The relative absence of "peace" and "nonviolence" as compared to "war" and "violence" in MacGregor's account of world history is representative of the Western representation and interpretation of history, culture, and society. History textbooks are dominated by narratives of war; the heroic and glorious are identified with the warrior who is celebrated in public statues. War and military museums are prominent national institutions in many countries. The themes of peace, nonviolence, and antiwar, on the other hand, are conspicuous by their absence—not least in museums (widely regarded as guardians of high culture and which fulfill a major role in public education). The world still awaits the opening of the first national peace museum. Yet, an essential part of the development of a culture of peace, and of peace education, is making peace and nonviolence more tangible and more visible. Only in this way it will be possible to inform, encourage, and inspire many people. Peace museums are ideal vehicles for the furtherance of a culture of peace and nonviolence in society at large. The various aspects of peacemaking and the wide variety of peacemakers can be attractively illustrated through objects which, together, provide the foundations for a peace museum. A brief description of the nature and significance of ten artifacts, and representing various aspects of peace, suggests that peace also has a history, no less fascinating than that of war, and which deserves to be remembered and celebrated. The examples that follow are drawn largely from the Western world and the modern era, and are presented in broadly chronological order.

## William Penn, the Belt of *Wampum* (1682)

One of the most famous and remarkable instances of intercultural peace-making in modern history concerns the early colonization of Pennsylvania and the role played by its proprietor and first governor, the English Quaker William Penn. The Quakers, a Christian sect that emerged in the middle of the seventeenth century in England, were being harshly persecuted. One of their early leaders, Penn was well connected and obtained from King Charles II a tract of land in the New World, which became a haven for several thousand Quakers (as well as for dissenting Christians from continental Europe who also faced persecution). They could now practice their faith and live their lives without hindrance. The vast woodlands of eastern North America were sparsely populated by the Algonquin-speaking Indians, of whom the Lenni Lenape (or Delaware) was the most important tribe. Whereas earlier Dutch and Swedish immigrants had treated them brutally, the Quakers dealt with them on a basis of equality and fairness, not least as regards the purchase of Indian lands. When Penn arrived in October 1682, he had prepared the ground for meetings with the natives through his agent and the letters that Penn had sent and which expressed sentiments of friendship and cooperation that were unusual.[2] Until the 1750s, when the Quaker influence in the colony started to weaken, the new society that Penn had designed—his "Holy Experiment"—flourished. Its most significant feature was the harmonious relationship with the Indians, immortalized in the paintings by Benjamin West and Edward Hicks. A favorite subject was the first meeting between Penn and the Lenni Lenape in, reputedly, November 1682, under a large elm tree at Shackamaxon (near Philadelphia, a city which Penn was creating).[3] The great treaty, which was signed there has become famous, as has Voltaire's comment that this was "the only treaty between these nations and the Christians which was never sworn to and never broken."[4] According to legend, on this occasion and as a sign of their trust and friendship, the Indians gave Penn a belt of *Wampum*. The leather belt is fashioned from cylindrical beads of oyster-shell or fishbone (which were used as currency). This particular belt, measuring 26×9 inches, was presented by Granville John Penn, a nineteenth-century descendant of the original recipient, to the Historical Society of Pennsylvania. Like the paintings by West and Hicks, its image has often been reproduced in books on William Penn, Pennsylvania, colonial America, and Quakerism, and is widely recognized as a symbol of the peaceful living together of two very different peoples.[5]

## The Quaker Peace Testimony (1660)

At the heart of Quaker faith and practice is the principle of nonviolence as first set out in *A Declaration from the Harmless & Innocent People of God called Quakers*, addressed in 1660 to King Charles II and which has become known as the Peace Testimony.[6] The opening sentence states that "Our Principle is, and our Practices have always been, to seek peace." The rejection and denial of "all bloody Principles & Practices" the first paragraph concludes, "is our Testimony to the whole World." Meant to remove the fear and suspicion of Quakers as worldly "plotters and fighters," the letter stressed that "the spirit of Christ...will never move us to fight and war against any man with outward Weapons, neither for the Kingdom of Christ nor for the kingdoms of this world...our *Swords* are broken into *Plowshares*, and *Spears* into *Pruning-hooks*... Therefore we cannot learn War anymore." The declaration, issued on behalf of all Quakers, carried the signatures of 12 names, including that of their founder, George Fox. For 350 years, it has inspired the gradual development of a culture of peace, justice, and equality. This long and continuous tradition of Quaker peacemaking has left a rich legacy—in terms of concepts, practices, campaigns, organizations, institutions, as well as artifacts.[7] The Quaker Peace Testimony is therefore a most important object in the history of peacemaking. Highlights of the rich tradition of Quaker peacemaking are depicted in many of the 77 colorful embroidery panels presenting a visual history of Quakerism and which are on permanent display in the Quaker Tapestry Exhibition Centre in the Friends Meeting House in Kendal, Cumbria, in northern England.[8]

## Ludwig van Beethoven, *Ode to Joy*, Ninth Symphony (1824)

The ideal of human brotherhood has been expressed in all possible art forms and sometimes in a combination of several. Friedrich Schiller's poem, *To Joy*, first written in 1785 but later rewritten to include what would become its most famous line, "All men will be brothers," attracted the attention of a young Ludwig van Beethoven who in 1792 conceived the idea of setting the poem to music. This would become the famous choral part in the finale of his greatest and last symphony, the Ninth. Its premiere took place in Vienna in 1824 and was a spectacular success. This was one of the last public concerts conducted by the composer whose deafness was complete by this time. As early as 1837, a music critic referred to it as "the grand Masonic hymn of Europe," possibly the first time that the *Ode to Joy* was put forward as a European anthem, despite the universalist wording of Schiller's poem.[9] Almost a century later, in the aftermath of a catastrophic war that had laid waste to much of the continent, Beethoven's symphony was frequently proposed as a European or indeed universal symbol of peace. This was especially so following the foundation of the Pan-Europe movement by Count Richard Coudenhove-Kalergi in Vienna (1923); the hopeful developments of Franco-German reconciliation as suggested by the Locarno Pact (1925); and during the centenary celebrations, notably in Vienna, of Beethoven's death (1927). There was widespread yearning for peace, in Europe and beyond. Beethoven's masterpiece was frequently referred to as the most obvious and potent expression of this yearning. In 1929 Coudenhove-Kalergi had made *Ode to Joy* the anthem of his influential Pan-Europe movement and during the Beethoven celebrations, French internationalist statesman Edouard Herriot and leading intellectual and pacifist, Romain Rolland, campaigned to make the *Ode* the anthem of a reborn and pacified Europe, as well of the world. After the Second World War, Coudenhove-Kalergi and Herriot continued their campaign, now in the context of the Council of Europe, founded in 1949. It was not until 1971 that the Council adopted a resolution that made Beethoven's music (but not Schiller's words, with their universal reach) the European anthem. In 1985, the European Community followed suit. His Ninth Symphony has often been played to celebrate momentous political events such as the fall of the Berlin Wall and the end of the Cold War it heralded (1989) and in this respect, its appeal to a virtually global audience is unique. The (silent) artifact that relates to it is the score, first published in 1826. While Beethoven's original manuscript has been lost, the one that he used during the symphony's first performance—the work of a copyist, with many revisions and annotations in the composer's hand—was sold in 2003 by Sotheby's in London for £ 2.1 million, the highest price ever paid for a single musical work. The auctioneer called the object "an incomparable manuscript of an incomparable work."[10]

## Victor Hugo, the United States of Europe (1849)

France's greatest poet, Victor Hugo, played a major role in making the Second General Peace Congress, held in Paris in August 1849, famous and successful. The congress, initiated by Anglo-American pacifists, was one of the highlights of the nineteenth-century organized peace movement. Not only did he lend his name and considerable prestige to the meeting by agreeing to preside over it during each of the three days of the congress, but his powerful oratory, both in his opening and concluding speeches, inspired delegates as well as idealists everywhere (and for generations to come). His inaugural address has become known as "The United States of Europe," thereby popularizing an expression that had first been used the previous year by Carlo Cattaneo, an Italian republican whose federalist and democratic ideas also projected a European federation of democratic republics. Hugo pointed to the history of France, which at one time was a collection of warring provinces but which had grown into a single political entity which preserved the cultural diversity of its former provinces, as a model for all of Europe. He predicted that the nations of Europe, without losing their "distinctive qualities" or their "glorious individuality," would one day "be blended into a superior unity and constitute a European fraternity, just as Normandy, Brittany, Burgundy, Lorraine, [and] Alsace have been blended into France." He foresaw a day when this unity would eliminate the horrendous and wasteful arms race and constant threat of war, when competition of ideas and markets would replace struggles over territory. In a particular effective and rousing piece of oratory, Hugo introduced his prophecies of a future European peace by repeating, again and again, the phrase, "A day will come.... "

The printed proceedings of the congress mention that Hugo's address was frequently interrupted by outbursts of applause, and that at the close "the whole assembly rose and greeted the speaker with three cheers given after the English fashion."[11] Hugo's vision and oratory continued to inspire large numbers of people. His inaugural speech in 1849 has been called "the best-known document of the 19th century peace movement,"[12] and "perhaps the most beautiful page in the entire literature of pacifism."[13]

## Bertha von Suttner, *Die Waffen nieder!* [Lay Down Your Arms] (1889)

The nineteenth-century peace movement (1815–1914) spawned many peace societies, organized national and international peace conferences, and issued numerous publications. Particularly in the period 1889–1914, the movement was successful in having elements of its agenda—the main plank of which was the substitution of war by peaceful conflict resolution, through arbitration and the development of international law, disarmament, the federation of Europe, and the creation of a league of nations—increasingly accepted by public opinion and governments. This was in no small part due to the publication in 1889 of the novel *Die Waffen nieder!* (Lay Down Your Arms) by the Austrian baroness Bertha von Suttner. Its success made her the leading figure in the international peace movement until her death in June 1914. For instance, she founded the Austrian Peace Society and cofounded the German and Hungarian Peace Societies, and played a major role in the International Peace Bureau, the chief organ of the international peace movement. The novel caused a sensation. Tolstoy wrote to her, "The abolition of slavery was preceded by a famous novel written by a woman. May God grant that the abolition of war will follow on your novel." Indeed, it became known as the *Uncle Tom's Cabin* of the peace movement. Both books had been written to promote a cause and were successful in gaining a wide hearing for it and in attracting many readers to the social movement that each book was meant to serve. *Die Waffen nieder!* was translated into many languages and made its author world famous. The impact on one reader in particular, proved to be highly significant.

At one time, von Suttner had briefly been Alfred Nobel's secretary in Paris. After the success of the book had catapulted its author to the forefront of the peace movement, she tried to convince a skeptic Nobel that it had a realistic program, and begged for his support. That her efforts were not in vain became clear shortly after Nobel's death on December 10, 1896, when the contents of his last will and testament were revealed. The Swedish inventor of dynamite had left most of his vast fortune for the establishment of five annual prizes, one of which was to be awarded "to the person who shall have done the most or the best work for fraternity between nations, for the abolition or reduction of standing armies, and for the holding and promotion of peace congresses." It was widely recognized at the time that this inestimable legacy to the peace movement was due to Bertha von Suttner. It was also clear that he had her in mind as an early recipient of the prize. Her novel, as already indicated by its title, was a passionate plea for disarmament and she was also in the forefront of organizing and presiding over conferences of the peace movement—two of the three kinds of peace work Nobel had specified in his will. When the first Nobel prizes were awarded in 1901, Bertha von Suttner was not among the laureates; she had to wait until 1905 before she was honored with the prize for "champions of peace" (the expression Nobel used in his will). Von Suttner was not only the first woman to receive this prize, but also the person who influenced Nobel to leave a large legacy for peace work. The Nobel Peace Prize has become the most coveted and prestigious award of the modern world and *Lay Down Your Arms* can be seen as the book behind its creation.[14] It is therefore a key object in the modern history of peace. Von Suttner's novel has aptly been called the world's only disarmament best seller; in an age threatened by the proliferation of weapons of mass destruction, its message has lost nothing of its urgency. Copies of the original edition of *Die Waffen nieder!* are very rare[15] one is kept in Nobel's library in his Swedish home in Karlskoga (now Nobel museum). Bertha von Suttner is largely forgotten, unlike her rich friend, although her image appears on the Austrian two Euro coin. There are several Nobel museums; Bertha von Suttner deserves one, at least one.[16]

## Alfred Nobel's Testament (1895)

Alfred Nobel's testament itself, drawn up and signed in Paris on November 27, 1895, is another important object in the history of peace.[17] Much can be learned about the twentieth century, particularly as regards the evolution of peace-thinking and peacemaking, through the lives of the peace laureates (comprising individuals as well as organizations). Through the creation of this prize, Nobel—a prolific inventor and astute businessman—greatly contributed to make the pursuit of peace more respectable and legitimate, as well as more visible. The esteem in which the prize is held has stimulated the creation of an ever-growing number of other awards for "champions of peace" which, however, seem destined to live in the shadow of the Nobel Peace Prize.[18]

## Albert Einstein, 2% Speech (1930)

Albert Einstein was the twentieth century's greatest scientist, and one of the greatest scientists of all time. He was chosen as "Person of the Century" in the December 31, 1999 issue of *Time* magazine. His passion for peace and social justice throughout his life greatly contributed to make him a universally admired figure. As his long-term friend and secretary Otto Nathan has written, "except for his devotion to science, no cause was more important or closest to his heart than the determination that the institution of war be forever abolished." Evidence of this is provided in the substantial volume, *Einstein on Peace*, edited by Otto Nathan and Heinz Norden, which brings together all his numerous writings, statements, and letters on the subject with valuable background information by the editors.[19] Until the Nazis came to power in his native Germany (1933), Einstein was a passionate advocate of war resistance and conscientious objection to military service. According to Nathan, "A climactic point in Einstein's career as a militant pacifist came on December 14, 1930, when he spoke at a meeting in New York's Ritz-Carlton Hotel, under the auspices of the New History Society."[20] Einstein said, "Deeds...are needed...Under the present military system everyone is compelled to commit the crime of killing for his country. The aim of all pacifists must be to convince others of the immorality of war and rid the world of the shameful slavery of military service...Even if only two percent of those assigned to perform military service should announce their refusal to fight, as well as urge means other than war of settling international disputes, governments would be powerless, they would not dare send such a large number of people to jail."[21] According to Nathan, "Einstein's speech was greeted by pacifists with great enthusiasm, first in America and then throughout the world. Indeed, it established him as one of the outstanding international heroes of pacifism. He received many congratulatory messages, and in the ensuing months buttons with the legend '2%' began to blossom from the lapels of young men on American streets and campuses."[22] The idea for such a button had been conceived by Sydney Strong, a New York City peace activist who believed that it could serve as a symbol of the rejection of conscription and of the refusal to play any part in war. "The Button dramatizes the great Peace Idea, and marks the first step, personal commitment, in effective anti-war tactics."[23] He reported that in a short time, several thousand buttons had already been used in New York, and several hundred others are displayed on the Pacific Coast (where Einstein had repeated his remarks in Pasadena). Einstein would have been horrified to know of the trial, ten years after his death, of Don Lorenzo Milani, and especially that it was instigated by a group of clergymen who obviously believed that blind obedience to the state overruled religious scruple and personal conscience.[24]

## The CND/Peace Symbol (1958)

Following the Second World War, Einstein resumed his campaigning for the abolition of war which now, in a nuclear age, had become an imperative for survival. The Einstein-Russell declaration, issued in London in July 1955, was the last document he signed, just before his death in April. It stressed the great danger the world found itself in and appealed to world leaders and their peoples to find new ways of settling disagreements and to remember above all their common humanity. This declaration is the founding document of the Pugwash movement of concerned scientists of East and West, which became an important pressure group for the restraint of the nuclear arms race during the Cold War. Bertrand Russell, the leading British philosopher, social critic, and pacifist, also became involved in mass protest of the Campaign for Nuclear Disarmament (CND), founded in London in 1958. CND went on to become the most important British peace movement, celebrating its fiftieth anniversary in 2008.[25] The symbol on the button—"just a circle with three lines on it"[26]—which CND first used during a protest march in 1958 has since become famous the world over as the symbol of peace. It had been designed in 1958 by the British textile designer, conscientious objector and peace activist, Gerald Holtom, whose original drawings are preserved in the Commonweal peace library and archives at the University of Bradford.[27] Whereas Einstein's "2%" button has been forgotten, the popularity of the CND symbol worldwide has resulted in its use in a wide variety of contexts (not always related to peace or disarmament). It is a most important object in the global story of peace of the last half century.

## United Nations Peacekeeping Forces: Blue Helmets (1956)

Whereas the idea of the need for a permanent international organization of states to reduce and eliminate violent conflict between them is old, its realization had to wait until the twentieth century. The Treaty of Versailles (1919), which settled the First World War also made provision for the establishment of the League of Nations—a first attempt at creating such a body which, however, proved unable to prevent the outbreak of another world war two decades later. For all its faults and weaknesses, its successor, the United Nations, has become a major player in global politics. For the first four decades of its existence, the UN was greatly hampered by the international environment in which it had to operate, the Cold War, involving great antagonism between the two superpowers and a dangerous and all-pervasive ideological and military confrontation that brought the world to the brink of disaster more than once. Yet, even in these difficult circumstances the UN managed to play a constructive role (often against the will of its most powerful member states). The most remarkable and successful innovation the UN pioneered in these early days was the creation of a peacekeeping force. Its origins go back to the Suez crisis when, in October 1956, Israel, Britain, and France invaded Egypt, following President Nasser's nationalization of the Suez Canal. Britain and France were able to extricate themselves (and their troops) from this illegal, ill-conceived, and catastrophic venture after the deployment of a UN Emergency Force (UNEF) to keep the peace. UN secretary-general Dag Hammarsjkold had been authorized by the General Assembly to negotiate a cease-fire and also had been invited to explore the idea of sending a UN force to keep the peace. He immediately produced a report, which has been called a "conceptual masterpiece in a completely new field, the blueprint for a non-violent, international military operation."[28]

Brian Urquhart, the only person in the UN secretariat with extensive military experience, played a central role in creating such an unprecedented force, all aspects of which had to be invented from first principles, and with very little time. For instance, "One of the first problems was how to identify the UN troops. With three foreign armies fighting on Egyptian soil it was important that the UN Force should be clearly distinguishable [especially when] its soldiers would be wearing their own national uniforms. Distinctive headgear seemed to be the key, and we agreed on blue berets, only to find that it would take weeks to get enough of them made. There were large stores of American Army helmet liners available in Europe, and to spray-paint them UN blue was a simple matter. Thus, the 'Blue Helmets' came into being."[29] Amazingly, already by mid-November the first units of the UNEF took to the field, and the British and French troops left Egypt before the end of the year. The UNEF lasted over ten years and its value and importance in keeping the peace in Sinai and Gaza during this period was only fully realized following its dramatic termination in 1967. Although there have been many setbacks, and UN peacekeeping operations have sometimes been deployed in inappropriate circumstances, and the soldiers involved have not always lived up to standards of behavior one might expect from a UN force, peacekeeping has become a central part of the work of the UN—in spite of the fact that this term is not to be found in its Charter (itself a good candidate to be among the 100 objects), which does not even envisage the activity involved. UN peacekeepers traditionally have been only lightly armed, only for the purposes of self-defense. As indicated already, the original idea was to identify UN peacekeepers by their soft bonnets, rather than by hard helmets. Only practical necessities made the latter, rather than the former, the symbol of a new kind of military force: not to fight, but to act as a buffer between hostile forces, and to monitor cease-fire agreements. Often, a cease-fire enabled peace negotiations to be initiated and the ground to be laid for a peaceful resolution of the conflict. The blue helmet thus became a symbol of a new kind of soldier with a new kind of mission. As UN secretary-general Javier Perez de Cuellar stated in his speech accepting the Nobel Peace Prize for the UN Peacekeeping Forces (1988): "The technique [of] peacekeeping uses soldiers as the servants of peace rather than as instruments of war. It introduces to the military sphere the principle of nonviolence."[30]

## Conclusion

The small selection introduced above is only the tip of the proverbial iceberg—peace history is still largely unknown and hidden, and overwhelmed in the public perception by war and its symbols and artifacts. However, the general public is familiar with such towering figures from recent history as Gandhi, Martin Luther King, and Nelson Mandela, or with such living legends as Desmond Tutu and Aung San Suu Kyi (all Nobel Peace laureates, except Gandhi). From the more distant European past, there are also great figures whose significance for peace, however, is not always recognized, such as Erasmus, Kant, and Tolstoy. From such a crowded field the tenth object, left unidentified here, is not easy to select. To tell the history of peace from the beginning, and from a global perspective—including ancient China, as well as the civilizations of ancient Greece and Rome, among others[31]—it will not be difficult to identify 90 other significant objects. The collection, display and interpretation of 100 such objects would be an obvious and ideal way to create a world peace museum. Of course, many of the objects would only be available as copies or reproductions since their private or public owners (including museums such as the British Museum) may be reluctant to part with artifacts. It is no exaggeration to claim that a peace museum, which aims to tell the world history of peace through objects that are important and interesting enough to be displayed, could draw on at least 1,000 objects. Most of the nearly 200 member states of the United Nations would struggle to limit their individual submission to just five items. From the very small sample provided above—which includes the music of Beethoven, the oratory of Victor Hugo, and symbols of campaigns of protest—it is clear that such a museum would be a lively place for learning about, as well as celebrating, peace. It would be one of the most beautiful of all museums, honoring the peacemakers of the past and present. It would also be one of the most useful (and necessary) museums, inspiring and encouraging its visitors to believe in peace and recognize their role in helping to bring it about.

## Notes

1. MacGregor, N. (2011). *A History of the World in 100 Objects* (London: Allen Lane/Penguin Books).
2. Soderlund, J. R. (ed.) (1983). *William Penn and the Founding of Pennsylvania 1680–1684. A Documentary History* (Philadelphia: University of Pennsylvania Press).
3. Cook Myers, A. (ed.) (1970). *William Penn's Own Account of the Lenni Lenape or Delaware Indians.* Revised Edition (Wallingford, PA: Middle Atlantic Press).
4. Taylor, E. E. (1936). *Peace Pacts Honoured: Two Examples from History* (London: Friends' Book Centre), p.6.

5. See, for instance, Merrell, J. H. (1999). *Into the American Woods: Negotiators on the Pennsylvania Frontier* (New York: W.W. Norton).
6. Most recently, it has been reprinted in Weitsch, M. (ed.) (2010). *"Be Patterns, Be Examples". Reflecting on 350 years of working for peace in Europe* (Brussels: The Quaker Council for European Affairs), pp.4–6.
7. Brock, P. (1990). *The Quaker Peace Testimony 1660 to 1914* (York, England: Sessions Book Trust).
8. Cf. www.quaker-tapestry.co.uk/the-exhibition/about-the-tapestry.
9. Buch, E. (2003). *Beethoven's Ninth: A Political History* (Chicago: University of Chicago Press), p.123. The account that follows is largely based on this book. The politicization of this as well as other compositions by the same composer is illustrated in Dennis, D. B. (1996). *Beethoven in German Politics, 1870–1989* (New Haven, CT: Yale University Press).
10. "Score of Beethoven Ninth Sold for £ 2.1 Million," *The Times* [London], May 23, 2003.
11. A contemporary English translation of the speech is in *Report of the Proceedings of the Second Peace Congress Held in Paris on the 22nd, 23rd and 24th of August, 1849* (London: Charles Gilpin, 1849), pp.10–14. The original French text is in the French edition of the same publication: *Congres des Amis de la Paix Universelle Reuni a Paris en 1849. Compte-Rendu* (Paris: Guillaumin, 1850), pp.3–5. The full text in English is available in Cooper, S. E. (ed.) (1972). *Five Views on European Peace* (New York: Garland); see also her introduction, pp.14–17. A shortened version is in Chatfield, C. and Ilukhina, R. (eds.) (1994). *Peace/Mir. An Anthology of Historic Alternatives to War* (Syracuse, NY: Syracuse University Press), pp.100–102.
12. Cooper, S. E. (1991). *Patriotic Pacifism: Waging War on War in Europe, 1815–1914* (New York: Oxford University Press), p.24.
13. Ruyssen, T. (1961). *Les Sources doctrinales de l'Internationalisme* vol. 3, (Paris : Presses Universitaires de France), p.551.
14. Heffermehl, F. S. (2010). *The Nobel Peace Prize: What Nobel Really Wanted* (Santa Barbara, CA: Praeger).
15. Van den Dungen, P. (2000). "The Price of Peace: Rare Books of Peace." In *Antiquarian Book Monthly*, 27, pp.10–17.
16. Van den Dungen, P. (2010). "Towards a Bertha von Suttner Peace Museum in Vienna (1914–2014)." In Johann G. Lughofer (ed.), *Im Prisma: Bertha von Suttner. "Die Waffen nieder!"* (Wien-St. Wolfgang: Edition Art Science), pp.211–237.
17. It is reprinted, and extensively discussed, in Sohlman, R. (1983). *The Legacy of Alfred Nobel: The Story behind the Nobel Prizes* (London: The Bodley Head), pp.136–139. Sohlman was Nobel's last secretary and coexecutor of his will.
18. Van den Dungen, P. (2000). *The Nobel Peace Prize and the Global Proliferation of Peace Prizes in the 20th Century.* vol. 1, no. 6 (Oslo: The Norwegian Nobel Institute Series), available at: www.nppri.org/pdf/Vol1_No6.pdf.
19. Nathan, Otto and Norden, Heinz (1960). *Einstein on Peace* (New York: Simon and Schuster). Nathan was Einstein's secretary, and executor of his will.
20. Ibid., p.116.
21. Ibid., pp.116–117. The speech was included under the title "Militant Pacifism" in the early anthology of Einstein's pacifist writings edited in 1933 by Alfred Lief, *Albert Einstein: The Fight against War* (New York: John Day), pp.34–37. Nathan and Norden reprinted this text with extensive (and rather unnecessary) stylistic changes. Cf. *Einstein on Peace*, p.656, n.29.
22. Nathan and Norden, *Einstein on Peace*, p. 118. Ronald W. Clark evidently did not see the button when he wrote that it carried the words "two percent." Cf. *Einstein: The Life and Times* (New York: World Publishing, 1971), p.368.

23. Sydney Strong (1931), quoted in *Peace Militant* (New York City: New History Foundation), p.29. The booklet was dedicated "To Albert Einstein—Commander-in-Chief of the Forces of Militant Pacifism."
24. He would also have been impressed by Milani's powerful argument about the possible duty to disobey the state, as put forth in the letters to the Military Chaplains and to the Judges. Long extracts from these letters, together with other material, ("Don Lorenzo Milani, Conscientious Objection in Italy"), have been reprinted in Ronald G. Musto (ed.) (1996). *Catholic Peacemakers: A Documentary History. Vol. 2: From the Renaissance to the Twentieth Century. Part 1* (New York: Garland), pp.417–430. Milani's letters are still most relevant today.
25. At least two splendid volumes were published in this year: Ken Kolsbun (with Mike Sweeney) (2008). *Peace: The Biography of a Symbol* (Washington, DC: National Geographic); Barry Miles (2008). *Peace. 50 Years of Protest 1958–2008* (London: Collins & Brown).
26. Kolsbun, *Peace: The Biography of a Symbol*, p.17.
27. Rigby, A. (1997). "Symbols of Peace: The Commonweal Collection." In Carol Rank (ed.), *City of Peace: Bradford's Story* (Bradford: Bradford Libraries), pp.151–159. Many objects from the peace archives at Bradford University feature in the "100 Objects from Special Collections at the University of Bradford" online exhibition started in January 2011 by the University's Special Collections librarian, Alison Cullingford (and inspired by the British Museum/BBC project). The CND/Peace symbol is object no. 2. Cf. http://100objectsbradford.wordpress.com/.
28. Urquhart, B. (1987). *A Life in Peace and War* (London: Weidenfeld & Nicolson), p.133.
29. Ibid., p.134.
30. Abrams, I. (ed.) (1997). *Nobel Lectures Peace, 1981–1990* (Singapore: World Scientific Publishing), p.221.
31. An excellent recent global history of the peace idea, going beyond the modern European era, is Gittings, J. (2012). *The Glorious Art of Peace* (Oxford: Oxford University Press).

# 6

# Responding to the Call of Peace: In Memory of a Future That Might Have Been

*Clive Zammit*

## Introduction

History teaches us that war is inevitable and that to strive idealistically for lasting peace in the realm of real politics is dangerously naive. In this chapter I investigate the possible sources for the origin of this apparently natural link between history and war. I draw on Roland Barthes' analysis of myth to question the nature of this link and its implications for the realm of ethics and responsibility. The results of this investigation are used to assess the relevance and merit of the actions and events that this book sets out to commemorate.

## A Call for Commemoration

> "I continue to be troubled by the unsettling spectacle offered by an excess of memory here, and an excess of forgetting elsewhere, to say nothing of the influence of commemorations and abuses of memory—and of forgetting.[1]

Here is a collection of essays in honor of Don Lorenzo Milani's contribution to peace. This publication is an act of commemoration. Its readers and its writers collaborate in paying tribute to actions of significant value in virtue of which their agent, Don Lorenzo Milani, is deemed to merit honor and respect. The work is motivated by the conviction that the person and events it commemorates deserve what Paul Ricoeur calls "a just allotment of memory."[2] The chapters strive to allot a place in collective memory to Milani's insistence on the right of conscientious objection and the pursuit of justice through peaceful means. They make a claim on behalf of Milani's actions and convictions, ensuring and securing their archival allotment.

Events call for commemoration when they do not sit well in the past. These are events that escape or transgress the conventional temporal parameters of past, present, and future. Because they exceed the past, these events have a claim on the present. A commemoration sets time out of joint,[3] disrupting its passage by exhuming the past and (re)-presenting it for the future.

In choosing to respond to a call from the past, a commemoration follows a decision that draws on and suggests a system of values, which informs the selection, placing and archiving of such events. What claim do these particular events have on a place within the archive? What, in our predicament, would justify responding to this call to exhume the past and to burden the present and risk contaminating the future with its remains?

## Our Present Predicament

> During the twentieth century, we saw the eruption of violence on an unprecedented scale. Sadly, our ability to harm and mutilate one another has kept apace with our extraordinary economic and scientific progress. We seem to lack the wisdom to hold our aggression in check.[4]

Is there any doubt that our predicament is that of being caught in a spiral of war?

> Does not lucidity, the openness upon the true, consist in catching sight of the permanent possibility of war?[5]

Having borne the full burden of the Second World War, the Lithuanian philosopher Emmanuel Levinas suggested that the inevitability of war may be written in the genetic code of the conceptual structures that founds and supports our thought processes. According to Levinas, within the tradition of Western thought, reality can only be conceived as war. As a consequence, our thinking has evolved mainly as a tool to respond to this reality, tuned and geared primarily for confrontation and violence. The main objective of thinking is therefore that of "foreseeing war: and "winning it by every means." Levinas insists that it is high time that we realize that Western thinking is held within a dynamic of conflict of oppositions in which progress can only be achieved through totalization of one opposite by another.

If Levinas is right in thinking that the inevitability of war is the result of a genetic inscription in our thought processes, then it may be possible to search for the source of this inscription and question whether other possible alternative avenues for the development of thought may have been forgone. Could there still be a way to retrieve such possibilities and to re-inseminate Western thinking, to enable it to develop along alternative future routes?

## The Axial Age—an Aporetic Place of Inspiration

In our current predicament, I believe that we can find inspiration in the period that the German philosopher Karl Jaspers called the Axial Age because it was pivotal to the spiritual development of humanity. From about 900 to 200 BCE, in four distinct regions, the great world traditions that have continued to nourish humanity came into being: Confucianism and Daoism in China; Hinduism and Buddhism in India; monotheism in Israel; and philosophical rationalism in Greece.[6]

We seem to be caught in an aporia, a treacherous place of nonpassage, where we can neither carry on along our traditional destructive paths of thinking nor sensibly forgo this same tradition that has also acted as the foundation of indisputable successful development in all fields of human endeavor. On the one hand, there is little doubt that we need to depart from the traditional mode of thinking. On the other, one cannot help doubting whether there can be anything to gain from backtracking over two and a half millennia, undoing everything that has been achieved in the process in order to try and uncover some dream of an ideal golden age that was already the subject of myth in the time of myth. Such harking back can only be regarded with extreme caution if not with outright suspicion. Recent thinkers, such as Martin Heidegger, who have followed that route of dismissing the entirety of the Western tradition in the hope of reviving some threatened European heritage, are not particularly exemplary in the political ramifications of their thinking and their political affiliations. Is it not futile to retread the unsavory paths followed by such thinkers, when history itself teaches us that war is inevitable?

> Doesn't history teach us the futility of all such efforts? To say that it does is to give to history a wholly mythical power, for history has no such lessons of futility to teach. It is only by our present consent that the past can set limits to the future. So can we dare to hope for peace on earth? Freud's answer is an unequivocal mandate for our time: we can dare nothing less.[7]

## Seeking Issue at the Archive

In our present predicament we have no option but to run the risks involved in going back to the source of our thinking in a quest for inspiration from a type of thinking that is still uncaught and uncouth. What we seek, therefore, is the "archive," which is the source of the genetic structure of our system of thought.

> Arkhe, we recall, names at once the commencement and the commandment.[8]

As Derrida notes, the arkhe is that place in our history, which not only sets our thought in motion but also continues to guide or lead it along its preset foundational parameters. Just like the hidden underlying foundations of an architectural structure, these guiding parameters have receded from view and fallen into forgetfulness. This receding may give the impression that our thoughts have now been liberated from guiding constraints of their arkhe. In truth, however, this is a functional receding that shelters and protects the arkhe and ensures both its preservation and its continued influence. In its archival form, the arkhe takes on an archaic semblance, a semblance of the irrelevance of the antiquated. In true fact, it continues to lead and dominate from its safe haven wherein it remains protected from the flux and turmoil of the exposed outskirts of developing thought. This critical point of cultural and social transition, a point that although mostly shrouded in myth remains seminal in all aspects of our thinking. This is where we locate the arkhe of our tradition. The hand that leads remains hidden and invisible, except to the select few who may have access to the domicile of the archons.

> The archons are first of all the documents' guardians. They do not only ensure the physical security of what is deposited and of the substrate. They are accorded the hermeneutic right and competence. They have the power to interpret the archives. Entrusted to such archons, these documents in effect speak the law.[9]

It seems that a possible way through the aporia of our present predicament would be to gain access to this guiding arkhe and to identify those genetic traits, which give our thinking its destructive confrontational nature. In the Western tradition the beginning of the "Axial Age" coincides with the development of writing as a tool to record. First it is mythological narratives that are recorded. Soon after it is the significant events and deeds of men that eventually became our history.

## A Time of the Possibility of Peace—a Time of Difference

Needless to say, mythologies abound with memories of a golden age, an age of peace and bounty, an age before strife and suffering. The idea of a golden age of perpetual peace finds its natural place precisely in a time before history, a time before time. Being a nontime and a nonplace it is consigned safely and fittingly to mythology. [10]

But if it is history and human events that we are concerned with as the arkhe of Western thought and its supposedly inherently destructive character, we must focus squarely on Herodotus. At the very outset, the point of issue of his History, Herodotus declares that his objective is specifically to record and commemorate the noble and heroic deeds of men, to ensure "that the causes may be remembered for which these waged war with one another." From its very first page, the written history of Western civilization is a history of war.

Having declared his mission and objectives as boldly as possible, Herodotus cannot help but drop a hint, an intimation, of the existence of a time prior to the inevitable state of war.

> Up to this point, they say, nothing more happened than the carrying away of women on both sides; but after this the Hellenes were very greatly to blame; for they set the first example of war, making an expedition into Asia before the Barbarians made any into Europe.[11]

We can read Herodotus' opening reference to a time before the war in a number of ways. It can be just a warming up note, a few lines written to get him started, to give him the required momentum required to tackle the harder stuff. Similarly, his intention could also have been to ease the reader into the more serious stuff that lies ahead. They can also, however, be an unintentional hint of an alternative space. This could have been a remnant, or a trace, of what at this time was receding from the consciousness of Western thinkers in order to make a space for the new emergent thinking that would eventually become the Western tradition. If one were to indulge in more Derridean terminology, this could be described as "a Freudian impression," a "mal d'Archive"; the bruised imprint left by the tightening grasp of an arkhe, which may at this time have started slipping and losing its grip.

## The Emergence of the Willing Agent

> Now they say that in their judgment, though it is an act of wrong to carry away women by force, it is a folly to set one's heart on taking vengeance for their rape, and the wise course is to pay no regard when they have been carried away; for it is evident that they would never be carried away if they were not themselves willing to go. And the Persians say that they, namely the people of Asia, when their women were carried away by force, had made it a matter of no account. [12]

From Herodotus' account it seems that what was once regarded as "an act of wrong," which those of wise judgment would hold as "a matter of no account," at some point became a matter of such offence that the Hellenes felt justified to embark on a major expedition into Asia to destroy Priam's great city. One must remember that this was not a casual skirmish or a whimsical foray, but an invasion of such magnitude that it drew a permanent line that was to set two cultures in antagonistic opposition for all time. Herodotus need not remind us that "from this time forward they had always considered the Hellenic race to be their enemy" because in fact, over three and a half millennia later, the war drums are still beating along the same geographical and cultural lines.

Herodotus' opening verses bear witness to a shift in the way that the early Greeks experienced human actions and how acts of wrongdoing were to be engaged with. They point to a time when the role of the greater forces at play beneath the acts of folly of man was still given its due recognition. This awareness and acceptance of the limit of our control on human and worldly events reduced the weight and consequence of man's acts of transgression which, when judged wisely, were therefore more likely to be regarded as matters of no account.

This experience of reality was, however, to shift at this seminal time for our tradition. As a consequence of this shift, human acts of transgression took on enough weight to cause tectonic shifts of permanent cataclysmic proportions. If, following Armstrong's suggestion, we are to draw inspiration from the thinkers of the axial period, then we would need to understand some of the factors that underlie this shift.

In his analysis of this shifting worldview, Jean-Pierre Vernant focuses on the time of the emergence of Greek tragedy describing it as the time when mythological thought is fast losing ground to rationality and the emergence of the free standing human agent.

> This experimentation, still wavering and indecisive, of what was subsequently in the psychological history of Western man to become the category of the will—as is well known, in ancient Greece there was no true vocabulary to cover willing—is expressed in tragedy in the form of an anxious questioning concerning the relation of the agent to his actions.[13]

It seems that this turbulent period of development from a worldview characterized by mythological thought, to one characterized by rationality and willful agency, provided the creative energy required to give birth to political, cultural, and intellectual models, which were to found and nourish the development of the Western world. It may also well have been this same creative tension between two competing worldviews that gave the resulting tradition its insistence on the serious consequence of human actions and the eventual grip of a violent and confrontational mindset that continues to hold our tradition in its sway.

## From Inspiration to Authority

If we were to use Hesiod's writings as a way to step back further into the dawn of our civilization by a couple of centuries, this change in the experience of man's role in worldly events and the weight of consequence attributed to them becomes immediately evident.

Hesiod (eighth century BC) starts his Theogony by invoking the muses who are the daughters of memory.

> From the Heliconian Muses let us begin to sing, who hold the great and holy mount of Helicon, and dance on soft feet about the deep-blue spring and the altar of the almighty son of Cronos.[14,15]

He praises and reveres them for "they taught Hesiod glorious song while he was shepherding his lambs."[16]

The gift of the muses is not merely one of song and merriment. The man who receives their gift will speak well and make good judgments. He will be honored and held in high esteem.

> All the people look towards him while he settles causes with true judgements: and he, speaking surely, would soon make wise end even of a great quarrel; for therefore are there princes wise in heart, because when the people are being misguided in their assembly, they set right the matter again with ease, persuading them with gentle words.[17]

When the bard sings of the glorious deeds of past heroes and the gods, his song entwines both a remembering and forgetting. The purpose of remembering is to enable the heart to forget its present heaviness by remembering great deeds done in the face of greater threats and losses. But besides relief from the oppressing pain and sorrow, the gift of the muses also enables good judgment worthy of noble princes; "for they bring forgetfulness of evil, rest from pain."[18] Is this the judgment of the times before the onset of war, when such wrong as the carrying off of women was not a thing to make much of?

Through their gift of song and by juggling between memory and forgetting, the muses offer the possibility of transcendence from harsh reality. Hesiod invokes the muses to lift his spirit and let him be the instrument of their gift of forgetting by singing their memories. Hesiod, however, quickly moves on to warn us of the coming of another very different type of forgetfulness:

> Then deadly Night gave birth to Nemesis...and strong-willed Strife. And hateful Strife gave birth to wretched Work, Forgetfulness, and Famine, tearful Pains.[19]

This is by far not a sweet forgetfulness, but the very daughter of Strife, granddaughter of Night and a sibling of Work, Famine and Pain. What sort of forgetfulness is this then that is so far removed from the sweet song of the muses that can help man to transcend the harshness of reality? This is Lethe[20] who dissimulates truth and sends peace of mind into oblivion. This forgetfulness has nothing to do with Memory or her daughters. Rather than offering a passage for transcendence, Lethe chains man to all that is harsh and painful in his mortal condition and banishes any chance of forgetfulness. Lethe is in fact a forgetfulness of forgetfulness. It insists on remembering the harshness of the human condition, and forbids the memory of any possible relief through forgetfulness. Being at war even with itself, Lethe drives the possibility of forgetfulness into oblivion, shutting off the possibility of transcendence from the human condition.

Furthermore, Lethe shuts off man's memory of the greater deeds of princes and heroes who could discern wisely between matters of true concern and matters of no account. It makes man forgetful of his better judgment by which he could put wrongs into a wider perspective and thus glimpse possible alternatives to rash or unprofitable courses of action. As a consequence, Lethe locks mortals in an unrelenting spiral of strife and suffering.

Hesiod and Herodotus inhabit different regions of an era in which our worldview shifted from the mythological to the philosophical. Hesiod seeks inspiration from the Muses, placing himself within the flow of a dance whose source is beyond his own self and his memory. His song is the song of the Muses for whom he is the instrument by which they bring about harmony and tranquility.

Herodotus, by contrast, proclaims his authority on the accounts of the events that constitute his history.

> This is the Showing forth of the Inquiry of Herodotus of Halicarnassos, to the end that neither the deeds of men may be forgotten by lapse of time, nor the works great and marvellous, which have been produced some by Hellenes and some by Barbarians, may lose their renown; and especially that the causes may be remembered for which these waged war with one another.[21]

Herodotus' opening declaration stamps his authority. He is the source of his writings, and his stated objective is the conquest of memory over forgetfulness. History starts by explicitly cutting itself free from the sources of myth. As it turns out, the history of Herodotus is not only an account of war, but it is itself, in essence, a declaration of war against the mythological worldview. This is a glorification of memory and a declaration of war on forgetfulness. But in the thinking that is being ushered through this shift in worldview, memory and forgetfulness have now taken their place as conceptual opposites. The memory that Herodotus glorifies bears no relation to the lighthearted Muses that dance with forgetfulness. This memory is a memory that must forget forgetfulness. It turns out, ironically, that the memory that Herodotus insists on, is a memory that insists on forgetting. It becomes evident, therefore, that by insisting on memory Herodotus is actually drawing on Lethe.

Herodotus' unknowing collusion with Lethe results in the closure of any alternative other than war. Drawing on Lethe, history is fixed on war. We are now left with no option but to remember the facts of history, and also to insist that these objective facts can have no possible alternative interpretation. Lethe also dictates that we must forget that there may be the possibility of finding someone who in Hesiod's words "would soon make wise end even of a great quarrel." This possibility would require someone who has the gift of the Muses, that is, the gift of joining the playful dance of the memory of forgetfulness. Someone with this gift could have helped to make the incipient historical event of Helen's abduction a matter of no account rather than the cause of a great war.

These contrasting opening stances, Hesiod's invocation to be inspired by Muses and Herodotus' declaration of authority and his stated objective of insisting on memory, are reflective of a shifting worldview. Hesiod and Herodotus occupy different locations within this turbulent shifting landscape. Moving away from a mythological understanding of reality, Western thinking seems to turn to History with the call of "lest we forget." We must not forget who started the war and why we are at war. Although it would be simplistic to blame the perpetual continuation of war on the insistence on memory, it is a fact that this insistence has not led us out of war.

## Perpetual Peace—a Satirical Inscription

> Whether this satirical inscription on a Dutch innkeeper's sign upon which a burial ground was painted had for its object mankind in general, or the rulers of states in particular, who are insatiable of war, or merely the philosophers who dream this sweet dream, it is not for us to decide.[22]

Kant immortalizes the wit of this unknown Dutch innkeeper's sign by using it as a cue for *Perpetual Peace: A Philosophical Sketch*. The very thought of the possibility of perpetual peace must be the subject either of lighthearted satire or the "sweet dreams" of philosophers. Kant writes his sketch on the express condition that the reader makes a clear distinction between the "empty ideas" contained in it and the "empirical principles" by which world-wise statesmen must run the affairs of the state.

Questioning the inevitability of war can only be dared on two conditions. First, one must state that these are only empty ideas, the games that philosophers play, mere sweet dreams. Secondly, one must ensure that such empty dreams "in no way threaten the security of the state." It turns out that questioning the inevitability of war is no mere innocent folly. It is, in fact, a serious transgression as it can easily pose a danger to the security of the state. Ultimately, we must not only not forget that war is inevitable, but we must also remember that questioning this inevitability and even dreaming of the possibility of peace actually poses a threat to the state.

By his cautious remarks in the introduction of *Perpetual Peace*, Kant wants to make it clear that he knows he is treading on dangerous ground. History teaches or is thought to teach us that war is a natural and a permanent state, and to question this is to threaten the natural order of things. Kant shows that he has learnt the lessons of history.

## The Inevitability of War—a Mythical Inflexion

It sounds very natural to say that one has learnt the lessons of history. History has, after all, acquired this "wholly mythical power," which allows it to teach lessons to us humans. How did history come to acquire this power?

In his visionary essay "Myth Today," Roland Barthes explains how myths draw their power from our semiological systems, and delves on their effect on our experience of reality.[23]

> The elaboration of a second order semiological system will enable myth to escape this dilemma: driven to having either to unveil or to liquidate the concept, it will naturalize it. We reach here the very principle of myth: it transforms history into nature.[24]

According to Barthes, myth is a second-order semiological system, which feeds parasitically on the first-order system which is primarily, but not exclusively, language. In the first-order system signifiers, (usually acoustic images), are linked with signifieds (mental concepts). This linking nourishes the enrichment of both the signifier and the signified. This mutual constitution of signified and signifier results in the sign which is "the associated total of the first two terms." [25]

> Take a bunch of roses: I use it to signify my passion. Do we have here, then, only a signifier and a signified, the roses and my passion? Not even that: to put it accurately, there are here only "passionified" roses. But on the plane of analysis, we do have three terms; for these roses weighted with passion perfectly and correctly allow themselves to be decomposed into roses and passion: the former and the latter existed before uniting and forming this third object, which is the sign.[26]

Following Ferdinand De Saussure, Barthes maintains that the link between the signifier, (the acoustic image: roses) and the signified (the mental concept: roses) is arbitrary. This link is not motivated by any connection between the natural attributes of the image and the concept. The linking of the two creates a sign which is embedded into, and at the same time enriches, the linguistic system of which it makes part. This linguistic system gives shape and structure to our experience of and engagement with reality. Our life-world is both constituted and accessed through our sign systems.

These sign systems are "language-objects," and as language-objects they are both true and also unreal. Simply put, the link between the acoustic image (rose) and the mental concept (rose) is true by virtue, and within the parameters, of the conventions of the sign system to which it belongs. This truth is attributed by the sign system not by some objective reality outside the system.

Barthes argues that a second-order system or metalanguage feeds on the signs produced by the first-order system and replicates its structure, to produce what he terms Myth. When myth takes hold of the meaningful signs of the first-order language, it empties them of their meaning but retains their form which it then uses as the bare framework on which it builds its own signification.

A meaningful sign within the first-order language, "Perpetual Peace," for example, is appropriated by myth that feeds on its first-order meaning. Myth impoverishes the first-order meaning of this sign to make space for the second-order signification which it will give it. Through myth, the sign "perpetual peace" is linked with the mental imagery or concepts of a graveyard and an inn's name. The atrophied sign is now enriched by the new attribution to the second-order signified (graveyard, death, joke, wit), resulting in the constitution of the myth with its new signification. This new signification is that perpetual peace is an impossibility in the land of the living; that the thought of it is mere folly, the stuff of laughter. Through the work of myth, "perpetual peace" now belongs to an afterlife. It is what only the dead can have. For the living to long for perpetual peace now amounts to longing for death and giving up on life.

## From Historical Contingency to Natural Causality

> Where there is only an equivalence, he sees a kind of causal process: the signifier and the signified have, in his eyes, a natural relationship...any semiological system is a system of values; now the myth consumer takes the signification for a system of facts.[27]

Following Herodotus' cue, the chronicles of Western history are full of evidence that war is a constant reality. This is an inductive truth. There has always been war; our history has been recording conflicts since the beginning of writing. But even if there are enough histories of war to occupy every corner in all present and future archives, there is still not one iota of evidence to suggest that the inevitability of war is an objective fact imposed by the logical structure of reality. The inevitability of war is evidently true historically, but it is still unreal. Its reality is a product of the work of myth.[28] Myth feeds on the "equivalence" between history and war and produces "a causal process...a natural relationship...a system of facts."

> Myth has a double function: it points out and it notifies, it makes understood something and it imposes it on is.[29]

By imposing these true facts upon us, Myth actually imposes a system of values. This is achieved by turning an archive of memories into what in our eyes we start experiencing as natural inescapable causal relations. Myth inflects reality, changing history to nature. As a result, "language objects, photos, shapes, rituals, objects" are attributed a natural causal link with a given mythological signifier. Images of alterity, acts or rituals and objects of an alien nature, cultural transgressions, political maneuvers from across the line of enmity, are attributed a natural inescapable causal link with the signified mental concept: war, self-defense, retaliation, military intervention.

These perceived causal relations will also define and dictate our response. In so doing, myth mediates and possibly compromises our "response-ability." Through myth, a signifier, for example, a picture of an industrial plant in the Iranian desert, or a group of women wearing burkhas in the high street, is associated with a signified mental concept such as "religious fundamentalism," "pariah states," "defensive retaliation." The resulting signification is the myth of the necessity and inevitability of war, and hence its justification.

## Conclusion: Beyond the Myth of War; a Memory of Peace

The commemoration of Don Lorenzo Milani turns out to be the commemoration of a reader of myths, whose work reveals their function. Milani's insistence on the right of conscientious objection reminds us of the distortion of the myth of war. More essentially he reminds us that the imposition of this myth calls for continual vigilant resistance to the reality it imposes. Can such minor and rare acts of resistance have any real bearing on the immensity of the tradition which they attempt to resist?

> We often belittle, call childish this need to be wonderstruck...but we set right off again in search of the wonderful. That which we hold worthy of our love is always that which overwhelms us: it is the unhoped-for, the thing that is beyond hoping for. It is though, paradoxically, our essential self clung to a nostalgia of attaining what our reasoning self had judged unattainable, impossible.[30]

We have seen that at the seminal axial age of the tradition, an "arkhe-ic" abduction took place whereby the archive of our tradition is carried away from the domicile of myth[31] to that of history, from the realms of the playful Muses to the insistence of the records of memory. Through his questioning resistance to this abduction, Milani calls for the repatriation of this archive. His response to the call of war transcends the causal instinctual reaction imposed on us by history. Milani's response opens the door for the long forgotten possibility of peace.

By remembering this possibility of peace, Milani bears witness to an impossible future that might yet be.

## Notes

1. Ricoeur (2004), p. xv.
2. Ibid.
3. Derrida (1994).
4. Armstrong (2006), p. xi.
5. Levinas (1969), p.11.
6. Armstrong (2006), p. xii.
7. Gordon (2008), p.1. In his reply to Einstein's question "Why War?" Freud states that although in theory human society may evolve away from violence and toward more rational means to settle disputes, in reality war will remain as it is the result of one of the two main human drives of destruction, (the other drive being Eros). Freud regards both these drives as essential and necessary for life, however, he also suggests that "anything that encourages the growth of emotional ties between humans" will serve to curb the destructive instinct from manifesting itself as war.

8. Derrida (1996), p.1.
9. Ibid., p.2.
10. Myths are narratives that normally contain a particular worldview, that is, a distinctive mode of experiencing and relating with reality. Later in the chapter, the term "myth" is used with a different meaning, in relation to the philosophy of Ronald Barthes. The shift to this second use will be duly noted.
11. Herodotus (1988), l. 4.
12. Ibid.
13. Vernant (1988), p.46.
14. Cronos is a Titan that represents time. Mount Helicon is a mountain located off the gulf of Corinth. It contained two springs that were considered as sacred to the Muses.
15. Hesiod (1988), ll. pp.1–25.
16. Ibid.
17. Ibid
18. Ibid.
19. Ibid.
20. In Hesiod Lethe is the personification of oblivion and forgetfulness.
21. Herodotus (1988).
22. Kant, I. (1994).
23. Barthes uses the term "myth" to refer to the second-order semiological structure, which he analyses in "Myth Today." Barthes suggests that "myth" conditions our experience of reality. The term "myth" as used by Barthes, is to be distinguished from "mythology," which is what the term "myth" referred to in this chapter prior to this point. As stated, the latter normally refers to the worldview, (a mode of experiencing and relating with reality), which was reflected in mythological narratives such as those of Homer and Hesiod.
24. Barthes (2000), p.129.
25. Ibid, p.113.
26. Ibid.
27. Ibid., p.131.
28. In Barthes' sense of "myth."
29. Barthes (2000), p.117.
30. Bataille (1995), p.15.
31. In the first sense used in the chapter, that is, a narrative that contains a distinctive way of experiencing and relating with reality.

# References

Armstrong, K. (2006). *The Great Transformation: The World in the Times of Buddha, Socrates and Jeremiah*. London: Atlantic Books.
Barthes, R. (2000). *Mythologies*. Trans. Annette Lavers. London: Vintage.
Bataille, G. (1995). *Lascaux or the Birth of Art*. Trans. Austryn Wainhouse. Lausanne, Switzerland: Skira.
Derrida, J. (1996). *Archive Fever, A Freudian Impression*. Trans. Eric Prenowitz. Chicago: University of Chicago Press.
Derrida, J. (1994). *Spectres of Marx*. Trans. Peggy Kamuf. New York: Routledge.
Gordon, J. (2008). Available at: www.philosophynow.org/issue66/Is_War_Inevitable. Sept/Oct 2011. Accessed on November 11, 2011.
Hesiod (1988). *The Theogony*. Trans. A. T. Murray. Vol. 1 The Loeb Classical Library. Ed. G. P. Goold. Harvard: Harvard University Press.

Herodotus (1988). *The History Of Herodotus*. Trans. George Rawlinson. Vol. 6 The Loeb Classical Library. Ed. G. P. Goold. Harvard: Harvard University Press.

Kant, I. (1994). *Perpetual Peace and Other Essays*. Trans. T. Humphrey. Cambridge: Hackett Press.

Levinas, E. (1969). *Totality and Infinity*. Trans. Alfonso Lingis. Pittsburgh: Duquesne University Press.

Ricoeur, P. (2004). Preface. *Memory, History, Forgetting*. Trans. Kathleen Blamey and David Pellauer. Chicago: The University of Chicago Press.

Vernant, J. P. and Vidal-Naquet P. (1988). *Myth and Tragedy in Ancient Greece*. Trans. Janet Lloyd. New York: Zone Books.

# 7

## Peace Education in a Culture of War

*Antonia Darder*

Throughout my lifetime, the US government has been in a permanent state of war. Over a hundred overt military campaigns of varying degrees have been undertaken in the name of peace; and who knows how many covert operations have been launched. As a Puerto Rican child, my very identity from the beginning has been intimately intertwined with a legacy of war. My citizenship is the direct result of the Spanish-American War, which converted my country into a colony of the United States. The year I was born, 1952, the United States was embroiled in both the Cold War and the Korean War. As a preteen, reports about the Cuban Missile Crisis and the action at the Bay of Pigs were interspersed with fears of nuclear war on the evening news. During my teen years, civil rights conflicts erupted on the domestic arena, as I watched Black Panthers being shot in their home, on television screen. Growing up in Los Angeles, I also found myself smack in the midst of the Watts Riots, and later, as a witness to violent police attacks on Chicana and Chicano activists who had congregated at Laguna Park, after a peaceful march along Whittier Boulevard. As a young mother, radio reports of the Vietnam War comingled with the lullabies I sang my babies.

Beyond these war campaigns, US military actions over the last 60 years have also included participation in the First Indochina War; the Lebanon Crisis; the Cambodian Civil War; the Invasion of the Dominican Republic; the Invasion of Grenada; the Lebanese Civil War; the Action in the Gulf of Sidra; the Contras (Counterinsurgency) attack of Nicaragua; the Bombing of Libya; the Iran-Iraq War; the Invasion of Panama; the Gulf War; the Somali Civil War; the Bosnian War; Operation Uphold Democracy in Haiti; the Bombing of Afghanistan and Sudan; the Kosovo War; the War on Terror; the War in Afghanistan; Operation Enduring Freedom in the Philippines, Horn of Africa, and Trans Sahara; The Iraq War; War in North-West Pakistan; Yemeni al-Qaeda Operations; the second Liberian War; the Haitian Rebellion; the Libyan Civil War; the Lord's Resistance

Army Insurgency in Uganda and the Southern Sudan; and, just days ago, an attack in Mohmand Province near the border of Pakistan and Afghanistan. In each instance, the toll to working and poor populations of these regions has been staggering, while the elite filled their coffers, as US forces bombed their people—bringing to mind Sartre's words: "When the rich wage war, it's the poor who die."[1]

## The Hidden Curriculum of Violence

Most of these military offensives remain obscured or unknown to the majority of US citizens—although not to the working-class men and women in the US military who soldiered these offensives and the families who lost their children on foreign soil. Yet, despite this history of permanent war, students attending public schools are socialized to be deeply ignorant and detached from the realities of war, through a discourse that rationalizes military aggression in the name of victory, freedom, and security at home. Veiled and fragmented perspectives of war (and thus, of peace) are carried out through both a hidden curriculum within schools that claims to be apolitical, neutral, and objective and a public pedagogy of the media that glorifies violence and conquest as virtuous human production. Negated, of course, is the obvious wholesale human destruction carried out solely in the interest of capital.

In the process of public schooling, students—particularly working-class students who are both objectified and instrumentalized as reserved armies of the elite—are exposed to a hidden curriculum that effectively alienates them from the suffering of others. As agents of the war industry, schools also function effectively to block critical engagement with the dehumanizing brutality of aggression and the grand profits it affords the ruling class. Similarly, the media function as pedagogical venues that conveniently normalize and reinforce the necessity of war. Hence, the violence becomes twofold, in that the judgment of working-class students is swayed against their own best interest. Instead, they are initiated into a culture of permanent war, which surreptitiously obscures and underhandedly perpetuates conservative patriotic discourses and patriarchal exultations of hypermasculinity and military aggression—in both men and women—as simultaneously equivalent to invincible power, sexual prowess, and homeland security.

Or, at least, this is the case until the brutal casualties of young US soldiers begin to cross the class and color divide of affluence, suddenly disrupting the Disneyland veneer of "middle-class" existence. Such was the case during the Vietnam War, when televised body bags rolling down a conveyor belt held not only the children of the urban ghettos and barrios, but also the bodies of "red-blooded American boys" of the suburbs. This was a historical moment in which people, across class and color lines, finally began to take to the streets in an effort to end the war in Southeast Asia. We saw aspects of this phenomenon also at work in the Occupy movements, as formerly "middle class" or well-established people who lost their jobs and homes in the last decade, took to the streets to shout in unison, "We are the 99 percent!"

## Peace: A Critical Moral Imperative

On the other side of the equation is often found a liberal formulation of peace education, detached from conditions of human suffering and gross inequalities that are experienced by the majority of the world's population. As such, a critical discourse of peace seldom finds its way into the mainstream public school classroom, despite the presence of a Peace Movement in the US that has persisted for over 30 years. This is the case, because central to a critical politics of peace is a radical moral imperative—the transformation of contemporary structures of inequality and social exclusions that rationalize war, through a contradictory rhetoric that embraces militarism essential to peace.

Accordingly, what often blocks critical peace education efforts is precisely its uncompromising commitment to the establishment of social, economic, and political relationships that support a deeply communal ethics of justice, liberty, and human dignity—all essential to a *dialectical* exercise of peace in our personal and public lives, as both educators and cultural citizens of the world. This constitutes radical peace initiatives that extend our political reasoning beyond simplistic idealism or dematerialized intellectual refrains, in order to unearth those critical questions of morality buried by the "free market" logic of neoliberalism. In contrast, the focus of a critical peace education must be placed on contending with the tough moral questions, through which we can move closer towards humanizing strategies and political solutions that confront the exploitation and domination that underlie the structural roots of violence.

Toward this end, critical approaches to peace education must unfailingly retain a dialectic connection in their interrogations of peace and violence. This is particularly important in that mainstream peace studies, although well-meaning and correct in many instances, often fail to acknowledge in substantive ways the historical, cultural, political, and economic asymmetries that persist and give rise to violent outbreaks and military aggression in this country and around the globe. Not all actions of violence, therefore, can be homogenized and distilled to make simple the cause of peace, particularly where meanings protect the power and privilege of the status quo.

This dynamic, Freire (2006) contends, is well evidenced where "[t]he dominant elites consider the remedy [for dissent] to be more domination and repression, carried out in the name of freedom, order, and social peace (that is, the peace of the elites). Thus, they can condemn—logically, from their point of view—the violence of a strike by workers and can call upon the state in the same breath to use violence in putting down the strike" (p.78). This conservative view of peace is informed by a positivist ideology that is steeped in an instrumentally technocratic rationality that glorifies forms of logic and political approaches that obscures power and privilege through deceitful intonations of objectivity and neutrality. Most recently, we witnessed this positivist logic of peace at work in state efforts to dismantle the Occupy movement's encampments within cities and on university campuses. The use of pepper spray against students at the University of California Davis and the incarceration of hundreds of occupiers in New York and California, alone, were justified by political rhetoric that claimed these actions were necessary to security on the streets and peace on the campus; messages carefully spun in unison by police, university, and government officials, alike.

Hence, without thoughtful and grounded engagement with those moral questions that surround the social and material conditions at work in the lives of oppressed communities, traditional Western notions of peace falsely obfuscate gross inequalities, by prescribing to a definition of peace that is apolitical, absolute, universal, and devoid of concern for the existing structures, policies and practices within education, labor, housing, and beyond that inform the manifestations of violence. Without interrogating discussions of peace and war through a critical lens, the essential truth—that oppressed populations are often thrust into dynamics of war and violence, not of their own making, but rather by the oppressive structures and practices that dehumanize and strip them of their dignity as individuals and as a people—remains hidden.

## Making a Peacefully Just World Possible

In order to support the development of critical peace education, educators must be willing to speak of the silenced histories of violence and oppression that have remained shrouded by the powerful agents of the capitalist state. Unveiling the world requires us to acknowledge the crimes against humanity—genocide, slavery, colonization, incarceration and impoverishment—so that we might labor toward reparations and a genuine politics and practice of peace can be forged. This entails a critical pedagogy of peace that acknowledges openly that all power relationships among human beings are forged within terrains of struggle and thus, requires a fundamental political commitment to a revolutionary love, anchored in an ethics of self-vigilance, a commitment to global human rights, the exercise of dignity and respect, and an embodied solidarity across our differences. More specifically, as suggested above, a fundamental intent of critical peace education constitutes the integration of curricular content, classroom structures, and pedagogical approaches that challenge the individual, collective, and structural forms of violence at the heart of unbridled militarism, racism, class warfare, gender and sexual oppression, and the exercise of aggression as the ultimate solution to domestic and international disputes.

Hence, an education for peace in the face of permanent conditions of war must raise complex questions and controversial notions about war and peace that are generally marginalized within the field of education. As such, educators and activists must grapple with the permanent realities of war in the United States and the ideological and structural policies and practices that inform this condition. But it is not enough to stop there. Instead, critical educators must create ample opportunities, in both classrooms and out in the streets, to critically rethink the meaning of peace education within US schools and across global contexts, anchored in both critical philosophical principles *and* important empirical research that offers groundbreaking insights into long-standing concerns in the field.

Moving across different educational contexts, what is clearly evident is the manner in which students are systematically socialized from very early in their academic formation to attach ideologically specific meanings to narratives of peace and war, given the power relations, cultural differences, and class distinctions that shape their particular social location within their own communities and the larger national sphere. As such, educators and activists must make key connections between the dominant ideology of public schooling and a culture of militarism that privileges the sensibilities and material interests of the hegemonic culture and class. The conflation of military interests and the educational formation of working-class youth, as a common phenomenon around the world is a good case in point.

In their recent work, Paul Carr and Brad Porfilio[2] raise significant concerns about the manner in which policies and practices are designed within public schools—particularly within working-class and racialized communities—to increasingly allow high school campuses to be utilized as convenient venues for military recruitment. This is readily visible in the increasing establishment of Junior Reserve Officers' Training Corps (JROTC) programs in public schools, where the military curriculum readily cultivates allegiances to an imperialist vision, while it thwarts critical interrogations of pro-military views and their negative impact on both individuals and the larger society. To challenge such practices and policies, critical peace educators must employ counter-recruitment strategies within their communities to challenge conservative ideologies and epistemologies of war and violence, in order to halt the long-standing US military occupation of public school campuses, as armed services recruitment sites targeting young working-class men and women who often feel they have few options for improving the material conditions of their lives.

Similarly, important connections and critiques must be launched regarding the intellectual work of scholars within the corporatized university, that can also function as an extension of the military industrial complex. Such interrogations must carefully consider the ways in which neoliberal university policies actively sustain the culture of violence and, thus, a permanent economy of war, through political and economic mechanisms that fuel the internationalization of capital and its discontents. Moreover, engaging historical university struggles, such as those that took place during the Vietnam War, can help peace educators and activists reveal essential lessons about the use of collective responsibility as a means for working toward peace-centered initiative within higher education.

Hence, in our labor as critical educators we must work to uncover the unexpected ways in which discourses of peace and war are inextricably linked to ideologies of power and, thus, engage with greater complexity what it means to work for peace, within domestic and global regions where suffering and poverty persist and values of dignity, liberty, and critical democratic life remain obscured. Given the difficulties under which we must labor to realize a critical peace education in public schools, we must move beyond prescription, into the complex and murky waters of domination that disrupt peace and, from whence, violence is born.

But more importantly, we must critically consider a range of innovative policy, curricular, pedagogical, and sociological interpretations aimed at generating a robust critical dialogue about peace education locally, nationally, and internationally. This calls for a radical politics of peace education that can effectively dismantle the existing paradigm of war—where violence is considered the predominate solution for resolving conflict—and, in its place, embrace a critical paradigm of peace, where issues of human rights, social justice, and ecological concerns guide domestic and international solutions. Inherent in such a transformative paradigm of peace is also an important political and pedagogical message; one that calls forth civic courage, uncompromising commitment, and revolutionary action, so that we, as educators and cultural workers, may work both philosophically *and* practically on the ground to dismantle the existing culture of war and usher in a genuine culture of peace—a culture where policies and practices aligned with social justice, human rights, and economic democracy can flourish in our schools, our communities, and the world. Underlying this call is the recognition that through the power of collective political commitment, critical consciousness, and the *power of love*, we, together, can make a peacefully just world possible.

## Notes

1. Sartre. J. P. (1951). *Le Diable es le Bon Dieu* (Fammarion et Cie).
2. See Carr, P. and Porfilio, B. (2012). *Educating for Peace in a Time of "Permanent War"* New York: Routledge.

# 8

## On Education, Negotiation, and Peace

*Marianna Papastephanou*

## Introduction

Peace education is often associated with cosmopolitan education because global peace is typically considered the most important component of the cosmopolitan ideal. Presuppositions of peace such as conflict resolution are then viewed from what can be termed "an agreement perspective on cosmopolitanism" By this I mean that many political theorists, peace educators or organizers of conflict resolution initiatives imagine the solution of local or world problems as consensus-reaching decisions through negotiation processes that focus on a pragmatic give-and-take with little or no attention to issues of justice[1] and fair settlement of ethical debts. Within such a framework it is assumed that the ultimate cosmopolitan objective of dialogue is cognitive: to get to know others, to learn about them and, just by knowing them, all pending issues will be solved. The main tendency is to confine cosmopolitanism to the everyday and factual contact with what is not familiar; and to emphasize its pragmatic stakes, that is, interaction, movement, habit, and *modus vivendi* and *coexistendi*. Thus, for many contemporary thinkers, cosmopolitan is the subject who allows the pragmatic dimension of her existence to be shaped not only by what is available in her culture but also by elements of other cultures and lifestyles of other people. This simple, "collection-like" and "touristic" contact with otherness presupposes capital, technology and a planetarism[2] in the double sense of nomadic wandering and globality.

Against such a planetary understanding of cosmopolitanism, we may emphasize, with Sharon Todd, that "a cosmopolitan ethic invites both an appreciation of the rich diversity of values, traditions and ways of life *and* a commitment to broad, universal principles of human rights that can secure the flourishing of that diversity" (2007, p.25). Hence, for some theorists, the cosmopolitan self should educationally be shaped to respect difference, human rights, and international legality, to engage in debates over global material aid and to promote global peace and reconciliation. The latter reaffirms the connection between peace education and cosmopolitan education but in a more complex fashion. This is how the argument goes: to be willing to move globally, especially when this willingness reflects self-serving purposes, is not on its own a cosmopolitan attitude. And, to be willing to construct and enrich one's life plans or forms of being and sensing through diverse cultural influences does not make one automatically a cosmopolitan person. For, cosmopolitanism involves also a commitment to political ideals such as peace, justice, and cooperation under conditions of respect for peoples' diverse accounts of what counts as meaningful and worthwhile.

However, even when cosmopolitanism is preserved as an ethico-political ideal of global action coordination on grounds of human rights, the appropriate distance from an ethically inflated planetarism[3] is not guaranteed. The current association of cosmopolitanism with peace-loving and fluid identities is arbitrary, insofar as those terms are placed within a pragmatic monological idiom that fails to recognize a deeper significance of politics, a significance that raises demands upon the self that truly go beyond the call to enrich one's existential choice and, simply, to respect others.

Thus, this chapter criticizes the monologism of the isolated self; a self that is disengaged from others; since what connects all of them (the self and the others) is a solitary desire for a rich variety of goods. Pragmatic monological planetarism places the actor in a subject-object relation to the material that belongs to other cultures, and then jumps into unwarranted ethical conclusions about the intersubjective relation itself. Though, at first glance, the vision of peace and international legality seems to escape monologism by binding people in a relation of mutually restricted freedom, solipsism operates even when the pragmatic conception acknowledges the significance of legal cosmopolitanism. This happens because, within pragmatic cosmopolitanism, legality is interpreted in a self-centered way that suppresses the political relational character of peace and downplays legality's interplay with ethics. In such a context, law acquires only a protective quality that serves primarily the self. And ethics is reduced to a narrow sense of morality, one that secures for the "cosmopolitan" an uplifting moralist self-image. Within the agreement perspective, the peace-loving person becomes the one who does not intentionally harm others, who respects and tolerates their idiosyncrasies, and who, at times, performs acts of charity.

To illustrate my argument about the inadequacy of the pragmatic agreement perspective, I contrast the idealized figure of the global peacemaker, the negotiator, with the embodied cosmopolitanism of public intellectuals and educators such as Lorenzo Milani and Camilo Torres. This contrast shows that the demands that the figure of the peacemaker with truly cosmopolitan virtues raises upon selfhood are higher than those usually assumed within the agreement perspective.

## Peace Education and the Cosmopolitan Self

The conception of peace that I associate with the "agreement perspective" has several shortcomings that have already been discussed in the relevant literature. Indicatively, it has become clear that the usual focus on the cognitive aspects of peace education tends to "overlook the interactional, affective, and material aspects of justice and peace building" (Zembylas, 2008, p.114). Further, some theoretical and pedagogic accounts of peace education have been charged with a methodological localism that fails "to treat peace and war as political categories" (Sigal Ben-Porath, 2006, p.58). It declares cosmopolitan the individual who acknowledges an obligation (first and foremost to oneself) to be open to various lifestyles scattered around the world, to adopt, select, or experiment with some of them, or at least, to tolerate their unobstructed existence. Based on the latter and determined simply to reduce interpersonal violence, this educational methodology produces apolitical curricula that "work in light of a conception of 'peace' that is merely personal or, at best, civic. 'Conflict' in this description refers to peer relations rather than to international relations" and it has little to do with fostering "peace in its political sense" (ibid, p.62).

Various initiatives display a naive reduction of political tensions to failures in interpersonal communication while taking the guise of unquestioningly well-meant and progressive efforts to peace and democracy. Yet, the protagonists of such peace education efforts fail to see "that *'peace' in a less than perfect world is a terrible human condition*, to be morally and practically challenged—and that overcoming such an immoral human condition might justify even violent resistance to 'peace'" (Gur-Ze'ev, 2011, p.4). Some peace education, conflict resolution, and educational synchronization initiatives are often misguided enough[4] to be part of the problem that the local communities face (instead of being conducive to its solution). Ironically, instead of promoting peace, they frequently serve an agenda of "militarized globalization" (Saltman, 2007, p. 11). Such an agenda includes the "so-called war on terror, the U.S. military presence in more than 140 countries, and the encirclement of the world's oil resources with the world's most powerful military." Saltman sees this as going hand in hand with "a continued culture of militarism that educates citizens to identify with militarized solutions to problems." In other words, peace discourse masks a deep-down aggressive resolve to enforce "solutions" that are as facile and callous as they are extreme and polemical. In a more applied educational sense, this militarism takes the form of "education as enforcement" (ibid).[5]

To sum up, when promoted in accordance with a broader, wrongheaded cosmopolitanism, peace education fails carefully to examine the real, political causes of a conflict and to raise higher demands upon subjectivities. In the end, such peace education becomes only too effective in cultivating pacification rather than peace. It may even join forces with global tendencies to appease public anger and peoples' discontent for the sake of global risk management and easier economic border-crossing. Within its confines, the cosmopolitan self is typically personalized in the figure of the peace-loving partner in dialogue, the peacemaker and the negotiator (for instance, the third party, the international referee or the goodwilled, impartial judge of a conflict). The encounter of the We and Others is likewise theorized as a cognitive or purely communicative, synchronic challenge. The irenic, that is, what tends to promote peace or reconciliation, is then exclusively conceptualized as disentangled and uncomplicated coexistence. Ultimately, the dominant "agreement perspective" on cosmopolitanism assumes a rather uniform meaning of peace, much against the multifaceted nature of what might count as peace. In turn, education addresses the task of cultivating the peaceful personality in equally superficial and reductive terms.

## The Negotiator, the Peacemaker, and the Educated

Even those approaches, which present cosmopolitanism as an ideal of equality, democracy, and care sometimes exhaust relationality[6] in respecting diversity and in endorsing liberal discourses of rights. They thus bypass some deeper cosmopolitan challenges that the relation of the I and the Other presents for selfhood. Consider, for instance, David Held's view that

> those born after the Second World War are more likely to see themselves as cosmopolitans, to support the UN system and lend their support to the free trade system and the free movement of migrants.[7]

Apart from being an interesting question for empirical research rather than a self-evident assertion, this view invites criticisms as to what counts as cosmopolitan and whether we should accept the self-description/self-image of post–Second World War subjects uncritically as truly cosmopolitan.[8] Is the support to the United Nations[9] and/or the support to free trade system and to free movement all it takes for one to be cosmopolitan? Even if those commitments are a necessary condition, are they also a sufficient one for developing cosmopolitan subjectivities? Is cosmopolitanism a solipsistic matter of what ideas the thinking subject entertains? We may object that such monological legalism and flat liberalism can deliver at most globalized rather than cosmopolitan selves.

The following explains further the above objection and shows why the negligence of ethico-political cosmopolitanism and the suppression of the relational quality of the legal dimension render legalist cosmopolitanism problematic or, at least, incomplete. In one of his texts Bruce Ackerman (1994) deploys a legal approach to rooted cosmopolitanism against the standard conception of cosmopolitanism as universalist convergence on certain values. As he writes:

> I remain an unrepentant cosmopolitan. But there are risks lurking in this existential stance—a clear and present danger of pretentiousness, precocity,

and solipsism, as I find that others refuse to engage on the terms that ego finds so reasonable.[10]

The question he poses is how different and independent egos would consent on maxims of action without each one of them absolutizing solipsistically one's own standpoint or fearing that the other will do so.

My response to this question challenges first and foremost the centrality of the question itself. The difficulty with Ackerman's "agreement perspective" (a perspective that makes the above question—and concern—so central) is that we wait to figure out whether the others would agree with us in order to reaffirm our cosmopolitanism and act accordingly. In both modern legalist (interpreting international right in a flat way) as well as post-structuralist conceptions of negotiation of meanings, be they universalist or relativist, what remains unshakable is the priority of cosmopolitanism as agreement[11] over cosmopolitanism as focus on treatment, practical reorientation, and amends for past crimes. The problem of others (supposedly cumbersome eccentrics or unmanageable fanatics) failing to agree with what the "cosmopolitan" ego finds so reasonable will keep haunting all "cosmopolitan" efforts so long as those are exclusively preoccupied with the tensions of dialogue among different people. This preoccupation occurs at the expense of attention: to material conditions of life that shape much difference in the first place; and to the role that our attitude[12] plays in the formation of such difference. Similar problems will persist if we carry on assuming that by changing our attitude toward others, those others will take advantage of us and that, to avoid this possible exploitation of our benevolence, we should first make them negotiate with us and share our values.

Our diachronic and synchronic entanglement with others and with the whole world and the indispensability of the role of the other for examining our life constitute a kind of cosmopolitan spectrality (Derrida, 1994) that puts cosmopolitan ideality to the test. If we acknowledge the importance of facing such spectrality, we realize that we need first to question whether we are indeed cosmopolitan instead of declaring our cosmopolitanism an objective, indisputable fact. Prior to worrying whether others would converge in possibly common values, we should ask more carefully what it means to be truly cosmopolitan. If we always assume that negotiation on world affairs is irrelevant or even prior to changes in our ways of treating others (or treating the environment) then we will never escape the above dilemmas. For one thing, dialogue is facilitated where there is trust and care—not in lip service but in reality, through provable and visible commitments to justice. Against imperial conceptions of peace that sacrifice the individual on the altar of pacifying and protective social concord and global reconciliation, we should remember that "the offended individual" (in our context, the one suffering the consequences of conflict or war, the poor and underprivileged, the one lacking appropriate educational attention, etc.): "must always be appeased, approached, and consoled individually."[13]

In a Levinassian formulation that radicalizes human rights discourse:

> God is perhaps nothing but this permanent refusal of a history which would come to terms with our private tears. Peace does not dwell in a world without consolations.[14]

After all, one cannot trust another whose cosmopolitan declarations serve more her need to uphold a positive self-image rather than concrete, practical measures of changes in treating *cosmos*.

The inadequacies of the agreement perspective are also reflected in the educational aspirations to cultivate the cosmopolitan citizen. Such conceptions of the cosmopolitan chime with the outlook on conflicts that much peace education maintains. The broader political claim that cosmopolitanism is served when independent parties judge conflicting claims[15] becomes more concrete within educational contexts where the peace educator reserves for herself the image of the impartial third party, the "cosmopolitan" who is in a better position to judge than those involved in, or affected by, the conflict. And she is, supposedly, capable of all this just by being the third party, without having to delve deeply into the specifics of the conflict or to harken to those who may have experienced the whole issue in a less detached and more informed way. What most discourse of this kind assumes is that, just as *super partes* political authorities should consist of "cosmopolitans," and by the latter they mean those people who are committed to international order, peace, and reconciliation (ibid.), likewise, peace educators should be impartial dialogue facilitators whose northwestern perception of things does not intervene, supposedly, in any crucial fashion and thus invites no requirements of change or redirection whatever. So long as they declare their commitment to peace and order, they can bestow on themselves the enabling title of the "cosmopolitan" and acquire the role of the arbiter of just solutions. Apart from resting on a vague sense of commitment,[16] this assumption links the northwestern glorification of the supposed objectivity and impartiality of its bourgeois cohorts with cosmopolitanism *tout court*. Evidently, all this focuses on how to reach agreement or make the involved sides agree rather than on how to search for the most viable and just settlement that would build trust on fair treatment and a common vision of a better life. Those educated along such lines seem free to "negotiate" their future but are, in truth, conditioned to want the specific future that northwestern dialogue "facilitators" deem realistic, appropriate, and risk-free.

Many "cosmopolitan" peace negotiators entertain a conception of justice as "a matter of harmonizing the interplay of conflicting interests."[17] Against this conception, we may follow Badiou's objection that:

> justice, which is the theoretical name for an axiom of equality, necessarily refers to a wholly disinterested subjectivity.[18]

Despite claims to impartiality, the peace negotiators' conception of justice downplays the requirement of disinterestedness because it measures everything in terms of gains and losses in the typical northwestern fashion and tailors conflict resolution accordingly. It considers global conflict (sadly often reduced to cultural conflict at the explanatory level) only an object of negotiation. Negotiation, etymologically coming from the Latin *nec* and *otium*, no free time, is precisely the negation of leisure that urgent action demands, the cancellation of the pause for thought that is usually necessary when one considers issues of justice and of doling out justice. For the busybody international negotiator who views reconciliation as "give-and-take," any pause for thought, any detailed study of the particularities of a conflict that touch upon justice (rather than upon technicalities) is just a waste of time. It is a waste of the time that is precious: for pressuring those who can tolerate pressure (usually the weaker party of a conflict which, more often than not, though surely not always, happens to have a lesser share of culpability than the stronger party); and for achieving agreement, an agreement that will bring us closer to global peace (and the negotiator to a peace Nobel prize), to a conflict-free world in which all will indulge safely and merrily in "cosmopolitan" illusions of grandeur. Calgacus's complaint about the Romans creating wilderness and calling it peace (as stated in the well-known narrative by Tacitus) has had a lasting pertinence. But cosmopolitanism as a relational regulative ideal is not a problem of self-serving agreement with the other but, rather, a problem of how the other has been treated and how this should change.

Hence, cosmopolitanism requires the lived time and the thinking about time that question invested time. It requires the pause for thought that may urge the thought of the cosmopolitically educated to a new orientation beyond negotiation and narrowly defined interest:

> Cosmopolitanism as a set of ideas that seek more peaceful forms of living together on a global scale is in need of a theoretical framework that faces directly the difficulties of living in a dissonant world.[19]

Taking into account the specificities of living in a dissonant world protects the ideality of the sought peaceful forms of living together on a global scale from relying on a facile notion of peace that ignores conflict and dissent in a multidimensional reality. Besides, more peaceful forms of living can be the ideal of that Old Order that is largely known as *Pax Romana* or even of a New Order that resembles it. For any ideal of peace not to slide into pacification, a more critical outlook on global realities, a more deeply cosmopolitan education, and a new specification of what counts as true peace are needed.

## The Cases of Milani and Torres

This has a special bearing on peace education. For, at its best, peace education relies on a conceptual distinction that introduces nuance and treats more reflectively what counts as peace. The distinction in question is between negative peace and positive peace (as formulated by J. Galtung[20]). The former refers to the absence of war, conflict, and violence. The latter refers to "the existence of economic, cultural, and political practices that contribute to the well-being of the citizens on all sides."[21]

Important as this may be, it still leaves much space for exploring the meaning of well-being, which is crucial for judging whether the cultivated peace is of the *Pax Romana* kind or of a more demanding kind. In other words, an account of the good life is an inescapable theoretical challenge that peace education confronts in its cosmopolitan aspirations.

For instance, the education that was combated by Milani[22] and by Torres[23] claimed that it did promote the well-being of all sides (successful students and drop outs/poor). It defined those sides as: those capable of learning and ascending the social ladder; and those others who were incapable of doing so due to inherent inabilities and to whose best interests was to drop out from school and take the social place that is most appropriate to their, supposedly, limited capacities. Against such an education and against its implicit conception of well-being, Milani argued that:

> poverty had created academic disadvantages impossible for those children to overcome. Such students should not be failed, but given compassionate understanding and additional school time.[24]

He went even further, claiming that:

> the socioeconomic order, of which the educational system functioned as an integral part, had to be completely changed in favor of the justice and equality now completely missing from the world.[25]

Hence, he developed an educational project of radical pedagogy that provided full time schooling to students who had dropped out from public schooling.[26]

Just as for Milani, for Torres too, aspirations to a *modus vivendi* of undisturbed coexistence of the strong and the weak were unacceptable. Education should be preparation for a better world, not initiation into the current world of expedient seizing of opportunities and of profitable negotiation of gains and losses on grounds of power and control: "Like Don Milani, Torres became an inveterate organizer of schooling projects for poor people"[27] and expected from each person to work for the radical change of society.[28] Both saw pastoral action as political action, that is, not only as provision of comfort, solace, and charity,[29] but also as denunciation of social conditions (e.g., poverty and oppression) that set obstacles to human solidarity and human flourishing.[30] Unlike the idealized figure of the "cosmopolitan" present-day negotiator and peacemaker who works for the harmonization of the interests of conflicting parties, Milani and Torres worked for the dismantling of the fixed and uneven social space allocated to the rich and the poor. Instead of envisaging a world as an ordered and harmonized whole of opposing-though-co-ordinated parties, they had been against any division of the world.

Milani and Torres might not qualify as peacemakers from the fashionable perspective on peace that we have criticized above. They neither promoted a pragmatic, *modus vivendi* consensus, nor did they employ a pacifying rhetoric of conflict resolution. Instead, they held a very demanding conception of justice and conditioned peace on the realization of such a justice. In his *Letter to the Military Chaplains*,[31] Milani rejected the diplomatic language—so dear to today's negotiators and peace facilitators—that avoids the real stakes of a debate: "enough of high-sounding, vague speeches. Get down to the nitty-gritty."[32]

He was far from irenic in his defense of underprivileged children or of conscientious objectors. He resorted to intellectual warfare in order to make his positions absolutely clear. His *Esperienze Pastorali* has been characterized as a *book of Savonarolian wrath*. He even stated:

> If you have the right to teach [...] that Italians and foreigners can legitimately, even heroically, butcher each other, then I claim the right to say that the poor, too, can and ought to fight against the rich.[33]

As for Torres, initially, he held his own concept of the insurrection of the poor, which was meant to be an "'ideal, peaceful revolution', according to the model of the Christian Democrats in Chile."[34]

But, later, unlike Milani, whose militant intervention operated at the verbal and activist level, Torres defended armed intervention and revolutionary violence as the only possible way that the poor could obtain justice in the world.[35] As a priest and academic, Torres encouraged young people in Colombia to become involved with the poor. He had tried for about 18 years to convince the church to meet its social obligations to the poor, and the government to begin programs that would really help the poor. When all this turned out to be of no effect, Torres saw that the oligarchy in his country was unshakeable and that revolution was a last, though inevitable, resort.

But, in fact, Milani and Torres promoted a vision of true peace, one that goes beyond pacifying language, polite yet vacuous idioms, and superficial (or deep-down self-serving) conceptions of cross-cultural dialogue. To illustrate this, let us contrast peace as connected with elitism, property and power with peace as can be extrapolated from Milani and Torres' thought. The former kind of peace is encapsulated in the following statement by Boissy d' Anglas, the Thermidorean figure who personalizes, according to Badiou, the sacrifice of virtue on the altar of property:

> We should be governed by the best...[Y]et, with very few exceptions, you will find such men only among those who, owning property, are bound to the country in which it lies, to the laws that protect it, to the peace that preserves it.[36]

What Boissy d'Anglas rejected among other things, as Badiou remarks, is political virtue. He did not require "leaders to be virtuous politicians, only that they be governmental representatives of the 'best'"—something that can be said about many contemporary negotiators or peacemakers who undertake to impose the policies and promote the "world" that big powers favor. And "best," for Boissy d'Anglas, is "absolutely conditioned by the objective figure of property."[37] Peace preserves property, secures that laws protecting property will remain intact and turns into *patria* any country in which property can be made or found.[38]

By contrast, Milani rejected the obedience to the kind of protective law that cannot be universalized because it serves the interests of the few. In his own words:

> I cannot tell my pupils that the only way to revere the law is to obey it. I can only tell them that they should hold mankind's laws in such esteem as to observe them when they are fair (that is, when they uphold the weak). When they see that they are not fair (that is, when the laws sanction abuse of power by the strong) they should fight to change them.[39]

Against a monological and solipsist notion of peace as centripetally oriented agreement with the other, Milani's implicit conception of peace raised demands of transformed consciousness of all people. Efforts along such lines would enable learners to redefine wealth itself[40] with a view to enhancing the quality of life on and with the rest of the cosmos.[41] so that laws forfeit their interest-driven and protective role for the sake of more universalizable qualities. Likewise, Torres believed that, though lawless action "cannot be justified by its supposedly romantic virtue" it has nevertheless " to be taken as soberly and realistically as possible and can be justified only under very specific conditions."[42]

We may infer those specific conditions from his statement:

> The people [...] are desperate and have made up their minds to risk everything, even life itself, in order that the next generation of Colombians may not be a generation of slaves; in order that the children of those who today are prepared to offer their lives may receive education, a decent home, food, clothing, and above all human dignity.[43]

Cosmopolitanism for Torres and Milani, then, is not a commitment to any land where property lies; nor is patriotism a blind support to war operations of one's country. Much against the current, wholesale incrimination of any national feeling on the part of some peace negotiators or educationists, Torres deemed that risk should be taken:

> in order that future Colombians may live in a homeland which is really theirs, free from American domination.[44]

But Torres' emphasis on the national as declaration of otherness' vis-á-vis an oppressor's culture was not at odds with cosmopolitanism as commitment to the whole world. However, this kind of national patriotism was not and could not have been Milani's "in the chauvinist atmosphere of fascist Italy."[45] Or of the years that followed WW2. For Milani: "there really were only two nations: the rich and the poor.[46]

We have reached a point now where our contrast of Milani with present-day cosmopolitans and peace negotiators founders upon an apparent similarity: the antinationalist spirit of the above quotation and of the entire letter to the chaplains may seem to bring Milani close to those who think that all it takes for effecting peace is just to brand nationalist all commitments to a patria. But, as Timothy Brennan writes, to demolish:

> the pretence of national sovereignty for the purpose of accusing those who have sold it out

is one thing; to question:

> "whether independence itself is meaningful or desirable"

is quite another. While "the new cosmopolitanism blurs the two,"[47] Milani avoided any such conflation of aggressive and defensive action. In fact, Milani separated aggressive from defensive war. This becomes evident when one thinks through the implication of the following position of Milani: he condemned Italy's engagement in aggressive war as well as the Chauvinist education that rationalized that engagement; but this antinationalism did not stop him from defending the sovereignty of Ethiopia [48] and the national struggles of those suffering imperial oppression. In cases such as that of the Ethiopian war, Milani saw the legitimacy of a nation's defense against imperial aggressors.

## Conclusion

Milani and Torres' cosmopolitan visions are more nuanced, sensitive to situatedness, and oriented to questions about the treatment of others (and not about mere, pragmatic agreement with them) than those of many contemporary thinkers. They avoided both: the socialization of citizens into accepting military aggression, and the contemporary equation of peace-loving with the unqualified negation of communal-national affect. They never associated peace-loving with the mindset that glorifies the pursuit of private happiness, security, and protection at the expense of redemptive politics. Milani did not only insist that "all wars resulted in a tragic waste of human life" but, like Torres, he also reminded people that peace does not dwell in a world divided into rich and poor. Through their activism, both exemplify what it means "to love efficaciously."[49] As public intellectuals, they negated what has been described in this chapter as a monologism that makes cosmopolitanism an anodyne, lukewarm ideal of a society that feels that it owes nothing else to the world but respect for harmless, inoperative difference and believes that this is the most serious change that it has to undergo. Milani and Torres' embodying cosmopolitanism as an attitude of serious engagement with the other, rather than just symbiosis or personal enrichment, is a lesson of lasting significance for cosmopolitan and peace education.

## Notes

1. I am referring here mostly to issues of redistributive and restorative justice.
2. *Planēs* in Greek is both the wanderer and the global. The planetary conception of cosmopolitanism forgets that cosmopolitanism in antiquity (and later, as it had been revived in early modernity through the political and legal twist that Stoicism underwent in Rousseauist and Kantian reformulations) emerged from much stronger ethico-affective and cognitive concerns.
3. I do not argue against planetarism altogether; on the contrary, some of its aspects have a true cosmopolitan significance. But my objection concerns the ethical inflation and political exaggeration of that significance of planetarism to the point of identifying it with cosmopolitanism as such. I argue, against it, that the image of the traveler, of the dissident or the stranger (nowhere and everywhere in the world) is not an ethical image per se. It has, rather, a monological touch, since the "cosmopolitan" acts and qualities associated with this image are beneficial or significant for the wanderer herself first and foremost. They are beneficial for others only potentially and by implication.
4. For instance, Kenneth Saltman identifies some USAID programs as typical of such misguided and ultimately detrimental intervention in global affairs.
5. By the latter term, Saltman describes the educational militarism that enforces "global neoliberal imperatives through numerous educational means" (Saltman [2007], p.11).
6. The term "relationality" here refers to the political significance of the relation of two or more parties, involved or entangled in a situation that cannot or should not be seen just from the perspective of one affected party. To the monology of the latter possibility, the relational is the antipode, as it stresses the role of mutual engagement in political situations.
7. Held (2003), p.469.
8. For more on this objection, see Papastefanou (2012).
9. Derrida (2003, p.111) and Habermas (2003b, p.39) have criticized the UN because it is gradually becoming more like a paper tiger in the thrall of the strong global players rather than a truly justice-oriented organization of international right.
10. Ackerman (1994), p.535.
11. This includes its opposite, that is, cosmopolitanism as dissent and *Gelassenheit* (let-be) acknowledgment of disagreement.
12. Derrida asks, "does killing necessarily mean putting to death? Isn't it also 'letting die'? Can't 'letting die', 'not wanting to know that one is letting others die'—hundreds of millions of human beings, from hunger, AIDS, lack of medical treatment, and so on—also be part of a 'more or less' conscious and deliberate terrorist strategy?" (2003, p.208).
13. Levinas (1994), p.20.
14. Ibid.
15. Archibugi (2003), pp.489–500.
16. How is this commitment judged? Is it just a verbal assurance on the part of the appointed mediator or does it require more tangible proof?

17. Badiou (2005), p.100.
18. Ibid.
19. Todd (2010), p. 216.
20. See Gur Ze'ev (2011), p.16.
21. Ben-Porath (2006), p.58.
22. I avoid any introductory reference to Don Milani because this ground has already been covered in this book.
23. Camilo Torres, an activist Colombian priest and academic (sociologist), founded a movement, the United Front, which aimed to lead all progressive forces to the pursuit of political change in Colombia. But Torres' initiative was nipped in the bud, as he was killed in early 1966 in a skirmish with an army patrol. Levine (1979), p. 15.
24. Drake (2008), p.459.
25. Ibid.
26. Mayo (2007), p.529.
27. Drake (2008), p.466.
28. Drekonja (1971), p.60.
29. In Torres' view "individual acts of kindness and charity were negated by the unjust structures of society. And since these structures were founded on power, only power (not appeals to conscience or good will alone) could change them." (Levine [1979], p.16).
30. Levine (1979), pp.7–8 and p.13.
31. In 1965, a group of military chaplains publicly attacked conscientious objectors for their lack of patriotism and Milani responded to them with a letter. 1965 is also the year in which Torres resorted to guerilla action.
32. Milani (2008), p. 3. Although it had a more specific role in his text, I take Milani's exhortation as a plea for a direct questioning of the "production" of those Others to whom we seem today to owe nothing other than respect and toleration of their existence.
33. Ibid., p.2. But he added a disclaimer of revolutionary bloodshed: "At least in their choice of means they are better than you. The arms you approve are horrible instruments for killing, mutilating, destroying, creating orphans and widows. The only arms I approve are noble and without bloodshed: the strike and the ballot box" (ibid).
34. Drekonja (1971), p.59.
35. Drake (2008), p.463.
36. Boissy d' Anglas, cf. Badiou (2005), p.128.
37. Badiou (2005), p.129.
38. For more on how and why Boissy d' Anglas defended colonialism on such grounds, see Ibid.
39. Milani (2008), p.12.
40. Milani, B. (2002).
41. Borg and Mayo (2008), p.713.
42. Drekonja (1971), p.62.
43. Torres, available at: www3.uakron.edu/worldciv/pascher/torres-idania.html.
44. Ibid.
45. Brennan (1989), p.15.
46. Drake (2008), p.457. "He wanted the poor of the world to defend themselves against their exploiters, not to serve them by joining the armies of capitalism" (ibid.).
47. Brennan (1989), p.6.
48. Milani (2008).
49. Torres's phrase.

# References

Ackerman, B. (1994). "Rooted Cosmopolitanism." *Ethics*, 104, 3, pp.516–535.
Archibugi, D. (2003). "A Critical Analysis of the Self-determination of Peoples: A Cosmopolitan Perspective." *Constellations* 10, 4, pp.488–505.
Badiou, A. (2005). *Metapolitics.* Trans. J. Barker. London and New York: Verso.
Ben-Porath, S. (2006). *Citizenship under Fire: Democratic Education in Times of Conflict.* Princeton and Oxford: Princeton University Press.
Borg, C. and Mayo, P. (2008). "Globalisation, Southern Europe and European Adult Education Policy." *Policy Futures in Education* 6, 6, pp.701–717.
Brennan, T. (1989). "Cosmopolitans and Celebrities." *Race and Class* 31, 1, pp.1–19.
Derrida, J. (1994). *Specters of Marx: The State of Debt, the Work of Mourning, and the New International.* Trans. Peggy Kamuf. New York and London: Routledge.
Derrida, J. (2003). "Autoimmunity: Real and Symbolic Suicides: A Dialogue with j. Derrida" (interviewer: G. Borradori). In G. Borradori (ed.), *Philosophy in a Time of Terror.* Chicago: The University of Chicago Press.
Drake, R. (2008). "Catholics and the Italian Revolutionary Left of the 1960s." *The Catholic Historical Review* 94, 3, pp.450–475.
Drekonja, G. (1971). "Religion and Social Change in Latin America." *Latin American Research Review* 6, 1, pp.53–72.
Gur-Ze'ev, I. (2011). "Beyond Peace Education: Toward Co-poiesis and Enduring Improvisation." Available at: http://construct.haifa.ac.il/~ilangz/ Accessed on February 15, 2011.
Habermas, J. (2003). "Fundamentalism and Terror: A Dialogue with j. Habermas (interviewer: G. Borradori). In G. Borradori (ed.), *Philosophy in a Time of Terror.* Chicago: The University of Chicago Press.
Held, D. (2003). "Cosmopolitanism: Globalisation Tamed?" *Review of International Studies* 29, pp.465–480.
Levinas, E. (1994). *Nine Talmudic Readings.* Bloomington: Indiana University Press.
Levine, D. H. (1979). "Religion and Politics, Politics and Religion: An Introduction." *Journal of Interamerican Studies and World Affairs* 21, 1, pp.5–29.
Mayo, P. (2007). "Critical Approaches to Education in the Work of Lorenzo Milani and Paulo Freire." *Studies in Philosophy and Education* 26, pp.525–544.
Milani, B. (2002). "From Opposition to Alternatives. Postindustrial Potentials and Transformative Learning." In Edmund O'Sullivan, Amish Morrell, and Mary Ann O'Connor (eds.), *Expanding the Boundaries of Transformative Learning.* New York and London: Palgrave-Macmillan.
Milani, L. (2008). *Letter to the Judges.* Trans. Gerry Blaylock. pp.1 – 23. Available at: www.semisottolaneve.org/ssn/a/26987.html.
Papastefanou, M. (2012). *Eccentric Cosmopolitanism and a Globalized World.* London: Paradigm Publishers.
Saltman, K. J. (2007). *Capitalizing on Disaster.* London: Paradigm Publishers.
Todd, S. (2007). "Teachers Judging without Scripts, or Thinking Cosmopolitan." *Ethics and Education* 2, 1, pp.25–38.
Torres, C. Statement to the Press. Available at: www3.uakron.edu/worldciv/pascher/torres-idania.html. Accessed on February 15, 2011.
Zembylas, M. (2008). *The Politics of Trauma.* New York: Palgrave Macmillan.

# 9

# From Conflict to Conflict Resolution: Teaching the History of Cyprus in the Buffer Zone

*Isabelle Calleja Ragonesi*

## Introduction

The study of International Relations has been dominated from its inception by the realist school, which contends that the international political system is ultimately anarchic and lawless, and that countries must therefore be ready to fight and defend themselves. In the twentieth century we see the rise of Wilsonian Idealism that holds that cooperation between countries built round common economic and political goals, and cemented through institutional dynamics, furthers a global peace agenda. This chapter uses the case of Cyprus, where a doctrine of realism has long been entrenched and reflected in the island's division. This division is maintained through standing armies, the use of force, and a dialectic of animosity and threat. This chapter makes an attempt to illustrate the importance of peace studies and the doctrine of idealism to affect conflict resolution. In particular it focuses on the recent changes in educational trends particularly in the "buffer zone." The chapter assesses both the contribution of these to the present climate characterized by a "cold peace" and their potential to create a future scenario where the island can make the transition to a "real peace"; a scenario where Cypriots learn to understand, accept, and live with diversity.

## The Cyprus Conflict; Realist versus Institutional Approaches

In 2013 another round of peace talks aimed at uniting the North and South of Cyprus seemed to, once again, have reached an impasse. They failed, it is argued, as a result of a process that does not utilize the principles of inclusiveness and participation based on procedures of multiple alternatives, public consultation, and security and confidence-building measures.

While official attempts to resolve the crisis may lack certain peacemaking mechanisms and may have resulted in little change at the constitutional and executive levels, to talk of a stalemate and continuance of the status quo would be a very inaccurate reading of recent events in Cyprus. It would imply that only one international relations discourse, that of the realist school, predicated on sovereign-state relations, can give an accurate rendering of recent history in Cyprus. Admittedly, viewed through the lens of the realist school, little has changed in Cyprus. Two small polities with different governing elites and institutions continue to coexist within a framework largely of conflict. This conflict was brought home to us by Turkey's refusal to open up her borders to goods from the Republic of Cyprus in line with her European Union (EU) treaty obligation,[1] her decision in 2012 to boycott the Cyprus EU presidency,[2] and The Republic of Cyprus' attempts to exclude Turkey from EU initiatives.[3]

However, if we abandon a dialectic premised on sovereign-state relations and on the realist school, and instead focus our attention on what is happening on the ground at the level of grassroot endeavors, a very different picture of the Cypriot situation emerges. An international relations discourse influenced by liberalist and constructivist doctrines might lead us to conceive things in a different way. This approach is characterized by multiple actors including nonstate organizations who are brokers of power and who are interacting in the area that is not contiguous on the nation-state. A new type of global governance is operating in pluralist and postnationalist environment, transferring power away from the geographically defined nation-states to a wide range of actors including civil society, the private sector, and local and supra-regional governments. At the same time the solutions these actors advocate and are attempting to implement are focused on policy outcomes, rather than attempting to alter the structures of the two polities, or the relationship between them, through institutional and constitutional change. Through these methods the focus has been on social, economic, cultural, and historical issues, utilizing the principles of inclusiveness, participation, and confidence-building measures.[4]

The catalyst for change in Cyprus has been EU membership. Though the Republic of Cyprus (ROC) rejected the Annan plan (2004) leading to the exclusion of the Turkish Republic of Northern Cyprus (TRNC) from the union, the EU was determined that the whole island would benefit from accession. Membership reinforces the rights of citizenship of all Cypriots, and by extension their right to EU citizenship and an EU passport. All Cypriots born in Cyprus, of Cypriot parents, are Cypriot and EU nationals (Khadder, 2003). EU funding has also been allocated to the North of the island, and though the EU has suspended the application of the Aquis in the North, the Commission has been working with the Turkish Cypriot Chamber of Commerce, in order for the TRNC to align its legislation with that of the EU (Halil, 2010). However, perhaps the most important decision in terms of seeking reconciliation and conflict resolution on the island was the Green Line regulation (COUNCIL REGULATION [EC] No

866/2004 of April 29, 2004) voted on by the Council and put in place by the Commission prior to the entry of the ROC. The articles pertaining to this regulation determine the relationship between the North and South, utilizing a functionalist bottom-up approach,[5] formatted on the principles of the common market, the Strategic Environmental Assessment principles, and four freedoms. These regulations are also supervised, and updated through EU institutions ensuring that it is supranational rather than national governance that is now the name of the game.

## Buffer Zones as Peace Parks

This new relationship is illustrated by the transformation of that area that has for so long divided Cyprus, the Green Line and the buffer zone that surrounds it on either side. This zone was established in 1964 as a result of the civil war and became impassable after 1974 with the division of the island. It was further reinforced by Turkish forces who built a barrier on the zone's northern side, consisting mainly of barbed-wire fencing, concrete wall segments, watchtowers, antitank ditches, and minefields. The line then also started to be referred to as the Attila line after the Turkish code name for the military intervention in 1974. This buffer zone runs for more than 180.5 kilometers, and has an area of 346 square kilometers. The zone stretches for 180 kilometers from the western part of Kato Pyrgos to the east just south of Famagusta. It cuts through the center of the capital of Cyprus, Nicosia, separating the city into southern and northern sections. The width of the zone ranges from 3.3 meters in central Nicosia, to 7.4 kilometers at the village of Athienou. Over 10,000 people live here in villages and on farmland. The zone presently accounts for 3 percent of the total land area. There is also a buffer zone around the Kokkina enclave (located in the ROC but inhabited by Turkish-Cypriots) in Western Cyprus (UN Peacekeeping Force in Cyprus [UNFYCIP]).

The Green Line and buffer zone surrounding it have been a daily visual reminder of the continued conflict in Cyprus, and presented a very real obstacle to conflict resolution and unification. Indeed, in terms of realist theories of international relations, a buffer zone is classified as "a defined area, controlled by a peace operations force from which disputing or belligerent forces have been excluded."[6] A buffer zone is formed to create an area of separation between disputing or belligerent forces and reduce the risk of renewed conflict. In some UN operations it is also called an area of separation, and to undertake these tasks buffer zones also become demilitarized neutral zones.[7] However, in recent literature on peace studies, buffer zones are also seen as places where reconciliation takes place and the territory becomes the focus of peace rather than conflict.[8] Writing on Limpodo, Barrett talks of these Borderlands transitioning from zones of conflict to peace parks supporting thriving social ecological systems where through the removal of borders and the redesigning of space these previously desolate border areas become secure shared spaces allowing the restoration of their cultural and ecological integrity.[9] Barrett illustrates this by focusing on the role of the Limpodo buffer zone in South Africa, as it separates a number of states in the region where conflicts remain unresolved. She asserts that the "success" of a Peace Park is measured by how effective it is at both conservation and peace-building. Barrett adds:

> [T]he factors that determine this success include the location, conservation type, scale, history, players (international, governmental, indigenous and so on), finance, conflict type/intensity and the challenges that face the efforts collectively...[concluding that]...these factors are unique to each region, as is culture and historical allocation of wealth/resources. However the findings of these case studies, the nature, scale, longevity and frequency of the conflicts in question play a very large role in how these parks are at their conflict deterrence objectives.[10]

In theorizing on peace games Lejano corroborates this, stating that the employment of peace parks "corresponds to unseen shifts in the contending parties."[11] He adds that this territory where the emphasis is "on peace alters the priorities of the contending parties."[12] He attempts to illustrate this by utilizing game theory. Here, he posits that rational agents, each representing a state, is an agent promoting the greatest gain. This model, deriving from the two-person, noncooperative, zero sum game theory, is illustrated in this case by the decision to prevent conflict by relinquishing the right to cross over to disputed territory, and by giving up the beneficial use of the land in the buffer zone. The cost of using it would be too high and will resuscitate friction. Consequently, for instance, the Korean demilitarized zone remains vacant, and may even expand, as conflict possibilities remain high. However, Lejano argues that the risk of friction decreases with every round of play, that is, with repeated occurrences of cooperation, and he points to Cyprus where this zone has shrunk, as social and culture exchanges become hopeful signs of a new relationship between the North and the South.[13] In this scenario the methodological rules of traditional game theory solutions are overturned. Normally, these are called for action by national actors seeking solutions within the juridical and constitutional rules of the game. However, acting within the neutral buffer zone, where brokers of power are not contiguous on the nation-state, rational individuals slowly start to take on joint identities that both parties in the game share. Solutions become policy rather than polity oriented, focusing on social, economic, cultural, and historical issues, and are in the hands of local and international players rather than national ones.

## The Green Line and the Transformation of the Buffer Zone

Undoubtedly, in Cyprus today, while national politics and institutions remained intact, the Green Line regulation and the concurrent policies and funds put in place to enforce the aims of the regulation have transformed the island, increased the legal rights of Cypriot Nationals with regard to their access to resources on the island, despite the unresolved issues of land ownership, and, despite continued problems, have improved the relationship at the local level between the North and the South. In 2004, for the first time since 1974, Cypriots could move around freely throughout the whole island, as the Green Line regulation facilitated freedom of movement for Cypriots, EU, and third-country nationals. Free movement of goods destined for the South and the EU market were also facilitated (Cyprus Chamber of Commerce and Industry, 2011). Originally, movement was restricted to two crossings, today there are seven crossing points, (though not all may be active), the last one opened on Ledra Street in the center of Nicosia. Since 2004 the buffer zone is slowly being rehabilitated. Nowhere is this transformation more visible than in the daily hub of activity at Ledra Street. This recent opening has transformed the center; people freely move round Nicosia, the buffer zone between the two parts of the city is slowly being transformed from a no-man's-land to a thriving community where shops and restaurants are opening, Euros are accepted as payment, and taxis wait to take one further North. Slowly, the capital of Cyprus is coming together (Jacobson et al., 2009).

Facilitating the transformation of the area are a number of projects that have surfaced in the buffer zone. With extensive demining operations started by the UN in 2004, more than a third of the buffer zone's land has been opened to civilians, and many groves and farming lands have been revived. Much of the island's pork is produced here, in the largest pig farm in Cyprus.[14] Since 2008, the EU's Common Agricultural Policy applies to these lands, making them entitled to subsidies. Besides agriculture, urbanization is slowly reducing the buffer-zone areas, west of Nicosia, where the Green Line is not clearly demarcated. According to Michel Bonnardeaux, spokesman for UNFICYP, the UN peacekeeping mission for Cyprus:

> Before people were afraid to get close to the enemy, but with stability more and more they want to use their land in the buffer zone.[15]

Slowly, Cypriots are returning to their villages inside or adjacent to these Zones. The Greek-Cypriot villagers of Mammari, previously denied access by the UN force to avoid any incidents with nearby Turkish troops, have now returned to their land. In some areas the two communities now live side by side.

Reinforcing urbanization trends is the "No Man's Land Project" workshop (2010 and 2013) in the abandoned city of Famagusta, and is based on the hypothetical event of the return of the confiscated land and villages inside the Buffer Zone back to their former proprietors, following a 38-year period of abandonment. Targeting its rehabilitation, The School of architecture have told prospective participants of the project that they will be working on creating parametric systems,[16] that use as input efficiently quantified data; such as land parceling, transportation routes, or built growth, along with nonquantifiable elements, such as collective memory or regional or ethnic tension. The project aims to enhance the rich architectural heritage within this strip of land, identified by the project coordinators as the most important area within the historic center, and crucial for the future unification and integration of the city. The overall result would include historical analyses, surveys of buildings and public spaces, studies for emergency support of buildings and restoration proposals, and an enormous digital record used as a database for future projects. The project, once completed, would enable the conservation of the architectural heritage within the buffer zone and the revitalization of the historic center of Nicosia as a whole.[17]

Although accounting for only around 3 percent of the island's total area, this Zone is turning into a separate geopolitical entity of its own, and is playing a vital political and economic role, in a future reunification of the island's north and south.[18] Whether seen as a buffer zone, a no-man's-land, a demilitarized area, a neutral space or peace park, in this beautiful wilderness and grand abandonment, resonates, the voice of Lorenzo Milani protesting the ravages of war, fought in the name of such platitudes as nation and nationalism.

In this neutral space the disinherited and the oppressed are returning. They return, despite, or oblivious to, the cries of division that appeal to culture, religion, or history to reinforce difference and erode any attempts at creating a Cypriot identity. Here, a place has been created that allows and facilitates the interaction of Cypriots from the North and the South. A space, where institutional politics is replaced by socioeconomic and political grassroot activity, and where local players are freed from the exigencies of the national elites. A space has been born where individuals can truly interact as Cypriots. Thus, it was in the buffer zone between the two check points in Ledra Street, where a space was provided in 2011 and 2012 for activism by the "Occupy Buffer Zone" movement. These were weekly protests organized by Greek and Turkish Cypriots focusing on the problems of the global economic and political system, and on the division of Cyprus as a symptom of these problems.[19]

## Peace Education in the Buffer Zone

Made possible by and at the center of this transformation is peace education. Peace education is constantly being resorted to in order to bring the ideal of conflict to resolution to fruition. Teachers without borders[20] refer to the founding charter of United Nations Educational, Scientific and Cultural Organization (UNESCO) and its opening statement that wars begin in the minds of men as their guiding paradigm. If this is true it is only through our minds—through education—that war can be vanquished by peace. They believe that as teachers they have the duty to lead the way toward peace in their classrooms and communities. Consequently their Peace Education Program is designed to help them in this pursuit, by providing teachers with a framework for peace education. In this way they believe that they are contributing to the growing movement toward a global culture of peace. Peace Research Institute Oslo (PRIO), a leading organization in the field with offices in Cyprus elaborates on the importance of education in the context of conflict resolution. They cite studies that:

> demonstrate that formal education systems have a vital role to play in building peace in countries affected by armed conflict. Fieldwork conducted in three countries—Guatemala, Nepal, and Liberia—highlights a number of ways in which education is contributing to building the conditions for long-term, positive peace in those countries.[21]

The report centers around four conflict-transforming concepts that mediate the relationship between education and peace:

- Equitable educational *inclusion* within the formal education system can redress motivation, and eliminate opportunities to engage in armed conflict.
- School *socialization* processes can impact social acceptance of and constraints with regards to the use of violence. As a result of improved quality and safer, protective learning environments, individuals may have less motivation as well as fewer opportunities to engage in armed conflict.
- Building up trust and cooperation (*social capital*) through school-based organizations can rectify grievances over lack of participation and improve relationships between individuals and groups.
- The various *social benefits* of education (including hope and possibilities for the future, as well as improved levels of socioeconomic development) can raise the social, direct, and opportunity costs of engaging in armed conflict (Dupuy, p.26)

Crucial to the transformation of the buffer zone is the replication of a number of programs, centered on peace education.

In 2008, through their music studies program, the Cyprus Youth Council organized a concert with traditional Cypriot music performed by young people from the North and South in the buffer zone.[22]

The Peace Players Cyprus (PPI-CY)[23] run a sports program and use the game of basketball to facilitate positive dialogue and interaction between Turkish-Cypriot and Greek-Cypriot youth, with the ultimate goal being improved relations between the two communities in Cyprus. PPI-CY aims to break down social and cultural stereotypes, develop young leaders from both sides, and build community involvement and investment. However there is currently no basketball court located in the buffer zone, and many children and parents from both communities cannot or will not cross to the other side. They plan to build two courts in the buffer zone, which will be symbols of peace; a safe place where children from two divided communities can come together on neutral ground to play, learn, and grow for generations.[24]

In 2013 the UN announced the launch of a new study program looking at how bi-communal cooperation could help prevent wildfires that "know no borders."[25] The aim is completing an assessment of the wildfire problem within the buffer zone. Complementing these activities the University of Central Lancashire (51% stake holding) has opened up a Cypriot campus close to the village of Pyla in the buffer zone, the only locality where Greek- and Turkish-Cypriots live, aiming to draw students from both sides. Though presently its 140 students are predominantly Greek-Cypriot Cypriots, it envisages a growth of up to 5,000 students, many of whom they hope will be Turkish-Cypriots. The Goethe Institute and the US Fulbright Foundation now also have offices on the same street.

At the center of these new educational initiatives is an abandoned house in the Cypriot buffer zone acquired, renovated, and converted to create a social and cultural center that opened in 2011. Funding from several donor organizations and countries made possible the renovation of this disused building. Transformed by a Greek-Cypriot and Turkish-Cypriot team of architects, it contains a conference room, a library, multifunctional seminar rooms for training courses, events and presentations, and a café. In addition to the local population, local nongovernmental organizations (NGOs) also benefit from this project since they are permitted to use its various premises. The "home for cooperation" is the first center to be shared by both population groups of Cyprus, This project is the inspiration of the Association for Historical Dialogue and Research (AHDR), which was founded in 2003 (in the run up to EU membership) as an NGO by a group of historians, teachers, ethnologists, linguists, and research scientists.

## Teaching History: The Cold War and the Sovereign State

Located in the buffer zone, the AHDR is attempting to usher in a new phase in the writing and teaching of history. This is a crucial endeavor, for the teaching of history plays a central role in peace education. For ultimately it is the school history texts, as Stojanovic tells us, that are among the most important means for shaping national identity and historical awareness.[26] Through textbooks, pupils are at an early age imbued with images of their own nation, its place in history, its characteristics, as well as with images of other neighboring peoples. This fact indeed gives history teaching a special mission that surpasses its educational task, and turns it into an important instrument of both state and international policy. Indeed, history textbooks and the versions of history they relate have long been recognized as crucial instruments in establishing local, regional, and global identity, and the impact they may have on the relations within and between states. Post First World War, the revision of history school textbooks was seen as part of an important movement to reduce aggressive nationalism and promote peace. Post Second World War, efforts to reconcile warring nations were reflected in UNESCO's program of bilateral consultations between countries for the improvement of history textbooks. The task set was that of eradicating a truth that stopped at national frontiers, and adopting one that reflected an international conscience that overcame frontiers. Countries, including Germany and France, worked on a version of history that both could live with, and utilize for reconciliation and integration.[27]

There are numerous studies illustrating the use of history textbooks as political tools in Cyprus. Indeed, up to the 1990s when conflict between the two parts of the island continued to escalate and culminated in the declaration of the TRNC in 1983 of its status of sovereignty and independence, Cypriot textbooks were written to reinforce division and difference, to reiterate the Greek-ness and Turkish-ness of the two side of the island, and to solidify the relationship between client and patron states. The production of these separate textbooks for the two communities seems to have commenced in 1884 with the supply of textbooks from Turkey for the Turkish-Cypriots. The 1895 Education Law introduced two separate Boards of Education, one Christian and one Muslim. These textbooks were linked to the different versions of Cypriot community history found in the North and the South of the island. Many of these texts were produced in the motherlands, others were produced locally. As a Turkish-Cypriot student Erol Suleymanoglu pointed out Cypriot history is largely written by Greece and Turkey for each country's own political ends, harming the identity of Cypriots.[28]

In both communities, these history texts gave an inaccurate rendering of the relationships across the ethnic divide and even within it. The textbooks invariably portrayed the conflicts as intercommunal ones. They did not touch on intracommunal conflicts, or those between client states and the mother countries, important variables in order to understand the 1964 civil war, and the 1974 invasions. Thus, the history textbooks reinforced the image of solidarity between patron and client states, with little mention of the relationship of coercion and dependency between the two. While intercommunal relations are never mentioned other than in terms of conflict and brutal violence, school textbooks thus eulogize the external at the expense of intercommunal harmony. The end results were textbooks that deployed a nationalism fuelled by racist and exclusionary discourses. This is illustrated in the stories told by the victims of this history. In the service of this agenda, children through these textbooks were exposed to horrific caricatures of their neighbors living only meters away across the Green Line. They are not only the "primary other," but also the occupiers, the invaders, the enemy. These texts used a discourse of highly loaded and emotional language, full of imagery that sustains a notion of an "us" and a "them." There are images of ruthless murderers and innocent victims. This polarizing of the self and other was pointed out by the head of the Turkish-Cypriot Educational Planning and Program Development Department in July 2004:

> Our texts encourage the student to make enemies. In one part of a history text book it describes how Greek-Cypriots "gouged out the eyes, filled bodies

with holes" etc. This kind of language, as well as breeding hatred, can also cause lasting psychological damage to the young reader.[29]

## Teaching History: The Post Cold War and The International Community

With the end of the Cold War and the possibility of EU membership on the horizon and a corollary unification, a new phase in the writing and teaching of history in Cyprus was embarked upon. The TRNC overhauled their history textbooks and produced a new series informed by new rhetoric and new theoretical constructs. The ROC also participated in the process. However, this movement remained tied largely to an external remit. For post Cold War, we witness a new regionalization of Cypriot politics. This is the birth of a new Balkan region, no longer divided by the politics of bipolarity, but with space for the arrival of numerous small states. These states ensured their security and stability through eventual EU membership. Greece, a local hegemon, is by now an established member of the EU, Cypriot membership is on the horizon, as is the eventual start of accession negotiations for Turkey (Borowiec, 2000; Brewin, 2000; Jimenez et al., 2004). In this new dynamic, the security and regional interests of Greece and Turkey became complementary.

A push toward Cypriot identity politics was encouraged by the most important regional player, the EU. For the growth of this organization had heralded a shift in international politics from realist intergovernmental models based on national discourses and bilateral methodologies, toward a more institutionalist, functionalist, and integrationist approach, based on multilateral mechanisms. Localized models based on a multiethnic Cypriot identity now become feasible within the context of a federalized EU.[30] The complex and highly introvert and conflictual character of education in the region now had to be addressed in order to foster an education of understanding, for regime breakdown in the Balkans was a dangerous imperative in the EU's back yard as the cases of Kosovo and Bosnia illustrated.[31] The influence of Greece and Turkey over Cypriot history was being replaced by that of the EU, which sought a history that would legitimize and mythologize its role both within Cyprus and the region. The search is for a new community history, which would be focused on a discourse of supranationalism. This discourse would focus on a pedagogy of history that looked at the grand project of Europe, and would offset and discourage major historical narratives that are ethnocentric or even narrowly nationalistic. In effect, we have in the making a new normative and institutional memory of this "new" past, which codifies and homogenizes the collective memory in the context of the needs of a new external player, the EU; a player that requires a united Cyprus.[32]

In 1997, under the sponsorship of the Council of Europe, numerous associations from different Balkan nations came together to initiate a school of historical revisionism (The Southeast European Joint History Project),[33] that would allow the new states to cohabit adjacent and at times even shared spaces. Cypriot historians and teachers participated in these numerous seminars on the reassessment of Balkan history. Comparative research related to the study of school curricula and textbooks was encouraged. The dialectic here was to be that of peace studies, which promoted a history not of war, of political grandeur or political contingency, but rather sought a history of those variables that were central to peoples' existence, and brought them together rather than divided them. These included economic and social history, the geography of history, the environment of history, and a history also of different mentalities and different cultures. The ultimate aim was that of changing the image of the hostile neighbor.[34] The "Workbooks Project" is a manifestation of this organization's work. Its long-term aim being to encourage and support reconciliation in the region by allowing children to view the area's shared history from many points of view, thus opening up the past to discussion and debate through a participative and collaborative method of learning. In this way, we are told, the notion that there are many "truths" and versions of events, as well as many common experiences (rather than just a national viewpoint and an unfavorable image of "the other") will enable the process of reconciliation for the future to start. Through this innovative pedagogy, the children will also gain the skills and attitudes necessary for an open and democratic society to emerge.

The Council of Europe began a program specifically focused on history teaching in Cyprus in July 2003, on the initiative of the Secretary General and with the agreement of the Ministry of Foreign Affairs of the Republic of Cyprus. In 2004 the Council of Europe organized four activities in Cyprus comprising seminars and workshops, which brought together about 400 participants from the two main communities, as well as from Armenian schools. (The latter reflects the fact that Cyprus is a multicultural island, where you do not find just Cypriot-Greeks and Cypriot Turks.) The focus was on teaching history as multi-perspectivity. An approach reflected in "Recommendation 15 of 2001" on history teaching in twenty-first-century Europe adopted by the Committee of Ministers on October 31, 2001.[35] Further projects were proposed under the Reconciliation Commission,[36] which was to come into operation with the Anan Plan. The Commission was to be established to promote understanding, tolerance, and mutual respect between Greek-Cypriots and Turkish-Cypriots in the light of the Anan Plan. The work was to include: (i) the promotion of dialogue between Greek-Cypriots and Turkish-Cypriots regarding the past; (ii) preparation of a comprehensive report on the history of the Cyprus Problem as experienced and interpreted by Greek-Cypriots and Turkish-Cypriots, and (iii) recommendations to the federal government and the constituent states for action aimed at promoting reconciliation, which would include guidelines for publications and school textbooks.

Increasingly, teachers and students from the two sides of the Green Line were demanding history teaching that is fair to both communities.

In a bi-communal seminar at the Ledra Palace in 2000, the Bi-Communal Teachers Training Centre hosted "History: How Do We Teach it, How Should It Be Taught?" with support from the Fulbright Commission in order to promote intercommunal peace through education.[37] Dimitris Tsaousis, a 17-year-old student, asked why so much "blind gut hatred" exists among his Greek-Cypriot peers, none of whom were even born at the time of the invasion. He laid the guilt for this prejudice on a politicized education system that demonizes one side and naively praises the other.[38] In 2004, the head of the Turkish-Cypriot Educational Planning and Program Development Department, Hasan Alicik, made history with a project that aimed to bring sweeping changes to the way history is taught in Turkish-Cypriot schools. His task was to create a syllabus that would give "an objective view of Cypriot-history."[39] Thus, a school of historians have started analyzing the conceptualization of the minor differences, externalizations, projections, chosen traumas and glories, dehumanization, victimization, and ethnic identity.[40] This is being done to gain a greater understanding of the historical, psychological, and political barriers between Turkish-Cypriots and Greek-Cypriots.

Despite these changes, in March 2008, Andrekos Varnava in the Cyprus Mail stated that "Education reform is indeed linked to reunification. Changing how society views itself, however, starts with education of the young. Most of the textbooks produced in the island in the humanities and social sciences, especially the history textbooks, give a distorted picture of Cyprus' past. They monolithically project the idea that Cyprus has always been Greek, that the Greekness of Cyprus was preserved during times of foreign oppressive occupations, and blame others for the division of Cyprus. They deny the multicultural history of Cyprus; the involvement of 'Greek' elite in the ruling class of the country and the common hardships and joys of the various communities at the lower strata of society. They uncritically review contemporary history, breed hatred of Turkish-Cypriots and, in short, are one-sided in their pursuit of the Greek or Greek-Cypriot nationalist discourse, thus poisoning children's minds against other communities, particularly the Turkish."[41] This reflects a continued inability in Cyprus to effect reform in the teaching and writing of history, that remains written for, focused on and under the scrutiny of nation-state interests.

## Teaching History in the Buffer Zone

However, those working on this new type of teaching and writing of history in Cyprus, seem to have matured toward a more indigenous movement, fuelled by a new discourse, and new possibilities, facilitated by the neutral, nonsovereign politics of the buffer zone. Supported by a large number of organizations, this new school is spearheaded by the AHDR. In a climate where much of the history taught in Cypriot schools in the North and the South remains heavily biased according to cultural perceptions of events in the past wrapped up with the existence of these two micro states, the aim of the AHDR, which operates the Peace Centre in the buffer zone, is to teach history to Cypriot schools in a more multidimensional nonstate-centric context. This has finally become possible through a neutral space that has not only opened up numerous opportunities for joint endeavors across the line, but provides, maybe for the first time, a unique environment. One in which educational initiatives, namely those relating to history and culture, can be freed from the torpor of bias and prejudice that focuses on difference and extols the virtues of one's ethnicity and the vices of the other. It is freed from a history that assigns blame, holds the out-group to account, and yet absolves the in- group from the need for introspection, and the requirement to understand. To finally allow and make possible the writing and teaching of a history of Cypriots rather than of the States of Cyprus. Dr Meltem Onurkan Samani, vice- president of AHDR and a Turkish-Cypriot tells us that:

> Efforts to re-unite the country are now focusing on people-to-people contacts and joint history teaching in the buffer zone, rather than grand political solutions…[hoping that]…buffer zone will transform from being a place symbolizing division to a place of co-operation and dialogue.

This sentiment was also reiterated by Dervis Eroglu, president of the TRNC stating that he believes that "reconciliation between the two sides 'can be achieved and that history teaching is part of it.'"[42]

In this new phase, texts are written by Greek- and Turkish-Cypriots, in Greek, Turkish, and English. They are inspired by new schools of history; the Annales school[43] that looks to social, economic, and anthropological fields to enrich the study of history, schools that focus on cultural studies and archaeological and architectural studies. One recent text elaborated on historical change through developments in the study of music over space and time. Led by the AHDR board of Turkish and Greek-Cypriots the Association has held a number of events, beginning with a two-day educational seminar in February 2004 titled "What Does It Mean to Think Historically? Approaches to Teaching and Learning History." Historians from all over Cyprus, across disciplinary and linguistic boundaries came together to discuss ways in which historical thinking could be advanced. The Association has also set as one of its priorities teacher training on the epistemology and methodology of history teaching and learning. Many intercommunal educational discussions, seminars, workshops, and projects have been organized in collaboration with civil society and teacher trade unions across the divide in Cyprus and organizations abroad, such as EUROCLIO, CDRSEE, University of Oxford, and Council of Europe. A number of texts in English, Greek, and Turkish include; *Multi-Perspectivity in Teaching and Learning History*, published in 2005, *The Use of Sources in Teaching and Learning History* in 2009, *a Look at Our Past* in 2011 a supplementary interactive teaching pack on nonpolitical aspects of the history of Cyprus, *Representations of History and Intergroup Relations in Cyprus 2011*, *European Heritage for an Active Citizenship through Intercultural Dialogue 2011*, and *Revitalising the "Dead Zone". Home for Cooperation: an Educational and Research Centre 2011*. These publications have been prepared within the framework of teacher training activities, providing multidimensional insight into Cypriot history. In this way schoolchildren in Cyprus will gain an insight into the country's rich history, which in turn will generate mutual respect and understanding between the island's populations over the long term. The centre is also aiming to attract more than 2,000 visitors a year to its multicultural museum. Overall, these measures will contribute to greater tolerance and respect between the cultures in Cyprus. It is hoped that in the long term this grassroot initiative will contribute to reconciliation and peace-building.

## Conclusion

Conflict resolution in Cyprus remains elusive as the island remains divided. Two microstates continue to maintain this division by upholding two different versions of a Cyprus nation legitimized through different histories and national myths and memories.[44] In these historical memories and myths we all too often find the past, the present, and future of the nation.[45] The history books on Cyprus, and to a greater extent its school textbooks, illustrated the truth of these statements. For a nation's textbooks are the vehicle *par excellence* to reflect and transmit the national memory, which is illustrated through this community of myths.[46] The history textbooks on Cyprus have not been concerned with detailing the social, economic, political, and cultural exploits of the Cyprus people, which would have contributed to the fertilization of a history of a Cypriot nation,[47] for such a nation does not exist.[48] In 2013, the history being written and taught in the buffer zone, may be signs that these important attributes of nationhood are being created, providing the tools and facilitating the process, of conflict resolution. Is it possible that what we are witnessing in the buffer zone is a Cypriot State in the making?

## Notes

1. Kutlay (2009).
2. Yeong (2012).
3. Kyris (2012).
4. CYPRUS (2015); Ladisch (2006).
5. Functionalism is based on cooperation rather than integration of states. The common need for technocratic management of economic and social policy leads states to take common decisions, which requires them to cooperate and work increasingly together. Kurt, U. (2009). A Historical Glance at the EU from a Functionalist Perspective." *European Journal of Economic and Political Studies*, p.43.
6. Online Dictionary of Military and Associated Terms (2005).
7. Nolan (2002).

8. Barrett (2012).
9. Ibid.
10. Ibid., p.12.
11. Lejano (2007), p.45.
12. Ibid.
13. Lejano (2007).
14. France 24 (2012).
15. France 24 (2012).
16. Is a system being fed with variable information in order to achieve results, which keeps it within the system framework
17. Architecture Association (2013).
18. Cyprus Chamber of Commerce and Industry (2011), *Revitalising the Dead Zone.*
19. Aljazeera (2011).
20. "Teachers without Borders" is an international nonprofit organization that provides resources, tools, and training to enhance the knowledge, skills, and connectivity of teachers around the world. The organization was founded in 2000 by Dr. Fred Mednick, who believed that in addition to transmitting knowledge in their classrooms, teachers can effect positive change and development in their communities. Available at: www.teacherswithoutborders.org/.
21. Dupuy (2008) p.2.
22. Every body's Song (n.d., available at: www.everybodys-song.net/concert.php).
23. Peace Players International—Cyprus (PPI—CY) is a locally led, independently registered charity in Cyprus that uses the game of basketball to allow 11–15-year-old Greek-Cypriot and Turkish-Cypriot boys and girls to play together, learn together, and build positive relationships that overcome generations of mistrust and formidable physical barriers to interaction. Available at: www.peaceplayersintl.org/our-programs/cyprus.
24. PPI-CY Field Blog (October 15, 2010). blog.peaceplayersintl.org/2014/01/03/an-exciting-new-year-at-ppi-cy/.
25. Cyprus Mail (January 18, 2013).
26. Stojanovic (2001).
27. UNESCO (1953).
28. "Biased History Books Under Fire," (2000).
29. Bahceli (2004), available at: www.cyprus-mail.com/news/.
30. Zurn (2000).
31. Molis (2006); Friesendorf (2008).
32. Koussertari (2004); Richmond (2006).
33. Bonidis and Zarifis (2006).
34. Ibid.
35. Philippou (2005).
36. Taki (2004).
37. "Biased History."
38. Ibid.
39. Bahceli (2004).
40. Yuksel (2006).
41. Varnava (2008).
42. The EU observer online (May 09, 2011).
43. Annales school, School of history. Established by Lucien Febvre (1878–1956) and Marc Bloch1886–1944), its roots were in the journal *Annales: économies, sociétés, civilisations,* Febvre's reconstituted version of a journal he had earlier formed with Marc Bloch. Under Ferdinand Braudel's direction the Annales school promoted a new form of history, replacing the study of leaders with the lives of ordinary

people and replacing examination of politics, diplomacy, and wars with inquiries into climate, demography, agriculture, commerce, technology, transportation, and communication, as well as social groups and mentalities. While aiming at a "total history," it also yielded dazzling micro studies of villages and regions. Its international influence on historiography has been enormous. britannica.com/EBchecked/topic/1364891/Annales-school
44. Kizilyurek (2001).
45. *Education for Peace* (2004); Markides (2005).
46. *Disarming History* (1999).
47. Kizilyurek (2001).
48. Dodd (1998); Peristianis (1999).

# References

Aljazeera (2011). *Cyprus Occupy Buffer Zone*. November 15.
Anastasiou, H. (2000). "Negotiating the Solution to the Cyprus Problem: From Impasse to Post-Helsinki Hope." *The Cyprus Review*, 12, 1, pp.11–33.
———. (1996). "Conflict, Alienation, and the Hope of Peace: The Struggle for Peace in Militarised Cyprus." *The Cyprus Review*, 8, 2, pp.79–96.
Architecture Association, School of Architecture (2013). "Cyprus UN Buffer Zone: Rebuilding No Man's Land." Available at: www.aaschool.ac.uk/STUDY/VISITING/cyprus.
Attalides, M. (1979). *Cyprus: Nationalism and International Politics*. Edinburgh: Q Press Ltd.
Bahceli, S. (2004). "Making History." *Cyprus Mail*, July 15. Available at: www.cyprus-mail.com/news/.
Barrett, G. (2012). "Markets of Routine Exceptionalism: Peace Parks in Southern Africa." Paper presented at the Nature Inc. Conference, ISS, The Hague, June 29, 2011. Available at: www.ru.ac.za/.../Narture%20Inc%20Draft10021.
Bakshi, A. (n.d.). "The Home for Cooperation Opens in Nicosia's Buffer Zone." *Conflict in the Cities and the Contested State*. Available at: www.conflictincities.org/PDFs/CinC_Web%20report_Nicosia.pdf.
"Biased History Books Under Fire" (2000). *Cyprus Mail*, May 21. Available at: www.cyprus-mail.com/news/.
Bonidis T. H., and Zarifis, G. K. (2006). "Is There a Role for Education in the Way towards Stability and Democratization in the Balkans? a Critical Review of ba.so.ped's Aims and Publications." *European Journal of Education*, 41, 2, pp. 321–240.
Borowiec, A. (2000). *Cyprus: A Troubled Island*. West Port: Praeger Publications.
Brewin, C. (2000). *The European Union and Cyprus*. Cambridgeshire: Eothen Press.
Bryant, R. (2001). "Justice Or Respect: A Comparative Perspective on Politics in Cyprus." *Ethnic and Racial Studies*, 24, 6, pp.892–924.
Byrne, S. (2000). "Power Politics as Usual in Cyprus and Northern Ireland: Divided Islands and the Roles of External Ethnic-Guarantors." *Nationalism and Ethnic Politics*, 6, 1, pp.1–23.
Calotychos, V. (Ed.) (1998). *Cyprus and Its People: Nation, Identity and Experience in an Unimaginable Community*. Colombia: Westwiew Press.
Childs, P. and Williams, P. (1997). *An Introduction to Post-Colonial Theory*. Hertfordshire: Prentice Hall.
Chomsky Noam quotation available at: www.tumblr.com/tagged/noam%20chomsky?before=48.
Christodoulou, D. (1992). *Inside the Cyprus Miracle: Labours of an Embattled Mini Economy*. Volume 2. Minneapolis: University of Minnesota.

Christofides, M. and Lambrou, E. (2007). *The Island Everyone Wanted: An Illustrated History of Cyprus*. Nicosia: Verity Productions.
Christou, G. (2004). *The European Union and Enlargement: The Case of Cyprus*. New York: Macmillan.
Constantinou, C. M. (2006). *Aporias of Identity and the Cyprus Problem*. Paper presented at the ECPR Joint Sessions of Workshops. April 25–30.
Cyprus (2015). "Research and Dialogue for a Sustainable Future." Available at: www.cyprus2015.org/.
Cyprus Chamber of Commerce and Industry et al. (2011). *Economic Interdependence in Cyprus (2011) Current Assessment and Prospects for the Future*. Available at: www.undp-act.org/data/articles/interdependence_report_2011.pdf.
Demetriou, O. (2005). *EU and the Cyprus Conflict: Perceptions of the Border and Europe in the Cyprus Conflict*. Working Paper Series in EU Border Conflict Studies, June 18. Cyprus: Intercollege.
Dentash, R. R. (1972). *A Short Discourse on Cyprus*. Nicosia: Lefkosa.
Dictionary of Military and Associated Terms (2000). US Department of Defense. Available at: www.thefreedictionary.com/buffer+zone.
Diez, T. (2000). "Introduction: Cyprus and the European Union as a Political and Theoretical Problem." In T. Diez (ed.), *The European Union and the Cyprus Conflict*. Manchester: Manchester University Press.
*Disarming History*. (1999). "International Conference on Combating Stereotypes and Prejudice in History Textbooks of South-East Europe. Visby, Gotland (Sweden), September 23–25.
Djavit, A. (n.d.). *How History Should Be Taught in Cypriot Schools?* Available at: www.hisdialresearch.org/Articles/History.pdf.
Dodd, C. H. (ed.) (1999). *Cyprus: The Need for New Perspectives*. Cambridgeshire: Eothen Press.
———. (1998). *The Cyprus Imbroglio*. Cambridge: Eothen Press.
Dragonas, T. and Frangoudaki, A. (2001). "The Persistence of Ethnocentric School History." In C. Koulouri (ed.), *Teaching the History of Southeastern Europe*. Thessaloniki: Petros Th.Ballidis & Co.
Dupuy, K. (2008). *Education For Peace: Building Peace and Transforming Armed Conflict Through Education Systems*. International Peace Research Institute, Oslo (PRIO) for Save the Children Norway Report no. ISBN 82-7481-165-8.
*Education For Peace: Pilot Application for the History and Literature Books of the 5th Grade of the Elementary School* (2004). Organized with support from the Bi-Communal Development Program funded by USAID and UNDP and executed by UNOPS, Nicosia. A Report.
EU Commission (2005). Consolidated version of the Green Line Regulation including amendments COUNCIL REGULATION (EC) No 866/2004 of 29.4.2004 on a regime under Article 2 of Protocol No 10 of the Act of Accession as amended by Council Resolution (EC) No 293/2005 of February 17, 2005.
Everybody's Song Concert in the Buffer Zone Cyprus. Available at: www.everybodys-song.net/concert.php.
Forari, M. (2012). "Musical Encounters: Teaching History and Exploring Diversity CyprusPedagogicalInstitute." Availableat:www.pi.ac.cy/pi/files/epimorfosi/synedria/histrory_pestalozzI_2012/theodorou_eleni.pdf.
France 24 (2012). "Farmers Returning to the Cyprus Buffer Zone." Available at: 24.com/en/20121214-farmers-returning-cyprus-buffer-zone.
Friesendorf, C. (2008). "Kosovo's controversial independence: CSS analysis." *Security Policy*, 3, 9, pp.1–3.
"Greek Government Withdraws Controversial History Textbooks" (2007). *Cyprus Mail*, September 26. Available at: www.cyprus-mail.com/news/.

Green Line Regulations Crossing Points. Available at: www.mof.gov.cy/mof/customs/customs.nsf/All/05AEEF243C9BFC8BC22572BF002D0A28?OpenDocument.
Gregoriou, Z. (2004). "De-Scribing Hybridity in 'Unspoiled Cyprus': Postcolonial Tasks for the Theory of Education." *Comparative Education*, 40, 2, pp. 241–266.
Hadjiyanni, M. (2008). *Contesting the Past, Constructing the Future: A Comparative Study of the Cyprus Conflict in Secondary History Education*. Saarbrucken: VDM Verlag
Halil, J. (2010). "Second EU Harmonisation Package for North Cyprus." *Cyprus Forum. Com*. Available at: www.cyprus-forum.com/cyprus35797.html#p691043.
Hill Collins, P. (1990). *Black Feminist Thought, Consciousness and the Politics of Empowerment*. Australia: Allen & Unwin.
"History Is Not a Balance Sheet of Blame" (2004). *Cyprus Mail*, January 16. Available at: www.cyprus-mail.com/news/.
Hobsbawn, E. J. (1992). "Ethnicity and Nationalism in Europe Today." *Anthropology Today*, 8, 1, pp. 3–8.
Ioannides, C. P. (2001). *RealPolitik in the Eastern Mediterranean: From Kissinger and the Cyprus Crisis to Carter and the Lifting of the Turkish Arms Embargo*. New York: Pella Publications.
"It's Our Choice to Cultivate Hostility" (2007). *Cyprus Mail*, February 11. Available at: www.cyprus-mail.com/news/.
Jacobson. D. (2009). *The Opening of Ledra Street/ Locmaci Crossing in April 2008: Reactions from Citizens and Shopkeepers*. PRIO Cyprus Centre Paper 2.
Jimenez, A. M. R., Gorniak, J. J., Kosic, A., Kiss, P., and Kandulla, M. (2004). "European and National Identities in the eu's Old and New Member States: Ethnic, Civic, Instrumental and Symbolic Components." *European Integration online Papers (EioP)*, 8, 11, pp. 1–33. Available at: http://eiop.or.at/eiop/texte/2004–011a.htm.
Joseph, J. S. (1997). *Cyprus: Ethnic Conflict and International Politics*. London: Macmillan.
Khadder, T. (2003). "Turkish Cypriots Line up for Passports." *Cyprus Mail*, April 25. Available at: http://news.pseka.net/index.php?module=article&id=3837.
Kizilyurek, N. (2001). "History Textbooks and Nationalism." In C. Koulouri (ed.), *Teaching the History of Southeastern Europe*. Thessaloniki: Petros Th.Ballidis & Co.
Koulouri, C. (2001). "The Tyranny of History." In C. Koulouri (ed.), *Teaching the History of Southeastern Europe*. Thessaloniki: Petros Th.Ballidis & Co.
Koussertari, M. (2004). "Time to Rewrite the History Books." *Cyprus Mail*, January 15. Available at: http://www.cyprus-mail.com/news/.
Kutlay, M. (2009). "The Cyprus Question and the Future of Turkey-EU Relations." Available at: www.usak.org.tr/EN/makale.asp?id=1047.
Kurtz, S. (2001). "The Hegemonic Impulse of Post-Colonialism." *The Weekly Standard*, August 10. Available at: www.travelbrochuregraphics.com/extra/edward_Said_imperialist.htm.
Kyris, G. (2012). "N Cyprus the Other Side of the Green Line." *EU Observer. Com*. Available at: http://euobserver.com/opinion/115278.
Ladisch, V. (2006). "Towards the Reunification of Cyprus: Defining and Integrating Reconciliation into the Peace Process Princeton." Available at: www.princeton.edu/jpia/past-issues-1/2006/6.pdf.
Lejano, R. ( 2007). "Peace Games Theorising about Trans-boundary Conservation." In A. H. Saleem (ed.), *Peace Parks, Conservation and Conflict Resolution*. Cambridge: The MIT Press.
Maiz, R. (1999). "Democracy, Federalism, and Nationalism in Multinational States." *Nationalism and Ethnic Politics*, 5, 3 and 4, pp. 35–60.
Markides, C. (2005). "Exploding the Myths of Cyprus History." *Cyprus Mail*, December 18. Available at: www.cyprus-mail.com/news/.

Molis, A. (2006). "The Role and Interests of Small States in Developing European Security and Defence Policy." *Baltic Security and Defence Review*, 8, 1, pp.81–100.

Nolan, C. J. (2002). *The Greenwood Encyclopaedia of International Relations*, Volume 1. Available at: http://books.google.com.mt/books?id=Zp_yNYA20rgC&pg=PA205&lpg=PA205&dq=BUFFER+ZONES+IN+INTERNATIONAL+RELATIONS&source=bl&ots=qUcaYAqU6m&sig=.

"No Man's Land Project" workshop (2010 and 2013). Available at: www.nomanslandproject.com/.

Ozcelik, S. (2005). "An Analysis of the Cyprus Conflict with a Psychoanalytical Approach: Psychological, Historical and Political Barriers between Turkish and Greek Cypriots." *The Journal of Turkish Weekly*. Available at: www.turkishweekly.net/article/96/an-analysis-of-the-cyprus-conflict-with-a-psyhoanalytical-approach.html.

Panteli, S. (1990). *The Making of Modern Cyprus: From Obscurity to Statehood*. New Barnett: Interworld.

Peace Players International (2010). "PPI—Cyprus Proposes a Basket Ball Court in the Buffer Zone." Available at: http://blog.peaceplayersintl.org/2010/10/15/from-the-archive-ppi-cyprus-proposes-a-basketball-court-in-the-buffer-zone/.

Peristianis, N. (1999). "a Federal Cyprus in a Federal Europe." In A. Theophanous, N. Peristianis, and A. Ioannou (eds.), *Cyprus and the European Union*. Nicosia: Intercollege.

Philippou, S. (2005). "The Problem of the European Dimension in Education: A Principled Reconstruction of the Greek Cypriot Curriculum." *European Educational Research Journal*, 4, 4, pp. 343–367.

Preses, A. F. (2012). *Farmers Returning to Cyprus Buffer Zone*. Available at: http://lifestyle.xin.msn.com/en/beauty-fashion/farmers-returning-to-cyprus-buffer-zone.

Prodromou, E. H. (1994). "Towards an Understanding of Eastern Orthodoxy and Democracy Building in the Post-Cold War Balkans." *Mediterranean Quarterly: A Journal of Global Issues*, 5, 2, pp. 115–138.

Reynolds, D. (2005). *In Command of History: Churchill Fighting and Writing the Second World War*. New York: Random House.

Richmond, O. (2006). "Shared Sovereignty and the Politics of Peace: Evaluating the eu's 'Catalytic' Framework in the Eastern Mediterranean." *International Affairs*, 82, 1, pp. 149–176.

Said, E. W. (1978). *Orientalism*. New York: Random House.

Salem, N. (Ed.) (1992). *Cyprus: A Regional Conflict and its Resolution*. Ottawa: St. Martins Press.

Scherer, J. L. (1997). *Blocking the Sun*. Minneapolis: University of Minnesota.

Sonyel, S. R. (1997). *Cyprus: The Destruction of a Republic. British Documents 1960–1965*. Cambridgeshire: Eothen Press.

Spyrou, S. (n.d.). *Small Imaginations: Greek Cypriot Children's Constructions of "The Turk."* Available at: www.lse.ac.uk/collections/EPIC/documents/ICSpyrou.pdf.

Stojanovic, D. (2001). "History Textbooks and the Creation of National Identity." In C. Koulouri (ed.), *Teaching the History of Southeastern Europe*. Thessaloniki: Petros Th.Ballidis & Co.

Stoler, A. L. (2002). *Carnal Knowledge and Imperial Power: Race and the Intimate in Colonial Rule*. Berkeley and Los Angeles, CA: University of California Press.

Taki, Y. (2004). "The Reconciliation Commission." *Cyprus Mail*, March 28. Available at: www.cyprus-mail.com/news/.

Tatar, R. Z. (2004). "Changing the History Books: Papadopoulos Never Was Terribly Interested." *Cyprus Mail*, January 25. Available at: www.cyprus-mail.com/news/.

*Teaching Cyprus—In Search of Tolerance and Understanding* (2000). South-Eastern European Joint History Project Workshop II, Pyla, Cyprus, February 28–29.

*Teachers without Borders.* Available at: www.teacherswithoutborders.org/.
Terzis, N. P. (2000). "Objectives and Prospects for Historical Educational Research in the Countries of the Balkans." In N. P. Terzis (ed.), *Education in the Balkan: From the Enlightenment to the Founding of the Nation-States.* Thessaloniki: Kyriakides.
Theophanous, A. and Coufoudakis, V. (Eds.) (1997). *Security and Cooperation in The Eastern Mediterranean.* Nicosia: Inter college.
Theophylactou, D. A. (1995). *Security, Identity and Nation Building: Cyprus and the European Union in Comparative Perspective.* Aldershot: Avebury/Ashgate.
Trimikliniotis, N. (2010). *Country Report Cyprus.* EUDO Citizenship Observatory.
UNESCO (1953). *Educational Studies and Documents Bilateral Consultations for the Improvement of History Text Books.* New York: Author.
UNFYCIP United Nations Peacekeeping Forces in Cyprus. *The Buffer Zone.* Available at: www.unficyp.org/nqcontent.cfm?a_id=1592.
Varnava, A. (2008). "Moving Forward after the Presidential Election." *Cyprus Mail*, March 2. Available at: www.cyprus-mail.com/news/.
Yeong, L. H. (2012). "Turkey's Boycott of the Cyprus EU Presidency: Context, Meaning and Its Consequences." Working Paper No. 9, September EU Centre Singapore.
Yuksel. M. (2006). "Thinking about the Future: Leadership and Conflict Transformation." *E-Leader* Slovakia. Available at: www.g-casa.com/download/Yuksel_Leadership_conflict.pdf.
Zurn, M. (2000). "Democratic Governance beyond the Nation-State: The eu and Other International Institutions." *European Journal of International Relations*, 6, 2, pp. 183–221.

# 10

# Beyond Reality Dissonance: Improving Sustainability of Peace Education Effects

*Yigal Rosen*

## Introduction

Peace education in a region of intractable conflict faces a negative sociopolitical environment that works against its effects. The media, leadership, educational system, and other societal institutions continue to express a culture of conflict. In the light of these barriers, it would make sense to assume that peace education programs do not stand much of a chance of being truly effective. Indeed, recent studies show that the effects of peace education programs are short-lived and methods to sustain the effects over time are needed. The present chapter describes the societal-psychological climate of intractable conflict, the goals of peace education in such regions, the challenges of achieving these goals, and possible ways to overcome these challenges. Peace education programs should be designed to effectively manage the "reality dissonance" between the sought-for effects and sociopolitical environment. Mechanisms for sustaining educational change are described along with a model for program design. Finally the chapter offers several conclusions and directions for future research.

Intractable conflicts (e.g., Middle East) are usually characterized as lasting at least 25 years and as being fought over goals that are perceived as existential. Such conflicts are violent, perceived as unsolvable and of a zero-sum[1] nature. The parties involved invest much in their continuation.[2] Intractable conflicts persist for a long time, at least a generation. This means that at least one generation did not know another reality. The duration of the conflict forces members of these societies to adapt their lives to this continuously stressful situation. This type of conflict involves physical violence in which people are killed and wounded. The consequences of physical violence, especially the loss of life, have an immense emotional impact on all.

Despite these difficult circumstances, initiatives in peace education have thrived in settings such as Israel, Northern Ireland, and the Balkans. Different kinds of initiatives include Pathways into Reconciliation,[3] Education for Mutual Understanding (EMU),[4] and Education for Peace (EFP).[5]

Over time, peace movements in many places in the world took a variety of new and unique forms such as Lorenzo Milani's School of Barbiana. Although peace education initiatives in contexts of intractable conflict are commonplace, it is still important to ask whether they accomplish anything in such difficult circumstances. Careful research on peace education is limited, but by this point there is clear evidence of impact from some interventions. Several studies have documented positive impacts on perception of the other side, more positive emotions, willingness to have contact with the "others" and greater legitimization of "other's" collective narratives.[6] Other studies show that participation in the peace education programs leads to a greater acceptance of members of the other collective, more positive emotions, willingness to have contact with members of the other side, and greater legitimization of its collective narrative (Biton and Salomon, 2006).[7]

However, the news is not as heartening as it might seem at first. While most research has focused on immediate effects, some longer-term studies suggest that the impact dwindles over time.[8] The present chapter focuses on this phenomenon: In contexts of intractable conflict, how can we understand the forces that erode the near-term effects of peace education? This chapter offers a model of the forces at work summarized by the concept of "reality dissonance," the dissonance between the ideal views and practices promoted by typical programs of peace education and the sociopolitical environment that surrounds participants.

While part of the problem lies with reality dissonance itself, another part lies with the design of typical peace education initiatives, which on the whole do not incorporate features to combat reality dissonance. However, there are real prospects for doing better. In the last part of the article, we identify a number of program components that seem likely to promote more sustainable change, based on research in diverse areas.

## The Reality of Intractable Conflict

Attitudes in a setting of intractable conflict are far from homogeneous. Nonetheless, on the whole, members of such societies tend to be skeptical about peaceful resolution of conflicts. Both sides expect the conflict to continue and involve violent confrontations. Parties engaged in an intractable conflict make, at times, vast material (i.e., military, technological, and economic) and psychological investments in order to cope with the situation. Intractable conflicts are perceived as being about essential and basic needs and/or values that are regarded as indispensable for each side's existence and/or survival. The conflicts characteristically have a multifaceted nature, including matters of territory, self-determination, statehood, economy, religion, and/or culture. Each side focuses only on its own needs, considering any loss suffered by the other side as its own gain, and any gains of the other side a loss. Reconciliation in regions of intractable conflict goes beyond the agenda of formal conflict resolution to changing the motivations, goals, beliefs, attitudes, and emotions that prevail among the great majority of the society—regarding the conflict, the nature of the relationship between the parties, and of the parties themselves. Reconciliation consists of mutual recognition and acceptance, investing in the development of peaceful relations, mutual trust, and positive attitudes as well as fostering sensitivity and consideration of the other party's needs and interests. In essence, reconciliation requires setting new societal goals of peace, the construction of an image of the rival as a human being with equal rights, the active reformation of the collective memory, and the fostering of positive affects and emotions about peaceful relations with the past opponent. This is a profound challenge in view of the prolonged domination of a culture of conflict. It requires mass mobilization and support along with a sophisticated policy, planning and initiatives, and a wide variety of other activities—all in order to convince the members of one's society of the necessity, utility, value, and feasibility of the peace process.

Intractable conflicts occupy a central place in the lives of the individual members of such societies as well as the societies as a whole. Members are involved constantly and continuously involved with the conflict. Children and youth grow up in a pervasively belligerent climate that supports the prevailing culture of conflict, thus opposing the spirit of peace education.[9] The younger generation experiences this culture through family, through the societal channels of communication, including the mass media, and through other cultural agencies and products. An especially formative role is taken by the educational system, which serves as the major agent for socialization. Conflict influences school textbooks, instructional materials, teachers' instructions, school ceremonies, and so on. This form of socialization is so powerful because it reaches all of the younger generation in any society in which education is compulsory. Even so, peace education initiatives are a prominent and, at least, sometimes somewhat effective method for promoting a culture of peace.[10]

## Goals of Peace Education

Peace education aims to reconstruct students' values, beliefs, attitudes, emotions, motivations, skills and patterns of behavior, in a way that facilitates conflict resolution and other peace processes, and to prepare students to live in an era of peace and reconciliation.[11] When societies are involved in intractable conflict, the objective of peace education should be to advance and facilitate peace making and reconciliation. It should aim to influence the worldview (i.e., their values, beliefs, attitudes, emotions, motivations, skills, and patterns of behavior) of the members of society in a way that facilitates conflict resolution and peace process and prepares them to live in an era of peace and reconciliation. In order to achieve the objectives of peace education, a school system must go through major changes. It requires setting new educational objectives, preparing new curricula, writing school textbooks, developing instructional material, training teachers, creating a school climate that is conducive to peace education, and so on. Peace education, if successful, socializes young generations in such a way that it facilitates the process of reconciliation and eventually the construction of a culture. But the success of peace education depends on a number of conditions in the political-societal sphere as well as in the educational sphere.[12]

It is useful to conceptualize peace education initiatives as operating on three fronts: cognitive, emotional, and behavioral.[13] Although these are not perfectly distinct, the cognitive aspect can be understood as encompassing knowledge, perceptions, beliefs, attitudes, thoughts, values, and evaluations regarding the other and one's own collective. This includes: understanding the origins of violence between collectives and the need of reconciliation; understanding of and concern for human rights (civil, political, social, economic, cultural, environmental, and developmental rights); critical examination of one's own side's contribution to the conflict; balancing and personalizing the image of the "other"; openness to alternative information and tolerance toward collectives with contradictory worldviews. The emotional aspect consists of emotions and feelings toward the other and toward one's own collective: decreasing feelings of fear, anger and hatred toward the other; increasing hope, trust and mutual acceptance; experience the feelings (empathy) of members from the other collective and being able to empathize with the suffering of the other collective; recognizing the feelings and their roots on both sides, sharing them reflectively with one's own group and with members from the other group. The behavioral aspect consists of overt behavior patterns regarding the other and one's own collective.

The cognitive, emotional, and behavioral aspects of peace education are not disconnected from each other. Change in one of them can lead to a change in the others. Thus, changing the negative image of the other side (cognitive aspect) or reducing fear of members of the other collective (affective aspect) can influence openness to social contact with the other (behavioral aspect).

## The Mixed Effectiveness of Peace Education

On the affirmative side, research on peace education in the context of the Israeli-Palestine conflict shows positive impacts of educational programs on youth. For example, in her evaluative studies, Maoz found a positive attitudinal change among Jewish and Palestinian youth who participated in dialogue workshops.[14] Biton and Salomon studied the extent to which participation in a school-based peace education program affected youth's perceptions of "peace."[15] It was found that both Jewish-Israeli and Palestinian participants came to stress more the positive aspects of peace (cooperation, harmony) as a result of the program. Also, this study found that the program served as a barrier against the deterioration of perceptions and feelings during the times of escalated mutual hostilities (e.g., Intifada). Lustig studied the effects of a peace education program based on studying a foreign and remote conflict.[16] She showed that such study developed perspective-taking abilities regarding the home conflict. Rosen found positive impacts of a peace education program evidenced by greater acceptance of members of the other collective, more positive emotions, less negative stereotypes, openness to contact with the "others" and greater legitimization of the "other's" collective narrative.[17]

However, several findings indicate that the effects of peace education programs dissipate with time. For example, Bar and Bargal[18] reported an extensive study of peace education dialogue encounters where most of the effects of peace education programs were lost within a few months. Participants relapsed to previous negative or stereotypical attitudes and beliefs. Peace education as value-oriented education often faces societal barriers. Close analysis of peace education programs suggests that they face formidable barriers that would appear to prevent the attainment of their goals of mutual legitimization, changed attitudes, and empathy.

A study by Bar-Natan, Rosen and Salomon[19] revealed friendships with members from the other side created during the encounters increased readiness for social contact, and greater perceived legitimacy of the collective narrative of the other. However, the study found that these effects were short-lived as well as highly correlated with the initial attitudes and beliefs of the youths involved.

Finally, Rosen showed that peace education programs can effectively influence adolescents' more peripheral attitudes and beliefs, whereas the typical roadblocks facing peace education appear to pertain to the core beliefs of the groups' collective narratives.[20] Core attitudes and beliefs are more extreme than less central ones, are more stable over time, are held with more confidence, are more strongly associated with behavior, are more likely to influence other attitudes and beliefs, and—most importantly—are more resistant to external interventions.[21] Thus, peripheral attitudes and beliefs that are more easily affected by a peace education program can as easily change back in an adverse social and political atmosphere.

## Reality Dissonance

It is hardly surprising that impact would dwindle over time. Such phenomena are commonplace across many kinds of learning. That acknowledged, how can we best understand the erosive forces in the specific case of peace education in settings of intractable conflict? We argue that far more than simple forgetting is involved. The relapse reflects a pervasive and belligerent culture of war. The dissonance between more positive productive views and the sociopolitical reality wears away cognitive, emotional, and behavioral gains, particularly after participants have finished the intensive part of the program. For an overall term, we call this effect *reality dissonance*.

For example, Sommers, noting the active resistance of parents and other members of the students' larger communities to changes within participating youth, argues that "peace education positions itself between schoolchildren and adults in the same community making it virtually impossible for education to inculcate peaceful values in children when adult role models are built on conflict."[22] Outright confrontations aside, more subtle ways of undermining of gains accrues from the constant signals of belligerence sent through everyday conversations, newspaper stories, television news, and political speeches. It's hard to swim in this sea without getting wet! The pervasive sociopolitical reality tends to wash away islands of progress.

However, reality dissonance itself is only part of the problem. It is also the case that peace education programs typically do little to prepare learners for reentering the sociopolitical context. The programmatic shortfalls can be organized by the same three dimensions that characterize the goals of peace education: cognitive, emotional, and behavioral. Peace education programs generally suffer from what might be called cognitive oversimplification, emotional oversimplification, and behavioral oversimplification, as follows:[23]

*Cognitive oversimplification.* Peace education programs tend to emphasize superficial cognitive learning, giving short shrift to the complex multidimensional reality of conflict, peace efforts, and reconciliation processes. The content of peace education often amounts to a form of indoctrination provided by the government or NGOs.[24] Terms such as "tolerance" might be interpreted by some as ignoring the atrocities of the "other side."

To win learners away from an established culture of conflict, it is no doubt intuitively appealing to offer a strong simple counterview. However, we suggest that such a counterview, even if temporarily adopted in the context of an intensive peace education program, is not likely to prove robust as learners return to their normal life patterns. According to Bar-Tal,[25] information that is consistent with a deeply entrenched culture of conflict tends to be more attended and remembered, and inconsistent or confusing information reinterpreted to fit. Minimizing the multidimensional characteristics of the conflict in the name of peace can leave learners without ways of making sense of the complexity, and reality dissonance will most likely "reconvert" them to the culture of conflict.

Moreover, many programs focus on individual relationships, including relationships with members of the other group, but without deeply addressing or affecting perceptions of the other *as a group*. They also express an overly static view, incorporating little reflection about the future of the painful group relations.[26] When the participants try to understand fresh events that express the conflict, they tend not to transfer their knowledge to the new situations.[27] Connection to the person's reality as a point of departure for change is required in a process of change.[28]

Perkins has summarized the problem as "tribethink," the tendency to see the world in terms of the needs and aspirations of one's own tribe (group), standing against the other competing tribes.[29] The members of the tribe develop excessive cohesiveness, commitment, and compliance, sacrificing exploration of possibilities. The challenge of peace education is to overcome the limits of tribethink by dealing directly with the advantages of more open-minded views and the mutual benefits of peace. In many cases, programs do not do enough to make an alternative vision cognitively clear, accessible, and compelling for youth. Moreover, in many cases the immediate environment of family and friends continues to represent the culture of the conflict and draw participants back into tribethink.

So what might be done? We will return to this in more detail later, but basically there is a need for more cognitively complex and fact-oriented education about peace.[30] Peace education has to work harder to develop complexity of thinking about conflicts and possible ways for peacemaking and reconciliation.

*Emotional oversimplification.* A negative emotional orientation marks the societal-psychological infrastructure of intractable conflicts.[31] Despite this, most peace education programs do not refer directly to the affective aspects of the conflict and intergroup relations. For example, most of the programs do not deal with symbolic and realistic threat. Symbolic threats concern perceived conflict between groups' values and goals; realistic threats involve perceived competition for limited resources, often framed in zero-sum nature.[32] According to Bar-Tal,[33] hatred, anger, and fear are prominent in the psychological repertoire of societies involved in intractable conflict.

Moreover, peace education programs in regions of intractable conflict are by definition implemented amid unstable and sometimes violent situations that generate frequent emotional stress. Under stressful conditions, educational effects achieved earlier tend to revert to old patterns.[34]

So what might be done? Blindness toward the suffering and the emotional lives and feelings of others can be reduced by developing empathy, awareness of others' feelings and perspectives, which can change the ethnocentric emotional view developed as a part of a culture of a conflict[35] Also, peace education programs need to include learning of self-regulation emotional skills.[36]

*Behavioral oversimplification.* During and especially after a program, there is typically nothing much for participants to do with the newly learned attitudes and concepts. Participants have few ready-at-hand opportunities for political action, reflective expression, or contact with people from the other side. This near vacuum of significant actionability also applies to the educators involved, who see themselves as teachers and coaches, not as political or social leaders. New experiences, if they occurred during the participation in peace education program, are absorbed familiar and reliable construction of reality.[37]

So what might be done? True change may require people finding dissatisfaction, inconsistency, or intolerability in the current situation,[38] leading to some kind of productive action. What counts in the end is what people do. Peace education programs need to offer a kit of specific intergroup and intragroup activities that translate newly learned concepts and feelings into action on the ground, forming stable positive behavioral patterns over time.[39]

## General Mechanisms for Sustaining Educational Change

As already noted, the erosion of impact is not unique to the field of peace education. Similar setbacks, with both different and similar causes, have been noted in other fields as well. For instance, in science education, learners often regress to previously held misconceptions;[40] when teachers return to pretraining views of teaching;[41] drug addicts return to their addictions;[42] and schools and other organizations return to previously practiced modes of operation.[43]

Relapses in these and other fields such as social and organizational psychology have sometimes been successfully overcome or even prevented, and changes have been sustained in the face of adverse forces. Fullan argues that change is a never-ending proposition under conditions of dynamic complexity,[44] hence connection with the wider environment is critical.[45] According to Sims and Sims, long-term change in collectives involves the creation of key mechanisms, such as symbols, stories, language, ceremonies, and statement of principles.[46] These mechanisms enable transmitting and sustaining the newly developed culture. According to Senge et al., the challenges of sustaining transformation involve keeping the participants open-minded and managing fear and anxiety.[47]

Huberman and Miles make three suggestions regarding the continuation of change: (a) embed the change into the structure of the environment; (b) generate a critical mass of people committed to the change; and (c) create established procedures for continuing assistance, especially toward supporting new participants.[48] To assure the sustainability of change, groups create member commitment, seeking to inculcate a sense of emotional identification with the practices and values.[49]

Sometimes a change process can find a self-sustaining path from the very beginning; an initiative can "feed on itself" through positive feedback, which produces further change. Positive feedback mechanisms may be activated indirectly, by promoting successful experience, and directly by creating "as-time-goes-by" support.[50] An induced compliance technique involving dissonance arousal can serve as an "as-time-goes-by" mechanism.[51] The more a person tries the new learned behavior, the more he or she will like it, because the drive to reduce dissonance encourages people to change attitudes to make them more consonant with their behavior. Another "as-time-goes-by" mechanism is the "foot-in-the-door" effect—a willingness to engage in more significant behaviors after undertaking less dramatic ones.[52] Here, when someone carries out a small request, this increases considerably the likelihood of agreeing to a similar (or in many cases even dissimilar) larger request made by the same person (or in many cases even by another person).

Another potential self-sustaining mechanism involves peer-teaching. One of the best ways to understand deeply new concepts is by teaching them. Peer-teaching involves responsibility for collection and organization of information, deep understanding and identification with the body of knowledge, reflective thinking and leadership skills.[53]

Political support may be needed to sustain a prolonged change. Various studies have found that real change requires a significant amount of support from political overseers and other key external stakeholders.[54] Political overseers have the authority to pass legislation or put policies in place that mandate change, and they also control the flow of vital resources that are needed to sustain a transformation. Peace education can succeed when peace education as a policy is formally supported by leaders (e.g., prime minister or president) because they see it as a very important part of their peace-oriented policy. The Ministry of Education needs to have the authority, as well as the infrastructure and resources, to implement peace education. An organizational framework, lasting efforts, and continuous devotion are all required. The implementation is also related to availability of experts and professionals who can realize the institutionalization of peace education in schools. In addition, implementation requires continuous evaluation in order to find out what kinds of programs are efficient.[55]

Additionally, peace education initiatives require a substantial support among society members for conducting a peace process with the past rival. A majority, at least, have to support the peace process, including major political parties and organizations as well as most members of the civil society. Society members may be ready for the peace process, but not yet ripe for changing their conflict-related repertoire, which includes collective memory and ethos of conflict.

## Designing for Sustained Impact in Peace Education

It has to be acknowledged that addressing some weaknesses of peace education programs requires a change in the whole political-societal environment. According to Bar-Tal and Rosen[56] the following conditions are essential for implementing peace education widely in the context of intractable conflict: progress toward peace, support for a peace process by major political parties and the civil society, ripeness for reconciliation, and governmental and political support for peace education. However, even under less supportive conditions there is a place for the development and implementation of peace education programs based on what we would like to term a *Sustained Impact Model for Peace Education*.[57] Based on the analysis presented earlier, this model summarizes important elements and psychological-educational processes of peace education for sustained impact. The challenge of sustainability must be addressed from the beginning and throughout. As already argued, typical education for peace in settings of intractable conflict neglects the problem of reality dissonance. Without special preparation, participants encounter the gap between the new culture of peace promoted by the program and the pervasive reality of the conflict, which leads to losses of initial gains as participants readapt to the pressures around them.

Although severe reality dissonance is by definition a reality in such settings, programs can include features designed to mitigate some of the effect—features we call "sustaining components"—both during the main part of the program and afterward as part of a follow-up process. These components can prepare the participants for real-life situations where reality dissonance is likely to come to the fore. Follow-up components can help to refresh and maintain changes after the more intensive experiences of the main part of the program. We discuss briefly several promising sustaining components.

*Perspective-taking activities*: Frequently putting oneself in the others' place and seeing the world through their eyes, feeling their emotions, and even role-playing as they would behave in a particular situation. The "others" include people on the opposite side of the conflict but also more militant members of one's own society. This is based on the empirically proven method of induced compliance in the context of intractable conflict.[58] Habits of perspective-taking should help to build and sustain empathy toward the needs, suffering and intentions of others involved.

*Analyzing the recent events*: Guided uni-national and bi-national meetings for mutually analyzing the recent events of the conflict. Such meetings can foster transfer of the cognitive, emotional, and behavioral patterns cultivated by the program.

*Social networks:* Encouragement and support for participant activity within social networks and peace movements. Under the stressful conditions of a prolonged intractable conflict, societies set rigid limits for social proximity and distance. Internet-based social networks can help peace education participants overcome constraints of time, physical distance, and social distance.[59]

*Mutual projects:* Involvement in collaborative prolonged initiatives. Participants might engage in initiatives such as films, music, painting, theater, science, computer programming, sports.[60] Initial interest in the subject is essential for effective involvement.

*"Foot-in-the-door" experiences:* Less dramatic actions leading to more dramatic ones. The idea here is to create an initial platform leading toward greater commitment and participation. For example, this method could be used toward the end of a program by asking the participants to write short essays about their reflections on the program, sending them to other participants or educators. Most participants will then feel more obligated to the program and more likely to respond to invitations to volunteer for additional activities.

*Involving family and community:* Cognitive, emotional, and behavioral efforts to cultivate change addressing not just individuals but family and community. Youth are of course part of the community in which they live and are influenced by the views expressed in it. Therefore, it is important to reach out and involve families and the community in programs of peace education, even when the population is not at all homogeneous in its commitment to peaceful solutions. This can be done both during and after the major part of the program.

*Cross-age peer-teaching:* After participation in a peace education program, teaching younger children.[61] Peer-teaching fosters deep understanding, reflective thinking, and leadership skills.

*Mutual ceremonies:* Creation of mutual symbols, ceremonies and statements of principles. These mechanisms foster transmission and sustaining of the developing culture of peace.

*Positive expectancy:* Dealing explicitly with doubts and difficulties of conflict resolution and reconciliation processes. Participants have to expect challenges and setbacks, recognizing that they are part of the process and that they can be overcome.

A few comments on this list: First of all, we do not see this list as complete; certainly other strategies could be added. Second, we view these components as complementary; they contribute in different ways and can be used in combination. An extended program could even use them all, although it is perhaps more plausible that different well-designed programs would use different combinations of convenience. Finally, it is especially important that a program include some of these as follow-up components, to help learners weave the cognitive, emotional, and behavioral gains tightly into their everyday lives. Perhaps after the main part of the program, participants might adopt any of several sustaining routes, involving combinations of two or more components. These routes could in principle continue indefinitely, generating a prolonged supportive environment.

## Conclusions

Peace education is a principal tool toward peace and reconciliation within societies involved in ongoing conflict. Peace education in contexts of intractable conflict refuses to accept their supposed intractability, aiming to reconstruct the worldview of the young generation toward facilitating conflict resolution and peace processes and preparing youth to live in an era of peace and reconciliation. Those initiatives socialize new generations to a new climate in which a culture of peace can emerge as a result of the process of reconciliation. Educating new generations about the importance of peace and ways toward achieving it is probably one of the most important challenges for human beings wherever they live.

Research shows that peace education programs in the context of intractable conflict can have clear positive impact. However, research also suggests that the effects of peace education programs are temporary, with participants reverting to their original mindsets in the months after completion of a program. Losses with time after a period of education are a common phenomenon with several contributing factors. Our analysis seeks to explain these losses in the case of peace education, at least in part, through the general idea of reality dissonance. After a program, learners reenter the pervasively belligerent climate of a culture of conflict, with friends, parents, local and national political figures, and media stories commonly expressing views sharply contrary to the goals of peace education. Learners typically encounter push back from such sources, few chances to act concretely on their new commitments, and few opportunities to maintain thoughtful and empathetic discourse around themes of peace.

Although reality dissonance is a formidable force, there may be more hope for peace education initiatives than seems apparent at first. The fact of the matter is that typical peace education initiatives in regions of intractable conflict do little to recognize or cope with reality dissonance. An interdisciplinary analysis of the theoretical and empirical literature on change and its sustainability suggests a better general model for effective peace education. Programs could include a number of "sustaining components" that specifically address the challenges of reality dissonance in different ways.

Looking beyond peace education, in general, sustainability does not seem to get much attention from educational scholars and practitioners. Yet the problem is widespread. Moreover, reality dissonance plausibly figures in losses following other programs seeking cognitive, emotional, and behavioral changes; for instance programs designed to ameliorate substance abuse or violent or criminal behaviors, when people exit into the same social and physical environments that maintained these patterns. Likewise, it is reasonable to suggest that strong versions of such programs would incorporate a number of sustaining components to combat reality dissonance. Such components are a clear presence in Alcoholics Anonymous for instance.

Turning again to the challenge of peace, some of the sustaining components mentioned are empirically proven in the context of peace education (e.g., perspective-taking, social networks). Empirical studies are needed to examine the effects of other methods and combinations proposed here. Results of these studies can improve our understanding of sustainable change toward peace in cultures of conflict.

## Notes

1. Meaning that a gain on one side involves an equivalent loss on the other.
2. Bar-Tal, D. (1998). "Societal Beliefs in Times of Intractable Conflict: the Israeli Case." *The International Journal of Conflict Management,* 9, 22–50; Bar-Tal, D. (2007). "Socio-Psychological Foundations of Intractable Conflicts." *American Behavioral Scientist,* 50, 1430–1453; Kriesberg, L. (1998). "Intractable Conflicts," in E. Weiner (ed.), *The Handbook of Interethnic Coexistence* (New York: The Continuum Publishing Company), pp.332–342.
3. IPCRI (2004). *Pathways into Reconciliation* Israel/Palestine Center for Research and Information (IPCRI).
4. CCEA (1997). *Mutual Understanding and Cultural Understanding: Cross-Curricular Guidance Material* (Belfast: Council for the Curriculum, Examinations and Assessment).

5. Danesh, H. and Clarke-Habibi, S. (2007). *Education for Peace Curriculum: a Manual for Teachers and Students* (Neuchatel, Switzerland: EFP-International).
6. For example, Kupermintz, H. and Salomon, G. (2005). "Lessons to Be Learned from Research on Peace Education in the Context of Intractable Conflict." *Theory into Practice*, 44, 4, pp.293–302.
7. Husseisi, R. (2009). *The relationshp between legitimizing the adversary's collective narrative and adherence to one's own narrative as a function of participation in a peace education program*. PhD Dissertation, University of Haifa (Hebrew).
8. Rosen, Y. and Salomon, G. (2011). "Durability of Peace Education Effects in the Shadow of Conflict." *Social Psychology of Education: An International Journal*, 14, pp.135–147.
9. Bar-Tal, D. and Rosen, Y. (2009). "Direct and Indirect Models of Peace Education." *Review of Educational Research*, 79, 2, pp.557–575; Bar-Tal, D. and Salomon, G. (2006). "Israeli-Jewish Narratives of the Israeli-Palestinian Conflict: Evolvement, Contents, Functions and Consequences," in: R. Rotberg (ed.), *History's Double Helix: the Intertwined Narratives of Israel/Palestine* (Bloomington: Indiana University Press), pp.19–46.
10. Aall, P. R., Helsing, J. W., and Tidwell, A. C. (2007). "Addressing conflict through education," in I. W. Zartman (ed.), *Peace Making in International Conflict: Methods and Techniques* (Revised Edition) (Washington: United States Institute of Peace Press), pp.327–354.
11. Abu-Nimer, M. (2004). "Education for Coexistence and Arab-Jewish Encounters in Israel: Potential and Challenges," *Journal of Social Issues*, 60, 2, pp.405–422.
12. See Bar-Tal, D. and Rosen, Y. (2009). "Direct and Indirect Models of Peace Education," *Review of Educational Research*, 79, 2, pp.557–575.
13. For example, Bar-Tal and Rosen, "Direct and Indirect Models of Peace Education," pp.557–575; Iram, Y. (2006). "Culture of Peace: Definition, Scope, and Application," in Y. Iram (ed.), *Educating towards a Culture of Peace* (Greenwich, CT: Information Age Publishing), pp. 3–12; Salomon, G. (2004). "a Narrative-Based View of Coexistence Education." *Journal of Social Issues*, 60, 2, pp.273–287; Staub, E. (2002). "From Healing Past Wounds to the Development of Inclusive Caring: Contents and Processes of Peace Education," in G. Salomon and B. Nevo (eds.), *Peace Education: the Concept, Principles, and Practices around the World* (Mahwah, NJ: Lawrence Erlbaum Associates Publishers), pp.73–88.
14. Maoz, I. (2000). "An Experiment in Peace: Reconciliation-Aimed Workshops for Jewish-Israeli and Palestinian Youth," *Journal of Peace Research*, 37, 6, pp.721–736; Maoz, I. (2004). "Coexistence Is in the Eye of the Beholder: Evaluating Intergroup Encounter Interventions between Jews and Arabs in Israel," *Journal of Social Issues*, 60, 2, pp.437–452.
15. Biton, Y. and Salomon, G. (2006). "Peace in the Eyes of Israeli and Palestinian Youth: Effects of Collective Narratives and Peace Education." *Journal of Peace Research*, 43, 2, pp.167–180.
16. Lustig, I., (2002). "The Effects of Studying Distal Conflicts on the Perception of a Proximal One." Unpublished master's thesis, University of Haifa.
17. Rosen, Y. (2008). "Can Peace Education Change Core Beliefs?" Paper presented at the American Educational Research Association Annual Meeting, New York.
18. Bar, H. and Bargal, D. (1995). *Living with the Conflict* (Jerusalem: Jerusalem Institute for Israeli Studies).
19. Bar-Natan, I., Rosen, Y., and Salomon, G. (2008). "Aspects of Friendship between Adversaries," Center for Research on Peace Education, University of Haifa.
20. Rosen, *Can Peace Education Change Core Beliefs?*"
21. Thomsen, C., Borgida, E., and Lavine, H. (1995). "The Causes and Consequences of Personal Involvement," in: R. Petty, J. Krosnick (eds.), *Attitude Strength* (Mahwah, NJ: Lawrence Erlbaum Associates), pp.191–214.

22. Sommers, M. (2004). *Co-Ordinating Education during Emergencies and Reconstruction: Challenges and Responsibilities* (New York: UNESCO), p.180.
23. Rosen, Y. and Perkins, D. (2013). "Shallow Roots Require Constant Watering: the Challenge of Sustained Impact in Educational Programs." *International Journal of Higher Education*, 2, 4, pp.91–100.
24. See for example the case of Northern Ireland in Duffy, T. (2000). "Peace Education in a Divided Society: Creating a Culture of Peace in Northern Ireland," *Prospects*, 30, 1, pp.15–29.
25. Bar-Tal, "Socio-Psychological Foundations of Intractable Conflicts," pp.1430–1453.
26. Atieh, A., Ben-Nun, G., El-Shahed, G., Taha, R., and Tulliu, S. (2005). *Peace in the Middle East: p2p and the Israeli–Palestinian Conflict* (Geneva: United Nations).
27. Bar-Natan, Rosen, and Salomon, "Aspects of Friendship between Adversaries."
28. Gardner, H. (2004). *Changing Minds* (Boston: Harvard Business School Press).
29. Perkins, D. (2008). "The Five Languages of War," in D. Berliner and H. Kupermintz (eds.), *Fostering Change in Institutions, Environments, and People* (Mahwah, NJ: Lawrence Erlbaum), pp. 171–192.
30. Rosandic, R. (2000). "Grappling with Peace Education in Serbia." Peaceworks no. 33 (Washington: United Stated Institute of Peace Press).
31. For a summary see Bar-Tal, D., Halperin, E. and de Rivera, J. (2007). "Collective Emotions in Conflict: Societal Implications," *Journal of Social Issues*, 63, pp.441–460.
32. Stephan, W. G. and Stephan, C. W. (2000). "An Integrated Theory of Prejudice," in S. Oskamp (ed.), *Reducing Prejudice and Discrimination* (Hillsdale, NJ: Erlbaum), pp.23–45.
33. Bar-Tal, "Socio-Psychological Foundations of Intractable Conflicts," pp.1430–1453.
34. Biton, Y. and Salomon, G. (2006). "Peace in the Eyes of Israeli and Palestinian Youth: Effects of Collective Narratives and Peace Education," *Journal of Peace Research*, 43, 2, pp.167–180; Bar-Natan, Rosen, Salomon, "Aspects of Friendship between Adversaries."
35. For example, Rosen, Y. (2008). "Can Peace Education Change Core Beliefs?" Paper presented at the American Educational Research Association Annual Meeting, New York.
36. For example, Goldman, D. (1998). *Working with Emotional Intelligence* (New York: Bantam Books); Gross, J. J. and Thompson, R. A. (2007). "Emotion Regulation: Conceptual Foundations," in J. J. Gross (ed.), *Handbook of Emotion Regulation* (New York: The Gilford Press), pp. 3–24.
37. For example, Rosen, Y. and Salomon, G. (2011). "Durability of Peace Education Effects in the Shadow of Conflict," *Social Psychology of Education: An International Journal*, 14, pp.135–147.
38. Fullan, M. (2007). *The New Meaning of Educational Change* (4th ed.) (Teachers College Press).
39. Perkins, D. (2008). "The Five Languages of War," in D. Berliner and H. Kupermintz (eds.), *Fostering Change in Institutions, Environments, and People* (Mahwah, NJ: Lawrence Erlbaum), pp.171–192.
40. Chi, M. T. H. (2005). "Commonsense Conceptions of Emergent Processes: Why Some Misconceptions Are Robust," *Journal of the Learning Sciences*, 14, 2, pp.161–199.
41. Strauss, S. and Shiloni, T. (1994). "Teachers' Models of Children's Minds and Learning." in L. A. Hirschfeld and S. A. Gelman (eds)., *Mapping the Mind* (New York: Cambridge University Press).
42. Dakof, G. A. et al. (2003). "Enrolling and Retaining Mothers of Substance-Exposed Infants in Drug Abuse Treatment," *Journal of Consulting & Clinical Psychology*, 71, pp.764–772.

43. Argyris, C. and Schön, D. (1996). *Organizational Learning: Theory, Method and Practice*, (Reading, MA: Addison Wesley).
44. Fullan, M. (1997). "The Complexity of the Change Process," in M. Fullan (ed.), *The Challenge of School Change* (IRI/SkyLight), pp. 33–56; Fullan, M. (2007). *The New Meaning of Educational Change* (4th ed.) (Teachers College Press).
45. Sarason, S. (1971). *The Culture of the School and the Problem of Change* (Boston: Allyn & Bacon).
46. Sims, S. J. and Sims, R. R. (2004). *Managing School System Change: Charting a Course for Renewal* (Information Age).
47. Senge, P. et al. (1999). *The Dance of Change* (New York: Doubleday).
48. Huberman, M. and Miles, M. (1984). *Innovation Up Close* (New York: Plenum).
49. Kelman, S. (2005). *Unleasing Change: a Study of Organizational Renewal in Government* (Washington: The Brooking Institution).
50. Ibid.
51. Festinger, L. (1957). *A Theory of Cognitive Dissonance* (Stanford, California: Evanston, Stanford University Press); Harmon-Jones, E., and Mills, J. (1999). "An Introduction," in: E., Harmon-Jones. and J. Mills. (eds.), *Cognitive Dissonance: Progress on Pivotal Theory in Social Psychology* (Washington, DC: APA), (pp.3–25).
52. Freedman, J. L. and Fraser, S. C. (1966). "Compliance without Pressure: The Foot-in-the-Door Technique," *Journal of Personality and Social Psychology*, 4, pp.195–202; Burger, J. M. (1999). "The Foot-in-the-Door Compliance Procedure: a Multiple-Process Analysis and Review," *Personality and Social Psychology Review*, 3, pp.303–325.
53. Myrick, R. D. (1993). *Developmental Guidance and Counseling: a Practical Approach* (2nd ed.) (Minneapolis, MN: Educational Media Corporation); Dueck, G. (1993). "Picture Peer Partner Learning: Students Earning from and with Each Other," Instructional Strategies Series 10 (Saskatoon: Saskatchewan Professional Development Unit); Whiteman, N. A. (1988). "Peer Teaching: To Teach Is to Learn Twice," ASHE-ERIC Higher Education Report No. 4 (Washington, DC: Association for the Study of Higher Education); Ross, L. and Nisbett, R. E. (1991). *The Person and the Situation: Perspectives on Social Psychology* (New York: McGraw-Hill).
54. Berry, F. S. and Berry, W. D. (1999). "Innovation and Diffusion Models in Policy Research," in P. A. Sabatier (ed.), *Theories of the Policy Process* (Boulder, CO: Westview), pp.169–200; Chakerian, R. and Mavima, P. (2000). "Comprehensive Administrative Reform Implementation: Moving beyond Single Issue Implementation Research," *Journal of Public Administration Research and Theory*, 11, pp.353–377; Mazmanian, D. A. and Sabatier, P. A. (1989). *Implementation and Public Policy: With a New Postscript* (Latham, MD: University Press of America); Thompson, J. R. and Fulla, S. L. (2001). "Effecting Change in a Reform Context: The National Performance Review and the Contingencies of 'Microlevel' Reform Implementation," *Public Performance and Management Review*, 25, pp.155–175.
55. Kupermintz, H. and Salomon, G. (2005). "Lessons to Be Learned from Research on Peace Education in the Context of Intractable Conflict," *Theory into Practice*, 44, 4.
56. Bar-Tal and Rosen, "Direct and Indirect Models of Peace Education," pp.557–575.
57. Rosen, Y. and Perkins, D. (in press). "Shallow Roots Require Constant Watering: the Challenge of Sustained Impact in Educational Programs," *International Journal of Educational Research*.
58. Rosen, Y. (2008). "Can Peace Education Change Core Beliefs?" Paper presented at the American Educational Research Association Annual Meeting, New York.
59. Roth, A. (2005). "Structuring the Adversary's Narrative during An Intractable Conflict as Part of Peace Education through Internet-Based Exchanges," Unpublished Master's thesis, Faculty of Education, University of Haifa.

60. See for example, Zoubi. B. (2007). "The Effects of Participations in Bi-National Soccer Clubs on Perception of the Other Side in the Conflict Among Jewish and Arab Youth," Unpublished Master's thesis, Faculty of Education, University of Haifa, in the context of sports projects.
61. Jayusi, W. (2011). "Attitudinal Rehabilitation of Peace Education Participants by Peer-Tutoring," Unpublished doctoral dissertation, Faculty of Education, University of Haifa.

# 11

# Because "I Care": From an Encounter to a Political Option

*Francois Mifsud*

## Introduction

The encounter with "the other" creates a dilemma of how and in what way the self will respond to this "other." In this chapter, the concept of "the other" is used to signify those who differ from an individual or group ("the self" or "the we") in some way that the self/we perceives to be significant. This difference may refer to features like culture, religion, nationality, political ideology, or language. "The other" is interpreted both as a singular and as plural noun. Thus, "the other" can be either a she/he or a "they/them."

Don Lorenzo Milani responded to his meeting with "the other" with a radical political option by establishing the school of Barbiana. When Milani was sent as a pastor to the small village of Barbiana in the Tuscan mountains, he took with him a cultural and social baggage that marked him apart from the villagers. Milani was urbane, with an upper-middle-class background, while the villagers were peasants and mostly illiterate. Though Milani and the people of Barbiana were different in many ways, they developed a dialogical relationship that set the basis for their political struggle for equality and peace. Milani and the students of the School of Barbiana grounded their dialogical action and their political option in the ethical value of love and care for "the other." The book *Letter to a Teacher*, which they wrote collectively, clearly states that the school's educational goal is to engage in dialogical and relation activity with "the other." The school acknowledged that this dialogical and relational goal is motivated and realized through love; an insight they articulated in the school's motto: "I Care."

> The goal is to dedicate oneself to one's neighbour. And in this century, how can one wish to love if not through politics or though the trade union or

through education? We are sovereign. It's no longer time for begging, but for choices. Against the classists that you are, against hunger, illiteracy, racism, the colonial wars. But this is only the final goal, which must be remembered from time to time. The one to remember minute by minute is to understand others and to make oneself understood...Man needs to love one another even beyond borders.[1]

The radical political option for "the other" by the School of Barbiana is not an isolated case or a historical rarity. Throughout the years, many people transformed their encounter with "the other" into a political option for this "other." Yet, there were also instances, where the encounter with "the other" generated indifference and exclusion, even when the motives that lead to this encounter were moral or honest. Cases in point were many missionary and "expeditionary" adventures, originally undertaken with the best of intentions (seeking the good of this "other"), where however "the other" ended up being dehumanized, patronized, or exploited.

This chapter argues that the encounter with "the other" holds only a possibility of transforming this encounter into a political option and action for "the other." I argue that for the encounter to be developed into political action and into an option for "the other" it needs an ethical ideal. This ethical ideal is identified with the notion of *interest*. *Interest* is the key concept in this chapter. It is taken as that which transforms the encounter with "the other" into a political option for "the other." In the chapter I use "ethic" in the singular. This highlights a conception of ethics—of "the good life"—that is specific to every human being. It is an ethic where the self/us perceives itself in the encounter with "the other"; an encounter that supposes the possibility of relationality and dialogue between diversity. *Interest* is reflected in the maxim the School of Barbiana adopted: "I Care." In Milani's life and work; "I Care" becomes the moving and creative force behind the establishment of the School of Barbiana and behind his involvement in many political issues of post–Second World War Italy. The object of this article is not to recount historical and biographical facts about Milani, but to explore the necessity of ethic as a dialogical bridge between the awareness of the "the other," and the political option and action for "the other."

To identify better the role and necessity of ethic as interest in generating a political option for the other I contrast it to two other approaches through which the relation between the "we/self" and "the other" may be conceived. In the first section, I critically analyze Chantal Mouffe's political theory, focusing on the relation between "diversity" and "the political." Mouffe is an advocate for the modern dichotomy between ethics and politics, and consigns ethics to the private realm. In the second chapter I consider the positivistic approach to the issue of the relationship between the "I/self" and "the other."[2] I claim that whereas a positivistic approach to "the other" may recognize this as other, this recognition does not generate relationality with the "other," but the *intentional alienation*[3] of "the other" by the self.

The final section explains the necessity of ethic as *interest* in transforming the encounter with "the other" into a radical political option and action. The School of Barbiana with its maxim "I Care" evidences the dialogical and the relational space that ethic as *interest* can generate; transforming the encounter with "the other" into a political option for "the other." For the school of Barbiana "I Care" is not an ethical ideal to be attained, but a dialogical and relational space on which the alternation of teaching and learning occur. In this chapter, "I Care" is considered as a prime motivator for relationality and for a dialogical engagement with "the other"; accordingly ethic as *interest* is interpreted as *what* actualizes the possibility of dialogical engagement.

## Epistemology of "the Other" and "the Political"

What we can assert in this stage is that the we/they distinction, which is the condition of possibility of formation of political identities, can always become the locus of an antagonism. Since all forms of political identities entail a we/they distinction, this means that the possibility of emergence of antagonism can never be eliminated. It is therefore an illusion to believe in the advent of a society from which antagonism would have been eradicated.[4]

Chantal Mouffe recognizes that the tension that *we/they distinction* generates is inevitable; that it is intrinsic to the human relational nature. In this regard, she makes use of Carl Schmitt's political interpretation of human relations as a constant tension between binary oppositions. Mouffe however goes further. She identifies "the political" with the tension that the *we/they distinction* creates. The political is the space where the *we* and the *they* come across. Mouffe, however, does recognize a difference in the quality of tension that the *we/they distinction* generates. This tension can be either antagonistic or agonistic. Both antagonism and agonizm trace the origin of the *we/they distinction* in the otherness of the other. Without otherness (diversity) there is neither conflict nor communion since both conflict and communion subsist on the otherness of the subjects.

By antagonistic tension Mouffe understands a situation where the *we* perceive the *they* as an enemy. A case in point where the we/they tension is expressed in an antagonistic way is in a nondemocratic and nondialogical context. In an agonistic context on the other hand, the *we* perceive "the other's otherness" as legitimate. The tension between the *we* and the *they* assumes a more agonistic quality and the *we* would perceive the *they* as adversaries. This occurs, in a more dialogical and democratic context, as in a parliament between different political groups.

Mouffe believes that democracy is the type of political organization that has the potentiality of transforming an antagonistic relation between enemies (where the different other is to be eliminated) into an adversary relation. Democracy according to Mouffe has the potentiality of transforming antagonism into agonizm because democracy perceives diversity as legitimate and is protected by a legal framework. It is important to note that both antagonism and agonizm perceive the beginning of a *we/them* relation through the recognition of the otherness of the other, the only difference between the two being the quality of the relation between the *we* and the *they*.

> Envisaged from the point of view of "agonistic pluralism", the aim of democratic politics is to construct the "them" in such a way that it is no longer perceived as an enemy to be destroyed but as an "adversary", that is, somebody whose ideas we combat but whose right to defend those ideas we do not put into question. This is the real meaning of liberal-democratic tolerance, which does not entail condoning ideas that we oppose or being indifferent to standpoints that we disagree with, but treating those who defend them as legitimate opponents.[5]

"The political" for Mouffe becomes the arena or space where the *we* and the *they* come across, generating either antagonistic or agonistic relation. Both antagonism and agonizm need this. They need "the political" space to generate social structures, institutions, and practices which Mouffe identifies with "politics." The distinction between "politics" and "the political" is illustrated in the following way:

> [B]y "the political" I mean the dimension of antagonism which I take to be constitutive of human societies, while by "politics" I mean the set of practices and institutions through which an order is created, organizing human coexistence in the context of conflictuality provided by the political.[6]

Mouffe situates the distinction between the *we* and the *they* within an epistemological discourse, wherein the eye that perceives "the other" as "other" is never a naked eye but an eye that perceives through cultural and social constructs. Thus, in her thought there is an organic relationship between epistemology and "the political." For Mouffe, the epistemological act; the act through which we come to know, perceive and distinguish things in the world, including those who are perceived as *we* and those who are perceived as *they*, creates both the dichotomous perception of *we/they* and also political relationality; be it antagonism or agonizm. The inevitability of the two (the epistemological and the political) is expressed with an *ergo*[7]; an *obvious* relation between "the political" (antagonism or agonizm) and the *we/they distinction*:

> This point is decisive. It is because every object has inscribed in its very being something other than itself and that as a result, everything is constructed as difference, that its being cannot be conceived as pure "presence" or "objective". Since the constitutive outside is present within the inside as its always real possibility, every identity becomes purely contingent.[8]

Mouffe draws attention to this in various entries, for instance her criticism of Anthony Giddens's "Third Way" political theory. For Mouffe, postpolitical theories as Giddens's are theories that perceive contemporary

Western society as a society that exists beyond ideologies; beyond any division into "left" or "right," "progressive" and "reactionary," and so on. Mouffe on the other hand, calls the denial of ideologies as "ahistorical" and nondemocratic. Her conception of democracy is not of an abolition or assimilation of the *they* into *we* but of a political space that legitimizes the *they* as *other* and thus transform the *they* into an object of agonistic relation for the *we*.

Giddens's notion of a "Third Way" is unacceptable, because it is constructed on an "ahistorical" notion of a *we* that subsists without the *they*. Giddens's ideal of going beyond ideology is nondemocratic, because it eliminates other ideologies for the benefit of what ultimately is nothing but an ideology. Mouffe interprets the tragic events of 9/11 as evidence for both the unavoidable presence of the *we/they distinction* and of the historical inconsistency of Giddens's postpolitical ideal.

> It is also worth underlining that Giddens designates this new democratic state as "the state without enemies" and much of his argument is based on the idea that, with the passing of the bipolar era, states now face not enemies but dangers; hence the need to look for other sources of legitimacy than the ones provided by the threat of war. Those considerations were of course published before the events of 11 September 2001 and today, with the unleashing of the "war against terrorism", they seem hopelessly outdated.[9]

Mouffe's notion of "the political" entails the plurality and the diversity of the *we/they distinction*, and motivates her to exclude ethics from "the political." According to Mouffe in a modern political context there is no place for the Aristotelian merging between ethics and "the political."[10] For Mouffe, ethical discourse eradicates diversity and thus the *we/they distinction* on which antagonism or agonizm (the political) subsists. Mouffe considers ethical discourse as a prescriptive discourse. In contrast, discourse relating to "the political," which is generally more creative and critical. Thus Mouffe fully supports the liberal ideal where only "the political" should be situated in the public arena:

> The emergence of the individual, the separation of Church and State, the principle of religious tolerance, the development of civil society—all these elements have led us to distinguish the domain of morality from that of politics. If it is important to pose once again the question of the common good and that of civic virtue, this must be done in a modern fashion, without postulating a single moral good.[11]

## Positivistic Epistemology as *Intentional Alienation* of the Other

Positivism is a major approach in philosophy, the emergence of which is associated with Auguste Comte. The word "positivism," however, is also commonly used to denote one twentieth-century group of positivists, the

Logical Positivists.[12] In very crude and general terms, positivism claims that genuine knowledge "is scientific, in the sense of describing the co-existence and succession of observable phenomena."[13]

Hence, true knowledge is built from data that is exclusively derived from sensory experience. This data, however, can provide knowledge only if processed through logical and mathematical methods.

Positivist epistemology entails:

> an empiricism about scientific knowledge, which rests on observation as the moment of truth when hypotheses are tested against the facts of the world.[14]

Observation is the only justifiable epistemological method through which knowledge can be attained. Observation is categorically restricted to sensorial experience.[15] Now observation assumes:

> that the world exist independently of us, that perception gives knowledge of some particular items of its furniture and that there is no way of knowing a priori (i.e., independent of experience) what else it contains.[16]

This positivist premise is rooted in a dichotomy between human observation and the world that goes back to Descartes. Descartes's philosophy is characterized by a chasm between the perceiving subject and the world. The individual's cognition is the starting point of knowledge.[17] Epistemology hence, relates primarily to the individual's knowledge of the world, not to the subject's relationship to the world. The very existence of such world is not self-evident and requires argument to be ascertained.

Yet, positivism differs from Cartesian philosophy in an important respect. Though it assumes the dichotomy between human observation and world, it challenges the Cartesian tradition that takes the self, the "I," as the starting point and benchmark of knowledge. Within Cartesian philosophy, the subject has to verify knowledge she/he believes her/himself to obtain from the world; a world that contains not only inanimate objects, but also other human beings. In positivism on the other hand, in order to obtain sound epistemological knowledge, the subject need not seek to verify the existence of outside world. The world is thought to be accessible (only) through sensory experience, which is also the benchmark that guarantees any knowledge the subject thinks her/himself to possess. Experience, conceived to be made up of data received directly from the world through the senses, an insight positivism adopts from the empiricist tradition, and experiment are the yardsticks by means of which claims to knowledge are assessed; excluding any type knowledge (or indeed, any proposition), which is either held to be true a priori or not susceptible to empirical verification.

Positivist ideals applied to the sphere of society encourage neither antagonist nor agonistic encounters; any sort of engagement between the *we* and the *they*. Rather, positivist parameters set one method and ideal, and everyone has to fit and abide by this ideal. Consequently, positivist epistemology excludes any knowledge that is not ultimately verifiable or derived from experience. If some "others"; some *they*; uphold a different epistemology or way of engaging with the world, their epistemology and way of engaging with the world is dismissed. This creates further distance between the positivist *we* and the nonpositivist *they*. The latter are either dismissed or forced to converge into *we*. Hence, positivism ends up encouraging conformity rather than a relation (be it agonistic or antagonistic) where the diversity of different parties (including diversity in the way of conceiving and making sense of the world) is acknowledged. If one or both parties conceive the world according to parameters that are not those of the empirical sciences, this/these parties are enjoined to abandon their approach. We have the *Intentional alienation* of the other; the other ceasing to be either an enemy or an adversary, but being simply dismissed if his/her way of engaging with the world is not considered scientific. Hence there is not engagement, but estrangement.

Positivism reaches the same conclusion that Mouffe reaches, that is banishing it. Yet, the reasons why Positivism banishes ethical discourse are different from those that Mouffe presents. Whereas Mouffe excludes ethics in the name of the ideals of diversity and plurality, positivism excludes them because of its monolithic epistemology and conception of knowledge; considering any other form of knowledge that is not based upon or derived from empirical sources not just inferior, but false. Ethics is generally considered by Positivists to consist of a number of propositions that cannot be empirically verified. Hence, ethics is thought to contradict the positivist method.

## The Limits of Mouffe and of Positivism

Both approaches presented in the previous sections evidence important shortcomings. Mouffe for instance, underestimates an important element that links the *we* and the *they*,[18] the fact that the *we* may display an *interest* in the *they*. The etymological definition of *interest*; from the Latin *inter* and *esse* ("to be in between"); points to the potentiality that the *self* and/or *we* has/have of transcending itself to relationally engage with the *other/they*. It is a relation that is both epistemological and ethical. *Interest* is a deliberate response to the "other"; to the way in which the "other" lives, acts, and engages with the world. *Interest* then is the moving force that motivates the *we* into "the political" relation with the *them*.

*Interest* then, shows the limits of Mouffe's stance in confining ethics to the private realm; the limits of excluding ethical ideals from the public and "the political" dimension.[19] Mouffe's conception of "the political" as "engagement with the eclectic and the diverse" would justify the exclusion of the "ethical" only if "ethics" were conceived to entail a dogmatic and monolithic conception of the "good," and/or "the indivisibility of ethics and politics."[20] The notion of *interest* as an ethical ideal on the other hand, avoids both this dogmatism and the promotion of a monolithic conception of the good.

The ethical engagement of the *we* with the *them* does not necessarily contradict Mouffe's notion of "the political." Indeed *interest*, encapsulated in the maxim upheld by the School of Barbiana "I Care," entails that ethics may complement and enhance "the political" (in Mouffe's sense of the term).[21] The ethical ideal encapsulated in this slogan ("I Care") is not based on some abstract conception or ideal that generates a rigid and generalizing notion of ethics that seeks to perpetuate preconceived values and ideals. It is sensitive to the newness of the encounter of the *we/self* with the *other*. Indeed, the interest in and encounter with "the other" makes ethics (or "ethic") subjectively open for newness. It becomes the dynamic relational force that respects and enhances the diversity of "the other"; the link between the *we/they* and "the political." *Interest* for "the other" cannot be left out of the political sphere because it cannot be confined to a private or public realm. It needs to be present in every encounter with "the other." "Interest also has the power of transforming the instance (event) in which the 'we' or 'self' perceive/s 'the other' into a political option for 'the other.'"

This is in sharp contrast with what Mouffe maintains. As stated, for Mouffe:

> [T]he aim of democratic politics is to construct the "them" in such a way that it is no longer perceived as an enemy to be destroyed but as an "adversary."[22]

"Agonizm" is attained through a "construct" of the *them*, whereby the determining agent that includes diversity and transforms it into an agonistic relation is always the "self/we." In Mouffe "construction" is related to epistemology; to how one knows "the other." Since knowing "the other" does not entail encounter him/her/them but constructing "the other," her epistemology has one exclusive agent; the *we* that constructs the other. This excludes the epistemological newness that the encounter with "the other" generates.

Milani is not a philosopher who espouses a specific epistemology or presents a theory of knowledge. Yet, it is obvious that Mouffe's epistemology and politics, entailing that the *we* construct "the other" rather than engaging with him/her/they, is clearly incompatible with the ethos that the motto "I Care" encapsulates. The latter is more consonant with an epistemology that is conducive/open to the surprising encounter (newness) with "the other." But Mouffe's philosophy is not the only one that is incompatible with the ethos of the School of Barbiana. So is positivism.

Positivism evidences important shortcomings with regards to openness to "the Other." In claiming explicitly that its prescribed method is the only method (indeed "the method") that can guarantee knowledge, positivism excludes "the other." Other forms of gaining knowledge that do not follow positivistic procedures are simply dismissed as *not* or *less* epistemological. They are thought to provide inferior or invalid knowledge.

> The driving idea of Logical Positivism was that, because claims to knowledge of the world can be justified only by experience, we are never entitled to assert the existence of anything beyond all possible experience. It can never be probable, let alone certain, that these are, for instance, unobservable structures, forces, instincts or dialectical processes. Indeed it cannot even be possible, since to speak of them is technically meaningless, except as shorthand for observable regularities in experience. Knowledge is grounded in particular observations and can extend to general beliefs only in so far as experience can confirm them.[23]

The positivist perception of "knowledge" and its dismissal of types of knowledge that do not conform to positivist canons do not encourage diversity and relationality between different ways of conceiving the world and coming to know this.

Moreover, as stated, positivist epistemology claims that the epistemological role of the self is to "observe the world," while at the same time supposing a "neutral and detached" position from the reality being observed. These hold even when "observing" and coming to know "the other." Hence, positivism excludes the necessity of an encounter with "the other," or rather "the other" is encountered only as an "object"; as material to be observed and analyzed. A concrete example of the influence of observational and nonrelational discourse on politics is when countries evaluate and dictate the politics of other countries based on their own political ideals and agenda and not on a concrete grassroots relation with other countries.

Positivism then, begins with the *self/we* observing and scrutinizing, and concludes with the *self/we* collecting and comparing evidence, and maybe conjecturing some hypothesis that is strictly compatible with the collected data and the parameters of the natural science. Interest on the other hand, requires the reversal of this epistemological point of departure. Instead of having the *self/we* as subject and "the other" as the object of epistemology, interest requires an epistemological experience that deconstructs the *we* and *they distinction*. "The other" in the relation that is envisaged, is not a passive object of observation but a relational object. In ethics conceived as interest the self is letting her/himself be confronted by "the other's" needs; while the other instigates in the self an awareness of her/his involvement in causing "the other" to suffer. Such awareness can be attained because ethics as interest creates the epistemological conditions for the self to be surprised by the newness and otherness of "the other." The moment of this encounter is superbly illustrated by Levinas:

> From the depths of natural perseverance in the being of the being of a being who is assured of his right to be, from the heart of the original identity of the I—and against that perseverance, and against that identity—there arises, awakened before the face of the other, a responsibility for the other to whom I was committed before any committing, before being present to myself or coming back to self.[24]

## "I Care" as a Relational and Dialogical Space

Interest, encapsulated in the maxim "I Care," generates an awareness of "the other" that induces the *we/self* to be surprised by "the other." The more the *we/self* is surprised by the distinctiveness and newness of "the other" the more *interest* for "the other" is generated. It does not allow *we/self* to assimilate "the other" into the *we/self,* but instead it opts to relate with "the other" as other; to explore the otherness of "the other."[25] The subject this endeavor requires is not the *self/we* scrutinizing the world of positivism or Mouffe's self/we agonistically constructing the *they*. The subject it requires is born continuously anew out of the encounter of the *we/self* with the *them/other*. This encounter is splendidly expressed in the words of Levinas characterization of the crude encounter with "the face 'the other'":

> [T]he face facing me, in its expression—in its mortality—summons me, demands me, requires me: as if the invisible death faced by the face of the other—pure alterity, separate, somehow, from any whole- were "my business." As if, unknown by the other whom already, in the nakedness of his face, it concerns, it "regarded me" before its confrontation with me, before being the death that starts me, myself, in the face...It is precisely in that recalling me to my responsibility by the face that summons me, that demands me, that requires me—it is in that calling into question—that the other is my neighbour.[26]

## Notes

1. School of Barbian (2009), p.109.
2. Regarding "Positivism," the objective of this chapter is not to make an analysis of the limits and possibilities of positivism as a philosophical movement, but only consider positivism in relation to the influence it exerted on the ways in which one may conceive "the other" and relate with him/her/them.
3. This concept is explained later on in the chapter.
4. Mouffe (2008), p.16.
5. Mouffe (2009), p.102.
6. Mouffe (2008), p.9.
7. *Ergo* in Latin is stronger than the word therefore because it is an identification of two notions with each other. This leads one notion into assuming the other.
8. Mouffe (2009), p.21.
9. Mouffe (2008), p.59.
10. Chantal Mouffe beliefs that an Aristotelian merging of ethics and politics is not an ideal political approach for Modern and liberal diverse society, instead she opts for a Machiavellian dichotomy between ethics/morality and "the political."
11. Mouffe (2005), p.33.
12. The New Fontana Dictionary of Modern Thought (1999), p.669.
13. Ibid.
14. Hollis (1994), p.42.
15. It is categorical because only what is defined as sensorial and experiential by positivism is accepted as so.
16. Hollis (1994), pp.45–46.

17. "Descartes argues that the existence of sensible objects might be uncertain, because it would be possible for a deceitful demon to mislead us. We should substitute for a deceitful demon a cinema in technicolour. It is, of course, also possible that we may be dreaming. But he regards the existence of our thoughts as wholly unquestionable. When he says 'I think, therefore I am', the primitive certainties at which he may be supposed to have arrived are particular 'thoughts', in the large sense in which he uses the term. His own existence is an inference from his thoughts…In the context, what appears certain to him is that there is doubting." Russell (1992), p.188.
18. A relational engagement that, as we have seen, for Mouffe may be only agonistic or antagonistic.
19. The relational engagement between the *we* and the *they* or "other" is not automatic, entailing an *ergo*, as Mouffe suggested. One motive that may move one to relationally engage; indeed *the motive* that should move us to relationally engage with "the other," is interest as defined in this chapter.
20. Mouffe (2005), p.36.
21. That *interest* toward "the other" that "I Care" encapsulated is clearly evidenced in the critique the School of Barbarian made of the exam system in Italy (as evidenced in *Letter to A Teacher*). The school accuses formal education of being exclusive and a-educational, and of reinforcing the classist situation in Italy and isolating Italians from non-Italians. The school of Barbaina on the other hand, promoted voyages outside Italy as a pedagogical strategy, enabling students both to test their linguistic abilities and their ability to dialogue and relate with "the other." It also led them to question their culture and worldview.
22. Mouffe (2009), p.102.
23. Hollis (1994), pp.42–43.
24. Levinas (1999), pp.30–31.
25. It also induces the *we/self* to self-criticism; a criticism that frees the *we/self* from myths and fantasies, the most important being the myths of objectivity and those which exclude and make an object of "the other." Milani does not articulate clearly this, but implicitly evidences it in various ways. A case in point is the approach to history that the school of Barbiana adopts. The school's historical-critical analysis motivates students to trespass the patriotic frontiers, which were limiting the possibility of understanding and communication with "the other," and being open to the latter's vision and narrative. "History is the subject that has suffered most. There may be some books which are a little bit different. But I'd like to obtain information about the ones which are used most. Generally it's not history. It's a little provincial and biased story written by winners to the peasant. Italy is the centre of the world. The losers are all bad, the winners are all good. All that is mentioned are kings, generals, stupid wars between nations. The suffering and struggles of the workers are either ignored or given marginal importance. Woe to whoever is disliked by generals or producers or armaments. In the book which is considered to be most modern, Gandhi is mentioned briefly in 9 lines. Without a mention of his philosophy, let alone the method he used." School of Barbian (2009), p.135.
26. Levinas (1999), p.24.

# References

Carnap, R. (1995). *An Introduction to the Philosophy of Science*. Ed. M. Garner. New York: Dover Publications, Inc.

Chérif, M. (2008). *Islam and the West: A Conversation with Jacques Derrida*. Trans. T. Lavender Fagan. Chicago: The University of Chicago Press.

Derrida, J. (2007). *On Cosmopolitanism and Forgiveness*. Trans. M. Dooley and M. Hughes. New York: Routledge Taylor and Francis Group.
———. (2005). *The Politics of Friendship*. Trans. G. Collins. New York: Verso.
———. (2002). *Acts of Religion*. Ed. G. Anidjar. London: Routledge.
———. (2000). *Of Hospitality: Anne Defourmantelle Invites Jacques Derrida to Respond*. Trans. R. Bowlby. Stanford, CA: Stanford University Press.
———. (1998). *Monolingualism of the Other Or the Prosthesis of Origin*. Trans. P. Mensah. Stanford, CA: Stanford University Press.
Hollis, M. (1994). *The Philosophy of Social Science: An Introduction*. New York: Cambridge University Press.
Kapuściński, R. (2008). *The Other*. New York: Verso.
Levinas, E. (1999). *Alterity and Transcendence*. Trans. M. B. Smith. New York: Columbia University Press.
Meyers, R.G. (2006). *Understanding Empiricism*. Malta: Acumen.
Mouffe, C. (2009). *The Democratic Paradox*. New York: Verso.
———. (2008). *On The Political*. New York: Routledge.
———. (2005). *The Return of the Political*. New York: Verso.
Russel, B. (2004). *History of Western Philosophy*. New York: Routledge Classics.
———. (1992). *Human Knowledge: Its Scope and Limits*. London: Routledge.
School of Barbian (2009). "Letter to a Teacher." In C. Borg, M. Cardona, and S. Caruana (ed. and trans.), *Letter to a Teacher: Lorenzo Milani's Contribution to Critical Citizenship*. Malta: Agenda.
Tarnas, R. (1991). *The Passion of Western Mind: Understanding the Ideas That Have Shaped Our World View*. New York: Ballantine Books.

# Part III

# Peace, Democracy, Sexuality, Gender, and Aesthetics

# 12

# Peace Education and Critical Democracy: Some Challenges in Neoliberal Times

*John P. Portelli*

## Introduction

The concept of peace education is a contested and suspect concept.[1] Different scholars have conceived of peace and peace education in substantively different ways. As such it has been difficult to fully agree on a universal definition of peace education. However, referring to the work of Anderson, Trifonas, and Wright claim that his definition of peace may provide a working definition. Peace is:

> the absence of violence to any aspect of human life. [2]

Regarding peace education, the same authors note that this is at time viewed suspiciously given its "trope and historical baggage throughout the ages."[3] At times, the literature on peace education has lacked a certain rigor and reduced peace to a number of slogans like: no peace education without dialogue, no peace education without celebrating differences; no peace education without accepting "the other"; no peace education without democratic education. Each of these slogans captures a crucial aspect of peace education but none is sufficient to encapsulate the richness of peace education and the concept of peace. Moreover, unfortunate misunderstandings exist regarding most of the concepts included in these slogans.

The aim of this chapter is to identify and unpack challenges that democratic education faces in our neoliberal context. [4] An understanding and critical discussion of these challenges are meant to contribute to the ongoing conversation about the clarification and enacting of peace education.

One further introductory comment before I proceed with the argument of the chapter. As Bar-Tal[5] has noted, peace education is also an elusive concept. This is inevitably so since the concept intrinsically involves "a vision of a desirable society."[6] Bar-Tal argues that while there is common agreement that peace education aims at making "the world a better, more humane place," [7] such a commonly accepted vision is interpreted within the ideological beliefs of a certain country.[8] Given that such beliefs vary, it is inevitable that the meaning of the commonly accepted aim varies from context to context, and hence, naturally, the elusive nature of peace education. This is a fact that we have to accept in our considerations of the concept and any programs that are developed under its umbrella. It is also crucial that we identify the conceptual or ideational framework from which we operate. This paper is written from the perspective of critical democracy. As will be evident from the next section, critical democracy is consistent with peace education as:

> a social criticism applied to education. It criticizes those political decisions in education which instead of peace promote violence inside a given society as well as between societies. [9]

Lorenzo Milani strongly believed in and practiced the social criticism component in education. He was very perceptive of the political and educational decisions in his time. And he rigorously and collaboratively prepared the students in his school to understand the importance of and to practice social criticism. Another crucial tenet underlying Milani's practice is the importance of fulfilling the needs of students. As such both the collaborative approach he adopted and the content he dealt with were adapted to the needs of the students while at the same time aiming for the highest expectations. His focus on students' needs is another crucial point in critical democracy that will guide the argument of this chapter.

## Neoliberalism and Critical Democracy

Simply stated, democratic education is an education that takes democracy and its associated values seriously both in theory and in practice. However, both education and democracy are much contested concepts. In fact, there are differing and conflicting conceptions and practices of both. [10]

Democracy is both a moral and political ideal. And as such we know that it will never be fully achieved or finished. This is the very nature of ideals. As an ideal we believe that it is indeed worthwhile to struggle to achieve democracy and the beliefs, conditions, and practices that go with it. As a moral and political ideal, democracy substantively deals with how we as human beings ought to relate with each other. As John Dewey[11] has argued, democracy proposes a way of life that is the most humane. It is crucial here to note that when we talk about democratic education we are not referring to an education that follows so-called democratic governance. The focus is on the democratic *way of life* that needs to be enacted in educational institutions.

But what is involved in the democratic way of life? The literature on democracy has identified this way of life by using differing terms: liberal democracy, marketized democracy, minimalist democracy, participatory democracy, deliberative democracy, cosmopolitan democracy, critical democracy, thick and thin democracy, and strong democracy.[12] Each of these terms captures a different way of life associated with democracy. In general, adherents of democracy would concede that democracy, however it is conceived, is constantly being reconstructed,[13] or rewritten,[14] or rethought,[15] or rediscovered.[16] But the crucial question is whether or not democracy is anything we wish it to be. While definitely allowing for the reimagining of democracy as social conditions change, I contend that such reimagining does not imply that there are no core qualities associated with democracy that we cannot give up without exhibiting undemocratic values or actions. There is a democratic soul so to speak. For example, how can one claim to be democratic while abandoning human rights, or promoting racism (individual or systemic, consciously or unconsciously), or promoting the abuse of human beings? Surely one of the central litmus tests of democracy is how we deal with differences. Democracy is not a way of life or a moral and political ideal that promotes standardization or one-size-fits-all, or that promotes fear and shuts off the inquiry into differing albeit conflicting views. The authoritarian crushes disagreements and differences; the soft liberal puts disagreements aside as he or she believes they are all fine as long as they do not interfere with the rights of the individual; the genuine democrat acknowledges the differences, does not shy away from disagreements, and rather than crushing or hiding disagreements and differences, he or she meaningfully engages with disagreements and differences. The crucible that democracy accepts, of its very nature, is to deal with substantive differences in a humane manner. And this is exactly the connection with cosmopolitanism since it "calls for citizens who can respond in ways consistent with the inherent dignity of human beings"[17] while exposing citizens to "the diverse perspectives of others"[18] through which one's own views are challenged.

But are the procedures of dialogue, open inquiry, and tolerant and critical demeanors sufficient for the survival of the democratic way of life? Overall, pragmatists believe in the faith of the scientific method or procedures in dealing with substantive differences.[19] Others, including critical democrats,[20] argue that the democratic way of life demands more that procedures that are deemed to be neutral and objective. A robust democratic way of life has to go beyond procedural matters and deal with substantive issues.

Unfortunately the neoliberal culture that has dominated the "Western world" (and is now being forced on "other" worlds) has militated against the growth of a robust democratic culture. As the nineteenth-century liberal individualism and negative freedom shifted to the excessive individualism and the so-called free market, excessive competition and league tables, presumed neutrality and objectivity, standardization, narrow utility and accountability have dominated our way of life.[21] The way of life that has emerged from neoliberalism is not consistent with the soul of democracy, for it has put aside the power of the humanities[22] and thoughtful social sciences; it has promoted standardization and privileged rugged empirical evidence to the exclusion of the domains of the moral, critical, spiritual, artistic, and philosophical. As Apple notes:

> We live in a time when the very meaning of democracy is being radically changed. Rather than referring to ways in which political and institutional life are shaped by equitable, active, widespread and fully informed participation, democracy is increasingly being defined as possessive individualism in the context of a (supposedly) free market economy.[23]

Within such a context, enacting democratic education has become an onerous task—especially if, as it should be, it is based on equity rather than simply equality of opportunity, diversity rather than standardization, agonizm (adversaries) rather than antagonism (enemies), substantive and controversial issues rather than cold procedures and facts, taking a fair stand rather than pretending to be neutral and reproducing current injustices, and finally embracing social activism rather simply deliberation and discussion.

A democratic education that honors robust democracy has to consciously and, at times, subversively challenge the neoliberal practices in educational institutions (including universities). [24] We have the moral responsibility to question the myth that the "achievement gap" can be reduced by simply improving test scores of tests that purport to be neutral and objective while at the same time reproducing the neoliberal way of life without ever offering a reasonable justification for it. Of course we have to take numeracy and literacy seriously, but numeracy and literacy are not monolithic entities. There are in fact different forms of numeracy and literacy, and they all deserve to be taught and respected. To paraphrase Freire, reading the word (that is the technical aspect of language) is just as important as reading the world. And the reading of both has to include, for example, oral traditions, the poetic, the dialogic, the narrative, and not just the documentary. Democracy calls for a curriculum that takes life seriously in its entirety, and not just on aspects that continue to privilege certain groups of the citizenry.[25] A true polis is not one based on partial aspects of it; it has to include the cosmos in its fullest sense! And as such, it recognizes the importance of the particular and the universal, the tensions between them, and the need for an ethics of hospitality.[26]

## Challenges

There are several challenges that democratic education faces in neoliberal times. In this section I will focus on three major challenges that I have encountered in the practice (both at the elementary, secondary, and tertiary levels of education). These challenges are based on what I consider to be serious misinterpretations of the robust notion of democracy as it is applied to educational and pedagogical matters. In a sense these challenges arise from what one may refer to as "myths."

### Challenge 1: The Belief That Democratic Education Involves Only Procedural Matters

This belief rests on the view that democracy involves only procedural matters. That is, democracy deals only with *how* we proceed when we deal with issues about which there are disagreements. This view holds that once we apply the proper democratic procedures (usually associated with the scientific method of inquiry as proposed by Dewey), we will be able to rationally resolve problems.[27] Moreover, this position maintains that in classrooms it is crucial as pedagogues to focus on the procedures we use in our teaching: for example, who we allow to talk, how much time we allocate to students to talk, how we or they respond to each other, and so on. Such a view usually leads to the practice of setting class rules in a communal fashion and which are subjected to revisions depending on how the rules are working.

There is no doubt that procedural matters are an integral part of democracy and hence also democratic education. But it is fallacious to believe that all that matters is that we focus exclusively on procedural matters. Such a position, albeit unwittingly, promotes the belief that neutrality is possible. The position claims that if we find the proper technical matters and apply them accordingly then disagreements will be resolved. Ultimately the view has full faith in the technical and procedural irrespective of the substantive differences that arise. In practice, unfortunately, this leads to the practice of not dealing with substantive issues—because a lot of time is spent on matters of procedures and hence there is no time left to deal with substantive issues. Educators who adhere to this view, given their absolute faith in method, believe that they should not take a stand or pronounce a view about substantive matters. While such a stance is believed to be neutral or impartial or solely technical, in fact it is not. And hence the contradiction that arises if we fully associate democracy exclusively with matters of procedures.

A corollary of this position holds that democracy is simply a matter of voting, which is a procedural matter. A school principal recently chided me that democracy and education have nothing to do with each other in his school as, he rightfully claimed, he cannot convene the entire staff and students to vote on every decision he has to make. Unfortunately this naive conception of democracy, which though is very common in popular discourse, rests on the view that democracy and voting are synonymous. Of course, democracy deals with matters of governance, but, as pointed out earlier, there is much more to democracy than matters of governance. Nor does the democratic spirit imply that we have to vote on every single matter.

On the other hand, there are those who believe that the only acceptable procedure in a genuine democracy is to reach consensus on all decisions.

Again, while reaching consensus can be a worthwhile aim since it involves as many members of a community in the decision-making process, the faith in absolute consensus is another expression of the belief in democratic procedures. Hence, the same critiques that have been raised regarding the exclusive focus on democratic procedures can be made of the consensus view. Again, here I am reminded of another incident I experienced when I served as a parent on the school community committee that was mandated by the Ministry of Education of all schools in the province where I lived at the time. The committee members consisting of the school principal, a teacher representative, and eight parents met for a weekend with the aim of reaching full consensus about the wording of the mission statement of the school. While the procedure adopted was intended to create a democratic spirit, ultimately after all of us expressed our views and realized that we had major disagreements based on substantive educational and pedagogical differences, we could not come up with a consensus. However, the directions we were given emphasized that we had to reach consensus on the wording. As a result the outcome was a wording that we all agreed to but the mission statement was so watered down that it lacked any substance that made a difference. This was a classic outcome of forced consensus that is based solely on identifying common agreements. It seems to me that it would have been more representative of the true spirit of democracy if we simply listed the various substantive differences we had and acknowledged that we would do our best to support different practices at the same time in the school. However, this was not consistent with the directions we were given. As a result although at face value it seemed that we had reached a consensus, in fact this was an artificial consensus, which is not at all consistent with democracy.

## Challenge 2: Democratic Education Means No Real Role for the Teacher

A common misinterpretation of democratic education holds that since democracy is open to considering multiple and differing views, and it involves dialogue, then the role of the teacher is simply reduced to that of a facilitator who simply "navigates the traffic" in the classroom rather than explicitly offers direction, guidance, or even expresses her or his views. As such, according to this interpretation, the role and responsibility of the teacher is greatly diminished. In fact, however, the role and responsibility of the teacher in democratic teaching increases. From a nondemocratic perspective of teaching, the teacher assumes to have all the authority of deciding what is best in the interest of the students without considering what the students' and their community may hold about central educational issues. In other words, from the traditional perspective, the teacher makes the decisions irrespective of the context and only in relation to what has been a priori determined to be worthwhile for the students. Such a perspective which has been described as being an act of violence[28] falls prey to deficit mentality and as such it is believed that the student does not have anything to contribute to the educative process and learning. Without falling into the other extreme of laissez faire, the democratic educator, as both Freire and Dewey have argued, tries to deal with the tension of authoritarianism, on one hand, and, anything goes, on the other hand. A reasonable democratic and authoritative view of teaching adds more responsibility to the teacher and increases her or his role. As Freire has warned us:

> In some situations, in some circumstances, the democratic goal of liberating education can lead to irresponsibility if the students perceive it as expecting less from them. The responsible educator has to be at least six people as the teacher, leading as the professor and learning as the student, making an open atmosphere in a number of ways, but never, I repeat, never an atmosphere of laissez-faire, laissez-allez, never, but a democratic atmosphere yes. Then, by doing that, the students begin to learn a different way. They really learn how to participate. But what is impossible is to teach participation without participation! It is impossible just to speak about participation without experiencing it. We cannot learn how to swim in this room. We have to go to the water. Democracy is the same. You learn democracy by making democracy but with limits.[29]

Ultimately the misunderstanding identified above once again rests on the belief that teaching ought to be neutral and that neutrality is possible. It is commonly but fallaciously held that a democratic teacher should not influence the students because it is held that influencing students amounts to being indoctrinative. Such teachers believe that as teachers we should just stick to facts and entertain students' responses to facts, and make sure we do not offer any direction to students. Unfortunately what they fail to understand is that given our human predicament, every context influences us. As Dewey noted:

> Sometimes teachers seem to be afraid even to make suggestion to the members of a group as to what they should do. I have heard of cases in which children are surrounded with objects and materials and then left entirely to themselves, the teacher being loath to suggest even what might be done with the materials lest freedom be infringed upon. Why, the, even supply materials, since are a source of some suggestion or other?[30]

To avoid complete influence we would have to be living in a decontextualized context, which from the human experience is just impossible. As Counts stated: "Complete impartiality is utterly impossible."[31] What the democratic teacher focuses on, however, is the nature of the influence. In this regard a democratic teacher needs to be fair, offer different perspectives, and identify problems and issues as they arise within and about such perspectives. Moreover he or she needs to seriously take into account the views and experiences that the students bring with them to the class. He or she also needs to welcome critiques of his or her own views and reasoning, and welcome disagreements that need to be based on informed views rather than merely off the cuff opinions.

## Challenge 3: Democratic Education Demands One-Size-Fits-All

A final crucial misinterpretation that will be briefly explored is the view that democratic education demands that we adopt a common curriculum, a common set of standards, and a common mode of assessment and evaluation or else we are not treating individuals in the same manner, which is a requirement of a liberal democracy. This view has been expressed by most ministries of education in the Western world and adopted as a mantra by those who argue that we should remove the so-called achievement gap. The assumption underlying this position is that democracy implies equality and hence we should provide exactly the same things to students irrespective of where they come from, their race and ethnicity, their social class, their sex, gender or sexuality, and their abilities. What is best for who are considered to be "the best" should be promoted for all and hence we ensure equality for all.

The major problem with the one-size-fits-all view is that it assumes that equality and equity are identical. It is true that all human beings should have the same rights as human beings; we should all be treated the same in front of the law. However, having the same human rights expectations for all does not imply the same educational needs for all nor does it imply that different needs should be fulfilled in the same manner. Equity and sameness are not identical. Equity requires that we carefully and rigorously listen to all people's needs and attempt to understand what they mean and entail. Moreover, equity requires that we adopt whatever means needed to fulfill such identified needs. In education, just as in other human areas (e.g., health), adopting the same means and procedures does not always secure the same outcomes. In fact, in more instances than we realize, adopting the same means and procedures to different needs, ensures that we will never fulfill certain needs. The problem with standardization is that by definition it excludes the fulfillment of those needs that do not correspond to the mainstream ones that standardization expects to resolve. Imagine if in medicine we were to adopt the same procedures or treatment to different medical needs! I am only using the medical example as an analogy for I do not want to reproduce a pathological view of education. However, in education very often, we reproduce the same fallacious move that is so obvious in matters of health. In education equality is associated with what can be counted and measured (e.g., tests scores), and the focus is almost exclusively on equality of opportunity, which it is believed, will yield to equal and meritorious outcomes if all work hard enough—that is, irrespective of contextual needs that vary. The so-called meritocratic position assumes that beyond education we all have the same means (e.g., economical capital) that we need to accomplish educational needs. The lack of fulfillment of economic needs are not dissociated from social and political contexts that privilege some and marginalize others. Those that are marginalized have to struggle harder to succeed. In contrast, the robust notion of equity called for by critical democracy refers to what is most desirable and just with the aim of fulfilling different needs in whatever ways are needed and making sure that we have the appropriate access and resources to fulfill the needs. Of course, what this implies is that in reality students may do different things given different needs associated with different aims. And from the genuine democratic perspective all educational aims are considered to be worthwhile and none of them are privileged over others as happens within our neoliberal context that privileges narrow utilitarianism, reductionism, and cold empiricism.

Let me be very clear that the position I am arguing for and that is based on a robust notion of democracy and equity, *does neither entail nor promote* the lowering of standards or expectations. Lowering of standards and expectations would be a classic example of the deficit mentality, which has been argued is incompatible with equity.[32] Neither does my position entail that there should not be core or basic learning that should be made available to all, and that we ensure that all are given a real opportunity to learn. However, my position does question a narrow notion of core or basic based solely on certain hegemonic privilege. For example, it is crucial that literacy is made available to all and that we ensure the best possible achievements in literacy for all. However, to determine success in literacy solely by privileging documentary literacy over literary literacy for example, or written literacy over oral literacy will by definition always hold back certain people to succeed in literacy. Likewise, why should the linear, rational mode of expressing oneself be always privileged over the poetic and metaphoric? In our neoliberal times, there has been an overemphasis on "basic skills." No doubt "basic skills" are needed, but if the notion and practice associated with "basic skills" does not include the critical and reflective, then as Greene wisely admonished us some 35 years ago:

> [W]e shall leave a population passive, stunned, and literally thoughtless in front of television or with miniature speakers in their ears.[33]

In his work Milani himself noted the very point I am making. He was rightly concerned as to how the students would be classified depending on their learning or better still on how they were deemed to know or not know "school knowledge." For me he offers a classic example, when he observes that while the students in his school while attending regular public schooling were deemed not to have passed the gym exam because when the gym teacher had given them a ball and asked them to play basketball, the children were not able to do so and hence failed the gym exams. However these same children were very able to climb oak trees and carry heavy branches in the snow. The point here is that if the standards of physical education are solely determined by one's ability to play basketball the very "standardized expectation" used works against these children who in fact were very physically able and hence had reach the expectations of the gym classes. Milani was definitely not lowering the standards of physical education; he was challenging the way the students' learning and abilities were being assessed given the standardized norms that were by definition exclusionary.[34]

## Conclusion

In a recent interview, Tahar Ben Jelloun, the renowned Moroccan novelist/author stated: "Democracy is not like an aspirin you dissolve in water."[35] He made this point while discussing the situation in North African states regarding the recent attempts to remodel their political structures. Ben Jelloun's message is twofold. First, that democracy is not easy to accomplish or actualize. Second, the living of democracy will inevitably involve struggles that arise partly from differences in views and ways of life. His point connects with Mouffe's views that we cannot avoid conflict in democratic politics, and that moreover, democracy demands that we take conflict seriously. The issue, Mouffe argues, is how we view conflict and those who disagree with us:

> Democratic politics requires that the others be seen not as enemies to be destroyed but as adversaries whose ideas should be fought, even fiercely, but whose right to defend those ideas will never be questioned. Put differently, what is important is that conflict does not take the form of "antagonism" (struggle between enemies) but of "agonism" (struggle between adversaries). The aim of democratic politics is to transform potential antagonism into agonism. [36]

Of course living the spirit of agonizm is not an easy task. It is a task, however, that peace education has to continuously attempt to achieve. Peace education has to directly face the reality of conflict and also realize that robust democracy demands that we embrace it. It is not always the case that we can resolve conflict. Recognizing and honoring conflict is a central democratic disposition. But living with conflict also entails that we live with the conflict within us and within our communities. To live such a life in turn entails that we are not afraid to be critical of ourselves and our communities. In Ben Jelloun's novel *A Palace in the Old Village*, the main character, Mohammed, admonishes Bachir who "had an opinion about everything":

> If we don't criticize ourselves, we'll never get anywhere...So stop criticizing those who have the courage to criticize themselves.[37]

This latter point connects with Milani's point about the role of social criticism in education and politics. For Milani politics and education were intertwined and he did not shy away from the power dynamics aspect of education. Clearly for Milani, democratic education entailed a critical action component, which exhibited courage and subversion. In his school he invited noted Italian scholars to present their ideas to the students. But before their actual presentation in his schools, the students would have read and critically analyzed the work of the scholars. To the surprise (and in some instances the disgust) of the scholars, the students would voice their criticisms to the scholars. He was not afraid to prepare students to intelligently and consciously object to certain views that were conceptually, ethically, and politically problematic. As educators we own such a responsibility and duty. Educators in our neoliberal times occasionally, perhaps more than we wish, retort that they can't do otherwise because the system compels them to do so even if it is against their professional and ethical judgment. In *Letter to a Teacher*, Milani's students advise us to know the policies well and to analyze the wording and the spirit of the policies deeply. He gives examples of how knowing the policy well will allow us to find "loopholes," which in fact justify critical work.[38] In the spirit of Milani, I contend that if we do not challenge and carefully subvert the immoral and mythical qualities promoted by neoliberalism we would indeed be promoting a violence toward our students—a violence, which is conceptually and practically inconsistent with both peace education and democratic education.[39]

# Notes

1. Trifonas and Wright (2011).
2. Ibid., p.1.
3. Ibid.
4. Although democratic education is not identical to peace education, the two are closely connected. It can be argued that peace education requires democratic education
5. Bar Tal, D. (2002), pp.27–36.
6. Ibid., p.28.
7. Ibid.
8. And here one can add race, class, gender, sexuality, and so on.
9. Wintersteiner (2005), p. 55.
10. Portelli and Solomon (2001); Price (2007); Carr (2011).
11. Dewey (1938).
12. Portelli (2001); Held (2006).
13. Dewey (1916).
14. Ermarth (2007).
15. Kothari (2007).
16. McDonnell, Timpane, and Benjamin (2000).
17. Snauwaert (2002), p.11.
18. Snauwaert (2009), p.101.
19. In other words pragmatists believe that by adopting the scientific method or procedures that are consistent with the scientific way of inquiry we can resolve substantive problems and differences.
20. For example, Freire (1998).
21. Giroux and Giroux (2006); Mayo (2012).

22. Nussbaum (2011).
23. Apple (2011), p.21.
24. Portelli (2010).
25. Portelli and Vibert (2001).
26. Carlson (2003).
27. Dewey (1916) and (1938).
28. Freire (1972).
29. Freire and Shor (1987), p.88f.
30. Dewey (1938), p.71.
31. Counts (1932), p.16.
32. Valencia (1997).
33. Greene (1982), p.326.
34. Milani (2009), p.51f.
35. Ben Jelloun (2011a).
36. Mouffe (2002), p.8f.
37. Ben Jelloun (2011b), p.5.
38. See Milani (2009), p.53.
39. I would like to thank Professor Carmel Borg and Michael Grech for feedback on an earlier version of the chapter.

## References

Apple, M. W. (2011). "Democratic Education in Neoliberal and Neoconservative Times." *International Studies in Sociology of Education*, 21, 1, pp. 21–31.

Bar Tal, D. (2002). "The Elusive Nature of Peace Education." In G. Solomon and B. Nevo (eds.), *Peace Education: The Concept, the Principles and Practices in the World*. Mahwah. NJ: Lawrence Erlbaum, pp.27–36.

Ben Jelloun, T. (2011a). Interviewed by Ruth Schneider, *Exberliner*, October 17.

——— (2011b). *A Palace in the Old Village*. New York: Penguin Books.

Carlson, D. (2003). "Cosmopolitan Proressivism: Democratic Education in the Age of Globalization." *Journal of Curriculum Theorizing*, Winter, pp.7–31.

Carr, P. R. (2011). *Does Your Vote Count? Critical Pedagogy and Democracy*. New York: Peter Lang.

Counts, G. S. (1932). *Dare the School Build a New Social Order?* Carbondale, IL: Southern Illinois University Press.

Dewey, J. (1938). *Experience and Education*. New York: Macmillan.

———. (1916). *Democracy and Education*. New York: Free Press.

Ermarth, E. D. (ed.) (2007). *Rewriting Democracy: Cultural Politics in Postmodernity*. Aldershot, UK: Ashgate.

Freire, P. (1998). *Pedagogy of Freedom: Ethics, Democracy, and Civic Courage*. Lanham, MD: Rowman & Littlefield.

———. (1972). *Pedagogy of the Oppressed*. Harmondsworth, UK: Penguin Education.

Freire, P. and Shor, I. (1987) *A Pedagogy for Liberation: Dialogues on Transforming Education*. Westport, CT: Greenwood Publishers

Giroux, H. and Giroux, S. S. (2006). "Challenging Neoliberalism's New World Order: The Promise of Critical Pedagogy." *Cultural Studies—Cultural Methodologies*, 6, 1, pp.21–32.

Greene, M. (1982). "Literacy for What?" *The Phi Delta Kappan*, 63, 5, pp.326–329.

Held, D. (2006). *Models of Democracy*. Palo Alto, CA: Stanford University Press.

Kothari, R. (2007). *Rethinking Democracy*. New York: Zed Books.

Mayo, P. (2012). *Politics of Indignation: Imperialism, Postconlonial Disruptions and Social Change*. Winchester, UK: Zero Books.

McDonnell, L. M., Timpane, P. M., and Benjamin, R. (Eds.) (2000). *Rediscovering the Democratic Purposes of Education*. Lawrence, KS: University of Kansas Press.

Milani, L. (2009). *Letter to a Teacher*. Translated with notes and commentary by C. Borg, M. Cardona, and S. Caruana. Malta: Agenda.

Mouffe, C. (2002) *Politics and Passions: The Stakes of Democracy*. London: Centre for the Study of Democracy.

Nussbaum, M. C. (2010). *Not for Profit: Why Democracy Needs the Humanities*. Princenton, NJ: Princeton University Press.

Portelli, J. P. (2010). "Il-mentalita' tad-deficjenza u l-htiega tas-sovverzjoni: Riflessjonijiet dwar Milani" (Deficit Mentality and the Need of Subversion: Reflections on Milani). In C. Borg (ed.), *Lorenzo Milani: Bejn ilbierah u llum* (Lorenzo Milani: Between Yesterday and Today). Malta: Horizons Publications, pp.313–322.

———. (2001). "Democracy in Education: Beyond the Conservative Or Progressive Stances." In W. Hare and J. P. Portelli (eds.), *Philosophy of Education: Introductory Readings*. Calgary, AB: Detselig, pp.279–294.

Portelli, J. P. and Solomon, P. R. (2001). *The Erosion of Democracy in Education*. Calgary, AB: Detselig.

Portelli, J. P. and Vibert, A. (2002). "A Curriculum of Life." *Education Canada*, 42, 2, pp. 36–39.

Price, J. M. C. (2007). "Democracy: A Critical Red Ideal." *Journal of Thought*, 42, 1 and 2, pp.9–26.

Snauwaert, D. T. (2009). "Human Rights and Cosmopolitan Democratic Education." *Philosophical Studies in Education*, 40, pp.94–103.

———. (2002). "Cosmopolitan Democracy and Democratic Education." *Current Issues in Comparative Education*, 42, 2, pp.5–15.

Trifonas, P. P. and Wright, B. (2010). *Critical Issues in Peace and Education*. New York: Routledge.

Valencia, R. E. (ed.) (1997). *The Evolution of Deficit Thinking. Educational Thought and Practice*. London: The Falmer Press.

Wintersteiner, W. (2005). "Peace Education and Peace Politics: Education in the Era of Neoliberalism." In F. Pistolato (ed.), *Per Un' Idea di Pace (Conference Proceedings, April)*, pp.55–62.

# 13

# Does Democracy Promote Peace? A Rancière Reading of Politics and Democracy

*Duncan P. Mercieca*

## An Assumption: Democracy Leading to Peace

> *A steadfast concert for peace can never be maintained except by a partnership of democratic nations. No autocratic government could be trusted to keep faith within it or observe its covenants. It must be a league of honour, a partnership of opinion. Intrigue would eat its vitals away; the plottings of inner circles who could plan what they would and render account to no one would be a corruption seated at its very heart. Only free peoples can hold their purpose and their honour steady to a common end and prefer the interests of mankind to any narrow interest of their own.*
>
> Wilson's War Message to Congress, 1917.

> *Democracy is more than a collection of specific institutions, such as balloting and elections – these institutions are important too, but as part of a bigger engagement involving dialogue, freedom of information, and unrestricted discussion. These are also the central features of civil paths to peace.*[1]

The above two quotes capture the issue that this chapter addresses: the relationship of democracy to peace. With almost a difference of one hundred years and relatively different economic and political situations, Wilson and Sen seem to agree that democratic politics and practices lead to peace.

This affirmation is based on a number of assumptions. The first is that democracy is the best and most desired political system, and that all nations should be democratic. It is an assumption that some governments have used to justify some of their policies. In the last 40 years we have seen pressures on some countries (at times escalating to international military interventions) to change their political systems and adopt a democratic one. East European countries in the late 1980s, more recently in Afghanistan and now Egypt and Libya are just some examples.

Secondly, it is assumed by some that the democratization of the world will lead to the decline or possibly the elimination of borders between these countries. Thus, Rancière coins the term "law of limitless"[2] in which particular politics are dissolved into one big politics which is seen as limitless. A clear example is the idea of a European Union and the Eurozone.

Third, the assumption is often made that having a democratic and a limitless world will reduce and eliminate war, violence, and their threat at both international and local level. Hence, it would lead to peace.

Regarding peace, however, this seems always to live in the shadow of conflict, in the sense that, as Michael LeVan claims, peace:

> suffers... from being persistently conceived as a reaction, as an amelioration or ending of something else.[3]

Peace is always seen as "a matter of distance"; distance from some conflict or other.[4] Hence, ironically, the concept of conflict, which one seeks to avoid takes a central place in the very definition of peace. In this regard, LeVan uses the term "impotent peace" in order to capture the idea that frequently our focus is on conflict (which we seek to eliminate), rather than on peace itself. This focus on conflict and war displaces human beings from the center of politics. Discussion rotates around how conflict can be avoided rather than on what would be a better life for human beings. Thus, compromise is most likely to be the order of the day as the lesser of evils is sought. It is a kind of inverted conversation, so that one never gets round to talk which is more positive and proximal. If human beings were at the center then proximity rather than distance would come into play. Awareness and concern for the other might become the heart of political talk.

In the last 30 years, Jacques Rancière has been writing extensively about politics and democracy. Disagreement, "dissensus,"[5] and hatred are some of the words he uses to re-explain politics and democracy in his work. These terms seem to run contrary to the assumption that democracy leads to peace. In this chapter, two key and closely intertwined concepts from Jacques Rancière, that of politics and democracy, are considered. They are considered in light of the chapter's title question "Does democracy promote peace?" But before considering these, it is worth making a note about Rancière's style of writing and philosophy. These are based on the notion of "re-definition"; starting off with concepts and ideas with which readers are familiar, and then "renaming" these concepts and ideas.[6] It is a process that does not attempt to remove, solve, or eliminate the difficulties of understanding or using such concepts, but rather seeks to bring out the impossibilities and aporias these concepts entail. It also invites one to engage with these impossibilities and aporias.

In one such exercise Rancière renames politics as "police" and "democracy." This will be discussed in what follows. The chapter then proceeds to assess the implications of this to peace.

## Police and Politics

The term *equality* is at the heart of the Rancièrian project. Yet, in order to unpack this concept we have to look at Rancière's understanding of the term *politics*. Rancière does not reduce "politics" to voting procedures, referenda, and council systems, which are in place as part of our democratic society framework. These systems are for Rancière only a "mechanism" that distributes one's place in society. Thus, through voting, Peter who is a candidate may be posted in parliament, whereas Paul who is a voter, while contributing to Peter's election is assigned a place among those who may have a say on what is going on only once every five years. Rancière classes this as the "distribution of the sensible." It is the structure, which organizes everything and gives it purpose, a reason for being. For Rancière, the distribution of the sensible:

> [i]s a delimitation of space and times, of the visible and the invisible, of speech and noise, that simultaneously determines the place and the stakes of politics as a form of experience. Politics revolves around what is seen and what can be said about it, around who has the ability to see and the talent to speak, around the properties of space and the possibilities of time.[7]

A related term is what Rancière refers to as the "police." This roughly refers to "the structure and justification of a social hierarchy"[8] as well as to how we perceive "ourselves, one another, and the world."[9] Through such a structure, a lived reality becomes predictable and safe, in which assigned roles can be fulfilled and thus expectations met. Suffice it to mention the reliance which we have in present times on the expert who constantly determine the kind of life we live and the kind of relationships expected between nonexperts and experts, from a discussion of a child's school lunch, to the technocratic government in Italy. Hence, for Rancière:

> What generally goes by the name of politics is the set of procedures whereby the aggregation and consent of collectivities is achieved, the organization of powers, the distribution of places and roles, and the systems for legitimizing this distribution. I propose to give this system of distribution and legitimization another name. I propose to call it the police.[10]

As Gert Biesta puts it:

> One way to read this definition of police is to think of it as an order that is all-inclusive in that everyone has a particular place, role, or position in it; there is an identity for everyone.[11]

Rancière notes that one aspect of a policed society is "consensus." Consensus is "the sharing of a common and non-litigious experience."[12] This is a general feature of our time, shown in the fact that there is a general agreement that the distribution of the sensible: is a reasonable one, and that there is no reasonable alternative to it.[13]

Consensus is often placed at the heart of what we call democracy. Here, consensus discourse, often carried out by governments, through the intervention of experts, is translated into actions through a series of large-scale "economic, financial, demographic, and geostrategic equivalences."[14] For example, education discourse is currently being hijacked by international assessments such as Programme for International Student Assessment (PISA) and Trends in International Mathematics and Science Study (TIMSS), where there is consensus over what constitutes good education. One cannot not consent to this. It is a given. In fact, these actions are, as Rancière calls them, "objective givens."[15] These are the "pivots" in relation to which members of a community orient themselves and establishing "a life in common."[16]

Everyone in the community finds his place or better still is assigned a place within these "objective givens." Roles are assigned and taken up: Those who are supposed and those who are not supposed to think, those who work and those who give work, those who act out the performance and those who see the act, those who speak and those who listen. The competitors, those with various ideas, within this "life in common" are swallowed up. It is because of lives rotating round these "objective givens" that we experience a reduction in conflict and it is eliminated, which therefore gives us some tranquillity of peace. As Rancière argues, postmillennium consensus politics is conceived as a model of "social peace."[17] Everyone accepts the place she or he is assigned. This is not very different from many nondemocractic, or indeed antidemocratic set-ups, as Plato's utopia, where everyone is assigned a place and he or she has to accept it.[18]

Up to this point I have illustrated what politics is not according to Rancière. Yet, what is it that he considers to be politics? What is politics for Rancière? The following two quotes capture the main ideas concerning what politics is. For Rancière, politics:

> occurs when these mechanisms [the police as discussed above] are stopped in their tracks by the effect of a presupposition that is totally foreign to them yet without which none of them could ultimately function: the presupposition of the equality of anyone and everyone.[19]

More specifically, he elsewhere

> reserve[s] the term politics for an extremely determined activity antagonistic to policing: whatever breaks with the tangible configuration whereby parties and parts or lack of them are defined by a presupposition that, by definition, has no place in that configuration—that of the part that has no part[20]...political activity is always a mode of expression that undoes the perceptible divisions of the police order by implementing a basically heterogeneous assumption, that of the parts who have no part, an assumption that, at the end of the day, itself demonstrates the contingency of the order, the equality of any speaking being with any other speaking being.[21]

If we had to put Rancière's idea of politics in a nutshell then it would be captured in this phrase: *the parts who have no part*. We are all assigned a part in society and are expected to fulfill the part assigned to us. Politics occurs when through our actions we produce something outside of the part we are assigned and therefore produce something that has no part. Politics thus happens when there is a "break"[22] in the arrangement of the police; when there is dissensus rather than consensus. This means that "politics doesn't always happen, it happens very little or rarely."[23] Rancière uses a number of strong words to explain this breaking up. In his book *The Philosopher and His Poor* he uses the phrase "cutting up."[24] Pain and some form of violence may be at play here. This break/cutting up becomes concrete when a number of actions "that reconfigure the space where parties, parts, or lack of parts have been defined" occur.[25] An example is Rosa Parks' action in December 1955 where she refused to obey the bus driver's order that she give up her seat in the colored section to a white passenger, after the white section was filled. Her action broke/cut the part that she was assigned to her. Politics then happens when the two processes, that is, police and *the parts who have no part* come together. Politics is when *the parts who have no part* are able to supplement, "come into presence," "break," "divide," "cut up" the distributed order where everyone is fitted in.[26]

## The Equality Assumption: Changing the Starting Point

One concept that enables us to makes sense of Rancière's idea of policing, as "a system of distribution and legitimization," is the concept of "equality." Equality seems to be an end, a goal, that most democratic societies and governments (regardless of the difference in how they understand this concept) strive to achieve.

In this regard, Rancière suggests a shift. Rather than thinking of equality as an end product, an aim, a goal to be reached, equality should be considered as a *presupposition:*

> Equality is not a goal that governments and societies could succeed in reaching. To pose equality is to hand it over to the pedagogues of progress, who widen endlessly the distance they promise that they will abolish. Equality, is a presupposition, an initial axiom—or it is nothing.[27]

As May notes, equality "must be the expression of political actors [the people] rather than the possession of a political hierarchy." The shift being suggested here by Rancière is to see equality as something created by the *demos*, by the people, rather than for them. Because the people presuppose themselves as equal, they would act in that way. Their practices are practices of equality and they see the police order as contingent.[28]

A key element of Rancière's suggestion is the idea of "presupposition." That is, equality is understood as being there from the outset and not as being an end to be achieved. This, for Rancière, is the starting point of equality. Because the *demos* presuppose their equality, through their actions, they "come into presence" to use Biesta's words. They supplement (that is they give alternatives), they bring forth disagreement in the distribution of the sensible (the police). As in Rosa Parks' situation, through her action she gave an alternative to how things used to be and brought disagreement in the "police." This, as May reminds us, is a "*collective*[29] action emerging from the presupposition of equality."

In the remaining part of this section I consider how "equality" may be cherished but not respected in a supposedly democratic society, in one area in particular—education. I also illustrate how the concept may be concretely reread and reworked according to the lines Rancière suggests. In this regard I refer to his book *The Ignorant Schoolmaster: Five Lessons in Intellectual Emancipation.*[30]

In the book Rancière recounts the story of a school teacher Joseph Jacotot, an exiled French teacher working in Belgium. The Belgian educational system, as that in most European countries, conceived of equality in terms of equal access to the educational set-up. Yet, this educational set-up to which everyone had equal access, presupposed a fundamental division between those involved in it; students were assumed to be "ignorant" by not having valuable knowledge, and teachers who are considered to possesses knowledge, which they then hand to students. Despite the equality the educational set-up apparently cherishes, students are thought (and made) to be dependent on teachers. In Belgium, Jacotot found himself in an awkward situation.[31] He had to teach French to pupils whose native language he did not speak. Being caught in this position he tried an experiment, though he was skeptical about its possibility of successes.[32] Jacotot got for his students copies of the bilingual edition of *Tèlèmaque,* which was being published at that time in Brussels. Through a translator he instructed his students to see the words, repeat over and over, and read until they could recite it. Then he invited them to write what they thought they had read.[33] After some weeks, Jacotot met again the students and was, to his dismay, told that the students had learned to speak and write French without anyone explaining anything of them.[34] Explanation was not necessary.

Rancière notes that "explanation" entails a "double inaugural gesture" a gesture that reveals the limits of equality that is supposedly ingrained in established systems. On the one hand, "explanation" entails an *absolute beginning.* On the other hand, the teacher implicitly "throw[s] a veil of ignorance" on all knowledge that students bring along with them. He assumes it does not exist and/or it is not knowledge. He "appoints himself to the task of lifting it."[35] The teacher is the one who knows, while the student does not and needs the teacher to teach him. Rancière notes that, paradoxically, the more the teacher explains the more the gap between teacher and the student widens, even if in fact it should be narrowing. The teacher not only has the knowledge that the students lack. He can decide how this knowledge is distributed and arranged; a further source of power to the teacher that makes short shrift of the idea of equality.[36]

That the assumption contained in such system (namely student lack knowledge and are unable to obtain it themselves—the teacher possesses knowledge and will provide it to students) is fallacious is obvious, according to Rancière, if we consider the most complex things that we all learn which is our mother tongue. We learn this by chance, using a hit-and-miss approach. If we all learn this without help, we have at work:

> an intelligence that makes figures and comparisons to communicate its intellectual adventures and to understand what another intelligence is trying to communicate to it in turn.[37]

It is challenging this assumption that Rancière presupposes equality as the starting point and not the end point; an assumption that holds that we are all equally able (may be at different rates) to learn and muster different things, being "capable of formulating and carrying out our lives with one another."[38] In this respect, the school master's ignorance is a "quality" and a "virtue."[39] As Rancière puts it, only:

> one who is ignorant might perhaps permit another who is ignorant to know something unknown to both...The ignorant school master exercises no relation of intelligence to intelligence. He or she is only an authority, only a will that sets the ignorant person down a path, that is to say to instigate a capacity already possessed.[40]

What Rancière has said here about education may be applied to democracy and peace. Democracy and peace should not be considered as the end which some institution or international treaty set and which those involve in the institution/parties to treaty may or may not achieve. Peace and democracy must not be delivered by institutions to people. Democracy and peace must in some way be presupposed.

## The "Scandal of Democracy," and Radical Democracy as a Possible Way Forward for Peace

Just as with education and knowledge, democracy is a term that has been used in context that do not merely deliver what the term promises but entail things that are antithetical to this. Rancière refers to the "scandal of democracy":[41] Democracy is rule by the people. This, however, does not mean that in those societies that are called democratic each member of the *demos* is empowered in with regard to what goes on in the political life or indeed in his/her daily existence. Rather:

> [D]emocracy is rule by the people in the sense of "rule by those who rule", that is, rule by those who have no other claim to rule than random luck—the throw of the dice.[42]

The Nietzschean idea of the "throw of the dice," which Rancière is applying to democracy may disrupt our ideal understanding of democracy. Our politics today, hence our democratic states, still functions on the "six nondemocratic titles" Plato mentions in his *Laws*.[43] As Rancière argues, societies today are similar to the ones portrayed by Plato, were the minority always govern over the majority because they think they have "gold" placed in their soul. Hence:

> [T]he term democracy...[as it is normally used]...does not strictly designate either a form of society or a form of government. "Democratic society" is never anything but an imaginary portrayal designated to support this or that principle of good government. Societies, today as yesterday, are organised by the play of oligarchies. There is, strictly speaking no such thing as democratic government. Government is always exercised by the minority over the majority.[44]

For Rancière, on the other hand:

> Democracy is the designation of subjects that do not coincide with the parties of the state or society. [45]

Democracy occurs when the police order that assigns a place for each one of us (redistribution) is challenged through the acts of individuals or groups of people. These are, as Rancière argues in the above quote, subjects who due to their actions do not fit the police order anymore. This is democracy as radical "as it can get." It is a democracy that disrupts the established order.

Rancière's insistence that we live in oligarchies under particular police force is not to be understood as a limitation and a narrowing of the "political" in his sense of the term. As Chambers argues, Rancière's critique and redefining gives us possibilities that forms of democracies would take were it to occur.[46] Rancière is offering us different spaces of how to think of politics and of democracy that subvert the comfort and assumptions that we take for granted. Politics and democracy are understood as struggle that undermines the police force and oligarchy.

Hence, the question that this chapter started to address ("Does democracy promote peace?") needs to be redefined within a Rancièrian framework. Does peace come from "consensus," as current so-called democratic set-ups seem to entail? Or is peace on the other hand a matter of dissensus? A matter of what people do, and in particular, what they do to challenge the hierarchical orders of a given set of social arrangements?

The former is the very idea of democracy and consensus that Rancière has been attacking. It is a situation that entails living under an oligarchy, with some democratic trappings such as representative structures (voting in referenda and elections). Members of a democracy would have their place, role, voice that can be heard but not acknowledged as voice.[47] If peace is the result of a policing system that produces the "distribution of the sensible," then we have peace that is just reproducing and reaffirming inequality and not allowing for the different groups and members to achieve some level of emancipation.

An alternative is to think of peace as functioning within dissensus. Dissensus occurs when "politics is comprised of a surplus of subjects that introduce, within the saturated order of the police, a surplus of objects."[48] This supplement breaks the "autorepresentational logic of society"[49]; the logic of the distribution of the sensible. It is about altering the visible and the said. These "breaks," "divides" "cut ups" which produce a "gap in the sensible"[50] give the possibility of peace to start functioning. This supplement produces "political subjects,"[51] that is, subjects who have broken the police order, and that are a "community of equals." This supplement is what gives peace the possibility to start functioning.

## Conclusion

So, does democracy promote peace? Rancière argued that politics and democracy occur rarely. Hence, as May notes, within the Rancièrian concept democracy and politics are possible. Peace is possible as well.[52] However, democratic politics "does not reside with those who proclaim to lead us" nor does it reside within our institutions. It resides in us, in our decisions and in our capacity "to dissent from the police order."[53] It "is up to us, it appears when it does, out of our making."[54] We are the ones who create it. If we want democracy, we have to make it happen. If we want peace, we have to make that happen as well.

## Notes

1. Sen (2011), p.2.
2. Rancière (2006b), p.10.
3. LeVan (2011), p.49.
4. Ibid.
5. Dissensus is the opposite of consensus. It is thought by Rancière to involve disputing both what is taken as a "given" and the "the frame within which we sense something is given." Rancière (2010b), p.69.
6. See Chambers (2010), p.58.
7. Rancière (2004a), p.58.
8. May (2009), p.8.
9. Ibid.
10. Rancière (2004b), p.28.
11. Biesta (2010), p.48.
12. Rancière (2010b), p.7.
13. Ibid., p.123.
14. Panagia and Rancière (2000), p.123.
15. Ibid., p.214.
16. Ibid.
17. Ibid., p.119.

18. Rancière habitually goes back to the fathers of philosophy and begins his discussion with a historical excursus. In the Republic, Plato asks the key question "What is justice?" claiming that the answer is "everyone doing the job s/he is naturally suited for." This implies that nature determines the place we should occupy in society, including the management of the state. Thus, in Plato's utopia the top few (whom he calls Philosopher-Kings) make decisions for the rest of society. For people to accept their role, Plato resorts to a noble lie; a story whereby the demigods create our souls and randomly place in them one of three elements: gold, or silver, or bronze. If you have happen to have gold then you become a philosopher-king, if silver you become a warrior and if bronze you become a worker.
19. Rancière (1999), p.17.
20. Emphasis added.
21. Rancière (2004b), pp.29–30.
22. Rancière (2003), p.30.
23. Rancière (2004b), p.35. It is important to note that police, while it is not politics, has its value and Rancierre does not place politics/policing in a good/bad binary relationship.
24. Rancière (2003), p.225.
25. Ibid.
26. See Biesta (2006).
27. Rancière (2003), p.223.
28. Rancière (2004a).
29. My emphasis.
30. Rancière (1991). In various writings and interviews, Rancière claims that this book has brought a shift in the course of his thinking and hence, he regularly refers back to it.
31. When reading *The Ignorant School Master*, it is very difficult to say when Rancière is writing in his own voice and when he is quoting Joseph Jacotot. This is why I write Rancière/Jacotot.
32. "He expected horrendous barbarism, or maybe a complete inability to perform." Rancière (1991), p.2.
33. Ibid.
34. Ibid., p.9.
35. Ibid., p.6f.
36. Rancière (2010a), p.3.
37. Ibid.
38. May (2009), p.7.
39. Rancière (2010a), p.1.
40. Ibid., p.2f.
41. Rancière (2006b), p.51.
42. Chambers (2010), p.65.
43. In the *Laws* Plato lists seven titles that belong to those who rule; titles that are supposed to determine who is naturally entitled to rule and who is not. The six titles I refer to are the following. four depending on birth: (the title of parents over children; of the old over the young; of masters over slaves; and of nobles over commoners) and two on nature (the strong over the weak and the intelligent over the ignorant). We therefore have a natural division between those who count and those who do not count in the running of the state. Those "who are best" (Rancière [2006] p.40) rule by merit of nature and "science '*qua*' knowledge" (Rancière [2001] p.9)
44. Rancière (2006b), p.52.
45. Rancière (2003), p.99f.
46. Chambers (2010).

47. LaVen (2011).
48. Panagia and Rancière (2000), p.123.
49. Ibid., p.125.
50. Ibid.
51. Ibid. It needs to be reminded that what Rancière is arguing about is not to do away with the police and the distribution of the sensible, but to produce gaps in these logics.
52. May (2009).
53. Ibid.
54. Ibid.

# References

Biesta, G. (2010). "A New Logic of Emancipation: The Methodology of Jacques Rancière." *Educational Theory*, 60, 1, pp.39–59.

———. (2006). *Beyond Learning: Democratic Education for a Human Future*. Boulder, CO: Paradigm Publishers.

Chambers, S. A. (2010). "Police and Oligarchy." In Jean-Philippe Deranty (ed.). *Jacques Rancière: Key Concepts*. Durham, NC: Acumen.

Derycke, M. (2010). "Ignorance and Translation, 'Artifacts' for Practice of Equality." *Educational Philosophy and |Theory*, 42, 5–6.

Guenoun, S., Kavanagh, J., and Rancière, J. (2000). "Jacques Rancière: Literature, Politics, Aesthetics: Approaches to Democratic Disagreement." *SubStance*, 92.

LeVan, M. (2011). "Four Notes for a Politics of Peace." *Peace Studies Journal*, 4, 3, pp.49–53.

May, T. (2010). "Wrong, Disagreement, Subjectification." In Jean-Philippe Deranty (ed.), *Jacques Rancière: Key Concepts*. Durham, NC: Acumen.

———. (2009). "Democracy Is Where We Make It: The Relevance of Jacques Rancière." *Symposium. Canadian Journal of Continental Philosophy / Revue canadienne de philosophiecontinentale*,13, 1, pp.3–21.

Panagia, D. and Rancière, J. (2000). "Dissention Words. A Conversation with Jacques Rancière." *Diacritics*, 30, 2, pp.113–126.

Rancière, J. (2010a). *On Ignorant Schoolmasters*. In Charles Bingham and GiertBiesta, G. (eds.), *Rancière. Education, Truth, Emancipation*. London: Continuum.

———. (2010b). *Dissensus: On Politics and Aesthetics*. Ed. and trans. Steven Corcoran. London: Continuum.

———. (2007a). *On the Shores of Politics*. London and New York: Verso.

———. (2007b). "The Emancipated Spectator." *Art Form*. Available at: http://digital.mica.edu/departmental/gradphoto/public/Upload/200811/Ranciere%20%20spectator.pdf, on August 8, 2011.

———. (2006a). "The Ethical Turn of Aesthetics and Politics." *Critical Horizons*, 9, 1, pp.1–20.

———. (2006b). *Hatred of Democracy*. London and New York: Verso.

———. (2004a). *The Politics of Aesthetics: The Distribution of the Sensible*. London: Continuum.

———. (2004b). *Disagreement: Politics and Philosophy*. Minnesota: University of Minnesota.

———. (2003). *The Philosopher and His Poor*. Durham and London: Duke University Press.

———. (2001). "Ten Thesis on Politics." *Theory and Event*, 5, 3.

———. (1999). *Disagreement: Politics and Philosophy*. Minneapolis: University of Minnesota Press.

Rancière, J. (1991). *The Ignorant Schoolmaster: Five Lessons in Intellectual Emancipation*. Stanford, CA: Stanford University Press.
Ross, K. (1991). "Rancière and the Practice of Equality." *Social Text*, 29, pp.57–71.
Sen, A. (2011). *Peace and Democracy*. Cambridge, UK: Open Book Publishers.
——. (1992). *Inequality Reexamined*. Cambridge, MA: Harvard University Press.
Wilson's War Message to Congress, 1917. Available at: wwi.lib.byu.edu/index.php/Wilson%27s_War_Message_to_Congress, on November 30, 2012.

# 14
# Peace and Sexuality—Two Reflections

*Mario Gerada, Clayton Mercieca, and Diane Xuereb*

## Reflection 1

We must admit that when we were asked to write something about peace and sexuality we were surprised. We never thought of these two concepts and human experiences together. Moreover, as Drachma LGBT (Drachma LGBT is a Maltese association of Gay, Lesbian, Bisexual, and Transgender Christians) we are not very familiar with Don Milani. However, from the little we know of him, we can say that what we are doing may, in some ways, remind some of his philosophy, way of life and methodology. As LGBT people, we often find ourselves being the objects of someone else's reflections, theologies, judgments, and statements. Some of these are well thought theories. Others are terrible. Many fail to reflect our reality. In a manner that is reminiscent of Milani and his community, at Drachma we practice the bottom-up approach, we play with democracy and liberation. We do not reject tradition or conservative teachings either. But we do not allow these to become cages. We use them as platforms that help us grow in love and service. We also struggle to find our own voices; sexual, spiritual, theological, and biblical. In the light of this, our attempt to write this chapter is an experiment; a way of being together and write. Fra Gwann Xerri taught us much about this way of being. This exercise turned out to be a creative process, which further stimulated our thoughts and introduced us to new concepts. We are gay and lesbian persons raised within the Catholic tradition here in Malta; as we find ourselves reflecting together about sexuality and peace, from where we are in life, society and religion—the three of us identify ourselves as Christian also by choice, one of us choosing to identify himself as belonging to the Roman Catholic Church, in faith and tradition. Our reflections do not necessarily follow a logical framework but rather allow free, spontaneous, playful, childlike thoughts to emerge, dance and play together to enrich ourselves and hopefully others with our experiences and reflections.

Hence, we want to specify that we are not writing this chapter as academic experts on the matter, but rather as human beings, who cherish their Christian faith and are honest about who they are. This includes being honest about our own sexuality—our intimate relationships. The three of us form an integral part of Drachma. Though having different perspectives and life stories, the three are active and cooperate within the same group. Diane is also very active at a European level, within the forum of gay and lesbian Christian groups.

As human beings raised as Catholics we had to confront our sexuality (an ongoing process), identity and gender in the light of society's prejudices and organized religion's often unhelpful messages. As human beings we are neither better nor worse off than the rest of the population. Yet as a group we have to carry a heavier burden because of our different sexual orientation. This is the great injustice placed on the shoulders of the LGBT person. A burden that sometimes crushes some of our own community leading them into unhealthy spaces, at other times even to suicide. This is the reason why we witness our faith and sexuality. This is the reason why we are activists. To hopefully send signs of hope that it can and it does get better. To proclaim that faith itself can help the LGBT person and his or her family to struggle with this conflict, which often takes shape internally as well. Often internalized homophobia haunts us from within. Prejudice, hostility, negativity, and hate toward us assail us from outside. But the rainbow-father God, the one who promises hope and life, is also found in the midst all of this darkness.

Upon reflecting about the title we realized that in fact there is a kind of war going on. Peace for the gay community and even more so for the Christian LGBT community is a far away promised land, long for desired. As a gay community we experience many forms of exodus. For others it means leaving Christianity or all forms of religion completely. For some of us it means leaving behind oppressive and violent interpretations while holding strongly to our faith. We believe that both options are a struggle, both hard. Having said that, along the years much has been written and many LGBT Christian groups have sprung and are springing all over the globe. We are not yet there but the promised land is in sight. Historical speeches defending LGBT rights, such as those of former secretary of state Hilary Rodham Clinton and Secretary-General of the United Nations Ban Ki-Moon, are encouraging. The road ahead is still a long one though we have come a long way, but are we out of the desert yet?

The struggle is at various levels. It is between church hierarchies and gay communities. It is between the state and the gay community. It is between society and the gay community though here at grassroot levels one finds most signs of hope. It is between gay people who are claiming liberation and homosexual persons forming part of institutions—be they civil or religious, who still want to subjugate themselves to forms of oppression and hold back the rest of the community alongside them. The struggle is within the gay community itself, often those who "left" religion feeling very betrayed by those of us who "remain" and profess faith. The struggle is also within the community's internalized patriarchal forms of relations, oppression, and sometimes exploitation as well. The war is inside of us, with our own internalized homophobia, guilt and shame, fears of our own sexual desires for intimacy and love. And yet, amid all of this, peace is possible and also already a joyful reality among us as well. Much is going on here in Malta as well. More organizations are forming and the collaboration is a joyful one. More people are supportive and understanding of the struggles of the LGBT community. More politicians are coming round and some members within the church hierarchy may be listening more. Malta Gay Rights Movement's (MGRM) campaign, recently launched, is another positive sign witnessing how we are finding more spaces within this society and claiming our place within it. MGRM's collaboration with Drachma Parents' Group is also another example of elegant collaboration between the various organizations who also may have different ideological starting points.

In some countries and amid all of these struggles the gay community has managed to achieve much. Others are on the way. The LGBT faith community is also actively undergoing much rethinking of faith itself. This rethinking is happening not only in the Christian faith but in other faiths as well.

For those of us who reflect about our own experience also from the perspective of the Christian faith we are finding that lust may not be very helpful and that there might be more to sexuality, as after all church teachings say. However, lust is not a gay problem but a human experience. It can be the start of a relation but, if this relationship is simply based on this, it may not go very far. And yet, in our community we are also finding that sexuality and sex between gay couples can also be spaces of union and communion, of sacredness, spaces where one needs to walk with clean feet. They are encounters where the living spirit of God—love is honored, cherished, and shared. Encounters where people are at peace with the world and themselves. Many in the Catholic Church fail to see this and perceive all gay relationships as sinful or far away from God's plan for humanity. Others are claiming the opposite. Our own experiences witness that God is among us and also within our intimate loving relationships. Of course we are sinners as well and, like the rest of humanity, we struggle with this as well.

Some people in the gay community are struggling like other human beings to find relationships within which one can flourish. Love and life are always a mystery. Society may not always help (neither the gay nor the straight). Violent neoliberal ideologies such as consuming irresponsibly, success and profit at all costs, definite contracts and the domination of resources and human bodies have their toll on society's understanding of intimate human relationships as well. They are a threat to peace. The gay person is not immune from these threats either. Like others we are a part of and participate within these same societies of ours, with their own ideologies, political visions, and directions or lack of.

Within such a landscape many theologies about us have dismembered us. In many dominant theologies our person and our bodies are completely missing. But our bodies speak of theology as well. God is also found within our hearts, within our relationships embodied in our queer bodies. God is a source of peace.

In a discussion of peace and sexuality, we cannot fail to honor our ancestors who struggled and their fight allowed us to breathe, to find new life, to encounter ancient yet novel thoughts, to be able to dream of dreams and have visions together and not be afraid to imagine new possibilities and horizons. Queer and gay affirmative theologies, written against all odds helped us look at our bodies anew, reread our own experiences, look at the Gospels with fresh eyes and a spirit of love. They taught us to reject the spirit of fear, despair, oppression, and rejection. Our forefather and mothers have helped us find our own human and theological voices. They gave us life. They opened for us possibilities that gaze toward eternity. We honor these parents of ours as faith teaches us to do. We also honor those who struggled in the civil and human rights spheres. Some may have been atheists or inspired by other spiritualities. Some may have experienced deep rejection by their own churches and could never overcome that deep hurt. And yet, their "faith"' remained shining within and expressing itself in civil and human rights works across the globe. We honor all those who strive to uphold the dignity of each and every human person and those who believe in love in all of its forms. Religious belonging is secondary to fraternal, peaceful, and loving relationships.

Being gay is a joyful gift. Not only a gift to oneself but a gift for others as well. It enriches the human landscape and diversity. This human experience helps us experience our Creator anew and look at love with fresh eyes. It helps us to be at peace with ourselves and with others. Life, love, intimacy, and relationships are to be cherished. No matter what. The gay community has been reminding societies and churches about this fact.

> My partner and I woke up in the middle of the night and started to talk about the paper at three-thirty in the morning. We did not talk much about it, we just realised something quite profound. Marjon had her hand on my head and I had my hand on her side, and all of a sudden Marjon said I can feel God here through our connection through the energy of our hands and it was peaceful, it was very peaceful.

## Reflection 2

Peace is a peculiar concept. Nations have justified wars in order to achieve it. On an individual level, many have relentlessly tried to experience peace in various activities that eventually fall short of their promise. On the other hand, sexuality is such a personal experience that at times it is hard to talk about it between a couple who are in a long-term committed relationship let alone among persons who barely know each other. Sometimes, we relate to each other as if people are "sexless." Institutions often harshly speak out loud to their congregation about the way one should live one's sexuality, often missing on so much beauty, romance, and poetry that is found within intimate sexual relationships. This is very antithetical to peace.

The notion of peace and sexuality is interesting not only for the gay community, but for society in general. Through our experience at Drachma LGBT we realized that sexual and spiritual integration is a human struggle as well. The reconciliation between peace and sexuality is a journey for all.

Questions about sexuality are intimate personal questions: Is it ok to be terrified of sexual intercourse? What about my fantasies about someone I have loved in the past while being with my partner? Should I masturbate to relieve myself of tension? Why am I feeling attracted to someone of my own sex although I don't identify myself as gay or lesbian? So many questions....

Sexuality can stir many internal conflicts that shatter one's peace. These conflicts may arise as we start getting to know ourselves better. We also find it hard to admit that at time such conflicts start at a very tender age, 12 or even earlier for some of us. We are afraid to speak about such thoughts, and then they torment us. Such thoughts can become a monster, which grows powerfully within us, overwhelming us at some point causing us feelings of revulsion and anxiety. Peace becomes a distant notion, which can only be achieved when sexuality is addressed for what it is, a gift that needs much nurturing and address.

Sexuality and peace are often strangers to each other and, of course, to us as well. The risk is that we stop questioning, take things as they happen and react in an ad hoc manner. What is worse is that we rely on misinformed sources to tell us what is expected of us and how we should express our sexuality. As a result we let that monster inside of us feed on our insecurities and negative self-regard making us incapable of creating solid and well-formed relationships.

Socrates once said "the un-examined life is not worth living." The unexamined life can only lead to a travesty of peace, both on a personal and social level. Socrates' injunction has something to say about our own sexualities too. Being passive toward life will not help us achieve internal peace. Yet how can we achieve peace when questioning our own being becomes so dangerous?

Sex and the expression of one's sexual identity has always been a topic fervently scrutinized by most religions. For too many years, many people have listened to preachers condemning sexual acts and behaviors without questioning them. No one ever dared to challenge the preacher because his (most of the times, male preacher's) description of sexuality somewhat differed from how the listener would experience his or her sexuality.

Institutions and authorities created and legitimated the "right" way to express one's sexuality, and implicitly condemned as "wrong" and "evil" all other ways. Most of the time people saw themselves as falling under the "evil" category and attempted to renounce such evil ways to conform with the good ones. Only in this way could one feel that they were not cut off from God's grace. Others throw away the baby of faith with the bath water. But were they in peace with themselves? Peace was in many cases forsaken.

The following statements became common:

> I am not allowed to feel same-sex attractions because they are "intrinsically evil" and thus I am called to live a chaste life by which God will help me to control my urges and provide me with other forms of grace.

And:

> I have to repress my sexual fantasies which I wish to share with my girlfriend/boyfriend because she will definitely be put off.

And:

> It is dirty and perverse to explore my own body by masturbating because I am only allowed to offer my body to someone else within marriage for the purpose of procreation.

The list can go on and on. If one dares to act differently from what the norm presumes, he or she becomes the outcast; the reason why society is faced with so many problems. S/he becomes the target and scapegoat of society. S/he may even victimize him/herself. Peace with the entirety of oneself is impossible if the person remains confined with these premises.

When one of us accepted his sexuality as a gay man at the age of 16, the immediate option he was faced with was to forsake the religion, which he grew up with and abandon any spiritual beliefs. This felt like being catapulted on the other side of the pole. While he was finally coming to terms with his sexual identity, peace was still far from achieved. The option to abandon his spirituality did not give him any peace at all. It was crucial for him to have them both without perceiving them to be in conflict with each other. Yet again, this seemed like an impossible mission. He was now living the "gay lifestyle" and this seemed to make his God unhappy. Was this true? The search and yearning for the truth seemed to be the most important thing in order to achieve that peace.

It took him two hours of listening to James Alison; an author/theologian, Catholic and openly gay person, to finally start understanding what it means to be at peace with one's sexuality. The idea that there were other convinced Catholics and openly gay persons was already a breath of fresh air. To listen to the witness and words of a world renowned theologian and author made it even more astonishing. What remained imprinted in his heart and will remain until the end of his days were the words, which Jesus himself said to Pontius Pilate during his trial—"I AM"—two words that make up a total of three letters; two words that seem incomplete and lack significance but open up a new theology, which liberates people from their own oppressions. These words signify the importance of embracing one's true self. By affirming one's real identity, one is being a reflection of the Divine. We strongly believe that the words "I am" should be the mantra that allows the person to delve into one's own presence and realize God's presence within himself. Peace becomes finally materialized and felt in every nerve of the body. One's true sexuality comes to be seen as a gift, which is so beautiful and powerful when expressed in its way.

# 15

# On Art and Politics: Exploring the Philosophical Implications of the Creative Order of Art on the Organization of Social Relations

*Mark Debono*

## Introduction

The following chapter takes its cue from Milani's effort to equip individuals with the ability to question critically the authoritarian forces that turn the world into a more "oppressive, cynical and dangerous"[1] place to live in. Though the Church and the state did not endorse Milani's notion that one should resist subordination, Milani, himself a priest in exile at Barbiana, continued to insist on the notion that education remains significant if it keeps provoking individuals to live an authentic life.

The first part of this chapter explores two paintings, *Guernica,* by Pablo Picasso, and *Judith beheading Holifernes* by Jamie Miller. I intend to situate the context of these paintings, the Gernika bombing and the Abu Ghraib tortures, in a larger framework so as to question the effect of authoritarian politics on peoples' freedom.[2] It appears that such politics by its logic of war and abuse tends to reduce any opening for freedom. This chapter suggests that art, in its seeking of alternative routes of how to connect its various elements, can turn out to be an enterprise of imagination,[3] which promotes an expression of freedom.[4]

The second part of this chapter focuses on the artist's role in the world and on how art's creative aggregation of its parts can serve politics to find other means of regulation besides the limited one of the might of the fittest.

# I

The image of ruin in Picasso's *Guernica* takes us back to April 26, 1937, the day the Basque town of Gernika was bombed by the German and Italian airforces. This bombing gives rise to the question, "What type of politics occasioned such barbarism on European soil?" "Was this an isolated incident of an authoritarian type of politics or was there something more to the event?"

The Vienna and Prague lectures of 1935 by Edmund Husserl point to the deterioration of the social fabric of Europe as a consequence of the domination of technical progress. Martin Heidegger, Husserl's pupil, amplifies the discord that technology brings to our everyday existence, particularly when it turns into a "provocation," a "nightmare that threatens to enslave or even destroy its begetter."[5] Heidegger goes on to describe this condition as a crisis that brings about "the forgetting of being,"[6] one where the self loses its trustworthiness and enters into a diverted rapport with the world and with other people. According to Heidegger, this type of rapport will eventually generate a fatal disburdening of "moral autonomy and therefore, of moral responsibility."[7] This lacuna implies that we will not be able to account for our own identity in a meaningful way, bringing about a situation that hinders an adequate rapport with other persons.

Regarding the bombing of Gernika, Gijs van Hensbergen[8] notes that Western political powers had already been utilizing their technological mastery for genocidal purposes in territories under their colonial control. Hensbergen quotes Sven Lindqvist who in *History of Bombing* claims that:

> Bombs were a means of civilization. Those of us who were already civilized would not be bombed.[9]

The bombing of Gernika also reveals the speed, accuracy, and efficiency with which entire populations can be erased effectively, in the shortest time possible. Hensbergen claims that, after a three-hour attack from the air, Gernika had almost been entirely obliterated.[10] In this scenario, the political handling of technological mastery and the tragedies, which it gave rise to among the inhabitants of this community of the Basque town were an almost negligible detail in comparison with the mass executions that occurred later in the Nazi death camps; an experience where, according to Adorno, our identities became synonymous with death.[11]

It is against this background, that one revisits Picasso's *Guernica*, and asks why, in this particular painting, all the objects depicted, from the wounded horse to the fallen corpses, express ruin? Through these striking images of ruin Picasso perhaps wanted to tell us that his *Guernica* is something more than just a reminder of the event of the bombing of a town. Was Picasso trying to perform the almost impossible task of salvaging ruin in an artistic manner? Whatever the historical conditions that produced the painting, the somberness of its monochromatic texture keeps capturing a sense of mourning. And the lack of color in Picasso's pure image of ruin, recalls the Socratic notion that "the chromatic distracts us from the pure idea of the beautiful and soils the beautiful idea of the pure, from which we mortals are so mournfully remote."[12] It is this condition of ruin which:

unites memory and mourning: it is itself a monument to the impossible restitution of what never was fully present to us in the first place.[13]

The elements of destruction and lack of freedom in the *Guernica* carry us to that type of "earth as no one has ever seen it, the earth has a splendor that it never has had, and as everything destroys itself in the twentieth century and nothing continues, so then the twentieth century has a splendor which is its own."[14] In *Guernica*, Picasso cultivates the tragic loss of the Gernika bombing and mysteriously gives us an unexpected vision of how people come close to destroy each other and the world. This may be one reason why on a daily basis thousands of people keep visiting the *Guernica* at Reina Sofía, because they are:

> mesmerized by the power and scale of the image as they stare wide-eyed at the painful drama acted out before them. Transfixed, they gaze in reverential contemplation. Guernica's power to shock has, despite the millions of reproductions, never gone away. Its rejection of human barbarity and its cry for liberty and peace remain as insistent today as the day Picasso put down his brush back in 1937.[15]

Can we, today, feel the same about the artistic image of ruin in the *Guernica*? Is Picasso, through this painting, moving beyond the devastation that politics can bring? Regarding the silence in the picture, does this tell us that plans by politics to organize a more decent world for us to live in freedom and care are doomed to failure? The silence in the picture is like a plea that addresses the question about what continues to charm us in politics. Why do the untrustworthy promises of politics always appear so colorful? Can we, today, maybe as never before, a decade after the 9/11 event, perceive politics as the failure of its promises through and through particularly in the circumstance where international politics accepted America's "war on terror" to promote global security and peace? In his acceptance speech of the 2006 Nobel Prize for Peace, "Poverty is a Threat to Peace," Muhammed Yunus specifies the reasons why politicians' decisions to make war a priority shattered the hope to eradicate poverty in the world. He claims that the year 2000 started with a great global dream:

> World leaders gathered at the United Nations in 2000 and adopted, among others, a historic goal to reduce poverty by half by 2015. Never in human history had such a bold goal been adopted by the entire world in one voice, one that specified time and size. But then came September 11 and the Iraq war, and suddenly the world became derailed from the pursuit of this dream, with the attention of world leaders shifting from the war on poverty to the war on terrorism.[16]

According to Susan Sontag, this "war on terror" took its wrong turn when the pictures of the abuse committed by American soldiers on prisoners in Saddam Hussein's Abu Ghraib prison were publicly disseminated.

Sontag claims that what these photographs illustrate is as much "the culture of shamelessness as the reigning admiration for unapologetic brutality."[17] Could this same violence justify the violence that occurred on 9/11? According to Timothy Radcliffe, the violence of 9/11 was terrible, one that blocks all dialogue:

> It was a brutal power that denied all communication. In fact those engines of communication, jet airlines, smashed into those hubs of economic and military communication. It was an act of dumb violence, which spoke of the absence of all speaking, an unaccountable power. What also became visible that day was the violence of our global village. All the pain and suffering of humanity, which normally we keep far away and invisible, exploded in our face that day. The hidden violence that is implicit in the global market became visible in an instant.[18]

Can art, today, like Picasso's reaction to the Gernika bombing, respond to these events? Jamie Miller is an artist who attempts to express this wrong turn in American politics (particularly the tortures that happened at Abu Ghraib prison) in his painting *Judith beheading Holifernes*. Without shame and excuse, Miller deliberately copies the painting by Caravaggio with notable alteration. He replaces Holifernes' head with that of former president George W. Bush.[19] What is the decapitation evoking? Is the artist's intentional "copying" telling us that in today's world art lacks the creative force to generate the new? Or is the artist's "impoverishment" drawing our attention to the fact that politics has lost its imaginative power to suggest alternative routes for organizing social order besides that of the might of the fittest?

These questions open up a debate about how politics can take other routes than that of war. One of these routes is that of tentatively looking at the creative processes whereby art produces a balanced blend of its form and content. This discussion will occupy the second part of this chapter.

# 2

The philosopher and novelist Iris Murdoch depicts the artist as someone who possesses a knowledge of "oneself in the world (as part of it, subject to it, connected with it)" and who has the "the firmest grasp of the real."[20] This seems to hold in the case of Picasso and Miller. For both artists, the bombing and torture episodes turn out to be an indispensable tool for painting *Guernica* and *Judith beheading Holifernes*. This is the reason why, according to Murdoch, artists reveal to us:

> the place of necessity in human life, what must be endured, what makes and breaks, and to purify our imagination so as to contemplate the real world (usually veiled by anxiety and fantasy) including what is terrible and absurd.[21]

"Necessity" refers to the fact that though humanity could be better without the Gernika bombing or the tortures of Abu Ghraib, yet in art these world events acquire a definite form. In this sense, art rather than distracting us from the world as it really is, brings us face to face with the real, even if this reality disturbs us. In Walter Benjamin's sense, both artists appear as "historical materialists," who produce their paintings out of a "freezing" technique—a method of "grasping" and "stopping" the actual ongoing shifts of history, where happenings are crystallized into "a shape and be constructed as something immediately present." Regarding the historical subject, Benjamin writes: "In this structure he recognizes the sign of a messianic arrest of happening." By virtue of his "constructive principle," by means of this "shock" which he gives to history, the historical materialist causes it to crystallize into a monad, bringing about the "arrest of happening."[22]

In this manner the paintings show us the continuity of history's timeline because they serve as a reflection on a past event. They invite us (who live in the present) to ponder on how easy it is for politics to turn authoritarian and generate abuse. These works however, remain valid for future generations. Adopting Critchley's argument then, we may see works of art as an opening:

> in the name of another history, in the name of justice, which would not be [...] an end to history, but the continual working over of history as a work of infinite mourning, a politics of memory, the insomniac experience of being haunted by the spectres of the past.[23]

Works of art, can serve as a means whereby we stop, read a book, watch a film, see a play, listen to a piece of music, enjoy viewing paintings and sculpture. In stopping and dedicating some time to art we may glimpse the manner in which artists distribute the various elements in their works of art. Artists either give equal weight to the parts involved in the content to generate a harmonious form or else they try to produce such balance out of an asymmetrical positioning of the various parts. Art therefore, because it seeks to continue distributing fairly its parts, continues to channel us to an unlimited number of possibilities about how to connect the various parts together. If, therefore, we take art to be the form which is endlessly seeking the means to bring its various ramifications together in a genuine manner, we can say that art may be one of the few "havens" where one finds an expression of freedom.[24] And if art imparts this freedom, what effect can this have on authoritarian politics?

Today, this argument as to whether politics can bring freedom to people deserves more attention than ever, because we feel that nothing is certain anymore. "Our world has become inordinately complex, and not just for the onlookers but above all, for those who seek to rule it. It seems that these cannot sort its problems without creating more serious problems."[25] Notwithstanding this fact, many people, particularly those who rule, claim that politics can still harbinger freedom. It is against this fragile background, where freedom of people is no longer sovereign or where it is diluted, that one questions whether politics can move on the same lines of art by trying either to give equal sharing to the individual members to produce as much harmony in society as possible or by weighing how to generate equilibrium by whittling every individual difference.

At this stage, one is led to ask why does art manage to keep inventing modes of connecting its diverse content and why politics fails to connect the diversity of people. Does politics fail because in the words of Paulo Freire it lacks the ability to invent and reinvent[26] its ways to overcome its tyrannical apparatus? Why is it so difficult for politics to tolerate dissent? How will politics look without having a privileged authority to connect people socially? Can we still hold the belief that politics is able to organize the social relations between people in a free manner? The warning by Steiner that wherever there is tyranny, be it

> political, ecclesiastical, tribal—literature (music to a more fitful degree) is the agent of declared or Aesopian opposition, of subversive irony and clandestine hopes. It is, as Russian parlance has it, "the alternative state". Poets, thinkers, have been slain, their writings burned and pulped, their possibilities of publication gagged, since antiquity.[27]

And tyranny can take various forms. It can even disguise itself as democracy.

Contrary to these political moves, art continues to offer us alternative routes and this is the reason why, in its various manifestations, we continue to glimpse an infinite expression of creation and restoration; an unstoppable flow of freedom verging on the threshold of the excessive. Art transfigures the historical moment, and though it gives such historical happenings like the Gernika bombing and the Abu Ghraib tortures a different dimension, it always leaves the viewer guessing as to what the paintings focusing on these events have to say to us. Unlike politics, which always tries to manipulate the way we look at the world, art continues to provide us different "faces," which we glimpse in our world. Aren't our own different faces themselves suggestive of such difference?[28]

Why does politics always try to contain the different expressions of the individual members of society under one heading? Those who resist expressing uniform gestures as politics maybe desires, will be telling us that there are other means how everyday reality can be handled. This acceptance may give rise to greater tolerance among human beings in society.

## Conclusion

In a damaged world where some of us wake up to harsher realities than we used to be accustomed to, we may understand, that it is not fully in our hands to have:

> power to eliminate conflicts and escape our human condition, but it is in our power to create the practices, discourses and institutions that would allow those conflicts to take an agonistic form.[29]

The tension between the order of art and that of politics remains charged by the provocation that the creative order of art, unlike that of politics, appears to provide a sense of freedom and care to our disjointed social relations. The questions about the part played by artists, art, politicians and politics in society remain provoking the context that we are still learning to live to accept and live with one another's difference in freedom and care.

# Notes

1. Carmel Borg, Mario Cardona, and Sandro Caruana (2009). "Introduction: Lorenzo Milani—The Man and His Legacy," in *Letter to a Teacher: Lorenzo Milani's Contribution to Critical Citizenship* (Malta: Agenda), p.19.
2. For this chapter I limit the discussion to the manner these two paintings illustrate authoritarian politics—since politics and art contain manifold meanings.
3. Iris Murdoch (1999). "The Sublime and the Good," in *Existentialists and Mystics Writings on Philosophy and Literature*, Part V, Peter Conradi (ed.), George Steiner (Foreword) (London: Penguin Books), p.211.
4. George Steiner (2002). *Grammars of Creation*, Chapter III (London: Faber and Faber), p.107.
5. George Steiner (1992). "The Presence of Heidegger," *Heidegger, iii*, (London: Fontana Press), p.140.
6. Martin Heidegger (1992). *Being and Time,* John Macquarrie and Edward Robinson (trans.) (Oxford: Blackwell). In Part One, Section VI, "Care as the Being of Dasein," Section 40—"The basic state-of-mind of anxiety as a distinctive way in which Dasein is disclosed" (pp.228–235), Heidegger elaborates the issue about how the fleeing from that which connects us to life can lead to inauthentic living.
7. Steiner, "Being and Time," *Heidegger ii*, p.93.
8. Gijs van Hensbergen (2005). *Guernica: The Biography of a Twentieth-Century Icon* (London: Bloomsbury).
9. Sven Lindqvist (2001). "The Nightmare Made Real," *History of Bombing* (London: Granta Books), p.43. Hensbergen, on this same page, provides us with a list of some of the major bombings that happened outside Europe before 1937 by Western and non-Western powers. He mentions the 1911 bombing of a Tripoli oasis by the Italians; the 1919 bombing of Dacca, Jalalabad and Kabul by the British; the 1920 bombing by the British of Iran, Trans-Jordan and Baghdad; the 1922 bombing by South Africans of the Hottentots. Moreover: "In 1925 volunteer American planes, under orders from the French Flying Corps, and in service of the Spanish, destroyed Chechaouen in Morocco; while the French killed more than 1,000 in Damascus. Between 1928 and 1931 the Italians managed to reduce the Arab population in Libya by 37 per cent by aerial attack; in 1932 the Japanese bombed Shangai, and in 1936 the Italians bombed Ethiopians with gas and chemicals."
10. Ibid., Chapter 1, pp.36–37.
11. Theodor W. Adorno (1990). "After Auschwitz," in E. B. Ashton (trans.), *Negative Dialectics*, Part Three: "Models, Section III: Meditations on Metaphysics, 1," (London: Routledge), p.362. Adorno was referring to Auschwitz, one of the major death camps
12. David Farell Krell (2000). "Broken Frames," Chapter 1, *The Purest of Bastards—Works of Mourning, Art and Affirmation in the Thought of Jacques Derrida*. Part One: "Mourning the Work of Art" (University Park: The Pennsylvania State University Press), p.30. In the *Phaedo*, Plato, through the figure of Socrates, discusses how the senses can distract the soul from contemplating beauty and goodness in purity.

13. Ibid., "Echo, Narcissus, Echo," Chapter 2, Part One: "Mourning the Work of Art," p.77.
14. Gertrude Stein (1984). *Picasso* (New York: Dover Publications Inc.), p.50.
15. "The Final Journey," *Guernica—The Biography of a Twentieth-Century Icon*, Chapter 11, p.332.
16. Retrieved from www.nobelprize.org/nobel_prizes/peace/laureates/2006/yunus-lecture-en.html
17. Susan Sontag (2007). "Regarding the Torture of Others," *At the Same Time: Essays and Speeches*, Paolo Dionardo and Anne Jump (ed.), David Rieff (Foreword) (London: Hamish Hamilton an imprint of Penguin Books), p. 137.
18. Timothy Radcliffe O. P. "Religious Life in the World That Is Coming to Be," available at: www.domcentral.org/library/coming2b.htm.
19. The image of this painting can be viewed on the website: http://twistedreality.ca/gallery3.htm.
20. Iris Murdoch (1978). *The Fire and the Sun—Why Plato Banished the Artists* (Oxford: Oxford University Press), p.84.
21. Ibid., p. 80.
22. Alfredo Lucero-Montano (2010). "On Walter Bejamin's Historical Materialism," in *Astrolabio. Revista internacional de filosofía*, 10, pp. 126–131, (p. 127).
23. Simon Critchley (2009). "The Hypothesis, the Context, the Messianic, the Political, the Economic, the Technological: On Derrida's *Spectres of Marx*," *Ethics-Politics-Subjectivity: Essays on Derrida, Levinas & Contemporary French Thought* (London; New York: Verso), p.155.
24. This discussion excludes cases where art is used for propagandistic reasons to sustain the powers that be. To understand in more detail the link between art and its branding purposes one can refer to the text by Steven Heller (2011). *Iron Fists: Branding the 20th Century Totalitarian State* (London: Phaidon).
25. Gabriel Kolko (2004). *Another Century of War?* (New York: The New Press), p.9.
26. Freire, P. (1990). *Pedagogy of the Oppressed*, Myra Bergman Ramos (trans.) (London: Penguin Books).
27. George Steiner (2002). *Grammars of Creation,* Chapter IV (London: Faber and Faber), p.187.
28. Our faces always convey: a sense of who we are in our very being—our thoughts, emotions, and identity. But what registers on the face is only a kind of mark, a "trace" of who we really are. Even our words convey only a very limited sense of our true being. Thus the face is a manifestation that appears truly but does so in a highly incomplete and partial way. The face is an appearance of other to us, but an appearance that signals an otherness lying behind it. "The face is present in its refusal to be contained," says Levinas (TAI 194). "The face resists possession, resists my powers. In its epiphany, in expression, the sensible, still graspable, turns into resistance to the grasp" (TAI 197). Jacques Derrida (2002). "Levinas and Derrida," in Bruce Ellis Benson (ed.), *Graven Ideologies—Nietzsche, Derrida & Marion on Modern Idolatory* (Illinois: InterVarsity Press), p.115. Bensons' quotations of Emmanuel Levinas are from the TAI—an abbreviation for Levinas' (1979) work, *Totality and Infinity: An Essay on Exteriority*, Alphonso Lingis (trans.) (The Hague: Martinus Nijhoff).
29. Mouffe, C. (2005). "Conclusion," *On the Politics* (London and New York: Routledge).

# 16

# Can We Learn from Comparing Violent Conflicts and Reconciliation Processes? For a Sociology of Conflict and Reconciliation Going beyond Sociology

*Nicos Trimikliniotis*

## Introduction

This chapter attempts to provide a basic framework for a sociology of ethnic conflict *and* reconciliation in deeply divided societies that have suffered from ethnic-related violence.[1] Despite the specialized knowledge and literature on the subject, ethnic conflict and reconciliation has received relatively little attention in sociological debates.

This inadequacy derives from a number of causes. First, interpretations of acts and practices of historic violence often fail to appreciate the institutional aspects, the duration and the variety in which "force" is manifested. For instance, borders and partitions (visible, overt and covert) are often manifestations of initial violent "acts" and "practices" of different forms, which may retain some of their historic rationale/functions (e.g., repressing and fragmenting), and are constantly transforming the shapes, forms, and magnitudes of violence in unexpected manners.[2] Secondly, in recent globalization-dominated literature there is inadequate sociological linkage between the macro and micro levels of violence in ethnically divided societies. Thirdly, the dialectic between "violence *versus* nonviolence" and "conflict *versus* cooperation" is somehow under-theorized and under-researched. We have rather simplistic assumptions about what is the "rule/norm" and what are the "exceptions." Fourthly, comparative studies of ethnic conflict-ridden societies generally lack sociological and contextual historical depth and/or are not based on deeper knowledge of all the "case studies" under examination. Moreover, reduction of societies into "case studies" reduces them into mere "examples" in already thought-out global paradigms or in other stereotypical regionalized models, often disguising eurocentric and ethnocentric readings, as well as other heuristic distortions, such as intellectual dependency and exceptionalism. Fifth, studies of "ethnic conflict" are dominated by conflict resolution paradigms taken from comparative *political* science. Here, as a rule, no reference is made to insights provided by contemporary sociological debates. Finally, the fragmentation derived from disciplinary expertise and specialization tends to disconnect the specificity of the conflict from the reconciliation processes, as these are studied by different sets of experts. Hence, the connections made are based on superficial modeling rather than in-depth comparative sociological studies of conflict and reconciliation as processes.

The aim of this chapter is to emphasize the need to link theoretically and empirically study of conflicts, focusing on specific ideas, modes, and practices of reconciliation that develop subsequently and dialectically in ethnically divided\polarized societies. This requires a sociology that is interdisciplinary; one which possesses the conceptual and methodological frames capable of bridging the gap between disciplines and specializations through which, "violence" and "conflict" have so far been separately studied. This sociology would draw on various dimensions of knowledge without becoming an eclectic ensemble. It would be a sociology that allows for creative integration of various approaches from different disciplines into a broad interdisciplinary perspective that is theoretically and empirically sound and policy-relevant. It would be a *sociology of conflict/reconciliation* that is global as well as contextual, universal as well as particular. Hence, it would have the potential to provide a frame for explaining and understanding violent conflicts and reconciliation processes *as distinct modes and processes within a single social phenomenon.*

The chapter starts by making some preliminary considerations on the notions of conflict and violence. Next it considers the Conflict Resolution (CR) approach, focusing on its history and limits. The final part of the chapter presents the basic frame of a sociology of conflict and reconciliation.

## Conflict and Violence

In sociological debates conflict is often juxtaposed to "order." Functionalists sought what maintains order in society (common values, social cohesion/ solidarity, and consent to hierarchical relations and ranking in society), while "conflict theorists" (Marxists, Weberians, followers of Simmel, and others) sought to understand how the nature and modalities of "conflict" derived from oppressive, exploitative, and unequal relations and from polarizations derived from conflicting interests, ideologies, priorities, and ways of life. Coser's classic work (1956) laid the foundations for studying "the functions of social conflict." Until the development of the specialized interest in ethnic-related phenomena, with the study of nations, nationalism, ethnicity, race, and racism,[3] it was mainly historical sociologists who had an interest in dealing with such phenomena. However, in contemporary studies of collective violence and war there has been neither proper interface with sociological scholarship,[4] nor much sociological interest in peace and reconciliation processes. Moreover, there has also been no comparative sociological study linking ethnic-conflict phenomena to peace and reconciliation practices and modalities.

Conflict is a generic term that entails different types, forms, and intensities of "violence" and "force"; from wars, mass murders, and genocides to "milder" forms like exploitation, oppression, restriction, exclusion, and discrimination. In dealing with violence-related ethnic conflicts, what is often missed is that violence operates in multiple ways, often unexpected and unintended. A case in point is the violence, which is institutional rather than direct, wherein the violent impact of rules and regulations are made to bear on the individual. Examples are borders, frontiers, and boundaries that are frequently a source of violence and exclusion.[5] There is little doubt that:

> whenever a delineation of boundaries takes place—as is the case with every ethnic and national collectivity processes of exclusion and inclusion are in operation.[6]

Violence, hence, is a *force in society and history*. It is a force that operates even in its absence. Fear of and anger at outbursts of violence may operate at an individual and collective level. Memories of violence are also powerful tools in shaping political, cultural, and social institutions and behavior. Wars or violent incidents of the past shape physical borders of states as well as mental and ideological boundaries of people. They are active forces in shaping population movements, settlements as well as perceptions of history, politics, and policy-making. A case in point is the situation in Palestine/Israel. Another case is the protracted de facto partition/ceasefire line in Cyprus.

What must be properly contextualized and seen in interconnected terms is the specificity of violence. This should be related to features like unequal socioeconomic positions and power relations, class, cast, gender, ethnicity, religion, age, disability, sexuality, and other features. Yet, however specific, localized and particular the forms of violence that exist are, they may also be compared and related to one another. In this regard, it is worth noting that in the twenty-first century, violence has become simultaneously more global and more localized at the same time. For instance the issue of torture of "terrorist suspects" by US security services in Guantanamo or Iraq is simultaneously a "global" as well as a "local" event, being both United States and Middle East related. Such human rights violations have certainly become more "globalized" as news of such happenings are spreading ever faster. Moreover, such events often generate political reactions in many parts of the world; responses by various groups that are endowing and politicizing these issues in their own "local" contexts. In the Middle East, for instance, such violence has an immediate effect in local politics.

## Violence, Sociology, and CR Theory

Sociological interest in the general category of violence is not new. Macro-sociological and historical-sociological systems of analysis have examined the role of violence in the shaping of nation-states.[7] Attention has recently shifted to micro-sociological aspects.[8] However, a sociology of ethnic conflict *and* reconciliation processes as a singular mode of reading these phenomena is distinctly absent.[9] Sociologists have either focused on the causes and logistics of conflict, or on reconciliation. Regarding the latter, a major role has been played by CR theory. Many CR approaches criticize compartmentalization and differentiation in social sciences, proposing a "multidisciplinary and holistic approach." They also blur the demarcation of "internal" and "external factors," adopting models of multiple causal factors and dynamics that refer to features like ethnicity, religion, language, or culture.

The sociological foundations of CR theory are found in Georg Simmel's work on conflict. Another seminal work is Coser's book on the functions of social conflict.[10] However, the field of CR as a distinct and influential area of study took off in the late 1950s and 1960s[11] with American conflict resolution scholars.[12] Across the Atlantic, the Norwegian sociologist Johan Galtung developed his own schema, through the formation of a peace institute[13] and the launching of a journal. [14]

Since the 1970s, there has been remarkable innovation with CR theory and practice, as scholars drew more from the various critiques and nuanced analyses within CR, as well as from other studies. Various approaches developed. The "needs-based" CR promoted by the Burton school is based on eight assumed fundamental needs (control, security, justice, stimulation, response, meaning, rationality, and esteem/recognition). Roger Fisher and the Harvard Negotiation Project developed the "interest-based negotiation" approach. Other approaches were also introduced.[15] In the 1990s one of the most innovative developments was the "conflict transformation school."

Post-1990s development within CR theory have seen an increasingly self-critical field of research. Many contemporary CR theorists have adopted Galtung's distinction between structural (i.e., the result of oppressive/unequal social, political, and economic structures), cultural (i.e., the expression cultural differences or practices in the ways of life of ethnic or social groups) and direct types of violence.[16] Lederach critically refers to the domination of International Relations (IR) and Political Science within CR theory and practice.[17] As a result of this criticism, subtler versions of CR theory appeared. Thus, Ramsbotham et al. provide a more sophisticated and dynamic model of CR. [18] Nevertheless, their study marks an evolution, rather than a paradigm shift or scientific revolution. Their hourglass model of conflict containment, conflict settlement and conflict transformation for instance, is seen to entail a long-drawn process rather than a highly nonlinear, fluid and contradictory process within a fragmented and polarized social structure, as is the case in many situations. [19] Assumptions about polarizations still tends to be ridden with "ethnicist" assumptions of communities assumed to be unified and homogenous, ignoring political, ideological, and social characteristics and identities such as gender, class, and religion. The rich debates around social identity and intersectionality are missing from CR theorization and praxis.[20]

Regarding the relation between CR and sociology some of the key innovative texts, (whenever these refer to "what sociologists say on conflict") send us back to the 1956 text of Lewis Coser on the functions of social conflict or to James Coleman's work on "community conflict."[21] This is not to undervalue the importance of the above texts, but merely to indicate how the CR studies persistently fail to refer to current, and I would argue rich, debates taking place within Sociology.

## Shortcomings of CR Theory

The CR perspective offers valuable analytical tools worth exploring and developing in the theory and in the practices that relate to conflict situations. However, there are a series of analytical and practical problems related to CR approaches, even in their most sophisticated versions.

The inadequacy of CR paradigms and reconciliation models has long been subjected to criticism. The feasibility of the peace models presented is seriously questioned on different counts. The CR theories of the 1980s and 1990s for instance, were problematic on the following counts:

(a) They relied heavily on "behaviorism." "Actors" are seen as a more or less preprogrammed creature. Human behavior was assumed to be predictable as it is acquired through "conditioning," which assumes that humans can be somehow programmed in to behaving in a particular ways, leaving no room for freedom to act otherwise, reacting to social conditions in unpredictable ways, rebelling or exercising their own will against the expected behavior. Ethnic or social groups or political actors are assumed to be caught in the so-called prisoner's dilemma where each side assumes that the "other" side is acting as an individualist and will behave in a manner to gain advantage in what is a zero-sum game. Take warring factions that have agreed to disarm for the benefit of peace. Each side assumes that the other is secretly cheating by arming to gain advantage; it will itself start to secretly stock weapons, increasing the risk of war.
(b) They suffered from "negative functionalism," whereby every social actor and action is generally assumed to have some utilitarian value to the actor.
(c) They made assumptions regarding the actors being rational and operating on the basis certain patterns of behavior, leaving little room for contradictory behavior, uncertainty, crisis-crossings, unintended consequences, and chaos in the models provided.
(d) The fact that they tend to refer to "actors" assumed some homogeneity within and between these. This is hardly the case with ethnic state conflicts. In these cases the "actors" in question are states, political parties, politicians, organizations, the UN, military establishments, social groups and classes, and individuals, all of which are diverse and dissimilar.

In the introduction to the third edition of what can be considered to be a key text, "the book of the year" by the Conflict Research Society,[22] Ramsbotham et al. attempt to respond to the critiques of CR through an innovative approach that seeks to incorporate the criticisms and enrich the CR theory into an all-encompassing synthesis.[23] They avoid the early behaviorism and accept the current prevailing thinking that "violence is not unavoidable and integral to the nature of conflict," taking conflict transformation[24] as the "deepest level of CR tradition rather than a separate venture." Moreover, they attempt to "rescue" the CR traditions from its "liberal peace underpinnings"[25] and advocate the need to "enrich western and non-western traditions through their mutual encounter."

Yet, even sophisticated versions of CR theory that recognize the importance of wider and diverse social, international, and political factors tend to essentialize and effectively reduce conflict to individual factors like psychology rather than addressing complex and multifaceted social, economic, and political aspects. A case in point are the recommendations for the creation of decentralized models of government and definite state structures that are based on the premise that these structures can be:

> designed to serve psychological, economic and relational needs of groups and individuals within nation-states.[26]

The designing of governmental structures in regime changes that followed US-led invasions or the various aid developmental reform programs in societies, which are ridden by ethnic conflicts are generally based on such essentialist perceptions. Rather than relying on the development of local or autonomous historical traditions and structures of governance, the funded programs tend to be models imposed from above. These models are designed by "experts" and are premised on political, economic, cultural, and socio-psychological assumptions that allegedly fit the "essential characteristics" of the people involved. Therefore, both the "diagnosis" and the "remedies" for ethnic conflicts are ridden with specific interests, biases, and simplistic assumptions about the kinds of "solutions" to the various conflicts.

One of the most common assumptions made by CR theorists concerning the nature of "ethnic conflict" is that these conflicts result primarily from "historical hatred" and "ethnic antagonism," that is, ethnic or national groups that are assumed to be homogenous and who, somehow, naturally compete with each other. This would be the "core" of the "problem," the essential aspect of the conflict. Both at a theoretical and at a concrete level this approach is highly questionable as it consistently underplays the role of other factors, including modern ones, in the continuation of the conflict. A consequence of this is that, whether by default or by intention, some "specialists" tend to remain rather uncritical of the role the West plays in many conflicts. This is because emphasis is shifted to factors that supposedly existed since time immemorial.[27]

Sophisticated models that contain different types of "actors" (such as individuals and states), include international linkages and involve state-related institutions as mediating forces, also tend to reduce "ethnic conflict" to "human needs" for identity and security. "Identity" is taken as a *given*. The "ethnic" dimension becomes an essential part, if not the core part, of "identity." In most cases even the social order is taken as "given" and "necessary." There is often a conservative bias toward a particular social order, even within CR theories. [28]

A cogent criticism of CR is that it promotes: "a standardization of peace interventions in civil war situations [and] often fails to 'deliver' or 'a widely enjoyed peace'"[29] which addresses the content of "peace," which is such that is best enjoyed by the mass of local populations. Such approaches:

> in many cases fail traditional and indigenous approaches to peace-making and reconciliation can offer a corrective to the failings of the Western peace-making model.[30]

The persistent failure of various peace and CR efforts in the Arab world is indicative. Hidden premises of Western conflict resolution about Arab political culture, for instance, illustrate the inadequacy of Western assumptions; assumptions like the supposition that the Arab world is "more conflict-prone or less conflict resolution-oriented than the West."[31] Transporting Western CR theories and techniques to the Arab world or elsewhere requires that the latter undergo considerable cultural adaptation if they are to be successful. [32]

Another area of failure of Western mediation is Africa. CR theorists in Africa emphasize *individualism* at the expense of traditional collective approaches, disregarding African traditional perspectives on family and kinship. Even the differentiations according to regions, known in subregional terms as the five Africas (West, southern, East and Central, Horn, and Maghreb North), are "stereotyped and simplified depictions," which "mask the important fact that Africa is diverse, heterogeneous and complex."[33] The dominant interpretations have failed to appreciate the importance of real societal processes and political problems in postcolonial settings as well as the potential for peace and reconciliation that lies in utilizing local resources and traditions. Even the so-called conflict-sensitivity approaches suffer from the "mainstreaming of conflict analysis in Africa." [34] A diagnosis often made is that there is an inability to strike a balance between identity, peace, and justice. However such "diagnoses," which may be credible in many cases, often fail to take into account the universal and local traditions and contexts. For instance, the exporting of the South African "liberal peace"[35] transition in Africa has been successful in Burundi and the Democratic Republic of Congo, but has failed to resolve the conflict in Côte d'Ivoire, and resulted in a chain of failures of interventions based on the liberal peace model in Angola following the death of Savimbi in 2002. [36]

## A Sociology of Conflict and Reconciliation: Going beyond Sociology?

For a deeper understanding of what are profoundly *social issues* we need *a sociology of conflict and reconciliation*. Introducing sociology to the peace specialists and practitioners, or highlighting the sociological contribution to the understanding of conflict, peace and reconciliation processes, is only one reason for developing further this branch of the discipline.[37] Sociology itself is a discipline, like all others. It is in constant need of renewal. The world is getting more complex, more unstable, more uncertain about its future, and, arguably, more polarized. Social scientists are forced to develop explanatory frames in areas, which constitute protracted "social problems" and are threatening the lives and well-being of people. While recognizing that there are crucial political, psychological and anthropological aspects requiring collective "solutions," which are political and legal, a sociological analysis should uncover essentialist social underpinnings, meanings, and practices.

The shape of such sociology of conflict and reconciliation is matter of debate; this chapter proposes the following as parameters for a framework of a sociology of conflict/reconciliation:

First, it must be a *public sociology* in the way Burawoy defines it—an engaging discipline that goes beyond the university community.[38] It will also "merge" and draw upon professional, critical, and policy-orientated sociology. The debates on "public sociology," with the pitfalls and nuances articulated within it, can be extremely valuable in defining the territory of a sociology of conflict/reconciliation. Activism, critical thinking, and professionalization of the fields of war, conflict resolution, and cooperation reconciliation make the debates all the more relevant. Moreover, increasing expert-specialization and professionalization generate professional, economic, and ideological interests in the field that require sociological unpacking. There are, however, contradictions in such an endeavor. On the one hand, there is a need for sustained critical engagement and activism where sociology draws on popular struggles and local traditions striving for rights. On the other, the "expertise," even if this is from the development of critical sociology, generates power relations, professional interests, and "disciplining." There is no easy answer to this problem. However, we can put some checks on these processes by making sociology engaging and insisting on popular participation, accountability, and scrutiny.

Secondly, it must *study reconciliation together with conflict* (i.e., conflict/nonconflict, postconflict as well as reconciliatory/cooperation initiatives, etc.) as the two cannot be separated. While it is recognized that there may be a focus on one of the aspects, it must be clear that the two are intimately connected. This implies that one cannot cut corners with superficial conflict analysis and without a deeper reading into the context in which conflict occurs. Any notion of transitional justice must be closely scrutinized and properly rooted in the sociohistorical, political, economic, and cultural setting. This requires a "thick" sociology produced within the specific society but fully versed and engaged with an ever more globalized sociology and knowledge.

Third, the *underlying assumptions* (philosophical, political, moral) and the related political agendas and policy-implications of various readings of conflicts and reconciliation processes, must be closely scrutinized, questioned, exposed, and criticized. Important critiques of established models of reading specific conflict, peace and reconciliation processes have emerged over the recent years, illustrating how political and ideological underpinnings can hinder understanding and how this encourages the promotion of specific models of conflict resolution and reconciliation as some kind of "recipe." For instance, the imposition of the "liberal peace model" in Africa is not only producing partial, distorted, and Western-biased readings of the conflicts and their resolution, but is neglecting and undervaluing the potential of homegrown resources and of traditions of struggle and reconciliation.[39] Where "local traditions" are utilized, these are often distorted by appropriating and subordinating them to Western models. Due to the structural prevalence of Western peacemaking models, even when "traditional" approaches are adopted as alternatives peacemaking methods, what we see is not the coexistence of both but: "the co-option of indigenous and traditional by Western approaches."[40] The disastrous Western entanglement in Afghanistan, Iran, the Middle East, the Balkans, and most recently Libya evidence the limits of such approach. The sociological enquiry into the subject should therefore take note of important critiques of Western traditions of conflict resolution.[41] It is high time that the debates around sociology draw on knowledge developed in the "global south"[42] where there is also serious scholarship and activism related to war, peace, and reconciliation.

At the same time, it is crucial that the various "non-western"/southern traditions are neither idealized, nor uncritically accepted as "the norm" in what are assumed to be "non-western"/southern settings. They must be subjected to a deep sociological enquiry and test.

Fourth, it must be *comparative*. Needless to say, from its inception sociology was a comparative discipline, as evidenced by the work of Durkheim. This is not to argue that single societies cannot or ought not to be investigated. On the contrary, the best sources for a *global sociology of conflict and reconciliation* must draw and depend on the richness of existing sociological studies, most of which delve into the specificities of particular societies. Such studies provide the kind of sociological depth necessary to draw out the comparisons in terms of the similarities and differences between various conflicts, peace, and reconciliation processes. Studies which compare and contrast cases require the necessary tools to properly analyze the context, but also to define the *differentia specifica* in the case studies. How else can we understand why and how certain violent conflicts develop, escalate or deescalate, or how reconciliation processes come about? Important conceptual tools can and are drawn from different disciplines—conflict resolution, comparative politics, international relations, social psychology, and anthropology. However, caution is required as to the reasoning *behind* the comparisons. It is trendy to compare in order to "go global," but there must be some rationale behind such comparisons. What is essential is that we need to locate and identify what the primary features of the conflict in a particular society are and only then decide what is comparable and what is not comparable with some other country or countries. As Ehrlich (2009) notes, only if we have a good grasp of specific context, the historical and structural aspects, the dynamics and balance of forces and their potentialities and contestations in the regions and states we can really engage in meaningful comparisons. Comparisons may fail to throw light, even though they are based on relevant features. For instance, a shared past under the same colonial master may make sense in understanding common features in different ethnic conflicts. However, this may be irrelevant in terms of presenting models for reconciliation. The conflicts in Israel/Palestine and Cyprus are a case in point. Both are located very near to each other and both have been subject to British colonialism. Both are "partitioned," and in both cases the partition is "dysfunctional" (i.e., causing harm and misery in different ways, making the status quo unsustainable). Yet, the possibilities for reconciliation and the trajectories that may be followed in both cases differ immensely. In the two cases, violence is quantitatively and qualitatively different and this influences the possibilities of resolution that exist in the two cases. In the case of Israel-Palestine; talk of reconciliation seems to be far fetched and there is violent death on an almost daily basis. In the case of Cyprus things are much milder.[43]

Fifth, the interdisciplinary nature of the exercise must be such that is cross-disciplined but not a-disciplined. The terms of engagement with other disciplines must be carefully observed to avoid becoming an eclectic ensemble with little coherence or sense. We need a sociology that draws on different aspects of knowledge that allows for creative integration that is theoretically sound, empirically robust, and policy-relevant. It will be a sociology that seeks to avoid self-referencing, examining the potential for reshaping ideas, practices and modes articulation.

Sixth, the sociology of conflict and reconciliation is best located *within* the rich debates generated by the sociology of ethnic-related phenomena, the study of nations and nationalism, ethnicity, race and racism, and war. These debates are entangled with questions relating to the interrelation between ethnicity/race, class and gender, the sociology of the state and power as well as global sociology, postcoloniality, and globalization.[44] The theorization of "nations" and nationalism as well as global/international power relations must be properly theorized. Questions relating to the various *political* projects and ideologies and to the complexities of state formations, contradictions, and class relations must be developed.[45] In order to address the global tasks before an ever-uncertain humanity, the sociology of conflict/reconciliation needs to feed on the above branches of sociology so as to understand wars, ethnic-related conflicts (intrastate and interstate), and the potential for peace, cooperation, and reconciliation.[46]

Seventh, the specificity of gender-related violence in conflicts, cooperation, and reconciliation processes must not be considered as an "add-on." The gender factor needs to be properly incorporated as an analytical category that allows for vital insights in such phenomena. The use of the image women as "biological producers of the nation" or the images of motherhood in conflicts produces gender perspectives on the nature of war, peace and "solution" to the conflicts.[47] As the wars in former Yugoslavia illustrate, part of the warfare and mobilization by different groups for support globally made great use of the image of violence specifically directed against women (e.g., rapes or threats of rape). Likewise, the US-led intervention in Afghanistan was justified using the oppression of women as a sound platform for intervention. Women have played a key role in peace and reconciliation initiatives as in Palestine/Israel or Northern Ireland.

Finally, this chapter is calling for *a* sociology beyond sociology and a reconciliation from below, which is as necessary as reconciliation "from above." I am calling for an expansion of the *scope* of reconciliation. I realize that this probably runs counter to what appears to be "common sense" among many practitioners and theorists of CR and reconciliation. They insist, with good reason, that the narrower the scope, the more effective the policy and practice of reconciliation, as (a) attention and resources are more focused and (b) one should not be involved in many fronts at the same time in building coalitions and consensus. This chapter is not denying the merits of having a sense of priority strategy, tactics, and timings. What I am proposing is that we need to *broaden* our conception of reconciliation *within society*. In other words, one must locate the processes of reconciliation within an existing dynamic, conflict-ridden, and polarized social reality. For instance, in attempting to reconcile two ethnic groups that have been in conflict for years we cannot ignore the presence of a possible third or fourth group (for instance the presence of a sizeable number of migrants) or of other issues that may affect social relations (gender-relations; class relations and struggles; homeless and excluded/marginalized/landless people; and migrant struggles). Such facts significantly alter social and political relations in ways which are not always predictable and linear.

Such factors often complicate and aggravate issues as they add various dimensions to conflicts and complex social realities. Gender, ethnicity, religion, and class are "hard variables" that may reinforce polarization and division. However, in other contexts gender, religion, and class can become issues that open up the terrains of struggle for peace and reconciliation. In this sense, women groups for peace (e.g., Women in Black in former Yugoslavia, Parents Circle in Israel/Palestine, Northern Ireland, and others) liberation theology-inspired reconciliation initiatives in South America, religious peace activism in Africa and Asia, and trade union–led worker and subaltern class initiatives in numerous countries and continents. Together, these are formidable forces for peace, transcending conflicts and making it possible to realize the emerging global and local "ethic of reconciliation."[48]

To retain hope in a fragmented and polarized world, we can and must learn from the historical and contemporary struggles. We must educate and be educated about world-peace-in-the-making. Sociology is a vital tool and component in this learning process.

## Notes

1. A more basic format of this chapter was presented at a plenary session on violence and reconciliation conference at the International Sociological Association held in Gothenburg (Sweden), July 11–17, 2010. The chapter grew from debates on reconciliation in Cyprus, South Africa, Israel/Palestine, India, and Ireland. Such matters were raised in the debates, which took place during the conference, *Learning from Comparing Conflicts and Reconciliation Processes: A Holistic Approach,* PRIO Cyprus Centre Annual Conference, June 18–20, 2009, Ledra Palace, Nicosia.
2. Balibar (2002b), (2004); Calame and Charlesworth (2009); Brown (2010).
3. It has become a broad, well-established, branch of study with various subcategories and a large number of journals and vast numbers of publications.
4. Malesevic (2010).
5. Balibar (2002a), (2004); Brown (2010); Calame and Chalesworth (2009).
6. Anthias and Yuval-Davies (1992), p.39.
7. Apart from the founders of sociology, in the late twentieth century, scholars like Barrington More (1966), Tilly (1990), Skocpol (1984), Mann (2005), Giddens (1985), Castells (1997), have contributed to the debates. Moreover, important in this field are the development of a critical reading in class, gender, and race studies.
8. Collins (2008).
9. In an effort to bring together these two aspects of social science and expertise the author organized a conference in 2009 (*Learning from Comparing Conflicts and Reconciliation Processes: A Holistic Approach,* PRIO Cyprus Centre Annual Conference, June 18–20, 2009, Ledra Palace, Nicosia).
10. Coser (1953) is often quoted and cited by the main textbooks on the subject, as the sociologist's insight into conflict.
11. See Ramsbotham et al. (2011).
12. For instance scholars like Jon Burton. The relevant the *Journal Conflict Resolution* was founded in 1957, available at: http://jcr.sagepub.com/.
13. The Peace Institute Oslo was founded in 1959, see www.prio.no/.
14. The *Journal of Peace Research* was founded in 1964, available at: http://jpr.sagepub.com/.
15. See Ramsbotham et al. (2011).
16. Galtung (2000).
17. Lederach (1997).
18. Ramsbotham et al. (2011).
19. Within so-called identity communities there may be fragmented groups, which have a developed or enhanced reconciliation with sections of the "enemy community," while other sections of the population may be highly polarized and hostile.
20. See Yuval-Davis et al. (2008).
21. Lederach (1997), p.182; Ramsbotham et al. (2011).
22. The Conflict Research Society (CRS) is the prime interdisciplinary forum linking professionals and academics concerned with cooperation and conflict and provides a meeting point for sharing their work, available at: www.conflictresearchsociety.org.uk/CRS%20book%20of%20the%20year.html.
23. Ramsbotham et al. (2011), p.7.

24. The term "conflict transformation" refers to the transformation of the structure of the conflicts, whereby one of the dimensions of the conflict (structure, attitudes and behavior) is altered (Mial [1992], p.55).
25. The notion of liberal peace is based on the idea of imposing the model of Western liberal of democracy as a framework of resolving conflicts. This model includes features like elections, the rule of law/ human rights and neoliberal market relations See Richmond (2008); Ramsbotham et al. (2011).
26. Azar (1986), pp.33–34.
27. Edward Said's concept "Orientalism," as a systematic way in which the East (the Orient) is distorted by Westerners, in many ways applies here (1978). Having said that, CR has also been criticized by American right-wing thinkers who consider it to be left-wing and to promote agendas foreign to the West's interests. Criticisms have come both from outside the realms of university system (claiming that "Peace studies do not produce practical prescriptions for managing or resolving global conflicts because 'ideology always trumps objectivity and pragmatism' and that CR is bent on putting a 'respectable face on Western self-loathing'") as well as from right-wing academics like Donald Horowitz. See http://en.wikipedia.org/wiki/Peace_and_conflict_studies
28. For example, Long and Brecke (2003).
29. See Mac Ginty (2008).
30. Ibid.
31. Salem (1993), (1997).
32. Ibid., (1993).
33. Francis (2008), p.4.
34. Porto (2008).
35. As per footnote 26, the concept of "liberal peace" has been defined as a Western the concept of liberal capitalist democracy as a universal model; in the African context, the assumption is that African elites and population need to be "trained" and "educated" to able to receive such a model.
36. Hagg and Kagwaja (2007), p.22.
37. Malesevic (2010), refers to these as rationales for their respective publications.
38. Burawoy, M. (2007), available at: http://burawoy.berkeley.edu/PS/Socio-Economic%20Review/PS%20vs.%20Market.pdf.
39. Francis (2008).
40. MacGinty (2008).
41. Ramsbotham et al. (2011), p.3.
42. See Sitas (2006); Alatas (2006); Patel (2006); Elizaga (2006).
43. See Sitas (2008); Trimikliniotis (2007), (2010), (2012); Ehrlich (2009).
44. See Balibar and Wallerstein (1991); Balibar (2002); Anthias (1992); Balakrishnan (1996); Gellner (1983).
45. An attempt to theorize such has been made in the context of Cyprus, see Trimikliniotis and Bozkurt (2012); Bozkurt and Trimikliniotis (2012); Trimikliniotis (2012).
46. See Trimikliniotis (2012).
47. Anthias and Davis (1992).
48. Sitas (2008), (2011).

# References

Alatas, S. F. (2006). "A Khaldunian Exemplar for a Historical Sociology for the South." *Current Sociology*, 54, 3, pp.397–411.

Anthias, F. (1992). "Connecting 'Race' and Ethnic Phenomena." *SOCIOLOGY*, 26, 3, August 1992.

Anthias F. and Yuval-Davis N. (1992). *Racialised Boundaries*. London: Routledge.
Azar, E. (1986). "Protracted Social Conflicts: An Analytical Framework." In E. Azar and J. W. Burton (eds.), *International Conflict Resolution: Theory and Practice*. Sussex: Wheatsheaf Books, pp.5–17.
Balakrishnan, G. (Ed.) (1996). *Mapping the Nation*. London: New Left Books.
Balibar, E. (2004). "World Borders, Political Borders." In E. Balibar (ed.), *We, the People of Europe, Reflections on Transnational Citizenship*. Princeton and London: Princeton University Press.
———. (2002a). "Ambiguous Universality." In E. Balibar (ed.), *Politics and the Other Scene*. London: Verso.
———. (2002b). "What Is a Border." In E. Balibar (ed.), *Politics and the Other Scene*. London: Verso.
Balibar, E. and Wallerstein, I. (1991). *Race, Nation, Class: Ambiguous Identities*. London and New York: Verso Press.
Brown, W. (2010). *Walled States, Waning Sovereignty*. New York: Zone books.
Calame, J. and Charlesworth, E. (2009). *Divided Cities, Belfast, Beirut, Jerusalem, Mostar, and Nicosia*. Philadelphia: University of Pennsylvania Press.
Collins, R. (2008). *Violence, a Micro-Sociological Approach*. Princeton, NJ: Princeton University Press.
Coser, L. (1956). *The Functions of Social Conflict*. New York: The Free Press.
Ehrlich (2009). "Comparative Research on Protracted Conflicts in Partitioned States: Methodological Considerations about Choosing Cases, Parameters and a Theoretical Framework." Paper for the conference *Learning from Comparing Conflicts and Reconciliation Processes: A Holistic Approach*, PRIO Cyprus Centre Annual Conference, June 18–20, 2009, Ledra Palace, Nicosia.
Elizaga, R. C. (2006). "Sociology and the South, The Latin American Experience," *Current Sociology*, 54, 3, pp.413–425.
Francis, D. J. (2008). "Introduction: Understanding Peace and Conflict in Africa," In D. J. Francis (ed.), *Peace and Conflict in Africa*. London: Zed Books, pp. 2–14.
Galtung, J. (2000). *Conflict Transformation by Peaceful Means, the Transcend Method*. New York: United Nations Disaster Management Program.
Gellner, G. (1983). *Nations and Nationalisms*. Oxford: Blackwell.
Hagg, G. and Kagwanja, P. (2007). "Identity and Peace: Reconfiguring Conflict Resolution in Africa." In *African Journal on Conflict Resolution*, 7, 2, pp.9–35.
Lederach, J. P. (1997). *Building Peace, Sustainable Reconciliation in Divided Societies*. Washington, DC: United States Institute of Peace Research.
Long, W. J. and Brecke, P. (2003). *War and Reconciliation: Reason and Emotion in Conflict Resolution*. Cambridge, MA: MIT Press.
MacGinty, R. (2008). "Indigenous Peace-Making Versus the Liberal Peace." *Cooperation and Conflict*, 43, 2, pp.139–163.
Malesevic, S. (2010). *The Sociology of War and Violence*. Cambridge: Cambridge University Press.
Mial, H. (1992). *The Peacemakers*. New York: St. Martin's Press.
Patel, S. (2006). "Beyond Binaries, A Case for Self-Reflexive Sociologies," *Current Sociology*, 54, 3, pp.381–395.
Porto, J. G. (2008). "The Mainstreaming of Conflict Analysis in Africa." In D. J. Francis (ed.), *Peace and Conflict in Africa*. London: Zed Books.
Ramsbotham, O., Woodhouse, T., and Miall, H. (2011). *Contemporary Conflict Resolution, the Prevention, Management and Transformation of Deadly Conflicts*, 3rd ed. London: Polity Press.
Richmond, O. (2008). *Peace in International Relations*. London: Routledge.
Said, E. (1978). *Orientalism*. London: Routledge & Kegan Paul Ltd.

Salem, P. (Ed.) (1997). *Conflict Resolution in the Arab World: Selected Essays*. New York: American University of Beirut.

———. (1993). "A Critique of Western Conflict Resolution from a Non-Western Perspective." Available at: www.ciel.usj.edu.lb/docs/CR/p_salem.pdf.

Sitas, A. (2008). *The Ethic of Reconciliation*. University of Kwazulu-Natal, Durban: Madiba Publishers.

Sitas, A. (2011). "Beyond The Mandela Decade: The Ethic of Reconciliation?" *Current Sociology*, 59, 5.

Trimikliniotis, N. (2012). "The Cyprus Problem and Imperial Games in the Hydrocarbon Era: From a Place of Arms to An Energy Player?." In Trimikliniotis, N. and Bozkurt, U. (eds.), *Beyond a Divided Cyprus: A State and Society in Transformation*. New York: Palgrave MacMillan, pp. 23–46.

———. (2010). *Η Διαλεκτική του Έθνους-Κράτους και το Καθεστώς Εξαίρεσης: Κοινωνιολογικές και Συνταγματικές Μελέτες για την Ευρω-Κυπριακή Συγκυρία και το Εθνικό Ζήτημα [The nation-state dialectic and the state of exception—sociological and constitutional studies on the Eurocyprian conjuncture and the national question]* Savalas, Athens 2010.

———. (2007). "Reconciliation and Social Action in Cyprus: Citizens' Inertia and the Protracted State of Limbo." *Cyprus Review, Special Edition on Reconciliation in Cyprus*, 19, 1, Spring 2007, pp.123–160.

Trimikliniotis, N. and Bozkurt, U. (Eds.) (2012). *Beyond a Divided Cyprus: A State and Society in Transformation*. New York and London: Palgrave MacMillan.

Yuval-Davis, N., Kannabiran, K. and Vieten, U. (2008). *The Situated Politics of Belonging*. London: SAGE.

# 17

# The "Modern" Muslim Woman in the Arab Peoples' Revolution of Freedom and Dignity

*Nathalie Grima*

## Introduction

In this article, I question the discourse and perceptions that place Arab women within the traditional-modern dichotomy. In the case of Muslim women, this is very often associated with whether they are following the Islamic dress of *hijab* or *niqab*, or whether they have rejected these garments. Apart from the simplistic association with tradition, Islamic dress is very often equated with gender oppression. My fieldwork with Arab Muslim women living in Malta has shown me that their situation is a much more flexible situation, which can be understood by looking at their perspectives rather than sticking to a rigid view. My respondents' narratives reveal that in general they tend to reject the idea that the only solution for gender equity is the one that is based on a Western, feminist, and apparently secular model. They rather tend to project the idea of a "modern" woman that can also be a practicing Muslim.

The second part of the article looks at the revolutionary events that took place in Tunisia and Egypt based on some of my respondents' contributions. Although they were not physically present during the protests, the women interviewed do share a strong sense of being part of a genuine collectivity that is united by the common cry for democracy, freedom of speech, and a just distribution of wealth in their homelands. What makes the collectivities of the Arab uprisings fascinating is the drive with which people of all ages, gender, religion, and political belief came together to stand up for their rights, proud of what they have accomplished against all odds. The spirit with which the Arab peoples are revolting against unjust systems of power can be compared to the activism and motivation of the Italian educator Don Lorenzo Milani, whose methods of teaching aimed to instigate the same political commitment among the oppressed, enabling them to stand up and challenge the status quo. The tens of thousands who have thronged the squares and streets in protest continue to resist the threat of reverting to the dictatorial or repressive rule, which they have put up with for decades. The issues discussed in the two parts are linked together in the final part of the chapter, where I explore the role of women in this struggle for peace and economic stability.

## The Paradigm—Islamic Feminism

With the collapse of the "iron curtain" in 1989, the dichotomy of the West and the Soviet bloc gradually shifted to that of the West and Islamism. Political issues such as the Palestinian-Israeli conflict, the "Rushdie affair," the Iraq war, the events of 9/11, the war in Afghanistan, and the "headscarf affair" have brought Islam into the limelight, greatly enhanced by extensive media coverage of a number of events, including live transmissions made possible with the introduction of satellite TV. The Bush administration's discourse of "war on terror" following the 9/11 terrorist attacks, may have reinforced a distorted image of Muslims especially among those who tend to look at Islam as purely fundamentalist. As may be expected with any form of generalized projections, the attempt to situate Muslims in a homogenous collectivity has been counterproductive. Roy refers to a "contemporary religious revival" or post-Islamism, especially among minority immigrant groups, generated by a reaction against what is perceived to be Islamophobia in certain quarters.[1]

Abu-Lughod[2] notes that when the Western powers, mainly British and American, decided to wage war on Afghanistan and Iraq during the first years of this century, one of the justifications they used was the need to liberate Muslim women from oppressive regimes. She refers to this as the "rhetoric of salvation"; a political rationale that serves to justify (at least in part) aggression or military invasion by focusing on women who supposedly need to be saved from the enemy power. For instance, in her radio address on November 17, 2001, Laura Bush included Afghan women, claiming that :

> the fight against terrorism is also a fight for the rights and dignity of women.[3]

These thoughts, that the rights and dignity and women are not respected in Afghanistan or other parts of the Muslim world, are common in the West and are in certain cases used to justify aggression by some power against a particular government or state. This generalized projection of Muslim women as passive agents has been criticized and challenged by scholars who have sought to deconstruct this misleading perception.

The deconstruction of this rhetoric of salvation has come from various sources. At one end we find the cultural relativist analysis, which seeks to explain local cultural patterns pertaining to particular communities without being judgmental, declaring that these should not be tampered with by the "'outsider" or serve as a "target of a 'civilizing mission.'"[4] Critics of this approach who are concerned with the rights and dignity of women, consider it to be apologetic and to provide a basis for retaining the status quo. Cultural relativists rebut that respect for these rights is not a universal value but pertains only to some societies. Such societies cannot impose these values on the former.

At the other end, we find the radical feminist analysis that seek to explain women's contexts in relation to patriarchal dominance. In their analysis, these feminists tend to start from the premise that women are always at a disadvantage in their life aspirations because they are victims of a male-dominated society. They have often used this approach to picture Muslim women as "invisible," "covered," "segregated," or "secluded." Their analysis has been criticized because, among other things, it remains focused on emphasizing the difference between men and women without providing solutions that can bring about gender equity.

In my fieldwork I prefer to use postfeminist concepts, which do not deny that women may suffer from various forms of injustice, including physical and psychological violence, but which nevertheless stress that Muslim societies cannot be simplistically divided into sharply delineated aggressive and victimized sectors. This is because both men and women may be victims, and also, because women are able to decide, act, and speak for themselves in the face of hardships or obstacles to gender equity.

One way of gaining a better understanding of these concepts is by taking into consideration the Islamic feminist standpoint that proposes that what may seem oppressive in the eyes of other feminists, such as the wearing of *hijab*, can be liberating as long as it is not imposed against their wishes (as the case of women in Iran). These Muslim feminists insist that Muslim women should not be patronized or romanticized as subjects that need to be protected or saved. After all, women in the Middle East and North Africa (MENA), alone or with the support of social networks, have very often voiced their concern about their day-to-day hardships, such as poverty, war, as well as access to health care, education, and to the labor market.

In this article, I draw on insights from this approach since it seems to be imbued by the people I interviewed, all of whom come from a Muslim background and analyze the Arab experience in relation to this. Though I might share similar values to the interviewees, the way in which we articulate these values may differ. The chapter however, seeks to respect these differences. It refrains from dividing the world into "We" and "Other" categories[5] and attempts to avoid an "imagined geography" wherein the Occident is clearly and sharply separated from the Orient.[6]

My chapter will be a dialogic exercise. This form of dialogue can be compared to what Yuval-Davis calls "transversal" dialogue which, rather than overcoming religious and ethnical barriers, acknowledges that "the world is seen differently"[7] by different people. As Toriello notes, this type of approach, seems to be ingrained in Milani's pedagogical practice based on inclusivity and dialogue.[8]

## The Findings—Gendered Spaces in Transition

In my fieldwork with Arab Muslim women living in Malta, my respondents very often referred to the transition of Islamic practices from the preindustrial to the modern times. According to their interpretation, this is linked to the transition from an economy based on agriculture in rural village settings, to one that became increasingly industrial bringing about a significant increase in mobility of people to the more crowded cities. In their villages, women participated in agricultural work and were actively involved in the subsistence of the extended family. Childcare was not assigned to a sole woman confined to the house, but shared among the other members of the family such as older wives, daughters, daughters-in-law, and cousins. Since women usually mixed with men who were members of the extended family, they did not wear the headscarf or *hijab* except for special occasions such as weddings or on the few occasions when they left the household to visit other relatives.

With the shift to industrialization, the status of the working woman began to change. This shift occurred mainly due to better access to higher education; a situation that saw more women improving their chances of employability, entrepreneurship, and undertaking professional careers. For some Muslims, however, this social change was a cause for concern because it entailed men and women mingling and socializing together in public spaces. Given the interpretations of the major Islamic schools of jurisprudence and exegeses,[9] many Muslims agree that this social mixing can be acceptable if both men and women dress and act modestly toward each other. This sense of morality in social relationships between men and women takes a material form, being embedded in the way that women dress in the presence of men who are not members of their nuclear family. Although these schools have not reached a consensus on the areas of the body that have to be covered, they agree on one point, "that women should cover in one way or another."[10] The *hijab* thus serves to create visible boundaries that transform a neutral public space into a gendered one. While men are expected to treat women with respect, they are not obliged to cover up in specific dress codes. Women's bodies on the other hand, are assumed to be a site of desire and temptation. The emphasis of covering falls on veiling that covers the hair and neck. The *hijab*, in itself a valueless piece of clothing, is transformed into a measurement of women's modesty and morality. What was originally a Qur'anic interpretation of modest behavior between men and women, has become an internalized cultural meaning in societies who have adapted new ways of retaining segregation in modern contexts where physical separation is no longer possible.[11]

This interpretation of a gendered space cannot stop here. During a short public presentation of my dissertation findings, I could not help noticing some of the Maltese non-Muslim participants who referred to women's veiling as "traditional." Claiming that veiling is only due to a tradition of segregation limits any attempt at a genuine and transversal dialogue. This stereotypical projection of the *hijab* probably extends beyond the boundaries of this particular public meeting, so I will now attempt to challenge it by presenting the views of the women I interviewed regarding the reasons why they decide to veil.

## The "Modern" Muslim Woman

My interviews with Arab, Muslim, women showed that the modern/traditional, religious/secular dichotomies may not apply, or may not apply in the way they are normally conceived to apply (the modern/secular supplants the traditional/religious), to the reality of many contemporary Muslim women.

A common observation among my respondents concerned the contrast between themselves and their own mothers with respect to their religious knowledge. While their mothers did not have good access to the Qur'anic text, "today, we have the possibility to know what the source of our religion is because we can read the text and also listen to Islamic teachings on the satellite TV programs." The possibility of pursuing a formal education together with the introduction of satellite TV, are both considered as significant progressive developments in the MENA region. Paradoxically, while governing leaders, such as those in Tunisia before the revolts, strove to create a secular state inclusive of a higher level of education and of technology, these progressive targets also served as a means of bringing religion closer and more central to people in the course of their everyday lives. Islamic teachings became more widespread due to a higher literacy and to the increasing viewership of sheikhs teaching on satellite TV and on internet sites.

Moreover, a study carried out by Cherribi[12] on the increased occurrence of women in *hijab* on the Al Jazeera Arab TV station, concludes that the Islamic veil on media serves to instill notions of Muslim identity. Seen in this way, education and technology can no longer be considered as structures that encourage secularization. In the Islamic context, the populist association of religion or religiosity with tradition and of secularization with modernity is deemed to fail. Religion can indeed be compatible with modernity,[13] because for many, it has become a "carrier of identity."[14]

In their personal accounts of veiling as a spiritual process, my respondents also reflected upon the connection between their individual religiosity and their identity. On the other hand they tended to condemn religious practice imposed by the state such as in Iran and Saudi Arabia. Their self-reflexivity as Muslims mostly fits the post-Islamist model, which Roy[15] defines as the development of religious spirituality on an individual level. This may lead to a "contemporary religious revival" which, rather than being imposed, is accompanied with the quest for one's identity. This revival can be observed not only in countries where Islam is not the predominant religion, but also in the repressive states such as prerevolutionary Tunisia, where some practices were frowned upon.

The issue of the *hijab* is frequently and simplistically caricatured as a religious imposition by various male-dominated institutions (family, state) on Muslim women who are frequently considered to be victims requiring to be liberated (in one way or another) from this imposition. While obviously one cannot deny that there are cases where this is the case, in many instances this characterization does not apply. Some Muslim women may perceive the *hijab* as oppressive. Many, however, consider it in different terms. Some consider it a duty to be freely adhered to. Others even perceive it as liberating or empowering. Moreover, apart from religious connotations, the *hijab* has others aspects; cultural or even aesthetic.[16]

Influences on women's everyday lives are multidirectional, and their actions cannot be explained merely in terms of Bourdieu's[17] concept of habitus, that is, as "habitual[ly] expect[ed] and assum[ed]" without the need for a process of reflection. They do not automatically "make their own" that which is practiced by the majority in their social environment, as if they were totally conditioned and shaped by others. A good number of women do not simply put on the veil unquestioningly. The narratives of the women I interviewed reveal that they take time to reflect upon what they consider as a personal commitment; a decision to be taken seriously, and which usually involves a decision-making process. Many consider their adhering to this almost-ascetic Islamic practice as compatible with their education system and with the possibility of obtaining a place in the labor market. That the wearing of the veil does not simplistically entail passivity is evidenced by the role women (many of whom wear a veil) played in Arab revolts;[18] seeking to bring about significant social changes after decades of dictatorial or repressive leaderships. It is on this that I focus in the next part of the chapter.

## A Significant Beginning—the Revolts in Tunisia and Egypt

Up till December 17, 2010, the hegemonic order in the Arab world had, to a certain extent, remained unquestioned. The United States were still seeking to capture the Al-Qaeda leader Bin Laden, considered as the number one threat to the stability, which was supposedly held in check by the world economic and military powers. South to North mobility across the Mediterranean was becoming more strictly controlled due to the bilateral agreements between Libya and Italy. The solution to the Palestinian question, still seems to-date a distant mirage.

The news of Mohammed Bouazizi's suicide shook the world not only out of empathy for his self-sacrifice, but also because it was immediately clear that the longtime status quo in the Arab world had been finally disrupted. Bouazizi's attempts to improve the standard of living of his family had been forcefully suppressed and he saw no way out of it but to end his life. What was incredible about this event was the way that it triggered a mass outrage and public action with people taking to the streets in protest. The revolts defy common assumptions that Arab peoples are passive and compliant.

They challenge the Eurocentric perspective of the Mediterranean construct that labels the region as a homogenous and nonresistant one. The uprisings, which were triggered off in the neighboring countries, together with the postrevolutionary reforms, already reveal the complexity of each differing context. which shows us how sociopolitically heterogenous the region is.

For example, in Tunisia, this was not the first time that the Tunisian people had taken action against the state's corrupt rule; a rule that had given rise to long-term unemployment, not to mention the police force's abusive violence. However, this time round, the people were determined they would break through the "media blackout"[19] by posting the filming of Bouazizi's self-immolation on Facebook. Rochdi Horchani, one of his relatives, reported that "the protesters took to the streets with a rock in one hand, a cell phone in the other."[20] Media censorship was a strong coercive force that the people of Tunisia had been facing to such an extent, that it was very difficult to achieve a homogenous spread of knowledge of the various small action groups emerging in different parts of the country. The state had been taking coercive measures in order to keep people in check and to block any signs of unified rebellion. However, the state underestimated two factors. First, the ability of the people to keep seeking new ways of informing and encouraging each other to take action (what in sociological terms one would identify as agency action). Secondly, censorship did not include Facebook, and so activists were quick to realize that this could be a very useful tool for spreading knowledge of what was going on and encouraging people all over the country to take to the streets in protest. People could share their hardships on a much wider scale, extending across time and space in a manner, which they couldn't have thought of a few years back. This alternative medium gave rise to a new form of power at the level of agency, which people set to use as a form of resistance to the repressive governing rule. Thus, with regard to Tunisia, even though only a third of Tunisia's population are internet users, this was enough to create the required ripple effect of what seems to be a counter-hegemonic act, this time brought about by the people themselves transformed into a general public willing to bring about the longed-for economic, political, and social changes.

A striking feature of these revolts was the role played by women. Images of women as very active participants in the revolts defied the perspective of Arab Muslim women as passive agents. The women's protest held in Egypt on December 23, 2011 with the call of, "women of Egypt raise your heads, you are more noble than those who stamp on you" is only one of the many examples of concrete action currently taking place in the face of injustice.[21] While these images may have surprised the Western viewer, Arab women themselves cannot understand the extent to which they are stereotyped, and as the Egyptian activist Hadil El-Khouly said:

> There was this sense of surprise, that "Oh, my god, women are actually participating!"...But of course women were there in Tahrir Square. I was there, because I'm Egyptian. Everyone was there. You really felt we were all one.[22]

Though not evident to many in the West, the revolts also had a religious dimension. At the beginning of these revolts, many in the West focused on the role played by modern technology, and on economic factors as causes of the troubles. These were undoubtedly major factors. The role of modern technology has already been discussed. Economic factors like the high rates of unemployment, especially among the younger generation, and the increasing inability of many to make ends meet, were undoubtedly major motives behind the revolts. However, there was another factor that helped trigger the revolt; a religious one.

In Tunisia, the revolution came about because the people's common end was to overthrow Ben Ali and to bring his corrupt governance to an end. The hardships brought about by unemployment together with religious suppression, were the two factors that may have united the people toward this common end. The widespread use of mobile phones and Facebook served as the means to transfer knowledge and encourage the people to take to the streets.

The role of religion, particularly with regard to the religious practice of women in Tunisia and elsewhere in the Muslim world, are discussed further in what follows.

## An Identity Crisis

Bourguiba's founding of a secular state in Tunisia did not reflect the consent of the majority. His original aim was a modern state where religion and governance could function independently of each other. This was considered a progressive attempt at enhancing education, gender equality, and religious freedom. In 1956, women were granted equal salaries, placing them at an advantage when compared to women in Europe and the United States. Unlike Bourguiba, Ben Ali did not completely disassociate himself from religion, but:

> deliberately and self-consciously appealed to Tunisia's Arab/Islamic heritage.[23]

However, when confronted by the strong opposition of the Islamic party *Ennahda*, he reintroduced the polito-religious separation and repressed this Islamic party.[24] Furthermore, he not merely repressed this party, but curbed certain Islamic practices *tout court*. This left a substantial part of the population wishing for a freedom "of" and not a freedom "from" religion. Individuals and groups sought ways of resistance, such as holding on to their right to wear *hijabs*, going to the mosque for prayers and speaking out against injustices incurred. One of my respondents, a Tunisian woman living in Malta, recounted how:

> it was difficult to practise your religion without attracting the bad attention of the government. If a woman or a man goes to a mosque frequently for the five times' prayers, you are automatically listed by the political police.

And, I asked, "labeled as fundamentalist?" to which she replied,

> Yes, that's the attitude of our government, the previous one. Hopefully now it will change.²⁵

She also spoke of how this repression led her for a very long time to feel as if she belonged nowhere. She was Muslim and Tunisian. Yet, due to Ben Ali's repressive regime, she felt no sense of belonging in Tunisia given that she could not freely practice her religion. Her account of her youthful years in Tunis was full of sad episodes of women friends who discontinued their education because they resisted removing the *hijab* when they were forbidden to wear it at schools and universities. In her opinion, the current Arab revolutions are a strong reaction to a crisis of identity. She believes that due to this kind of corrupt governance in most Arab countries and to the suppression of free religious practice in some, people ended up feeling neither fully Arab nor totally Muslim. For some, the Islamic text of the Qur'an became for some the only point of reference in reconstructing their identity. In her words,

> being Muslim and being Arab we were having a big setback because of 9/11, because of Israel, because of this and that...there is no systematic education in one language...the only identity is that of the Qur'an because nothing can touch it, nobody can change it. It's still there, it's like a unifying factor, at least for its values, not even for its religiosity. It's a set of sure values where people don't have to look somewhere else...don't have to keep on looking somewhere because of the closure of the political system because of the closure of everything.

Hence, given her interpretation, religious revival was not simply a matter of reacting to religious suppression but also a matter of reestablishing an identity. Speaking at the outset of the revolt she said:

> Now I am happy, I am happy to wave the flag, I am happy to sing the anthem.

In Tahrir Square and elsewhere in the Arab world, there were those who resisted what they saw as the imposition of the Western form of modernity. Most of my respondents speak out for democracy, higher wages, a better education for their children, and freedom of speech. They speak with a sense of pride about their decisions to go out to work, to drive a car, to wear the *hijab*, to buy nice clothes or new homes. Yet, at the same time, some of them also speak against certain aspects of the Western lifestyle especially when they refer to the latter's libertarian attitudes toward women's body and dress, sex before marriage, and cohabitation. Therefore they tend to support a conservative social order, embodying sexual borders and modest behavior, which, as explained earlier, goes beyond the traditional/modern dichotomy. They consistently emphasize that they are not living under any form of gender oppression. On the contrary, they go to great lengths to project themselves as autonomous beings who are able to decide for themselves on these issues. While they resist certain features of Western thought or behavior, they also speak out for gender equity that perhaps differs from the kind of equity emphasized by Western militant feminists. This challenges the intellectual, particularly feminist, discourse that normally views gender equity only within secular parameters.

Having emphasized this factor; that large numbers of Muslim Arabs (including many women) are turning to the Qur'anic text as a measure of identity (as explained by my respondent); the role of religion and religious groups should not be overexaggerated. The importance of religious factors does not entail that those who clamor for change seek to establish a theocracy, want to renounce to all aspects of modernity or that all those who seek change are affiliated to religiopolitical organizations.[26]

My Egyptian friend living in Cairo, Mona El Sayed, referred to "The Egyptian Movement for Change," better known by its slogan name "Kifaya" meaning "Enough."[27] According to her, this is a movement of Egyptian youth and ordinary people who do not associate themselves with religious groups or political parties. Although the Islamist al-Wasat party leader Abu al-'Ila Madi was involved in the movement's foundation in 2004, eventually the Islamists withdrew and contrary to some misconceptions, my friend Mona insists that the Muslim brothers and Al-Qaeda are not part of it. The second aim mentioned in the movement's manifesto is to work for a political reform in the light of "the repressive despotism that pervades all aspects of the Egyptian political system" and the "want for democratic governance" (as posted on Kifaya). This would seem to be inconsistent with any attempt to oppress in the name of religion (rather than oppressive religious practices, as was the case with secularized regimes).

Similarly, with the exception of one Libyan woman who showed an inclination for an Islamic state and Shari'a law, my conversations with some of my respondents prioritize the need for democracy, the end to corruption, fair wages, economic stability, and for developments in the educational and health systems. A social order based on religious affiliation retains its importance but this is considered to pertain to familiar matters such as marriage and one's behavior, rather than to political ones.

## Possible False Dawn?—a Place for Women Or a Return to Their Marginalization?

Having emphasized the role women play in the struggle for freedom from oppression, the reader should not be given the impression that the future poses no challenges. The title of an article posted on the movement's "Women in Black" mailing list written by Anna Louie Sussman, "Prominent During Revolution, Egyptian Women Vanish in New Order" points to the dangers that may lie ahead. Sussman writes about how women from all kinds of background who were so prominently active in Tahrir Square, were quickly "sidelined, pushed out of the political process" in postrevolutionary Egypt. This seems to be the challenge that Arab women involved in all the revolting countries will have to face in the coming years.

Egyptian women are at times feeling that they are not being included in the current processes of re-governance. Women are not questioning whether interested female candidates should be practicing Muslims or not. Neither are they questioning their Islamic dress. Their common aim is to have a higher female representation on this new and apparently long road to democracy. Their exclusion from this process is a clear indication that in the Arab world, there is much more to be done before pragmatic and not rhetoric equity can be reached. The current inclusivity of women in the public revolutionary actions should not cease once the revolutionary fervor is over. Otherwise women will continue to be subjected to gendered spaces in a world of political powers.

## Conclusion

Given what has been said, one can see that the Arab Spring presents phenomena that are not easily compatible with many Western narratives of progress, particularly with the traditional-modern dichotomy that these usually entail. It challenges Eurocentric ideas regarding Arab and Muslim passivity, particularly with regard to Arab and Muslim women. They also combine emancipation and religious fervor, rather than pose one as being antithetical to the other. Regarding religion, they debunk the widely held assumption that Islam and progress (in this case political progress) are incompatible with each other. These assumptions are held by many Europeans and Americans; laypersons and thinkers alike, on the political right as well as on the left. Few were those ready to challenge them.

The chapter also considers the possible threat that may lie ahead for Arab Muslim women who featured so prominently during the Arab Spring.[28]

## Notes

1. Roy (2004), p.3.
2. Abu-Lughod (2002), p.788.
3. Woolley and Peters (2001).
4. Mayo (2007), p.2.
5. Treacher and Shukrallah (2001), p.5.
6. Moghissi (1999), p.33.
7. Yuval-Davis (1999), p.94.
8. Toriello (2010), p.140f.
9. "The explanation of, and commentory on, the Quran, the sifting of different traditions to judge their validity, and the administration and elaboration of law...came to be enshrined in four great schools—the Hanbali, Hanafi, Shafe'i and Maliki" (Gilsenan [2005], p.30).
10. Roald (2001), p.271.
11. Anwar (2006), p.102.

12. Cherribi (2006), p.121.
13. Martin (2008).
14. Martin (1978), p.77.
15. Roy claims that this applies mostly in societies where state and religion are separate and follows the earlier Islamist phase of aiming to tie politics with religion (2004, p.3).
16. A higher frequency of images of women appearing in *hijab* has introduced the fashion element that suggests new and attractive ways of wearing it. Specialized shops offer a variety of headscarves and other Islamic clothing coming in different colors and designs. Seen from this perspective, the *hijab* reattains its fetish meaning of sensual and exotic. See Shirazi (2001), p.46; Entwistle (2002), p.143 However, the women who choose to abide by the Islamic discourse of modesty, resist this commercialization of the veil and adhere to the plain type of *hijab* pinned under the chin and do not put on any makeup. For these women, it is not only the amount of body covering that matters, but also the modesty in their dress and their attire.
17. Crossley (2005), p.108.
18. This article was written some months after the revolts set off in Arab countries between the end of 2010 and the beginning of 2011.
19. Ryan (2011).
20. Ibid.
21. The protest was held in reaction to the Egyptian army soldiers' assaults on women and after an online footage of a woman beaten and stripped was watched by viewers worldwide. More coverage of the protest can be read on www.truth-out.org/egypts-women-protest-despite-brutal-military-attacks/1324754474#.Tvs4LIEU06I.gmail.
22. As reported by Carla Power in her article "Silent No More: The Women of the Arab Revolutions," March 24, 2011.
23. Esposito and Voll (2001), p.104.
24. After succeeding Bourgouiba in 1987, Ben Ali promised the Tunisian Islamic Tendency Movement (MTI)—who later changed their name to *Ennahdha*—that he would officially recognize them as a political party. By December 1989, he had already categorically ruled out this recognition (Esposito and Voll (2001), p.104).
25. The interview was carried out after the Tunisian revolt.
26. Referring to the revolt in Egypt, Lynch refers to this as a "diverse coalition of oppositional movements" (2006) p.242, including liberals, Nasserists and Arabists revolving "around a core demand for change from below" Ibid.
27. Mona El Sayed is the director of "Fair Trade Egypt." During the peak days of revolution in Egypt in January 2011, she happened to be visiting Fair Trade organizations in Italy and before returning to Cairo to meet families and friends in celebration, she took the opportunity of sharing a Power-Point presentation summarizing the events. I was lucky enough to receive a digital copy of it via email.
28. I would like to thank Peter Mayo, Mark-Anthony Falzon, JosAnn Cutajar, Mona El Sayed, my fieldwork respondents, and my husband Adrian for their support.

# References

Abu-Lughod, L. (2002). "Do Muslim Women Really Need Saving? Anthropological Reflections
on Cultural Relativism and Its Others." *American Anthropologist*, 104, 3, pp.783–90.
Anon. "Declaration to the Nation." *Kifaya*. Available at: www.harakamasria.org/node/2944. Accessed on November 15, 2011.
Anon., Kifaya (The Egyptian Movement for Change). *Carnegie Endowment for International Peace*. Available at: http://egyptelections.carnegieendowment.org/2010/09/22/the-egyptian-movement-for-change-kifaya. Accessed on November 15, 2011.

Anwar, E. (2006). *Gender and Self in Islam*. London: Routledge.
Cherribi, S. (2006). "From Baghdad to Paris: Al-Jazeera and the Veil." *The Harvard International Journal of Press/Politics*, 11, 2, pp.121–138.
Crossley, N. (2005). *Key Concepts in Critical Social Theory*. London: SAGE Publications Ltd.
Entwistle, J. (2002). "The Dressed Body." In M. Evans and E. Lee (eds), *Real Bodies: A Sociological Introduction*. New York: Palgrave, Chapter 9.
Espostio, J. L. and Voll, J. O. (2001). *Makers of Contemporary Islam*. New York: Oxford University Press.
Gilsenan, M. (2005). *Recognizing Islam, Religion and Society in the Modern Middle East*. 2nd ed. London, New York: I. B.Tauris & Co Ltd.
Lynch, M. (2007). *Voices of the New Arab Public: Iraq, Al-Jazeera, and Middle East Politics Today*. New York: Columbia University Press.
Martin, D. (2008). *Differences between Pentecostalism and Fundamentalist Islam*. Available at: www.youtube.com/watch?v=-VkUnZC1xX0&feature=player_embedded#at=13. Accessed April 30, 2011.
———. (1978). *A General Theory of Secularization*. Oxford: Basil Blackwell.
Mayo, P. (2007). "Gramsci, the Southern Question and the Mediterranean." *Mediterranean Journal of Educational Studies*, 12, 2, pp.1–17.
Moghissi, H. (1999). *Feminism and Islamic Fundamentalism: The Limits of Postmodern Analysis*. London: Zed Books.
Power C. (2011). "Silent No More: The Women of the Arab Revolutions." *Time World*, March 24, 2011. Available at: www.time.com/time/world/article/0,8599,2059435,00.html. Accessed on November 28, 2011.
Roald, A. S. (2001). *Women in Islam: the Western Experience*. London: Routledge.
Roy, O. (2004). *Globalised Islam: The Search for a New Ummah*. London: C.Hurst & Co.
Ryan, Y. (2011). "How Tunisia's Revolution Began." *Aljazeera*, January 26, 2011. Available at: http://english.aljazeera.net/indepth/features/2011/01/2011126121815985483.html. Accessed on June 16, 2011.
Sabry, M. (2011). "Egypt's Women Protest Despite Brutal Military Attacks." *Truthout*, December 24, 2011. Available at: www.truth-out.org/news/item/5745:egypts-women-protest-despite-brutal-military-attacks#.Tvs4LIEU06I.gmail. Accessed on January 25, 2012.
Shirazi, F. (2003). *The Veil Unveiled: The Hijab in Modern Culture*. Gainesville, FL: University Press of Florida.
Sussman, A. L. (2011). "Prominent dring Revolution, Egyptian Women Vanish in New Order." *The Atlantic*, April 13, 2011. Available at: www.theatlantic.com/international/archive/2011/04/prominent-during-revolution-egyptian-women-vanish-in-new-order/237232/. Accessed on April 15, 2011.
Torriello, F. (2010). "Lettera a una Professoressa Aktar minn Erbgħin Sena wara: Interpretazzjoni Interkulturali." In C. Borg (ed.), *Lorenzo Milani: bejn Ilbieraħ u Llum*. Malta: Horizons.
Treacher, A. and Shukrallah, H. (2001). "Editorial: The Realm of the Possible: Middle Eastern Women in Political and Social Spaces." *Feminist Review*, 69, pp. 4–14.
Woolley, J. T. and Peters, G. (2001). Radio Address by Mrs.Bush. *The American Presidency Project*. Available at: www.presidency.ucsb.edu/ws/index.php?pid=24992. Accessed on January 14, 2011.
Yuval-Davis, N. (1999). "What Is 'Transversal Politics'?" *Soundings*, 12, pp.94–98.

# Critical Epilogue: Making Sense of Lorenzo Milani's Antiwar Project in Our Times

*Carmel Borg and Michael Grech*

The reader will certainly be impressed by the variety of reflections that Milani's "Letter to the Military Chaplains" occasioned. The topics of these reflections vary from sexuality to the Church, from art and myth to sociology, from discussions that occur within a Christian or a European context, to others that concern the Muslim and Jewish worlds. Peace is a multifaceted value. In these writings the authors try to consider some of these faces in the context of a postcolonial world.

In the 1950s and 1960s of the twentieth century many considered the collapse of the traditional European empire as a "sign of the times." The welfare state, the substantial implementation of which occurred on a wide scale following the Second World War, enabled an unprecedented percentage of Europeans to emerge out of perennial poverty. It was assumed by many that there was only one way where this social progress would develop—forward. Many thought that it would spread to other parts of the world and that within developed countries it would lead to an ever-increasing betterment in the standard of living and conditions of work. Admittedly the Cold War was in full flow. Yet, at the time of Milani's letter, events on both sides of the wall suggested to many that people might move forward in a direction that avoids the Scylla of unbridled capitalism and the Charybdis of Stalinism. Hope of peace—in the substantial meaning of the term, that also includes justice and well-being, and not merely the absence of conflict, abounded.

Today, some 50 years after colonialism supposedly ended, and 25 years after the fall of the Berlin Wall, the era of well-being failed to materialize. Most of the developing world failed to develop. Indeed, large parts of it are growing ever poorer. Even within the so-called developed countries, the standard of living of many declined. Peace, in all of the senses of the term, was not achieved. Indeed, as former US president Bush once admitted, people in the United States (and maybe in the West in general) might have to get accustomed to a situation of permanent war; something to which some people in other regions of the globe have been accustomed to for ages.

Given this scenario one might think that the most logical thing to do is abandon peace as an ideal; refrain from hoping and seeking to bring about new heavens on earth. Obviously, this would entail the futility of commemorating Milani's "Letter to the Military Chaplains." The authors, whose work is collected in this book, refuse to do so. They dare to hope and ponder on peace and its implications. In what follows we shall reflect on each piece, consider some limits and many possibilities that each chapter evidences. The thread that links all pieces together will be some aspect or another of Milani's militancy for peace and justice.

Milani's letter does not occur in a vacuum. The jingoistic discourse of the military chaplains to which he was reacting in his letter was not the only strand concerning war that existed within the Catholic tradition. Other figures adopted different discourses more favorable to peace. As the title suggests, Carmel Borg and Michael Grech's, "The Catholic, Italian and Tuscan Ecclesiastical Contexts of Don Milani's 'Letter to the Military Chaplains,'" attempts to present the national, regional, and international background to Milani and his work. The work and testimony of figures like Mazzolari, La Pira, Balducci, Day, and Jaegestatter among others is acknowledged. One limit of the piece, a limit the authors admit to at the outset, is that the ground which the writing has the task of covering is immense, and they can only give brushes, which might lack the depth and thoroughness that one who would like to come to grips with one (or one aspect of) these contexts might require. Moreover, while the piece adequately argues that under a number of aspects Milani was not unique, it probably fails to highlight sufficiently what is distinctive in Milani in contrast to the many Catholics who were involved in peace activities in Italy and elsewhere.

In his letter Milani denounces the (Catholic) religious blessing of war. He does not consider religion itself as a possible source of conflict. Hence, though in other aspects of his work (the display of different religious symbols at his school in Barbiana) he hints at the need of interreligious dialogue, Milani does not link this directly and explicitly to peace. This link is unequivocally made by Darren Dias in his chapter "Peace and the Religious in a Changing World: From Consensus to Difference." Though focusing on dialogue, Dias attempts to accomplish six tasks: illustrate the genealogy of the notion of peace from the Old and New Testaments to the contemporary Christian understanding; discuss the relationship between religion and violence (his conclusion apparently being that wars generally have economic and political causes, though the religious rationale that might be used to justify such conflicts provides a distinctive imprint on such struggles); considers the encounter between different religions in international forums and the attempt that some members of different denominations have made to extract a common set of core values that underlies the different religious traditions; analyses current Catholic approaches to peace and dialogue; examines the notion of dialogue and difference, highlighting the different nuances, approaches, and strategies. The last two sections are the ones where the themes are illustrated thoroughly and clearly, and where a valuable contribution to the debate on peace, religion, and dialogue is made. The former sections do contain important entries, though the themes and notions contained are not discussed in detail. For instance, at one point Dias (quoting David Little) claims that authentic religion never contributes to conflict, while flawed religion does. Such entry surely would have required some argument as to what makes a form of religion authentic or flawed. Or else, when discussing current Catholic approaches to peace and dialogue emphasis is made on statements of Popes and papal documents. The contribution of many Catholics on the ground is largely ignored. This notwithstanding, the already mentioned merits of the last two sections more than make up for these limits.

The "Letter to the Military Chaplains" implicitly seeks to free the Christian messages of peace from the (contradictory) accretions, which condoned and celebrated war that had accumulated throughout the years. The letter was published at a time when the Second Vatican Council was suggesting an *aggiornamento* aimed at presenting in a more authentic form the spirit of Christ's teachings. In his "Vatican II's Teaching on Peace and War: A Contribution to Conciliar Hermeneutics," Michael Attridge focuses on the encyclical *Gaudium et Spes,* focusing his attention on the themes of peace and conscientious objection. His interpretation of how *Gaudium et Spes* and Vatican II consider these themes is situated within a wider debate concerning the latter; the debate whether the teachings of Vatican II constitute a rupture in the teaching of the Church compared to what was being taught earlier, or whether its teachings were fundamentally a continuation of what was being taught earlier. Attridge considers this debate in relation to the themes on which he focuses, that is, peace and conscientious objection. He relates what *Gaudium et Spes* maintains to the opinions of two popes; John XXIII and Pius XII, and concludes that, while there are undoubtedly elements of continuity, *Gaudium et Spes'* teaching on these themes was markedly different from what was taught before. Attridge's article is extremely lucid and focused, though in its effort not to downplay the element of continuity between Vatican II and its popes (John XXIII and Paul VI), and their predecessor (Pius XII), the characterization of the latter is somewhat apologetic. For instance, Pius' failure to distinguish between nuclear and conventional weapons is conduced to his ignorance of the effects and nature of the former. For instance, it would have been interesting if one had to consider whether Pius' rabid anticommunism (in contrast to the firm but conciliatory attitude toward communism of his two most immediate successors) may have influenced the views he espoused on the issues in question.

The Church the military chaplains presented was not a beacon of hope; a sign of a possible peaceful future for humanity. It was the church of one nation whom it blessed in its struggles against others. Brian Wicker's "The Church as a Sacrament of the Future" explores a different possibility; of the

Catholic Church acting as a symbol and sacrament for the entire human race. Wicker exposes the limits of the most common political organization, the nation-state, and points to some features pertaining to arguably the greatest and oldest global organization, the Catholic Church, which may constitute a "sign and a promise" of how things ought to be; of how humans should be organized in light of current and later challenges. A case in point is the fact that unlike the head of a nation-state, who generally believes him/herself to be responsible only for the citizens of his/her state, the Pope, despite being the bishop of Rome, cannot put the interest of the members of his diocese ahead of those of others, but seeks the good of human kind.

Wicker presents the church as a sacrament for the future in a critical manner. While highlighting those current aspects in the Church's organization that might serve as a beacon to future political organization, he does not fail to point out the contradictions and shortcomings in the way in which this organization functions. One questionable aspect of the piece is the argument that seems to serve as a starting point of the article. From the fact that nation-states seem to be unable to face new global challenges like a worldwide environmental crisis, global terrorism, weapons of mass destruction, the inability of states to control their boarders, globalization of finance and global communication, he somehow concludes that "the institution of the sovereign state is...dying." This claim need not be wrong. It is simply questionable, in light of the opposing thesis that the state is simply undergoing a metamorphosis. But this does not impair the value of the article, most importantly in presenting a possible new way in which an institution functions.

In "The History of World Peace in 100 Objects: Visualizing Peace in a Peace Museum," Peter Van Den Dungen interrogates the dominant presence of narratives of war within public memory, and the totemic status enjoyed by war artifacts housed within prominent sites of public discourse. His proposal for the establishment of national peace museums constitutes an attempt to puncture the hegemonic status of war and militarism, actively reproduced through the institutions of civil society, including museums, and various memorials that glorify the subjugation and domestication of the defeated. His unmasking of the hidden curriculum of war is in sync with Milani's stance that no curriculum experience is ideologically neutral, and that education is intimately intersected with power. By engaging the artifacts, Van Den Dungen, like Milani, attempts to identify the structural and political assumptions upon which the pedagogy of war rests and to change the visitors' traditional interaction with memory. What may be pedagogically problematic in Van Den Dungen's curricular stance is his option to isolate and marginalize peace artifacts within the confines of a peace museum. Peace artifacts should be museum pieces. They should also, however, be mainstreamed and placed next to their war counterparts for a proper ethical and moral confrontation with the political content, economy and culture of violence. But then, his proposal may be just a beginning.

Referring to Paul Ricoeur, in his chapter "Responding to the Call of Peace: In Memory of a Future That Might Have Been," Clive Zammit captures the essence of this volume by describing it as a project that commemorates a provocation that does not sit comfortably in the past and, therefore, deserves "a just allotment of memory." Inspired by Derrida, Zammit argues that Milani's biography exceeds the past and, therefore, it deserves a claim on the present. He asserts that what is worth archiving and perpetuating is Milani's serious challenge to what Levinas refers to as the inevitability of war in the psyche of Western thinkers; a war culture that is "genetically inscribed"' in Western thought, to such an extent that engagement with war and violence has been normalized and perceived as inevitable. Informed by Milani's objection to automatic participation in violent acts against the enemy other, Zammit embarks on a preliminary journey in search of the archival sources that can provide a better understanding of the origins, perpetuation and consolidation of war, both as reality and as a myth. At the end of his piece, Zammit, while reaffirming the importance of Milani's antiwar project, questions the effects of such "rare acts of resistance" in providing a credible antidote to the war instinct. But then, is there any essentialist core that determines that it is a trait of Western culture that such acts have to be rare? Or is such discourse formulated in terms of a genetic code itself liable to be deconstructed.

Zammit's analysis and questioning are somehow in line with Antonia Darder's critique of liberal peace programs in "Peace Education in a Culture of War." The latter, (as well as Yigal Rosen's study on the long-term effects of peace education projects, which will be discussed later) throws some light on the limits of pedagogical projects aimed at reinventing a world that is not. Darder foregrounds the cultural politics of education processes that promote numbness toward the suffering of the working-class and non-white "others." In hegemonic terms, Darder argues that educational sites of practice, including the media, fabricate consent around the inevitability of the use of violence in the name of peace and freedom, while avoiding critical interrogation of the patriarchal, masculine, homophobic, racialized and social-class basis of the normalization of violence and triumphalism. Darder maintains that by engaging in simplistic and dematerialized, albeit well-meaning, idealism, liberal peace education programs tend to legitimate rather than interrupt the current status quo around consent for war. While acknowledging the difficulties in demarginalizing radical readings of hegemonic discourses, Darder argues that radical peace education programs, close to and dialectically engaged with human suffering and asymmetries of power, wealth and humanity, promote opportunities for a robust engagement with the historical, political, economic, and cultural roots of the perennial presence of war in our psyche. The absence in the foregoing chapter of concrete examples of programs that engage participants not only in critical reflection but also in radical action informed by such reflection, may dampen Darder's strong arguments for a radical approach to peace education. Distant from a praxial engagement with violence, it may be difficult to provide citizens with a solid base for Milani's vision of a mass of conscientious objectors.

In "On Education, Negotiation, and Peace," Marianna Papastephanou distinguishes between pacification and peace; between negative and positive peace. Inspired by Lorenzo Milani and Camilo Torres' uncomfortable relationship with the Catholic Church, and their consistent and persistent reminding that the Church should serve the poor first, Papastephanou exposes the futility of pseudo-cosmopolitan approaches to peace. Such approaches celebrate diversity and superficial border crossing without politicizing differences. As a result, they tend to pacify potential resistance to current local and global injustices rather than enabling the oppressed, at the receiving end of pacification, to engage in resisting an immoral and unethical peace that reproduces injustices and asymmetrical relations of power. Instead of politicizing the lack of peace, pseudo-cosmopolitan educational processes tend to personalize and psychologize peace. "Wrongheaded cosmopolitanism" fails strategically to examine the real, political causes of conflicts and to engage individuals in more challenging dialogues about the intersection of peace and social justice. Both Milani and Torres fit Papastephanou's definition of genuine cosmopolitanism. Both rejected the socialization of citizens into accepting the military logic while insisting that there could be no peace in a world divided into rich and poor. Milani and Torres' embodying genuine cosmopolitanism as a form of serious engagement with the other, rather than an simply engaging in personal enrichment, constitutes, in Papstephanou's own words, "a lesson of lasting significance for cosmopolitan and peace education." Quoting Sharon Todd, Papastefanou contends that true cosmopolitanism is characterized by both "an appreciation of the rich diversity of values, traditions and ways of life and a commitment to human rights." A question that may have been addressed is whether all values, traditions and ways of life are consistent with commitment to human rights?

The first part of Isabelle Calleja Ragonesi's chapter "From Conflict to Conflict Resolution: Teaching the History of Cyprus in the Buffer Zone," highlights the politics of the buffer zone. The chapter constructs the buffer zone that separates the Turkish-Cypriot from the Greek-Cypriot community as a metaphor for peace as work-in-progress; a site that is providing a genuine space for peace-oriented conversations and actions that transcend entrenched nationalisms and institutionalized politics. While one may problematize its peripheral, geographical status, such a zone illustrates how radical peace education, as argued by Darder, constitutes a true and concrete pedagogical possibility. "Occupy Buffer Zone," one of several projects of radical possibility mentioned in Calleja Ragonesi's piece, was based on the understanding that the absence of peace in Cyprus is symptomatic of a global economic and political arrangement that has widened the diameter of marginalization while concentrating wealth and power. In the context of a peace project aimed at reunification and reintegration, the role of history textbooks as instruments of peace is crucial. In this regard, the second part of Calleja Ragonesi's chapter is dedicated to a project that problematizes "state-centric" reading of history. Far from the institutional gaze, the historical narratives generated within the buffer zone are transformed into opportunities for intercommunal dialogue aimed at understanding rather than blaming the other. Writing the "history of Cypriots," as understood by Calleja Ragonesi, does not mean an attempt at creating a uniform interpretation of history to which citizens have to conform; it means unlocking a common process of participation in the creation of historical knowledge and meanings. Demystifying official knowledge, as constructed by powerful custodians of truth, was central to Milani's pedagogy of peace. In the case of Cyprus, this might entail demystifying the buffer zone itself. Contrary to Calleja Ragonesi's reading, this might entail pulling-down the buffer zone rather than reinventing it.

Yigal Rosen's chapter, "Beyond Reality Dissonance: Improving Sustainability of Peace Education Effects," focuses on the long-term effects of peace programs in contexts marked by "intractable conflicts"; curricular experiences administered by educators who want to continue to dialogue against the tribal, skeptical, and unidirectional grain. Rosen excavates deep into the strata of such programs, described by the author as holistic experiences aimed at changing attitudes, cultures, values, emotions, feelings, beliefs, and social relations, within schools, to evaluate their long-term effects. Rosen's archaeological work uncovers unsatisfactory results. For instance, the effects of peace programs in conflict-ridden contexts are generally short-lived. "Cognitive oversimplification," antithetical to Milani's call for rigor and depth in analyzing the root causes of local and international conflicts, "behavioural oversimplification"; curricula that, unlike the Barbiana experience, provide few opportunities to exercise learning and to connect concretely with reality, and "emotional oversimplification," shutting schools from the emotional stress that characterizes zones in conflict. These lead to what Rosen terms "reality dissonance" and, therefore, the long-term ineffectiveness of many peace education programs. The author's claim that peace education programs generally influence adolescents' peripheral attitudes rather than the more extreme, core attitudes, may confirm Milani's empirical observation that despite their pretentions, schools continue to serve rather than counter hegemonic discourses and relations. Rosen's chapter, therefore, highlights the limits of schools in shaping and reshaping societies. But, maybe, at times too much is expected from schools in this regard.

In his chapter, "Because 'I Care': From an Encounter to a Political Option," Francois Mifsud reflects on Chantal Mouffe's distinction between agonistic and antagonistic relations within political spaces. Agonistic relations allow for encounters that recognize the "other's otherness" as legitimate. In contrast, antagonistic experiences frame "the other" as adversary or enemy. Pedagogically, the former may lead to the possibility of genuine dialogue based on active listening and mutual respect. Mifsud argues that agonistic encounters, where the we/self meet/s the other as adversary, constitute the essence of Milani's pedagogy framed by the Barbiana school's motto "I Care." These encounters are open to newness and, therefore, may possibly lead to self/collective transformation. The antagonistic encounter on the other hand is devoid of the "I Care" spirit and is intended mainly to destroy the other according to a prescribed script. Such entrenchment allows minimal space for personal or social transformation.

Mifsud's second main argument focuses on the limits of positivist epistemology, focusing on the fact that in the name of some illusory monolithic objective truth, this approach eats into the possibility of subjectivities displaying an interest in and possibly engaging with each other. Such productive engagements problematize the illusion of one objective truth, allowing different truths to be recognized, informed and surprised by each other. While undeniably difficult and packed with tension, anxiety, uncertainty, and crudeness, relations based on genuine and subjective curiosity about the other are essentially communal and collective in nature. Such encounters, playing on Levinas' words, constitute good neighborliness. Whether Milani himself would have accepted this subjectivist twist, which Mifsud, in light of Levinas, proposes, is however hard to determine. The probability is that he would have preferred a more robust notion of truth, albeit a notion that does not confine one to academia, a seminary, or a sacristy.

The "Letter to the Military Chaplains," though associated to Milani, in fact evolved out of a dialogue he had with his students. It involved a group of learners, the different characteristics and capabilities of whom were fully recognized in his school and in collective efforts like the letter in question. His school imbued some of the ideals associated to democracy. John P. Portelli's article "Peace Education and Critical Democracy: Some Challenges in Neoliberal Times" deals primarily with the threats posed to democratic education in neoliberal contexts. Democracy is seen as a moral and political ideal relating to how we ought to deal with one another; a way of life rather than something that entails a number of procedures or mere equality of opportunity. The attempt to incarnate concretely this ideal is seen to entail a number of associated values (though these are not clearly outlined) and sociopolitical activism with regard to a number of issues. Indeed, Portelli believes that one of the three main challenges to democracy in education in a neoliberal society is the reduction of democracy to a set of procedures that are "neutrally" implemented in the class room. The other two challenges are the belief that democratic education devalues teachers to a fringe role and the claim that democratic education entails the implementation of one-size-fits-all strategies (enshrined in national minimum curricula) where differences concerning ability, culture, ethnicity, gender, and sexuality are not taken into consideration. Portelli confutes the three charges. He does not provide a definition of peace. He cites Trifonas and Wright who provide a working definition claiming that peace is "the absence of violence to any aspect of human life." Yet, even in light of other writings contained in this collection, this definition, albeit a working definition, will appear extremely narrow. Most writers emphasize that peace is not the mere absence of violence. One may reply that by "violence" the authors do not merely understand physical violence, as the phrase "any aspect of human life" indicates. Violence may be psychological or structural. But, if this is the case, the question that arises is can there be a nonviolent education in a class structured society; a society based on having one class/a number of classes engaged in hegemonic relations over others? Can such a society allow a peaceful and democratic education in the way Portelli understands it?

In the "Letter to the Military Chaplains," Milani sees democracy as one of the great inventions of humankind; one of the two "noble political systems that humanity has given itself." He does not, however, dogmatically conceive it as the teleological completion of some human ascent or a system that does not need to be bettered or improved. The link between democracy and peace is explored by Duncan Mercieca in "Does Democracy Promote Peace? A Rancière Reading of Politics and Democracy." Mercieca proposes a novel consideration of peace and democracy—considering these as the starting point of a process rather than a goal to be achieved. This is analogous to what Rancière does to the concept of equality, which is not considered a goal but a presupposition. The danger of considering equality and these other ideals as goals rather than starting points is, according to Mercieca's interpretation of Rancière, that equality and peace would be ideals that we cherish, but not respect. The effects of this change are illustrated through an example involving a classroom in Belgium whereby presupposing equality, rather than positing it as a goal, leads to a situation where concretely, the ideal is incarnated to a more perfect degree than it would if the ideal were set as an abstract target. Mercieca's article includes some interesting distinctions from Rancière, between what the latter calls "the police" (referring to the structures, justifications, and perception that relate and maintain a social hierarchy), the "distribution of the sensible" (which includes the procedures normally subsumed under the term politics), and what Rancière calls politics which, crudely, refers to those rare moments and activities when the order and structure imposed by "the police" is broken. It is when such order is broken, and not simply when people elect and vote their rulers in office, that democracy occurs. Democracy hence requires dissensus (challenging what is "given") rather than consensus. Mercieca speculates that if there is a link between democracy and peace then, in contrast to what many might assume, peace requires dissensus as well. The article hence provides many novel insights into the debate about peace. In some passages, however, the price for this originality is clarity, a shortcoming that may not be attributable only to Mercieca himself, given that clarity is not normally the supreme virtue of contemporary French philosophers. Moreover, one might have expected the link (or lack of it) between democracy and peace, which is the main theme of the chapter to have been spelled out more solidly and in more detail.

In the "Letter to the Military Chaplains," Milani and his school denounce the false imperative that commands obedience at all costs. The consequences of these imperatives and commands to peace in world are considered at length. The effect of fallacious inhuman commands on peace can reach another sphere; the personal and intimate sphere; a dimension that is frequently overlooked when peace is discussed. This facet of peace is discussed by Mario Gerada, Clayton Mercieca, and Diane Xuereb in their piece titled "Peace and Sexuality—Two Reflections." The three, who are members of the Maltese Christian LGBT group Drachma, not merely find obstacles to a peaceful existence, which are laid by a society that is deeply prejudiced against them, but live the tension that arises from the fact that they belong to the LGBT community and at the same time are committed Christians. They also point to phenomena like internal homophobia that can perturb one's peace. The personal style of the work is a fresh and welcome exception to the academic nature of the other pieces. The asset and the drawback of the piece is the fact that the claims made in the chapter and the suggestions proposed are based on personal insight and experience.

One conflict which, according to Milani's letter, could have been avoided had soldiers been instructed to follow their own conscience rather than blind orders was the Spanish Civil War. The destruction and loss of life this war entailed is best captured in the paining *Guernica* by Pablo Picasso. This painting is considered at length by Mark Debono in his chapter "On Art and Politics: Exploring the Philosophical Implications of the Creative Order of Art on the Organization of Social Relations," wherein the relationship between art and peace is discussed. Debono focuses on Picasso's *Guernica* as well as on Jamie Miller *Judith's Beheading Holifernes*. The former conveys both what is arguably the most famous and touching image of the effects of the modern means of destruction, and of the failure of politics which, in a century of supposed progress and rational planning, could not prevent (indeed induced) this and other massacres to happen. Debono claims that current politics is unable to suggest and promote a different social order. The rest of the chapter is devoted to the question as to whether art can succeed where politics fail; whether art can suggest or hint at different social organizations and at different relations between human beings, other than those which current politics can only replicate and reproduce. Debono seems to be very positive about this possibility. Yet, even admitting that art does have this possibility, can art lead to a concrete transformation on its own? Does it not require politics, not necessarily in the conventional and maybe distorted way, but perhaps in the way in which Milani understood it (seeking solutions to problems together rather than on one's own) to bring its alternative vision/s to fruition? Would not even a revolutionary type of art that is not linked to politics be a niche where a minority (generally bourgeois) engages in self-serving, radical intellectualism?

Milani not merely promoted the idea of peace. He made academic efforts at school to incarnate this ideal. Peace and the resolution of conflicts require not only good will but adequate theoretical tools that enable one to discern the causes of conflict and to envisage realistic targets that allow peace to be achieved. In his piece, "Can We Learn from Comparing Violent

Conflicts and Reconciliation Processes? For a Sociology of Conflict and Reconciliation Going beyond Sociology," Nicos Trimikliniotis attempts to do two things. In the first part he analyzes the shortcomings of various theories and approach that deal either with conflict or with the resolution of conflict. In particular, he focuses on the different versions of the Conflict Resolution theory and highlights the shortcomings that are common to these versions. These common shortcomings are an overreliance on behaviorist theories of human conduct, negative functionalism, illicit assumptions about actors, and their modes of behavior and failure to appreciate the diversity of different actors that conflicts and peace processes involves. Trimikliniotis does not merely identify the theoretical shortcomings of this model, but highlights the practical implications of these. On a more positive note, he advocates a sociology of conflict and reconciliation (he emphasizes the "and," highlighting that these two aspects are to be addressed together by this sociology), a sociology that must exhibit a number of features that are in direct contact with the world; studies conflict together with reconciliation; unearths the assumptions that the discourses that frame political agendas contain; be comparative without however overgeneralizing; be interdisciplinary in character; be open to the contribution of other discourses in the area; taking into consideration features like gender; addresses issues from below rather than from above. Timikliniotis' suggestion is original and deeply thought. It is not obvious, however, that some parts of his proposal do not repeat insights, which could have been included under one heading. Moreover, in the first part of the chapter (when discussing the approaches he is criticizing) it is not always obvious whether the critique is sociological or moral in character.

Milani emphasizes the need to come to grips with the narratives and histories of "the others"; of those who belong to other nations and fatherlands. Peace requires that one listens to and refrains from caricaturizing "the other." For many in the West "the other" is "Islam." Islam in general and Muslim women in particular are frequently caricatured in media, literature and popular culture. In her chapter, "The 'Modern' Muslim Woman in the Arab Peoples' Revolution for Freedom and Dignity," Nathalie Grima questions this picture that depicts Muslim and Arab women as passive, lacking initiative, and subdued. She also questions the "rhetoric of salvation," which requires that Muslim women be saved form their own culture and religion. In particular, Grima focuses on the *Hijab*, unearthing Western prejudices and misunderstanding, and showing that this iconic garment may mean different things to different Muslim women. Contrary to what many in the West might believe, the *Hijab* might be seen by some Muslim women as liberatory, enhancing their identity, rather than suppressing it. While Grima's writing seems to be excessively apologetic of the rationale behind the use of the *hijab,* the piece achieves the task of showing the limited nature of the categories most of us take for granted; categories like the dichotomous classifications modern/traditional, religious/secular; a limit of which we must be aware if the quest for peace is to be successfully undertaken.

At face value Grima's reflection seems to concern a reality—Muslim, North-African, Arab, and female—that is worlds apart from Milani's context (coming from a Jewish background, Christian, European, and a member of a male-dominated institution.). Yet, 47 seven years after his death, Milani's work is able to inspire worlds that seem to be light-years apart from the little Tuscan hamlet to which he was exiled. In the supposedly post–Cold War and supposedly postcolonial world of ours, Milani can still serve as a fount of inspiration.

Milani can inspire the Christian to recuperate the most genuine streaks within the Catholic tradition, as Attridge suggests, and track new paths forward in the journey toward piece, as Dias suggests in relation to inter-religious dialogue.

To Christians and non-Christians, his letter enjoins recuperating the memory of a dream of peace, as Zammit claims in his piece, a dream of peace that concerns not merely public and international spaces, but even the intimate sphere as Gerada, Clayton Mercieca, and Xuereb indicate. It also suggests the deconstruction of the semiotic value of buffer zones and borders, as in Calleja Ragonesi's piece, and the search for creative founts distinct from those of traditional politics, as in Debono's chapter. Not being mere daydreaming, this quest for peace requires adequate heuristic tools. Darder, Rosen, and Trimikliniotis' articles are a contribution in this regard.

In an era where globalization is the buzz word, Milani's work provokes reflections that invite us to envisage a new post–nation-state world order, as in Wicker's piece, or to beware of semblances cosmopolitanism, as in Papastephanu's chapter. At a time when democracy, whom together with socialism Milani sees as one of the greatest human feats in the political field, is being diluted by corporate politics, his work can inspire writers that invite us to seek a more substantial meaning of this term and to sift between genuine and fake democracy, as is evident in Portelli, Mifsud, and Duncan Mercieca's articles.

Maybe Milani's letter should be included in the peace museum Van Den Dungen suggests?

# Index

9/11, 151, 197, 198, 220, 227

Abu Ghraib Prison, 195
Abu-Lughod, Lila, 220
Ackerman, Bruce, 100, 101
*Ad Gentes*, 34
*Adesso*, 26
Adorno, Theodor, 196, 201
Afghanistan, War in, 58, 91, 175, 211, 213, 220
agonizm, 149–51, 154, 164, 170
agreement perspective, 97–102
Al Jazeera, 223
Alberigo, Giuseppe, 42
Alcoholics Anonymous, 142
Alicik, Hasan, 122
Alison, James, 192
Al-Qaeda, 91, 224, 228
Anan Plan, 121
anarchy/Anarchism, 18, 20, 21
*Ancien Regime*, 14
anger, 6, 99, 134, 137, 205
Annales school, 123, 125
antagonism/antagonistic tension, 149–51, 164, 170, 208
anticommunism, 2, 235. 
  *See also* "communism"
apolitical, 6, 92, 99
aporia/aporias, 79, 80, 127, 176
Apple, Michael, 164
Aquinas, Thomas of, 45
Arab Spring, 229
Aristotle/Aristotelianism, 36, 151, 156
arms race, 28, 34, 43, 46, 69, 72
Ashoka, Emperor, 65
Association for Historical Dialogue and Research (AHDR), 118, 122, 123

atomic war/weapons, 21, 28, 45, 46, 47, 49
Attridge, Michael, 39, 235, 244
Au, William, 45, 48
Augustine of Hippo, 15, 43–5
Axial Age, 79, 80, 82, 88, 237

Badiou, Alain, 102, 105, 106
Baghdad, British bombing of, 201
Balducci, Ernesto, 2, 24, 234
baptism, 2, 49
Bar, H, 135
Barbiana, 3–7, 29, 142, 147–9, 154, 157, 195, 234, 239, 240
Bargal, David, 135
Bar-Natan, Irit, 135
Barrett, Georgina, 113, 114
Barthes, Roland, 77, 85, 86, 89
Bay of Pigs, 48, 91
BBC radio, 65, 76
Beethoven, Ludwig van, 67, 68, 74, 75
behaviorism, 207, 208
behavioural oversimplification, 136, 137, 239
Ben Ali, Zine El Abidine, 226, 227, 230
Ben Jelloun, Tahar, 170
Benedict XV (Giacomo della Chiesa), 17, 18, 20
Benedict XVI (Joseph Ratzinger), 16, 31, 42, 60
Benjamin, Walter, 199
Berlin Wall, fall of, 68
Bernard of Clairvaux, 25
biblical, 31, 32, 187
Bi-Communal Teachers Training Centre, 122
Biesta, Gert, 177, 180

Bin Laden, Osama, 224
Biton, Yifat, 134
Black Panthers, 91
Bloch, Marc, 125
Blue Helmets, 72, 73
body, the, 56–8, 62, 92, 119, 189, 192, 193, 222, 227, 230
Bonnardeaux, Michel, 115
borders, 30, 100, 112, 113, 116, 118, 148, 176, 203, 205, 227, 238, 244
Borg, Carmel, 172, 234
Borghi, Bruno, 2
Bosnia-Herzegovina Inter-religious Council, 33
Bosnian War, 91, 120
Bouazizi, Mohammed, 224, 225
Bourdieu, Pierre, 224
Bourguiba, Habib, 226
Braudel, Ferdinand, 125
Brennan, Timothy, 107
British Museum, 65, 74, 76
buffer zone, 112–18, 122–4, 126, 127, 129, 130, 238, 239, 244
Burawoy, Michael, 210
Burton school, 206
Bush, George W., 198, 200, 233
Bush, Laura, 220

Calgacus, 103
Calleja Ragonesi, Isabelle, 238, 239, 244
Calli, Evaristo, 26
Cambodian Civil War, 91
Campaign for Nuclear Disarmament (CND), 72, 76
Capitini, Aldo, 2, 3, 20, 26
Caravaggio, Michelangelo da, 198
Carolingian, Royal House of, 25
Carr, Paul, 95
Catholic Action, 22, 24
Catholic press, 7
Catholic Scout movement, 22
Catholic Truth Society, 59
Cattaneo, Carlo, 58
Cavanaugh, William, 32
Centre Party, 14
Chambers, Samuel A., 182
Chaplains, 1, 6, 7, 13, 17, 24, 57, 105, 107, 109, 233, 235, 240, 241
charity, 15, 27, 54, 98, 104, 109, 125
Charles II, 66, 67

Chechaouen, bombing of, 201
Chelucci, Ireneo, 21
chemical weapons, 45, 47
Cherribi, S., 223
Christian Democracy, 14, 17, 22, 25, 27, 105
Christian World Order, 15, 21, 22, 25
church, Anglican, 60, 61
Church, Catholic, 2, 7, 9, 13–15, 17–19, 21–6, 30–2, 34, 38, 39, 41–6, 48–50, 53–62, 105, 187, 189, 195, 235, 236, 238
City of God, 15
City of Man, 15
*Civiltà Cattolica*, 21
class harmony, 25
class struggle, 14, 94, 213
Clerico-Fascism, 18, 20
climate change, 9, 55, 61
Clinton, Hilary, 188
cognitive oversimplification, 136, 239
Cold War, 16, 21, 31, 47, 48, 68, 72, 91, 118, 120, 233, 244
Coleman, James, 207
colonization, 3, 6, 9, 17, 18, 25, 31, 33, 39, 66, 91, 94, 109, 148, 196, 212, 233
commandment of love, 7
common sense, 2, 213
communism/communist, 2, 4, 7, 18, 20–2, 27, 43, 48, 235. *See also* "anticommunism"
Comte, Auguste, 151
Concordat, 14, 17–19, 26
Conflict Research Society, 208, 214
conflict resolution, 69, 97, 99, 103, 105, 111–13, 117, 124, 128, 133, 134, 141, 204, 206, 209–11, 214, 216, 217, 238, 243
conflict transformation, 206, 208, 215
Confucius, 5
conscientious objection, 1, 6, 16, 24, 41, 43–8, 71, 72, 77, 88, 105, 109, 235, 238
consensus, 18, 30, 33, 35, 36, 38, 97, 105, 165, 166, 177–9, 183, 213, 222, 234, 241
conservative/conservativism, 14, 16, 18, 20–2, 24, 27, 92, 93, 95, 187, 209, 227
Constantine, Emperor, 25, 57
contraception, 60, 61

Co-peace, 111
Coser, Lewis, 204, 206, 207
cosmopolitan, 9, 97–108, 163, 238, 244
cosmopolitanism, 97–103, 106–8, 110, 158, 163, 238, 244
Coste, Renè, 43, 44
Coudenhove-Kalergi, Richard, 68
Council of Europe, 68, 120, 121, 123
Council of the Parliament of World's Religions, 33
Counts, George, 167
Critchley, Simon, 199
critical democracy, 161–3, 169, 240
critical peace education/educators, 93–6
critical reading, 7, 214
Cronin, Kurth, 55
Crusades, The, 31
Cuban Missile Crisis, 46–9, 51, 91
Cutajar, JosAnn, 230
Cyprus, 112–30, 205, 212, 214, 216, 217, 238, 239
Cyprus Mail, 122

Dacca, bombing of, 201
d'Anglas, Boissy, 105, 106, 109
Darder, Antonia, 237, 238, 244
Darwin, Charles, 23, 27
Day, Dorothy, 16, 19, 234
De Saussure, Ferdinand, 86
Debono, Mark, 242, 244
Del Boca, Angelo, 5
democracy/democratic, 3, 5, 9, 14, 19, 22, 25, 46, 58, 59, 68, 91, 96, 99, 100, 121, 149–51, 154, 159, 161–71, 175–83, 187, 200, 215, 219, 227–9, 240, 241, 244
Derrida, Jacques, 79, 88, 89, 101, 108, 110, 157, 158, 201, 202, 237
Descartes, René, 152, 157
Dewey, John, 162, 165, 167
dialogue, 3, 5, 7, 9, 22, 23, 29, 33–8, 55, 96, 97, 100–2, 105, 117, 118, 121, 123, 134, 135, 148, 157, 161, 163, 166, 175, 198, 221, 222, 234, 235, 238–40, 244
*Dialogue and Proclamation*, 36
Dialogue Decalogue, 35
Dias, Darren, 234, 235, 244
*Die Waffen nieder! (Lay Down Your Arms)*, 69, 70

difference, 5, 9, 23, 29, 30, 33, 35–8, 54, 59, 80, 94, 95, 97, 101, 107, 116, 119, 122, 123, 147, 150, 161, 163, 165, 166, 170, 171, 200, 201, 206, 211, 221, 234, 238, 240
disarmament, 17, 22–4, 28, 31, 43, 59, 60, 69, 70, 72
Disneyland, 92
dissensus, 176, 179, 182, 183, 241
dissent, 66, 93, 103, 108, 183, 200
diversity, 148, 151
Dominican Republic, Invasion of, 91
Dossetti, Giuseppe, 22
Drachma, 187–9, 191, 242
Drachma Parents Group, 189

Eatherly, Claude, 5
Education for Peace, 132
Einstein, Albert, 21, 71, 72, 75, 76, 88
*Einstein on Peace*, 71
El-Khouly, Hadil, 225
El Sayed, Mona, 228, 230
emotional oversimplification, 136, 137, 239
Ennahda party, 226, 230
epistemology/epistemological, 95, 123, 149–55, 240
equality, 35, 66, 67, 100, 102, 104, 147, 164, 168, 177–81, 185, 186, 226, 240, 241
equality assumption, 179
Eroglu, Dervis, 123
ethics, 31, 39, 40, 59, 61, 78, 93, 94, 98, 110, 147, 148, 151, 153–6, 164, 172, 202
Ethiopia, Italian bombing of, 201
Ethiopia, Italian invasion of, 5, 18, 19, 107, 201
Eucharist, the, 56, 58
*European Heritage for an Active Citizenship through Intercultural Dialogue 2011*, 124
European Union, 112, 115, 120, 124, 126, 127, 129, 130, 176

face, the, 155, 156, 200, 202
Falzon, Mark-Anthony, 230
family, 42, 133, 137, 140, 188, 209, 222, 224

Fanfani, Amintore, 22
Fascism/Fascist, 1, 2, 5–8, 14, 18–22, 26, 107
fatalism, 9
fatherland, 1, 7, 16, 19, 26, 243. *See also* "patria"
Faulhaber, Michael Von, 16
Febvre, Lucien, 125
feminism/feminist, 219–21, 228
First World War, 16–19, 21, 72, 118
Fisher, David, 53
Fisher, Roger, 206
Freire, Paulo, 3, 4, 93, 164, 167, 200
French Revolution, 13, 14, 25
Freud, Sigmund, 79, 88
Freudian, 81
Fromm, Eric, 7
Fullan, Michael, 138
functionalism, 124, 204, 207, 243

Galtung, Johan, 104, 206
Gandhi, Mahatma, 3, 5, 20, 74, 157
*Gaudium et Spes*, 24, 33, 42–4, 47, 58, 235
Gelassenheit (let-be), 108
Gemelli, Agostino, 17, 18
gender, 4, 9, 55, 94, 159, 168, 171, 188, 205, 207, 212–14, 219, 221, 222, 226–9, 240, 243
genocide, 94, 205
Geoffrey, John, 55
Gerada, Mario, 242, 244
German Peace Society, 69
Gernika/*Guernica*, 195–202, 242
Giddens, Anthony, 150, 151
*Il giornale del mattino*, 24
Girard, Renè, 32
Golden Rule, 33
good will, 109, 242
Gospels, The, 1, 2, 34, 190
Gramsci, Antonio, 18
Grech, M., 172, 234
Green Line, 112, 115, 119, 121
Greene, M., 169
Greenpeace, 57
Grenada Invasion of, 91
Grima, Nathalie, 243, 244
Guantanamo, 205
Gulf of Sidra, military intervention, 91
Gulf War, 91

Habermas, Jürgen, 108
Haiti, military operation in, 91
Hammarsjkold, Dag, 73
Hanafi School, 229
Hanbali School, 229
Harvard Negotiation Project, 206
hegemony/hegemonic, 1, 18, 48, 95, 120, 169, 224, 225, 236, 237, 239, 241
Hehir, Bryan J., 44–7
Heidegger, Martin, 79, 196, 201
Held, David, 100
Hensbergen, Gijs van, 196, 201
hermeneutics, 42, 43, 48–50, 80, 235
Herodotus, 80, 81, 84, 85, 87, 89, 90
Herriot, Edouard, 68
Hesiod, 82–5, 89
Hicks, Edward, 66
*hijab*, 219, 221–4, 226, 227, 230, 243
Hiroshima, bombing of, 47, 49
historiography, 43, 126
*History: How Do We Teach it*, 122
Hitler, Adolf, 21
Ho Chi Minh, 22
Holtom, Gerald, 72
homosexuality, 60, 61, 188
Horchani, Rochdi, 225
Hottentots, South African bombing of, 201
*How Terrorism Ends*, 55
Huberman, Michael, 138
Hugo, Victor, 68, 69, 74
human rights, 22, 24, 31, 34, 94, 96–8, 102, 134, 163, 168, 190, 205, 215, 238
Hungarian Peace Society, 69
Hussein, Saddam, 197
Husserl, Edmund, 196

"I Care," 4, 147–9, 154, 156, 157, 239, 240
"I" the, 100, 148, 152, 155, 157
ideology/ideological, 2, 14, 16, 18, 22, 72, 93, 95, 96, 147, 151, 162, 189, 190, 204, 205, 207, 210–12, 215, 236
immigrants, 55, 66, 220
*In Search of Global Ethical Standards*, 33
incarceration, 94
Indo-China First War of, 91
inequality, 1, 6, 49, 93, 94, 183

institutional approach, 111–13
*Intentional alienation*, 148, 151, 153
interest (ethical), 148, 149, 153
International Sociology Association, 214
Intimacy: 189, 190
Institutional Aproach: 111–13
Intentional alienation: 148, 151, 153
Internet, 9, 55, 61, 140, 223, 225
Interreligious Coordinating Council in Israel, 33
intimacy, 189, 190
intractable conflicts, 131–3, 137, 239
Iran, British bombing of, 201
Iran-Iraq War, 91
Iraq War, 91
Islam/Islamic, 22, 53, 119, 219–24, 226–30, 233, 243, 244
Islamic feminism, 220, 221
Israel-Palestine conflict, 134, 212, 200, 205, 212–14, 220, 224
*Instituto per le scienze religiose*, 42
IVF (in vitro fertilization), 61

Jägerstätter, Franz, 16, 234
Jalalabad, bombing of, 201
Jaspers, Karl, 79
Jesus, The Christ, 16, 18, 26, 30, 34, 39, 44, 54, 56, 58, 62, 67, 193, 235
Jew/Jewish, 2, 19, 22, 30, 134, 135, 233, 244
John XXIII (Angelo Roncalli), 18, 22, 31, 41, 45–7, 50, 235
John Paul II (Karol Wojtyla), 31, 34, 59
Johnson, Lyndon Baines, 22
Joliot-Curie, Frèdèric, 21
*Judith beheading Holifernes*, 195, 198, 242
Junior Reserve Officers' Training Corps (JROTC), 95
*Just War on Terror? A Christian and Muslim Repsonse*, 54
just war theory, 16, 24, 31, 44–7, 53
justice, 1–3, 7, 8, 16, 17, 19, 20, 22, 24, 27, 28, 30–2, 34, 38, 43, 46, 47, 49, 59, 62, 67, 71, 77, 93, 96–9, 101–5, 108, 164, 184, 188, 199, 206, 209, 210, 221, 225, 226, 233, 234, 238

Kabul, bombing of, 201
Kant, Immanuel, 23, 27, 74, 85, 108

Kennedy, John Fitzgerald, 48
Kifaya (Egyptian Movement for Change), 228
Kimball, Charles, 32
Ki-Moon, Ban, 188
King, Martin Luther, 74
Korean War, 48, 91
Kosovo, War of, 91
Kung, Hans, 36, 54

La Pira, Giorgio, 2, 22, 24, 27, 234
language, 3, 5, 27, 42, 56, 62, 69, 86, 87, 105, 119, 120, 138, 147, 164, 180, 206, 227
Lateran Pacts, 17, 18
*The Laws*, 182
Lazzati, Giuseppe, 21
League of Nations, 18, 69, 72
Lebanese Civil War, 91
Lederach, John Paul, 206
Lejano, Raul, 114
Lethe (forgetfulness), 80, 83, 84, 89
*Letter to a Teacher*, 6, 9, 38, 147, 157, 158, 171, 173, 201
*Letter to the Military Chaplains*, 13–27, 105, 233–5, 240, 241
LeVan, Michael, 176
Levinas, Emmanuel, 78, 88, 90, 102, 108, 110, 155–8, 202, 237, 240
liberal peace, 208, 209, 211, 215, 237
liberation, 5, 37, 187, 188, 213
liberation theology, 213
Liberian, Second Civil War, 91
Libya bombing of, 91
Libya civil war, 91
Lindqvist, Sven, 196
Little, David, 235
Locarno Pact, 68
Logical Positivism, 152, 155
Lonergan, Bernard, 37, 38
*Looking at Our Past*, 123
love, 6, 7, 15, 18, 19, 28, 30, 31, 34, 43, 62, 88, 94, 96, 107, 147, 148, 187, 189–91
Lustig, Illana, 135

MacGregor, Neil, 65
Maliki School, 229
Malta Gay Rights Movement, 189
Mandela, Nelson, 74

Maoz, Ifat, 134
marriage, 42, 192, 227, 228
Marxism/Marxist, 21–3, 204
Mary, mother of Jesus, 18
Massimiliani, Roberto, 24
Matisse, Henri, 21
Mayo, Peter, 230
Mazzi, Enzo, 27
Mazzolari, Primo, 2, 19, 20, 22, 26
McCabe, Herbert, 54
memory, 8, 9, 77, 80, 82–5, 87, 88, 116, 120, 124, 133, 139, 197, 199, 205, 236, 237, 244
Mennonites, 31
Mercieca, Clayton, 242, 244
Mercieca, Duncan, 241, 244
meritocracy/meritocratic, 168
Mifsud, Francois, 239, 240, 244
Miglioli, Guido, 20
Milan, Edict of, 30
Milani, Lorenzo, 1–13, 17, 18, 22, 24, 26, 29, 41–3, 49, 71, 76, 77, 88, 98, 103–9, 116, 132, 147, 148, 154, 157, 162, 169–71, 187, 195, 219, 221, 233, 234, 236–44
Miles, Matthew, 138
militarism, 19, 93–5, 99, 106, 236, 241
Miller, Jamie, 195, 198, 242
monarchism, 14
monological, 98, 100, 106, 108
Mouffe, Chantal, 148–51, 153–8, 170, 172, 173, 202, 239
*Multi-Perspectivity in Teaching and Learning History*, 123
Murdoch, Iris, 198
Murray, John Courtney, 46, 47
Muslim women, 219–25, 229–30, 243
Mussolini, Benito, 2, 18, 19, 21, 26
myth, 16, 19, 77, 79, 80, 82, 84–9, 120, 124, 157, 164, 165, 171, 233, 237

Nagasaki, bombing of, 47, 49
Napoleonic wars, 14
Nasser, Gamal Abdel, 73, 230
Nathan, Otto, 71, 75
Nationalism, 14, 16–19, 24, 26, 68, 107, 116, 118–20, 122, 204, 212, 238
*La Nazione*, 1, 6
Nazism/Nazi, 14, 16, 20, 21, 26, 71, 196

negative peace, 104, 238.
 *See also* positive peace
Nenni, Pietro, 21
neoliberalism, 93, 162, 164, 171–3
Neruda, Pablo, 21
*New Testament*, 234
Ngo Dinh Diem, 48
Nicaragua Civil War, 91
*niqab*, 219
No Man's Land Project, 115
Nobel, Alfred, 70, 71, 75
Nobel Peace Prize, 21, 70, 73, 75, 103, 197, 202
*Non-Expedit*, 17
non-violence, 43, 48, 73
Norden, Heinz, 71
*Nostra Aetate*, 34
*Nuclear Deterrence: What Does the Church Teach?*, 59
nuclear war/weapons, 28, 31, 34, 44–7, 49, 59–62, 72, 91, 222, 235

obedience, 1, 7, 8, 16, 32, 34, 71, 106, 241
Occupy Buffer Zone, 116, 238
Occupy movement, 92, 94
*Ode to Joy*, 67, 68
*Old Testament*, 234
Operation Castle, 49
order, 43, 85, 86, 87, 89, 93, 102–4, 150, 177–9, 182, 183, 195, 198, 201, 204, 209, 224, 227, 228, 241, 242, 244
Orientalism, 215
*L'Osservatore Romano*, 18
other, the, 16, 32, 34, 35, 37, 97, 98, 100, 101, 103, 106, 108, 109, 119, 121, 132, 134–6, 147–57, 161, 163, 170, 176, 202, 207, 221, 235, 237, 239, 240, 243

*Pacem in Terris*, 22, 24, 31, 46, 47
pacification, 1, 99, 103, 338
pacifism, 15, 16, 44, 46–8, 69, 71
Pakistan, military operations in, 91
Panama, Invasion of, 91
Pan-Europe movement, 68
papal states, 17
Papastephanou, Marianna, 238
Parents Circle (Israel-Palestine), 213
Parks, Rosa, 179, 180

Parliament of the World Religions, 32
*Partito Popolare Italiano*, 14, 17, 20
*Partito Socialista Italiano*, 17
*Pastoral Experiences*, 41
*Pathways into Reconciliation Education for Mutual Understanding*, 132
*patria*, 18, 19, 24, 106, 107. *See also* "fatherland"
Paul VI (Giovanni Battista Montini), 31, 34, 235, 236
Paul of Tarsus, 56
Pavolini, Luca, 7
Pax Christi International, 21, 22
*Pax Romana*, 103, 104
peace education, 9, 65, 66, 91, 93–9, 102–4, 108, 110, 116–18, 131–46, 161, 162, 170–2, 237–40
peace parks, 113, 114, 116, 126, 128
Peace Players Cyprus (PPI-CY), 117, 125
Peace Research Institute Oslo (PRIO), 117
Penn, Granville John, 66
Penn, William, 66, 74
Perez de Cuellar, Javier, 73
Perkins, David, 137
Philippines, military operation in, 91
Picasso, Pablo, 21, 195–8, 202, 242
Pilate, Pontius, 193
Pius IX (Giovanni Maria Mastai-Ferretti), 14, 17
Pius X (Giuseppe Sarto), 17
Pius XI (Achille Ratti), 18, 26
Pius XII (Eugenio Pacelli), 2, 20, 31, 45–8, 235
planetarism, 97, 98, 108
Plato, 178, 182, 184, 201
police, The (Rancière's concept of), 176–80, 182–5, 241
political, the, 148–50, 153, 154
Pontifical Council for Interreligious Dialogue, 34. *See also* Secretariat for Non-Christians
poor, the, 1, 2, 4, 6, 7, 16, 24, 25, 29, 31, 32, 41, 42, 92, 101, 104, 105, 107, 109, 238
Pope, the, 25, 54, 58–61, 235, 236
*Populorum Progressio*, 31
Porfilio, Brad, 95
Portelli, John P., 240, 241, 244

positive peace, 104, 117, 238. *See also* negative peace
positivism, 151–6
postfeminism, 221
post-nationalism, 112
post-structural/post-structuralism, 101
power, 1–4, 9, 15, 25, 28–32, 43, 45, 46, 71, 79, 80, 85, 92–6, 104–6, 109, 112, 114, 154, 164, 170, 177, 180, 181, 196–8, 200, 202, 205, 210, 212, 219, 224, 225, 236–8
pragmatists/pragmatism, 163, 171, 215
presupposition, 178–80, 241
Priam, 81
Programme for International Student Assessment, 178

Quaker Tapestry Exhibition Centre, 67
Quakers, 31, 66, 67
Qu'ran, The, 222, 223, 227–9

racism/racist, 94, 119, 148, 163, 204, 212, 214
Radcliffe, Timothy, 198
Ramsbotham, Oliver, 206, 208
Rancière, Jacques, 175–86, 241
realist school/approach, 111–13, 120
reality dissonance, 131, 132, 135, 136, 140, 142, 239
Rebora, Clemente, 26
Recommendation 15 of 2001, 121
Reconciliation Commission, 121
Reconquest of Spain, 31
Redina, Massimo, 26
Reformation, The, 55
relationality, 36, 100, 108, 148–50, 155
Renaissance, The, 55
*Representations of History and Intergroup Relations in Cyprus*, 123, 124
*The Republic*, 184
resistance, 3, 5, 20, 21, 26, 71, 88, 91, 99, 136, 202, 225, 226, 237, 238
Revelation, 42
*Revitalising the "Dead Zone." Home for Cooperation: an Educational and Research Centre 2011*, 124
Ricoeur, Paul, 77, 237
*La Rinascita*, 7
Rolland, Romain, 68

Roman Curia, 42
Rosen, Yigal, 135, 139, 237, 239, 244
Roy, Oliver, 220
Rushdie affair, 220
Russell, Bertrand, 72
Russian revolution, 5

sacrament, 53–8, 62, 236
Said, Edward, 215
Salomon, Gavriel, 134
Saltman, Kenneth, 99, 108
Samani, Meltem Onurkan, 123
San Donato Di Calenzano, 3, 5, 29
San Suu Kyi, Aung, 74
Sartre, Jean Paul, 92
Savimbi, Jonas, 209
Savoy, Royal House of, 17
Schiller, Friedrich, 67, 68
Schloesser, Stephen, 48, 49
Schmitt, Carl, 149
Schuster, Alfredo Ildefonso, 18
Second General Peace Congress, 68
Second Vatican Council (Vatican II), 18, 33, 38, 41–9, 54, 58, 235
Second World War, 2, 14, 16, 20, 21, 26, 31, 39, 45–7, 49, 68, 72, 78, 100, 118, 148, 233
Secretariat for Non-Christians, 34. *See also* Pontifical Council for Interreligious Dialogue
self, 9, 19, 35, 37, 84, 88, 97–100, 102, 105, 119, 147, 148, 152–7, 193, 196, 223, 239, 240
Sen, Amartya, 175
sensible, The, 177, 180, 182, 183, 185, 241
sexual oppression, 94
sexuality, 9, 60, 61, 159, 168, 171, 187–93, 205, 233, 240, 242
Shafe'i School, 229
Shangai, Japanese bombing of, 201
Shari'a, 228
Shawn Copeland, M., 36
sign/sign of, 24, 34, 53–7, 62, 68, 85–7, 114, 124, 188, 189, 199, 233, 235, 236
silence/silent, 2, 4, 46, 68, 194, 197
Simmel, Georg, 204, 206
Sims, Ronald R., 138
Sims, Serbrenia J., 138
sin, 31, 34, 44, 60, 189

slavery, 69, 71, 94
socialism, 14, 17, 18, 20, 21, 244
socialization, 2, 107, 171, 133, 238
sociology of conflict, 203–4, 210, 212, 243
solipsism/solipsistic, 98, 100, 101, 106
Somali, Civil War, 91
Sommer, Marc, 136
Sontag, Susan, 197, 198
Soviet Supreme, 22
Soviets (Workers Councils), 18
Spanish-American War, 91
Spanish Civil War, 16, 242
Stalinism, 233
state, the, 8, 9, 15, 17–19, 23, 24, 29–33, 36, 43, 53–62, 68, 71, 72, 74, 76, 85, 87, 93, 94, 112, 114, 118–24, 133, 151, 170, 182, 184, 188, 195, 200, 205–9, 212, 220, 223–6, 228, 230, 233, 236, 239, 244
Steiner, George, 200
Strong, Sydney, 71
Sturzo, Luigi, 17
Suarez, Francisco, 45
subversion, 1, 9, 171
Sudan, bombing of, 91
Sudan, war in, 92
Suleymanoglu, Erol, 119
Sussman, Anna Louie, 228
*Sustained Impact Model for Peace Education*, 139
Suttner, Bertha von, 69, 70
Sylvester I, 25

Tacitus, Publius Cornelius, 103
Tahrir Square, 225, 227, 228
Teachers without Borders, 125
*Testimonianze*, 2
*The Catholic Worker*, 16
*The Ignorant Schoolmaster: Five Lessons in Intellectual Emancipation*, 180
*The Philosopher and His Poor*, 179
The Southeast European Joint History Project, 121
*The Use of Sources in Teaching and Learning History*, 123
The Workbooks Project, 121
*Time* magazine, 71

Todd, Sharon, 97, 238
tolerance, 121, 124, 134, 136, 150, 151, 200
Tolstoy, Lev Nikolayevich, 69, 74
Toriell, Filippo, 221
Torres, Camilo, 98, 103–10, 238
trace, 81, 205
trade unionism, 5, 20, 123, 137, 213
Trans-Jordan, British bombing of, 201
Treaty of Versailles, 72
Trends in International Mathematics and Science, 178
Trifonas, Peter, 161, 240
Trimikliniotis, Nicos, 243, 244
Tripoli, Italian bombing of, 201
Tsaousis, Dimitris, 122
Turkish-Cypriot Educational Planning and Program Development Department, 119, 122
Turoldo, David Maria, 22
Tutu, Desmond, 74

Uganda, troubles in, 91
UN Emergency Force (UNEW), 73
UN Millennium World Peace Summit of Religious and Spiritual Leaders, 33
UN Peacekeeping Force in Cyprus (UNFYCIP), 113, 115
*Uncle Tom's Cabin*, 69
United Nations, 31, 39, 59, 62, 72, 74, 100, 116, 130, 144, 188, 197, 216
United Nations General Assembly, 73
United States of Europe, 68
Urquhart, Brian, 73
Urquhart, Clara, 7
US Peace Movement, 93

Valensin, Auguste, 16
Van Den Dungen, Peter, 236, 244
Varnava, Andrekos, 122
verification, 152, 153
Vietnam War, 22, 91, 92, 95

Vitoria, Francisco de, 45
Viviani, Vincenzo, 2
Voltaire (François-Marie Arouet), 66
voluntarism, 13

Walmart, 57
war, 1, 2, 5–7, 13, 14, 16, 22, 24, 26–8, 30–4, 36, 38, 39, 41, 43–50, 53, 55, 59–61, 65–9, 71, 72, 74, 77–81, 83–5, 87, 88, 91–6, 99, 101, 104, 105–7, 113, 114, 118–21, 126, 135, 148, 151, 157, 175, 176, 188–90, 195, 197, 198, 205, 207, 209–13, 220, 221, 223–7, 242, 244
War of the Holy League, 31
War on Terror, 53, 99, 197, 220
Watts Riot, 91
We, the, 148–57, 221
Weiss, Alice, 2
West, Benjamin, 66
West the/Western, 17, 21, 22, 25, 29, 30, 32, 36, 39, 48, 65, 66, 72, 78–85, 87, 94, 102, 103, 151, 163, 168, 196, 201, 208, 209, 211, 215, 219, 220, 225–9, 233, 237, 243
Westphalia, Peace of, 55
Wicker, Brian, 235, 236, 244
William the Conqueror, 25
Wilson, Woodrow, 111, 175
Wilsonian Idealism, 111
Women in Black, 213
working class, 14, 21, 92, 95, 237
Wright, Bryan, 161, 240

Xerri, Gwann, 187
Xuereb, Diane, 188, 242, 244

Yemen, military operations in, 91
Yunus, Muhammed, 197
Yuval-Davis, Nira, 221

Zammit, Clive, 237, 244

**GPSR Compliance**

The European Union's (EU) General Product Safety Regulation (GPSR) is a set of rules that requires consumer products to be safe and our obligations to ensure this.

If you have any concerns about our products, you can contact us on

ProductSafety@springernature.com

In case Publisher is established outside the EU, the EU authorized representative is:

Springer Nature Customer Service Center GmbH
Europaplatz 3
69115 Heidelberg, Germany

www.ingramcontent.com/pod-product-compliance
Lightning Source LLC
LaVergne TN
LVHW051917060526
838200LV00004B/190